History of modern architecture

By the same author
The Origins of Modern Town Planning

History of modern architecture

Leonardo Benevolo

Volume two

The modern movement

The M.I.T. Press
Cambridge, Massachusetts

Third printing, 1985

First MIT Press Paperback Edition, 1977

First published in Italy in 1960
Storia dell'architettura moderna
© Giuseppe Laterza & Figli, 1960
Translated from the third revised
Italian edition, 1966
by H. J. Landry
This English translation first published
in Great Britain 1971: © Routledge & Kegan Paul, 1971

Published in the United States of America by
the M.I.T. Press, Cambridge, Massachusetts 1971

ISBN 0 262 02080 7 (hardcover)
ISBN 0 262 52045 1 (paperback)

Library of Congress Catalog Card number: 77-157667

Printed in the United States of America

Contents to volume one

volume one   **The tradition of modern architecture**

	Acknowledgements	vii
	Preface	ix
	Introduction Architecture and the industrial revolution	xv

section one   **Birth and development of the industrial town**

one	Changes in building technique during the industrial revolution	3
two	The age of reorganization and the origins of modern town-planning	38
three	Haussmann and the plan of Paris	61
four	Engineering and architecture in the second half of the nineteenth century	96

section two   **The debate on the industrial town**

five	The industrial town and its critics	127
six	Attempts at reforming the industrial town, from Owen to Morris	148

section three   **The industrial city in America**

seven	The American tradition	191
eight	The Chicago school and the American avant-garde	219

section four   **European avant-garde movements from 1890 to 1914**

	Introduction	253
nine	Art nouveau	262
ten	France's contribution: Auguste Perret and Tony Garnier	320
eleven	Experiments in town-planning from 1890 to 1914	343
	Notes	368

Contents to volume two

volume two   **The modern movement**

twelve	Conditions at the start	375
thirteen	The formation of the modern movement	412
fourteen	Early relations with the public	472
fifteen	Approach to town-planning problems	507
sixteen	Political compromise and the struggle with the authoritarian régimes	540
seventeen	Progress in European architecture between 1930 and 1940	586
eighteen	Modern architecture in America	629
nineteen	Europe after the Second World War	684
twenty	The new international field	748
	Conclusion	783
	Notes	841
	Bibliography	850
	Index	859

twelve

Conditions at the start

To make a fair assessment of the situation during the first two decades of the twentieth century – on which the movement of modern architecture was grafted, spanning the First World War – one must bear in mind that from 1890 onwards *avant-garde* culture had been putting new life into the theory and practice of architecture, but that, meanwhile, the technical, economic and social conditions on which the architect's work depended had changed even more rapidly, opening up a new and graver conflict between the transformations under way and the cultural models used to control them.

If architecture is the system of controls on which the arrangement of the urban scene is based, one may say that the changes in supply, provided by artists and *avant-garde* groups, remained greatly inferior to the changes in demand.

It is necessary to concentrate on this discrepancy, and to discuss it in the same way as we discussed that produced by the Industrial Revolution between 1760 and 1830, in the beginning of Volume 1. Now technical and economic processes upset the balance of settlements, introducing new factors and altering the quantities of already existing ones to such a degree as to produce situations that were qualitatively new; meanwhile, in a wider field, the battle between political theory and economic technique flared up once more and here again, as at the end of the eighteenth century, it was reflected in artistic activity and prevented the demands caused by current changes from being correctly interpreted.

This second industrial revolution was made possible by certain technical innovations: the spread of the Bessemer process (invented in 1856) in the iron industry, which meant that steel gradually replaced cast iron for almost all purposes; the invention of the dynamo (1869) to supply electricity at will and the experiments of Galileo Ferraris on the rotary magnetic field (1883) which made possible the use of hydraulic generators and which opened the way to numerous uses of electricity; the telephone (1876); and the invention of the internal combustion engine (1885) which made it possible to use petroleum for the propulsion of ships, land vehicles and, later, aeroplanes (1903).

Meanwhile the increase in railway building (which quadrupled between 1875 and 1905), the joining up of local networks into continuous systems (in 1872 the first transcontinental line across America was completed, in 1884 the St Gotthard tunnel, in

417   *L. Feininger,* Skyscrapers, *1919*

1902 the trans-Siberian railway), the opening of the Suez Canal (1869) and the rapid substitution of steam for sail in maritime transport (made inevitable by the lack of winds on the Suez Canal) lowered the cost of transport and made possible unprecedented developments in international trade, which increased threefold between 1880 and 1913.

These advances were made between 1870 and 1895, while prices continued to fall, and they were intensified at the turn of the century, when the discovery of gold-mines in the Transvaal initiated a period of exceptional economic prosperity during the period of peace and political stability preceding 1914.

But within this system which appeared so stable and progressive there was a contradiction between the liberal ideology, which had set these economic and political developments into motion, and the new forms of restriction made conceivable by the level of technical and organizational progress that had been attained; and this contradiction was becoming increasingly serious.

In the political field the liberal movement set the principle of nationality up in the place of that of divine right, and it enjoyed an almost unlimited triumph in Europe in the first half of the nineteenth century; but the same principle, applied to international relations, produced imperialism in the second half, and led to a state of balance based on the clash of irreconcilable interests.

In the economic field the economic difficulties of 1870 were enough to provoke a resumption of protectionism and colonialism; at the same time the transition from free trade to monopoly in certain big industries became evident.

Bertrand Russell wrote:

'Two men have been supreme in creating the modern world: Rockefeller and Bismarck. One in economics, the other in politics, refuted the liberal dream of universal happiness through individual competition, substituting monopoly and the corporate state.'[1]

The year 1870, when Bismarck managed to bring about the Franco-Prussian War, was also the year in which Rockefeller and Flager gained control of the Standard Oil Company.

The ambivalent meaning of the word 'freedom' is found again and again in the thought of the late nineteenth century. The freedom invoked by Van de Velde and Wagner, like that sought by Van Gogh and Rimbaud to the point of absolute self-sacrifice, retained a precise meaning only in relation to the traditional rules and circumstances that artists had decided to reject; this rejection had to have general validity, and at the same time it had to be backed by unquestionable personal commitment. Hence the appeal for universal communication, alternating with impatience with every concrete opportunity for comparison.

It is not possible to deal at all fully here with a series of problems which go beyond the limits of the history of architecture. We may simply note that the self-absorption common to members of the architectural *avant-garde* and many other experiments of the time, prevented accumulation of the results achieved by the most committed artists and groups, i.e. made it impossible for architectural thought to keep up with the changes in building technique, and even more so with the new organizational aspects of town-planning and tool production.

The technical innovations already described influenced building techniques, together with the new materials that could be used for supporting structures – steel instead of cast iron, and reinforced concrete – and with the means of internal communication – the lift, telephone, pneumatic post – which made possible the functioning of new building organisms, like hotels and multi-storey office blocks.

We have already noted that the culture of the time was not in a position, open-mindedly, to take in the possibilities offered by the new technical processes; cage-type structures were accepted by American builders and by Perret only by being interpreted as though they were traditional elements of the façade; the rhythmical and undefined character of the organism of the skyscraper emerged in Chicago building between 1880 and 1890, only in so far as the decorative finish was lessened, and it was lost in the activities of the more demanding designers, like Sullivan and Root.

But the shortcomings of *avant-garde* culture were particularly in evidence in connection with the problems of town-planning and industrial design.

In order to control the changes taking place in the towns, the town-planning techniques that had evolved during the second half of the century, fostered by the new economic and political planning, had produced typical modes of operation: the demolition of historic centres, extension of the suburbs, the dismantling of Baroque fortifications to build ring roads, flanked with gardens and public buildings. The formal models used in these operations were those of the classical tradition and *grand goût* on which, in the last years of the century, the curved and irregular street systems deriving from the English landscape tradition were grafted.

Building changes were carried out simultaneously with those of basic urban services – water-mains, sewers, electricity and gas-mains – applying the oft-tried parallelism between engineering and the eclectic tradition. This stock of solutions had already proved inadequate, in the first years of the twentieth century, when faced with certain unusual problems: the design of new capitals, for instance Canberra and New Delhi, the town-planning schemes for certain American cities, where the traditional grid-iron system could no longer hold the enormous dimensions that had been reached, for instance that by Burnham and Bennet for Chicago, of 1909. The problem grew even more serious when the spread of the motor car produced sprawling suburbs in America and later in Europe, extending the problems of urban organization into the general countryside.

Avant-garde thought not only disregarded these new problems, but it was not in a position to provide a coherent alternative to the traditional town-planning praxis for resolving the usual problems; the experiments of Garnier, Howard, Soria and Berlage were partial and hesitant attempts, which we must stress in view of subsequent developments, but which proved unimportant in comparison with those of orthodox town-planners like Stübben, Lutyens and Burnham, and pathetically out of scale in relation to the extent of the problems which were already emerging.

Thus in the field of the applied arts the prejudice of the reformers against mechanical processes was overcome only in the last decade of the nineteenth century, and was often replaced by an idealistic assessment of industrial values, which rebounded to become a formal exaltation of the mechanical mood. Thus *art nouveau*, although it was deeply interested in these problems, did not lead to any appreciable change in the productive organization of everyday objects, just at the moment when the demand for these goods was changing radically, because of the appearance of new and wider categories of consumers.

This failure to grasp the real facts explains the amazing speeding up of intellectual discussion in the decade before the First World War. New tendencies appeared in ever quicker succession and were outworn with equal speed; our task is not to list the single thrusts in the argument, but to pick out the really important points in this somewhat artificial dispute, those which bore long-term fruit.

418, 419 *Darmstadt, Matildenhöhe, House of P. Behrens (1900; from F. Höber, P. B., 1913)*

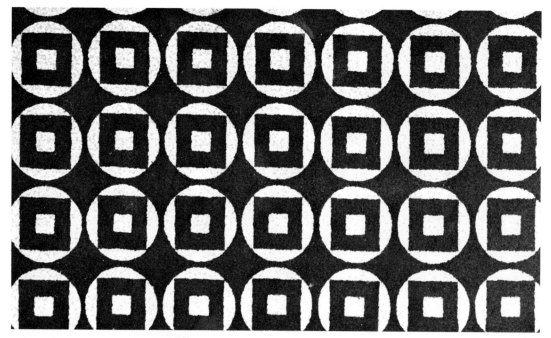

Die Zukunft unserer Industrie wird mit davon abhängen, ob wir entschlossen und im Stande sind, der nächsten Generation eine sorgfältige künstlerische Erziehung des Auges und der Empfindung angedeihen zu lassen. Bisher haben wir nur für die Ausbildung von Künstlern gesorgt.   Alfred Lichtwark.

420   *P. Behrens, Design for linoleum presented at the Brussels universal exhibition, 1910 (from Deutschlands Raumkunstgewerbe auf der Weltausstellung zu Brüssel, 1910)*
421   *Examples of Behrens' printing (from F. Höber, op. cit.)*

1   The Deutscher Werkbund and the new architecture

From 1900 onwards Germany was the centre of European architectural thought. The reasons for this were complex: in fact in Germany this culture was not backed by a tradition comparable to the French or the English, industrialization was recent and social structures more strongly linked with the past; but it was just this lack of precedent which made possible the emergence of an unbiased and progressive minority of entre-

preneurs, politicians and artists, and which placed them in a position not of open dis-agreement with the powers-that-were – as happened in almost all other European countries – but in a position to occupy key posts in the running of this changing society; thus it was with relative ease that *avant-garde* theorists and artists obtained teaching posts in state schools, editorships of impor-tant reviews or big publishing houses, that they came to organize exhibitions, influenced industrial production on a large scale and even, like Muthesius, had a certain degree of influence on the government's cultural policies. It was largely this organizational equipment that enabled Germany to attract the most gifted men from all over Europe: Van de Velde from Belgium, Olbrich from Austria and even, for some time, Wright from America.

The most important German cultural organization of the pre-war years was the 'Deutscher Werkbund', founded in 1907 by a group of artists and critics in association with certain manufacturers:

'The aim of the Werkbund [said the statute] was to ennoble craftsmanship, selecting the best representatives of art, industry, crafts and trades, combining all existing efforts towards quality in industrial work, and forming a rallying point for all those who are able and willing to work for quality'.[2]

This institution took up the heritage of the English associations inspired by Morris's teaching, with an important difference: it was not biased in favour of craftsmanship, nor did it set itself up in opposition to current methods of mass-production. This attitude was certainly opportune, because it did not set out to disregard any of the concrete factors at work but it promptly generated an uncertainty about method; in fact the English associations, wishing to remain faithful to manual methods, immediately had a precise practical path to follow, even if it was one-sided, and they could make use of medieval models, as did the Art Workers Guild, while the Werkbund, with its aim of combining art, industry and craftsmanship, which all operated with very different processes and habits, brought up a problem of method which remained temporarily indeterminate, covered by the ambiguous formula 'quality work' (*Qualitätsarbeit*).

In fact disagreement between the various factions within the Werkbund soon broke out: between the supporters of standardization and those of freedom of design, between the supporters of art and those of economy, and in 1914 between Muthesius and Van de Velde, already mentioned in Chapter 9.

Behind the traditional terms of this argument lurked the need to break through the particular self-interests of the *avant-garde*. Associations similar to the Werkbund were formed in many European countries: in 1910 the Austrian Werkbund, in 1913 the Swiss, in 1915 the Design and Industries Association in England.

The new generation of German architects grew up within the Werkbund between 1907 and 1914: Gropius, Mies van der Rohe, Taut. The mediators between this generation and the earlier one, which had initiated the regeneration of architectural thought, were two exceptional figures: Van de Velde, whom we have already discussed, and Peter Behrens (1868–1940). Van de Velde's contribution was mainly intellectual, while Behrens was influential in the practical field and was possibly, as Argan suggests,[3] the key figure for the understanding of this basic moment of transition in the history of modern architecture.

Behrens began his career as a painter; in 1899 he was one of the seven artists called to Darmstadt with Olbrich by the Grand Duke of Hessen, to start the colony of the Matildenhöhe, and here he built his house, inspired by Olbrich but with a rigidity of layout and a love of solid and heavy elements quite foreign to the whimsical Austrian (Figs. 418, 419).

After this Muthesius asked him to run the Academy of Art at Düsseldorf, and in 1907 Rathenau, the managing director of A. E. G., appointed him artistic adviser to his whole industry, from buildings to products and publicity. In this way Behrens became one of the most important practising architects in Germany; about 1908 Gropius, Mies van der Rohe and even Le Corbusier were working in his studio.

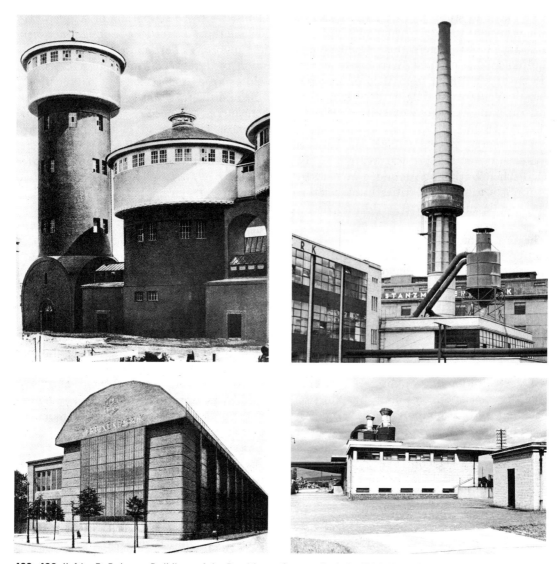

422, 423 *(left)   P. Behrens, Buildings of the Frankfurter Gasgesellschaft, 1911 (from G. A. Platz,* Die Baukunst der neuesten Zeit, *1927) and of the A. E. G. in Berlin, 1909 (from F. Höber, op. cit.)*
424, 425 *(right)   W. Gropius and A. Meyer, Two details of the Fagus works at Alfeld (1911)*

Behrens built various industrial buildings for the A.E.G. in Berlin and, even in such works, he never abandoned his attitude of artist-decorator, whose intention was to accommodate the functional elements with dignity and even a slightly outdated grace, Wagnerian in flavour. The general tone was sober and ponderous, with a vaguely literary allusion to the gloomy atmosphere of the traditional factory, while various salient

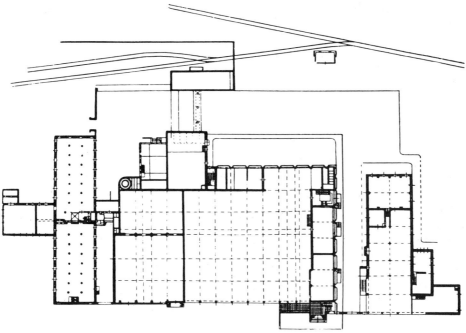

426, 427 *Alfeld an der Leine, The Fagus works (W. Gropius and A. Meyer 1911)*

428   *Alfeld an der Leine, The Fagus works*

episodes were treated in a distinctly decorative fashion, which concealed the functional nature of the structures: for instance, the head of the turbine factory, with its full pediment with the broken outline and glass wall beneath, which juts out from the masonry corners with their recurrent indented bands of brick, giving an effect of elaborate, abstract dovetailing (Fig. 423) or, elsewhere, the cylindrical volumes of the reservoirs, expressionistically accentuated, like menacing towers (Fig. 422).

On other occasions Behrens' architecture was light and cheerful, making use of Wagnerian two-colour technique to lighten surfaces of masonry, as in the Crematorium at Delstern and the Pavilion of Honour at the Werkbund exhibition at Cologne.

Behrens' repertoire was firmly rooted in the *avant-garde* tradition, particularly that of Austria. But he used the traditional forms sparingly, and spread over solemn monumental compositions they lost both force and concentration, not because of lack of energy on Behrens' part, but because of a sort of subtle distrust, of intellectual reserve, occasionally allowing values of quite another kind to come to the surface: the raw presentation of internal and functional mechanisms, uniform rhythms, indefinite repetitions of elementary motifs. Examples of this are the decorative designs studied for industrial production, where the *art nouveau* repertoire is drastically simplified and reduced to the

429 *W. Gropius, The Adler car designed in 1930 (from S. Giedion, W. G., 1954)*

combination of a few geometrical elements, to emphasize the grain and texture of the materials (Fig. 420).

It is important to remember that it was in Behrens' studio that Gropius and Mies van der Rohe were gaining experience, while working on the designs of the buildings already mentioned. The fact was this: the two experiments, that of the *avant-garde* which was dying out and that of the modern movement which was just emerging, were interlinked but basically incompatible; the passage from one to the other could therefore not come about by simple evolution, but by the weakening of the first experiment which died gradually as the elements of the second,

in a confused form for the moment, came to the surface.

Walter Gropius (1883–1969) the son of a wealthy Berlin architect and civil servant, worked in Behrens' studio but soon began to design on his own; in 1906 he designed a group of farm dwellings at Janikov, in 1913 he did some interior decorating, the design for a diesel locomotive and most important, in 1911, a splendid industrial building, the Fagus shoe-last factory at Alfeld an der Leine (Figs. 424–8, 430).

The Fagus factory rises in gracious isolation on the outskirts of Alfeld in a pleasant green hollow amid woods and hills; it is almost intact, like the town itself, being one of the few districts spared by the Second World War, and the present day visitor can almost imagine the building as it was fifty years ago, the moment it was opened. The most striking thing is the simplicity and confidence of this architecture, in contrast with the monumental posturings and dramatic harshness of similar works by Behrens and Poelzig; apart from the chimney, no volumetric element is accentuated more than any other, and the architectural tone is quiet and calm in the various bodies of the building corresponding to the various functions; even the general plan has no uncommon compositional features, the various parts being put together in the most simple and economical way possible.

This unimpeachable technical propriety has made perfect upkeep possible: only two materials, brick and burnished metal, have been used for the external surface, and the basic harmony of yellow and black dominates the whole composition. But the choice of details, particularly in the famous glass building, reveals numerous uncertainties: the ideal of making the glass protrude from the wall, the continuous glass at the corners, the main doorway and the block of the building in which it is set, lined with darker horizontal bands of brick, are plainly references to Behrens' style, made with a certain amount of embarrassment. Nonetheless it is plain that the interest of the designer does not lie here: there is even a sort of indifference, in the acceptance of certain basic stylistic facts, in contrast with the rigour of the more technically involved solutions; it is as though Gropius' interest had been apportioned in a way directly opposed to the normal, since it is less in the most striking parts and greater in those normally accepted as secondary.

In this building an extremely fleeting moment of transition was crystallized, and this may be the explanation of its particular attraction; it is as though, starting from the style of Behrens, the formal and stylistic

apparatus became ever slacker until it was narrowed down to a few formulae, which acted merely as means of chronological characterization, while the technical elements were organized in a taut, coherent way, though left almost completely bare, with all the freshness and tenseness that the situation allowed. Almost all the Fagus works can be read in a purely technological light, since the stylistic demands are reduced to an extremely slight outer covering. In this way the building acquires an absolute, rigid character; other works in Gropius' production which most resemble it are not buildings but industrial products, like the 1913 diesel car and the Adler motor car of 1930 (Fig. 429).

In Gropius' other important pre-war work, the model factory at the Werkbund exhibition in Cologne in 1914 (Fig. 431) the delicate balance of the Fagus was upset. Here aesthetic demands were obviously preponderant, and Gropius' style had absorbed a number of formal suggestions from Wright, Behrens and the Paris *halle des machines* of 1889, all of which were not always happily juxtaposed. However, his method of composition was still free and articulated, particularly in the courtyard with the two garages which link the body of the offices with the factory area. Many details are excellent, for instance the two spiral staircases, completely visible from the outside within their glass shells.

From the first, Gropius' personality tended to include and to mediate between conflicting theses and tendencies; for a brief period at this time this characteristic was in danger of degenerating into a sort of eclecticism, possibly connected with the atmosphere, inevitably eclectic, of the 1914 Werkbund exhibition, in which widely divergent forces were at work. It is interesting, in this context, to compare the other works built for the occasion: Behrens' assembly hall, Bruno Taut's pavilion for German glass industries, Hoffmann's Austrian pavilion, Van de Velde's theatre with its tripartite stage, each

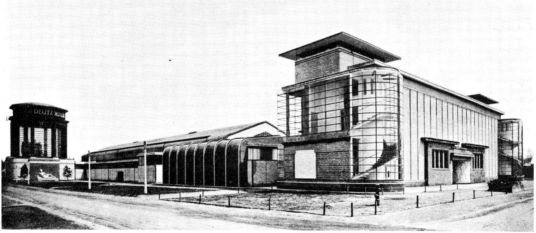

430, 431 *W. Gropius and A. Meyer, Detail of the Fagus works and the model factory at the exhibition of the Werkbund in Cologne, 1914 (from G. A. Platz, op. cit.)*

of which had its own marked and exclusive character.

At this time Gropius also began to write. His first article, published in Leipzig in 1911, has the following significant title: *In the building of industrial buildings, can artistic demands be reconciled with practical and economic ones?*[4]

In the Werkbund's Yearbook for 1913 Gropius published a study on the develop-

432 *Silos in Chicago, published in* Grandes Constructions *by A. Morancé*

ment of modern industrial architecture, where he illustrated and commented favourably upon certain utilitarian American buildings:

'The silos of Canada and South America, the coal carriers on the great railways and the most modern industrial establishments in North America . . . offer to the observer an architectural composition of such precision that their meaning is made forcibly and unambiguously plain to him. The natural perfection of these buildings certainly does not lie in the vastness of their material dimensions – plainly not to be taken into account as being among the qualities of a monumental work – but in the clear and independent vision their designers had of these great, impressive forms. They are not muddied by sentimental respect for tradition, nor by other intellectual scruples which debase our contemporary European architecture and preclude from it almost any real artistic originality'.[5]

These preferences help to explain Gropius' aims as a designer. Probably overestimating 'spontaneous' industrial architecture, he continued to move within the limits of *avant-garde* culture, but sensed that the solution to the antagonisms and difficulties was to be found by keeping close to practical requirements, not in some new ideological or formal system; his work contains something new and important with regard to the rest of European production: a calm and reasonable adherence to technical necessities, and a refusal to exaggerate the style deriving from this. For the moment, perhaps, he felt that this might be enough and that the new architecture might burst forth almost automatically, following objective necessities in a completely unbiased fashion.

But such a judgment is purely hypothetical; and Gropius' serene and optimistic experiments in the pre-war period were violently interrupted by the war itself and by the cultural crisis that followed it, and it was only after passing through this stage of crisis that the evolution of his thought was complete.

Ludwig Mies van der Rohe (1886–1969), was the son of a master mason; at first he worked as a designer in the studio of B. Paul from 1901 to 1907, then in 1908 with Behrens, and from 1911 in Holland with Berlage. In 1913 he opened an architectural studio in Berlin, but his work was soon interrupted by the war.

It is much harder to pass a judgment on the pre-war activities and tendencies of Mies than of Gropius. His first work, the Fuchs house of 1911, was still completely within Behrens' stylistic ambit, and the second, the Kröller-Müller house of 1912, was almost classical in character (though the terse and careful spacing of the windows anticipated the unique timbre of his best architecture). The young architect showed no desire for sensational novelties: rather, almost a craftsmanlike love of carefully studied constructional detail and concentration on the functional parts of the building, raising it to the rank of architecture simply by virtue of its carefully thought out proportions.

2 Movements for the reform of the figurative arts

Between 1905 and 1914 the activities of *avant-garde* painters had reached a crucial turning point, and aimed at a radical reform of the principles which regulate normal visual habits; the speed of developments and the similarity of the results achieved simultaneously by different artists following different paths, showed that a vital process was taking place, one that had been maturing for a long time, and that the interests of the whole of artistic culture were at stake.

In 1905, at the Salon d'Automne, the 'fauves' exhibited together for the first time (Derain, Friesz, Marquet, Manguin, Matisse, Puy, Rouault, Valtat, Vlaminck); in Dresden in the same year, working in a different direction, Bleyl, Kirchner, Heckel and Schmidt-Rottluff founded the group 'die Brücke' and were later joined by Nolde and others. Between 1907 and 1908 the first Cubist works of Picasso and Braque appeared, and were the starting point for the increasingly radical efforts of Léger, Gris, Gleizes and Delaunay. In 1909, with a group of German artists, Kandinsky founded the 'Neue Münchner Künstlervereinigung' and painted his first abstract water-colours in 1910; in 1911, together with Kubin, Marc and Münter he left the Munich group and formed the group 'der blaue Reiter', joined the following year by Klee. In 1910 Boccioni, Carrà, Russolo, Balla and Severini signed the first manifesto of futurist painting, following on from Marinetti's manifesto of 1909, and exhibited in Paris for the first time in 1912. In the same year Klee and Marc were in contact with Delaunay while in 1913, after a trip to Paris, Malevich arrived at complete abstraction with the famous *Black Square on a White Background*.

None of these experiments had any apparent link with architecture, indeed it was rather as though the painters of the time – with the exception of the futurists – preferred to drop contacts with other fields of activity and concentrate their energies on the problems of pure painting. But by doing this they found that they had broken through just those traditional outer limits of the field assigned to painting, and they established the foundations which were to release artistic culture – and, in a certain way, all culture – from the visual rules of the past.

The theoretical convictions and practical exercise of art had hitherto been founded on a sharp distinction between initial conception and material execution; the first had a universal and 'scientific' value and was linked with the same norms that ruled the representation of the natural world, while the second belonged to the reign of the particular and incidental. Though this dis-

tinction cannot be translated into philosophical terms at all, it was actually born within the ambit of Renaissance naturalism and was active in artistic thought as long as the problem of gnoseology and the search for forms regulating human knowledge *a priori* were dominant in philosophical thought.

The conceiving of visible forms was regulated by the norms of perspective, which corresponded supposedly to the natural laws of human vision; implicit in them was a hierarchy between geometric or primary features, and ones that were chromatic, tactile etc., which were regarded as secondary as in the Cartesian theory of the *res extensa*. For this reason, in painting, the representation of three-dimensional objects on the plane must allow in the first place for an unequivocal definition of their form and mutual positions, according to a system of reference linked to the position of the observer, and secondly an unequivocal link between form and colour, according to the examples offered by nature. In architecture the shape of each room was subordinated to a system of geometric proportions, to be adopted as a criterion of viewing by a single observer; the characters of each of the parts (form, texture, colour etc.) were dependent on the position occupied in this system and on the capacity of the human eye to perceive them at a glance or in a continued and definite series of successive glances; thus architecture becomes an extension of nature, an artificial world built on the same laws as the natural world.

Neo-classicism had cast doubt on the validity of the particular historical models which had hitherto been looked to, but not of the general rules of perspective; the new technical devices, furthermore, were born of a similar brand of scientific thought which conceived of all phenomena as set within an *a priori* system of spatial and temporal references. Thus the succession of stylistic revivals really caused variation only within

433 *Pablo Picasso,* Girl with Mandolin, *1910*

the choice of external details, and made it possible for a conventional parallelism to be set up between constructional techniques and perspective vision, that was all the more tenacious in that it was not explicitly felt; the great engineers of the nineteenth century, overlooking – i.e. taking for granted – formal appearances and concentrating on structural invention, only strengthened it. New building systems were born automatically conditioned by perspective, methods of calculation took heed of its precepts and the novel formal suggestions born of these technical experiments could not be looked at in an open-minded fashion (Le Corbusier's 'eyes which do not see').

This parallelism prevented new techniques from being adapted to the needs of modern society, because it brought with it a large number of limitations connected with the productive systems and hierarchical structure of pre-industrial society, and demanded a distribution of energies that was no longer compatible with the current professional situation of engineers and artists.

Designers working in the building field felt this state of affairs with varying degrees of unease, but pure artists – painters, sculptors etc. – suffered from it directly and felt themselves cut off from society, which appeared to be able to manage very well without them. For this reason they were forced to look inwards, and to strain increasingly and one-sidedly, against the conventions on which the representation of visible objects was based.

Their fulcrum was the hierarchy of primary and secondary elements; in fact *avant-garde* painting of the second half of the nineteenth century, from the impressionists to the fauves, worked around the central problem of the relationships between form and colour. The dispersal of the Fauvist movement and the contemporary birth of Cubism, around 1907, marked the peak of this process; the celebration of pure colour led to the doubting of the absoluteness of spatial reference in the representation of form and to the denial of the very basis of perspective.

The importance of this development, not only in the field of art but in the general balance between the various fields of modern culture, can be gauged today by the breadth of the consequences, rather than by the initial declarations of the artists and critics, eager to back up their experiments with general affirmations, which involved art and science, theory and practice. A discussion of the cultural syntheses suggested at this time would be out of place; but it is relevant to mention at least two experiments exactly contemporary with Cubism, which must be regarded as complementary to one another, although they were carried out quite separately.

1 The theoretical discussion of the absolute validity of the rules of perspective, which took place in art history between 1904 and 1912.

The first reservations about the absolute validity of the rules of perspective were expounded by G. Hauck at the end of the nineteenth century; a more solid and fruitful piece of criticism was carried out by G. I. Kern[6] – the protagonist of a memorable polemic with K. Doehlmann between 1911 and 1912 – and by J. Mesnil[7] who objectively reconstructed the origins of Renaissance perspective and set it definitely within the historical facts conditioned by time. E. Panofsky intervened in this debate as early as 1915[8] and drew his conclusions in his fundamental essay of 1927,[9] which opened the modern debate on the subject.

2 The crisis, in the scientific field, of the traditional concepts of time and space, linked historically to the conventions of perspective.

The discussion opened by the experiments of Michelson and Morley in 1881 on the earth's motion in relation to the ether, led Einstein to formulate the theory of relativity in 1905. The hypothesis of the quantum element of action, propounded by Planck in 1900 following research on black body radiation, was applied to optics by Einstein in 1905, and made it possible for Bohr to formulate his atomic theory in 1913, opening the way to the advances made by modern nuclear physics.

These theoretical developments, made inevitable by the continuity of the experimental research under way, led to a re-examination of the basis of scientific thought, which had been established for over two centuries, and particularly of the concepts of time and space, for which Minkowski and others tried to find a new general definition.

References to the broader cultural field, within which the figurative revolution of these years should be considered, must not obscure the specific values of the Cubist experiment, which is to be understood first of all in its own terms. The most important artists were not very forthcoming verbally (about 1910 Picasso answered an interviewer with the words: 'No talking to the driver') and the esoteric theories built up in their name by critics such as Apollinaire or colleagues such as A. Lhote, J. Gris, A. Gleizes, have acted largely as irrelevant targets.

At the beginning the Cubists expressed their intentions aggressively, breaking up the naturalistic continuity of images and presenting superimposed views which referred to various viewpoints, none of which was now used as an absolute point of reference; later they were to break up the totality of the image into its basic components: lines, surfaces, colours, sometimes arriving at an unbending abstraction, as did Gleizes.

The elements liberated in this way soon revealed new qualities and new meanings which had originally been hidden beneath conventional appearances, and new relations were seen to exist between the elements which then allowed them to be organized in a new way, according to new organic laws. But no-one thought of a new system of

definite precepts to be set beside the old ones, and people felt themselves involved in an open-minded process of enquiry, whose results could not be defined in advance. For the first time painters claimed that they had no preconceived intentions to carry out.

Picasso: 'A painting is not thought and laid out in advance; while you work, it changes in the same degree as the thought informing it';[10] Braque: 'a picture is an adventure every time, when I attack the blank canvas I never know what may spring out of it';[11] Gris: 'I never know in advance what the object represented is going to look like'.[12]

What then was the aim of these experiments? The objects of empirical reality were taken up by painters only after the common references linking them to that reality had been eliminated, including utilitarian ones (Braque: 'I try to see that an object gives up all claim to function, I take it up only when it no longer serves any purpose, like old objects at the moment when their usefulness is over'[13] and later Duchamp was to make use of *objets trouvés*, removed from their context). The metamorphosis of the object isolated in this fashion completely absorbed the attention of the painters; Apollinaire, interpreting their state of mind, spoke of pure painting, freed at last from their links with reality[14] and critical discussion moved around this basic point.

But there was also a complementary possibility. The object freed from its usual connections was ready to take on others, richer and broader, and painting, having given up the imitation of real things, might now invent and create them. The new modes of procedure might therefore affect all forms of productive activity, and the results might be extended, by means of technical knowledge and industry, to the whole urban scene, from a circle of initiates to the whole of society. Gris wrote: 'Cezanne makes a bottle into a cylinder, I make a cylinder into a bottle'.[15] Why then – even though Gleizes would not

434   *G. Balla,* Futurist composition, *1915–16*

agree – should this not be a real bottle, one that could be on everyone's table?

Cubism did therefore contain a sort of dichotomy; it was the last and most extreme product of the *avant-garde*, but it pointed towards possibilities of moving beyond *avant-garde* positions and putting an end to the unnatural isolation of the artist. The real

aim of the cultural process – which today, fifty years later, we can judge with sufficient detachment – was not a modification of the content of artistic representation, but a modification of the traditional concept of art as a representative activity, in opposition to the world of technical processes; the questioning of the rules of perspective and

435   *A. Sant'Elia,* The Electric Power Station, *1914 (from* Casabella*)*

their correspondence with the natural laws of vision, led to the collapse of the supposition that there existed a world of *a priori* rules, to which art owed its dignity and its substance as a separate entity.

This development had immediate repercussions on architecture; in the old system of values architecture was one of the specific applications of the broadest concepts of 'art'; in the new, art – if one is to continue using the same word – is one of the components of architecture, which once more appeared as a complete activity, as in Morris's definition.

But these consequences – which were to be drawn by Gropius and developed by the modern movement – were only implicit at the moment, or were felt only as confused aspirations, as was shown by the vicissitudes of the most aggressive group of the time, the Futurists.

Initially Futurism was a literary programme; the painters, sculptors and musicians who supported it set themselves to translate it, each in his own way, into his own field of activity. Severini wrote: 'Futurism was a general idea, or rather an intellectual attitude; but it gave us no means to express ourselves',[16] and indeed many and various activities took place beneath this banner, their unity being assumed or hoped for rather than actually attained. But precisely because of the slighter nature of their commitment, the Futurists were the first to realize that European *avant-garde* culture held within it the possibility of a new synthesis of the arts, and was preparing a new integrated setting for contemporary society.

Recently, recording the bicentenary of Marinetti's 1909 Futurist manifesto, R. Banham wrote: 'As we look back from the threshold of the space age, we see the Foundation Manifesto standing up, the farthest familiar landmark in the fog of history, the first point in which we can recognize an image of our own machine age attitudes'.[17]

In 1910, after Marinetti's manifesto, the two manifestos for painting appeared, in 1912 Boccioni's for sculpture and in 1914 that of Antonio Sant'Elia (1880–1915) for architecture, the first conscious attempt – even if incomplete and limited to verbal pronouncements – to bring the *avant-garde* revolutionary spirit into the architectural field.[18]

As is well-known, the first drafting of the manifesto was modified by Marinetti and Cinti[19] and was known in this version until G. Bernasconi re-published the original document in 1955.[20]

Sant'Elia's original text, stripped of the verbal extravagances of Marinetti's additions, is lucid and convincing, particularly at the beginning:

'The problem of modern architecture is not a problem of rearranging its lines; not a question of finding new mouldings, new architraves for doors and windows; nor of replacing columns, pilasters and corbels with caryatids, hornets and frogs; not a question of leaving a façade in brick or facing it in stone or plaster; in a word, it has nothing to do with settling on formalistic differences between new buildings and old ones. But to raise the new built structure on a sane plan, gleaning every benefit of science and technique, settling nobly every requirement of our habits and our spirits . . . . Such an architecture naturally cannot be subject to any law of historic continuity. It must be as new as our state of mind is new and the contingencies of our moment in history. The art of building has been able to evolve through time and pass from style to style, while maintaining the general character of architecture unchanged, because in history there have been numerous changes of taste brought on by shifts of religious conviction or successive political régimes, but few occasioned by profound changes in our conditions of life, that discard or overhaul the old ones, as have the discovery of natural laws, the perfection of technical methods, the rational and scientific use of materials. In modern life, the process of consequential stylistic development comes to a halt. Architecture, tired of tradition, begins again, forcibly, from the beginning'.

Sant'Elia's claims were backed only by a series of drawings – mostly perspectives, with a few plans and sections – which were plainly linked with the repertoire of *art nouveau* and which are comparable with the production of certain followers of Wagner, for instance E. Hoppe. The intentional audacity of the visions does not usually reach the point of breaking or weakening the traditional canons of perspective, as can be seen from the emphatic symmetry of almost all the drawings. It is therefore impossible to talk of futurist architecture, or even to compare these drawings with the activities of Boccioni and Balla, which were of quite another sort. But equally there is no doubt that Sant'Elia's tone – in the drawings as in the phrases of the Manifesto – is no longer that of the generation of *art nouveau*; there was a conscious desire for escape which stretched and transfigured the placid Wagnerian forms, even though it was not yet able to replace them with any coherent alternative.

The premature death of Sant'Elia during the war prevented this experiment from developing fully. For this reason his contribution was ambiguous and uncertain, and has been interpreted in many different ways, as an anticipation of Gropius[21] and Le Corbusier[22] or as an argument against international architecture and in favour of a hypothetical autonomous Italian tradition.[23]

A group of painters which was to have a decisive influence on the formation of the modern movement, even though it may seem very remote from architectural interest, was 'der blaue Reiter', born in 1911 of the meeting between Marc and Kandinsky and other artists of the Munich *avant-garde*.

These painters were not linked by any definite figurative tendency, nor by the desire to lay down a general method, but by a common commitment to going beyond appearances, to drawing close to their secret essence, not without mystical and esoteric undertones. Marc wrote:

'Do we not have a thousand years of experience telling us that things become the more obstinately silent the more obviously we hold the optical mirror of their phenomenal appearance before them? Appearance is always flat, but put it far from your soul – imagine that neither you nor your image of the world any longer exist – and the world takes on its true form again; a demon allows us to see through the cracks in the world, and leads us in a dream to the world behind its motley stage'.[24]

Kandinsky talked of the 'inner eye' which 'goes through the hard shell, through the outward "form" to penetrate to the very heart of things, and makes all our senses feel their inmost "beat".'[25] Because of this sharp perception of the contrast between appearance and reality, Marc and Kandinsky were more rigorous than the Cubists in excluding all relations between their art and practical life. In the catalogue of the 1913 exhibition of 'der blaue Reiter' we read:

'We do not live in an age when art is at the service of life. The real art that is born today seems rather to be the sediment of all the forces that life has not managed to absorb; it is the equation that abstract spirits draw from life, without desire, without aim, without strife. At other times art was the yeast which leavened the dough of the world; such times are now long past, and until they return, the artist must keep away from official life. This is the reason for our refusal, frankly taken, of the offers the world makes us; we do not wish to mingle with it'.[26]

It is interesting to consider that the three artists taking part in this exhibition, Feininger, Kandinsky and Klee, were shortly afterwards to work in the Bauhaus to re-establish just this link between art and life; the importance of their contribution, however, is proportionate to the concentration and rigour with which they first matured their art, without allowing themselves to be distracted by the clamour of the battles of the *avant-garde*.

3 The First World War and after

The 1914–18 war not only put an end to the activity of the architects and seriously restricted that of the painters, but it also affected their thought in various ways and set cultural activity moving along a somewhat different course.

At this point in the history of architecture internal and external factors, temporary and long-term ones are inextricably intermingled. We shall try to clarify the situation by distinguishing three orders of factors: the material consequences of the war, the psychological and moral consequences and the artistic experiments and theories which came of age during the war years.

The damage done during the war (even if it was not comparable to that done during the Second World War) and particularly the pause in productive activities during the war posed serious and urgent problems of rebuilding. There had been problems of accommodation everywhere even some years before the war, because of the renewed growth in the population. The vastness of the task was such that only the State could tackle it, so that subsidized building became an important factor, and the laws connected with it were developed accordingly.

The architect's clientèle changed too: he had fewer commissions from private clients and more from the State and public bodies, fewer separate houses and more districts and complexes. The importance of town-planning increased rapidly.

Meanwhile technical knowledge was producing the instruments needed for these tasks; the use of reinforced concrete became general after the war, because the regulations issued in the various countries appeared shortly before 1914. The war itself speeded up technical developments in many fields, for instance transport and metal-working.

In the defeated countries, Austria and Germany, as well as war damage there was also the overthrow of the old political régimes, the occupation and costs of reparation, which aggravated the already difficult economic situation. All these facts were reflected in the cultural field; political changes favoured cultural progress, because the progressive élite which had already come of age was automatically called upon to become the ruling class. The economic depression and particularly inflation forced the old classes to mix with one another, destroyed the habits rooted in the old social hierarchy and favoured innovating tendencies.

So it was in just these countries, where there was less friction with the old order, that the events most important for the new culture came to maturity.

Almost all the protagonists of the modern movement left their professions and went to war. This experience was crucial for many of them, in a cultural sense too; Gropius spoke for them all:

'The full consciousness of my responsibility in advancing ideas based on my own reflections only came home to me as a result of the war, in which these theoretical premises first took definite shape. After that violent interruption, which kept me, like many of my fellow architects, from work for four years, every thinking man felt the necessity for an intellectual change of front. Each in his own particular sphere of activity aspired to help in bridging the disastrous gulf between reality and idealism'.[27]

The objective to be aimed at had already received precise formulation in pre-war discussion; the problem was to bring cultural action into line with the technical, economic and social processes that had been developing from the industrial revolution onwards, to qualify and control them rather than to submit to their quantitative oppression. But there was still a clinging conviction, the legacy of the mentality that came out of the enlightenment: that there existed a sort of preordained harmony between the various demands, upset only by the persistence of old habits and institutions, and therefore able to be reinstated with essentially polemical action, by removing these institutions and habits. Technical knowledge, i.e. the immediate cause of the current changes, was regarded as having an intrinsically rational list and therefore as a guarantee of unlimited progress (or, in an equally unrealistic fashion, as a factor of regression by those who were unable to resign themselves to the passing of the old institutions).

The war produced a different concept of technical knowledge, more restricted and without ideological connotations. The same ideas that had been used to produce peaceful devices were now used to produce weapons of death and destruction, and technicians passed with surprising ease from one field of work to the other; also, psychological conditioning and the recourse of both sides to the same idealistic motives, for opposite aims, revealed the conventional character of many ideological formulae which had formerly been universally accepted. A disturbing gulf was thus opened between means and ends; technical progress showed itself to be an instrument of good and evil alike, and the excellence of the aims was no longer sufficiently guaranteed by the traditional discus-

sions on the 'great leap forward'. The atrocities committed on a large scale by men not particularly inclined to crime warned people how precarious were the safeguards of human society.

The war did not alter the terms of cultural debate, but it sharpened sensibilities to distinguishing form from substance, and proved the need for a radical rethinking of many of these terms, in order for the problems inherited to acquire any real meaning. Above all it made people realize that definitive solutions could not be found in theory – and that therefore it was not enough for them to be formulated by a small group of people – but that they must be tested in practice, involving all those concerned, and adapted to the changing circumstances with continual and unmitigating effort.

The bloody battle of interests, each well-justified within its own particular ambit, revealed that the really important interests were those common to all, and unceremoniously posed the need for a common plan of *entente*. 'It is vitally important that we understand each other clearly. Many say yes, but they do not really agree. Many are not asked, and many are in agreement in the wrong. Therefore: it is vitally important that we understand each other clearly,' says Brecht. It was no longer the conservatives who were speaking like this – they rather tended to drown their disappointment in a muddy scepticism – but the revolutionaries, who felt the need to base themselves on some still point, the faith in man as a being open to persuasion, the basis on which all the rest could be changed.

In this way reason came into its own once more. It was no longer the proud and optimistic reason of the previous age, but humble, cautious, and infinitely precious because it seemed to be the only remaining ideal after the disappearance of all the others, the only lasting legacy of past tradition and the only cause for faith in the future.

These feelings had a decisive influence on

436, 437   *H. Poelzig, Two designs for the Festspielhaus in Salzburg, 1919 (from G. A. Platz, op. cit.)*

the development of the *avant-garde* movements, polarizing them in two opposite directions. Either men lost faith in all theoretical organization, which rushed artistic experience towards anarchism and activism, or else they tried to organize the results of previous experiments on solid, objective bases, to build up a new stylistic

438, 439 *H. Finsterlin,* Sketches for an Arts Centre, *1919–20*

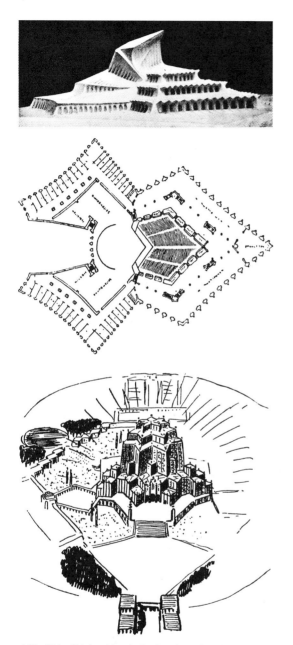

440, 441   *W. Luckhardt,* Design for a Popular Theatre, *1921*
442 *(below, left)   B. Taut,* Sketch for the House in the Sky, *1919*
443 *(right)   F. Marc,* Play of Shapes

language with general implications.

Futurism was almost immediately drawn towards political action. Marinetti was a propagandist for Italian intervention and many Futurists eagerly enrolled as volunteers; Boccioni and Sant'Elia were killed in

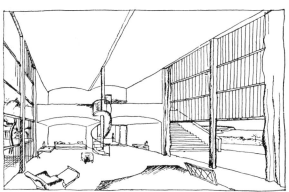

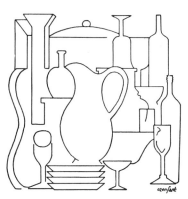

444   *F. Léger,* Two Women, *1925*
445, 446   *Le Corbusier,* Design for a Villa, *1916 (from* Oeuvre Complète*); Ozenfant,* Purist composition, *1925*

action; but the movement was very much weakened in the post-war period, and Marinetti shepherded its remains into the Fascist fold.

Dadaism, founded in Switzerland in 1916 by Tzara, Ball, Hulsenbeck and Arp, gathered together the most destructive artistic experiences that had emerged in reaction against the war (Duchamp, Picabia, Ernst, Ray); after the war Tzara settled in

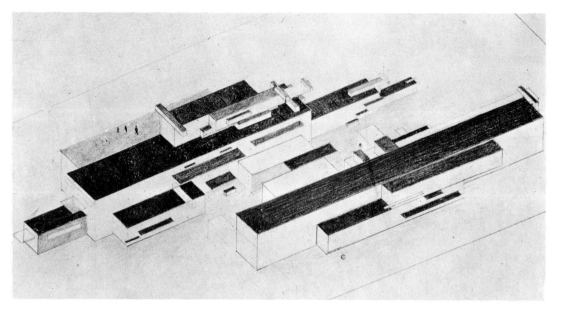

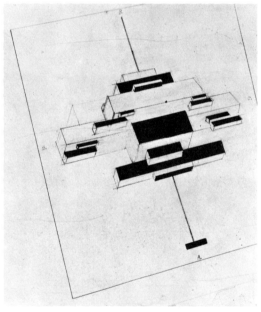

447, 448, 449 *K. Malevich, Three designs for houses of the future, 1923–4*

Paris where the movement developed along mainly literary lines, while Hulsenbeck and Ernst in Germany sought for direct participation in the political struggle until the main group in Cologne was dispersed in 1922. In 1924 Ray, Ernst and others joined the surrealist movement founded by Breton, which finally petered out in the mood of the thirties, after an unsuccessful attempt, between 1930 and 1933, at joining with the Communists.

This was the most obvious aspect of the post-war *avant-garde* and, for many, the quintessence of 'modern art'. The other side – which outlived the circumstances of the moment and which was what really

450   *G. Rietveld, Armchair, 1918*

counted for the fate of contemporary society – attempted to justify its innovating action in a reasonable fashion, distinguishing what should be retained from what was to be destroyed; modern architecture had its beginnings in this dividing line.

In the immediate post-war period the Cubist trunk put out various branches which aimed at abstracting from it a precise and universally communicable set of tenets, aiming thereby to go beyond the usual classification of the arts and extend into architecture.

The painter A. Ozenfant elaborated the principle of Purism from 1915 to 1917 in the review *Élan*, then met C. E. Jeanneret (1887–1965; the future Le Corbusier) and with him published the manifesto of the new movement in 1918, with the title *Après le Cubisme*. According to these two artists, Cubism had re-established the ability to appreciate, amid the mass of confused and approximate forms of the surrounding world, the simple and 'pure' forms which were the primary source of aesthetic sensations (Figs. 429–31). The simplification they hoped to bring about in artistic images was a particular example of the constructive spirit of synthesis which was ideally to influence all the branches of activity of our industrial society, from literature to science and technical matters.

In 1920, to test this intended unity, Ozenfant and Jeanneret founded the review *L'Esprit nouveau* which had *avant-garde* contributors from all fields, e.g. Aragon, Breton, Cendrars, Eluard, Ehrenburg, Epstein, Jacob, Milhaud, Rathenau, Satie, Tzara. In 1925 the review ceased publication and the two founders moved on along different paths. From now on Le Corbusier was devoting himself to architecture, while Ozenfant spent long years perfecting his murals.

In 1915 Malevich published his suprematist manifesto, in collaboration with Maiakovsky, Larianov and other revolution-ary writers; almost at the same time Tatlin was propounding constructivism and Rodcenko non-objectivism, which had in common the abandoning of all imitative references and the desire to start from scratch – from what Malevich called the 'desert' – to build up a new autonomous reality. Each tried to apply this procedure to architecture, and while Tatlin was outlining his contrived projects to celebrate the new Soviet institutions, Malevich was working on a series of marvellously consistent and rigorous abstract architectural images, with models called 'architectonen' and with designs for imaginary dwellings which he himself described and named 'planiti' (Figs. 447–9).

The Suprematist ideas were spread throughout Germany by E. Lissitzky, and Malevich himself went to the Bauhaus in 1926 to supervise the publication of his book *Die gegenstandslose Welt* in the series *Bauhausbücher*; but shortly afterwards the Russian *avant-garde* came into conflict with the political authorities and Malevich, though continuing to teach in the State schools in Leningrad, found himself completely isolated, so much so that very little is yet known about the last period of his activity, up to his death in 1935.

Neo-plasticism was founded in 1917 by the painters T. Van Doesburg, P. Mondrian, B. Van der Leck and V. Huszar, the architects J. J. P. Oud, J. Wils and R. Van t'Hoff, the sculptor G. Vantongerloo and the poet A. Kok; it was subsequently joined by the architects Gerrit Rietveld (1888–1964) and Cor Van Eesteren (b. 1897) and the cineast Hans Richter. The movement's mouthpiece was *De Stijl* which was published at irregular intervals until 1927.

The basic concepts were elaborated by Mondrian between 1913 and 1917, but theorized about and propagated mainly by Theo Van Doesburg (1883–1931). Within a short time they travelled the typical path from Cubism to complete abstraction, and

451 *G. Rietveld, Child's cart, 1918*
452 *T. Van Doesburg, The Aubette dance hall in Strasbourg (1926 in collaboration with J. Arp)*
453 *P. Mondrian,* Composition with planes of light colour and grey lines, *1919*

454   *P. Mondrian,* Composition in Blue, *1917*

set out to find a method to systematize this operation and to build up a new world of coherent and well-organized forms.

The basic idea was to start from the two-dimensional elements and to juxtapose them according to a new sense of their inter-relationship, from which a 'new plasticity' would spring. Van Doesburg saw clearly that this process was relevant not only to the painting of pictures or the creating of

455, 456 *T. Van Doesburg and C. Van Eesteren, Plans for a private house, 1920 (from* L'Architecture Vivante*)*

abstract sculptures but also to the reconstruction of the urban scene as a whole, in accordance with the technical and psychological needs of the time: 'The word "art" no longer means anything to us. In its place we demand the building up of our environment according to creative laws, deriving from a set principle. These laws, linked to those of economics, mathematics, engineering, hygiene etc., lead to a new plastic unity'.[28] And Mondrian, more explicitly:

'In future the realization of pure figurative expression within the encompassable reality of our environment will replace the work of art. But to attain this we must tend towards universal representation and detachment from the pressure of nature. Then we shall no longer have need of paintings and statues, because we shall be living within art. Art will disappear from life in the measure in which life itself gains in balance'.[29]

It was believed that this reconstruction of the environment could be made according to objective and universal laws, similar to those of science:

'It is impossible to imagine them, they exist and are felt only through collective and experimental work. The basis of these experiments is founded on the simple knowledge of the primary and universal elements of expression, in such a way as to arrive at a method of organizing them according to a new harmony. The basis of this harmony is the knowledge of the contrast, of the complex of contrasts, of the dissonances etc., which make visible all that surrounded us. The multiplicity of contrasts produces enormous tensions which, by cancelling each other out, create a balance and a feeling of restfulness. This balance of tensions forms the quintessence of the new architectural unity'.[30]

The first applications of this method to architecture were Van Doesburg's plan for a monument at Leemvarden in 1916, Rietveld's furniture (Figs. 450–1) and a house at Nordwijkerhout by Van Doesburg and Oud in 1917, in Oud's theoretical plans between 1917 and 1920 (Fig. 457) in the models by Van Doesburg and Van Eesteren between 1920 and 1923 (Figs. 455, 456), in the economic houses at the Hague by J. Wils in 1923, and very clearly in the house built by Rietveld in 1924 on the outskirts of Utrecht (Fig. 458) where the whole construc-

457   *J. J. P. Oud, Plan for housing estate on beach, 1917*

tion is aggressively resolved in a counterpoint of coloured slabs.

Oud's development is highly significant; after his youthful and theoretical plans for the houses at Scheveningen (1917), the workers' houses and factories at Purmerend (1918), he was appointed chief architect of the city of Rotterdam from 1918 to 1933; he thus found himself faced with tackling really important and demanding works, and the close adherence of the formal neo-plastic laws to technical, economic etc. laws – theoretically postulated by Van Doesburg – was posed as a practical problem. Naturally the results could not be as clear cut as in theoretical plans, nor could they be achieved at the first attempt, but only by means of intelligent mediation in the traditional constructional processes. From the first estate of working-class houses – Tusschendijken, 1920 – Van Doesburg protested with Oud because he used brick and juxtaposed uniform building types, while the 'balance of tensions' demanded that adjacent elements be all different. In the later complexes – Oud Mathenesse of 1922, Kiefhoek of 1925 and above all in the splendid terrace houses at Hook of Holland of 1924 – Oud broke definitively away from Van Doesburg and accepted traditional building types, at least as a framework; however, as will be seen

later on, it was precisely in these works that the neo-plastic method produced its first real fruits: decomposition was no longer flaunted and was absorbed with no visible trace into the blocks as a whole: yet the volumes, surfaces and colours were no longer those of before and emerged as quite new, as if seen for the first time, while harmony between form and construction re-emerged for the first time for over a century, on foundations very different from the original ones.

Oud himself explained his experiences as follows:

'The spirit of *De Stijl* was, at first, my spirit as well. It was born of an idea of Van Doesburg's and my own, and Van Doesburg was the driving force in the executive stage. The earliest numbers of the review published some of my works . . . which I regarded as the first examples of a real cubist architecture. Neo-plastic architecture (a probable allusion to the works of Rietveld, Wils etc.) and also Dudok's cubism derived from these works . . . . But my conclusions were different: through this process of decomposition I gained a new sense of proportion, of space, atmosphere, line and mass, colour and construction, but I

458 *G. Rietveld, Extension of the Schroeder house at Utrecht, 1924*
459 *A cover of* Mécano, *1922*

realized that the building that later derived from it was developing the most superficial aspect of my early works. Such a development seemed to me superficial for architecture: it had really more to do with painting and – as far as form was concerned – it was too hard and static. I abandoned it and began to move in another direction: a healthy, broad, universal social architecture could never come from this, i.e. from so abstract an aesthetic. There is no doubt, though, that neo-plasticism has given us architectural values which I would not like to see lost; but as far as I am concerned it has done this indirectly. My position is similar to that of the alchemists of the past, who did not find gold in their search for gold, but some other precious material'.[31]

Van Doesburg however, had decided to search for gold. In 1921 he joined the Dadaists, and with Arp, Tzara and Schwitters published a supplement to *Stijl* called *Mécano*, and went with them on a propagandist tour through Holland and Germany; in the same year he moved to Weimar and tried unsuccessfully to fit into the Bauhaus. Meanwhile, dissatisfied with the developments of neo-plasticism, he elaborated a new rival programme, elementarism, whose manifesto appeared in *Stijl* in 1926 (at this point Mondrian left the group and decided to carry on his rigorous pictorial experiment on his own); between 1926 and 1928, together with Arp, he furnished the Aubette dance hall in Strasbourg (Fig. 452) which was more or less the manifesto of his artistic beliefs; in 1930 he founded a last review, *L'Art concret* and before his death, the following year, planned to gather a new group of *avant-garde* artists together at Meudon for communal experimental work.

Neither Van Doesburg nor Mondrian felt personally inclined to leave their positions as *avant-garde* artists, but their contributions were crucial to the definition of the new architectural style: in a schematic and doctrinaire way, their experiments anticipated the problems that the modern movement had to face in the field of practical planning.

thirteen

The formation of the modern movement

Like every important historical transformation, the modern movement comprised a large number of individual and collective contributions, and it is impossible to pin down its origin to a single place or single cultural scene. What can be ascertained with certainty is the consistence of the various results from about 1927, when a common attitude between individuals and groups made itself felt. Behind this single point of emergence there existed a close-knit web of mutual stresses and exchanges, which it would be difficult and perhaps pointless to describe analytically.

One might first give a schematic description of the first decade of experiment, emphasizing firstly two revolutionary sets of experiments that were in conscious contrast with immediate tradition and certainly independent of one another, though interconnected in various ways: the teaching work of Gropius and his colleagues at the Bauhaus and the work of Le Corbusier as architect after the First World War. Secondly, one might list some experiments linked with the cultural movements of the pre- and post-war periods, but which occurred convergently, thus blurring the exclusive character of their points of departure so much that they become mutually commensurable and

could utilize each other's methods: among the most important were the work of Mendelsohn in Germany, Mies' progress from the Novembergruppe to the Werkbund, Oud's work for the administration of Rotterdam and Dudok's for Hilversum.

The distinctions were in fact schematic and demonstrative in kind: the parallel exhibitions of the Bauhaus and Le Corbusier, to pick the two most important facts of the second decade of the twentieth century, can be taken as an indication of the varied nature of the modern movement, and reveal two vastly differing types of contribution, the first collective and the second individual. The description of the early career of Mendelsohn and of the two Dutch masters should emphasize the possibility of the regeneration, within the modern movement, of the *avant-garde* trends that matured before and after the war, and it could be repeated for other individuals and other groups, for instance Van Eesteren, Bruno Taut, the Luckhardt brothers and Russian constructivists.

The historical result of this confluence of experiments was the inversion, after more than a century, of the centrifugal movement which had been devouring the innovatory activities of European and world culture. The new movement could no longer be

460 *L. Feininger's cover for the first Bauhaus manifesto, 1919*

labelled as the most recent of the movements that appeared so frequently on the scene; it bore witness to a more profound change, which acted on the complex of tendencies, channelling them in a new direction and forcing them to confront one another, in order to face up to the needs of a radically altered world.

1   The Bauhaus

Immediately after the end of the war, Walter Gropius was asked to run the Sächsische Hochschule für bildende Kunst and the Sächsische Kunstgewerbeschule, Van de Velde's school. He amalgamated the two institutions and thus founded the Staatliche Bauhaus in 1919.

The first manifesto, published in 1919, had a prophetic and obscure tone confirmed by the expressionistic cover by Feininger (Fig. 460).

'The complete building is the final aim of the visual arts. Their noblest function was once the decoration of buildings. Today they exist in isolation, from which they can be rescued only through the conscious, co-operative effort of all craftsmen. Architects, painters and sculptors must recognize anew the composite character of a building as an entity. Only then will their work be imbued with the architectonic spirit which it has lost as "salon art".

Architects, painters, sculptors, we must all turn to the crafts.

Art is not a "profession". There is no essential difference between the artist and the craftsman . . . Let us form a new guild of craftsmen without the class distinctions which raise an arrogant barrier between craftsman and artist. Together let us conceive and create the new building of the future, which will embrace architecture and sculpture and painting in one unity and which will rise one day towards heaven from the hands of a million workers like the crystal symbol of a new faith.'[1]

These phrases are no different from the numerous futuristic speeches that were being made at the time. However, the programme did not end with the manifesto of some new trend, but simply affirmed, in tortured and rambling terms, the need for a general methodology, based on natural laws and on those of the human mind, in which thought and action, material and spiritual needs might find a balance, transcending contrasting abstractions.

Gropius' first colleagues were Johannes Itten (b. 1888), a Swiss pupil of Hölzel, who held a course in formal education in Vienna from 1915 onwards – the American painter Lyonel Feininger (1871–1956) and the German sculptor and engraver Gerhard Marcks (b. 1889). In 1919 they were joined by Gropius' former collaborator Adolf Meyer (1881–1929), in 1920 by the painter Georg Muche (b. 1895), in 1921 by Paul Klee (1879–1940) and the painter and theatrical designer Oskar Schlemmer (1888–1943), in 1922 by Wassily Kandinsky (1866–1944) and in 1923 by the Hungarian painter Laszlo Moholy-Nagy (1895–1946). There were about 250 students, mostly German and Austrian. The study programme comprised:

A preliminary six months' course taken by Itten, and after 1923 by Moholy-Nagy and his ex-pupil Josef Albers (b. 1888) in which the student gained confidence with his materials and with various simple formal problems.

A three year course, partly technical ('Werklehre': the student had to attend one of the seven workshops for the working of stone, wood, metal, clay, glass, pigments and textile looms, and had theoretical lessons in book-keeping, costing and the drawing up of tenders), partly formal ('Formlehre': included the observation of formal effects in nature and in materials, the study of methods of representation and theory of composition).

After three years the pupil could take an examination to obtain a Journeyman's Certificate.

A further course, of varying length, based on architectural planning and practical work in the school's workshops; at the end the pupil could take an examination to qualify for a Master Builder's Diploma.

Commenting on the Bauhaus experiment some time after the event, Gropius noted three main features of the teaching:

–the parallelism between theoretical and practical teaching, because during the three year course the pupil studied simultaneously under two masters: a master of craft and a master of design:

'This idea of studying with two different groups of masters was a necessity, because neither artists possessing sufficient technical knowledge nor craftsmen endowed with sufficient imagination for artistic problems, who could have been made the leaders of the working departments, were to be found. A new generation capable of combining both these attributes had first to be trained. In later years the Bauhaus succeeded in placing as masters in charge of the workshops former students who were then equipped with such equivalent technical and artistic experience that the separation of the staff into masters of form and masters of technique was found to be superfluous'.[2]

– continuous contact with practical realities:

'The whole institution of the Bauhaus training shows the educational value which was attached to practical problems, which impel the students to overcome all internal and external friction . . . For that reason, I endeavoured to secure practical commissions for the Bauhaus, in which both masters and students could put their work to a test . . . The demonstration of all kinds of new models made in our workshops, which we were able to show in practical use in the building, so thoroughly convinced manufacturers that they entered into royalty contracts with the Bauhaus which, as the turnover increased, proved a valuable source of revenue to the latter. The institution of obligatory practical work simultaneously afforded the possibility of paying students for saleable articles and models which they had worked out. This provided many a capable student with some means of existence'.[3]

– the presence of creative masters:

'The selection of the right teacher is the decisive factor in the results obtained by a training institute. Their personal attributes as men play an even more decisive part than their technical knowledge and ability . . . If men of outstanding artistic ability are to be won for an institute, they must from the outset be afforded wide possibilities for their own further development, by giving them time and space for private work. The mere fact that such men continue to develop their own work in the institute produces that creative atmosphere which is so essential for a school of design and in which youthful talent can develop'.[4]

The basic idea was to utilize craftsmanship no longer as a Romantic aim or ideal, but as the means for the education of modern designers, capable of giving industrial products a definite formal bias. Faced with the controversy between craftsmanship and industry which had been raging for a decade within the Werkbund, Gropius chose neither one term nor the other, realizing that this was a battle between two opposing abstractions. In reality the difference between the two types of activity was only one of degree, as craftsmanship was not pure conception (since the idea must always pass through a technical expedient in order to reach reality) nor was industry purely mechanical (since the machine itself, in so far as it produces forms, posed a problem of creativity); they were two different ways of carrying out the same activity, at once intellectual and mechanical; the first was more direct and less extensive, the second less direct and more extensive. The transformation concerned not so much the material instrument as the distribution of human energies:

'The difference between industry and craftsmanship is due far less to the different nature of the tools employed in each, than to sub-division of labour in the one and undivided control by a single workman in the other. This compulsory restriction of personal initiative is the threatening cultural danger of the present day form of industry. The only remedy is a completely changed attitude towards work which, though based on the sensible realization that the development of technique has shown how a collective form of labour can lead humanity to greater total efficiency than the autocratic labour of the isolated individual, should not detract from the power and importance of personal effort'.[5]

Here education was a crucial factor: indeed the knowledge of the whole process, by means of direct and manual experience, would allow those who were to carry out the single phases to see their own work within the framework of the whole: then they would no longer be uncaring cogs in the works, but would form a group of responsible operators, aware of the nature of their association and the original spiritual values attached to technical work would be re-established, being transferred from individual work to group work.

Passing from educational terms to social ones, the problem was to heal the breach between culture and production brought about by the industrial revolution. Hauser wrote:

'The obstruction which has occurred in this development since the Industrial Revolution, the lead that technical achievements have gained over intellectual, is to be attributed not so much to the fact that more complicated and more diverse machines began to be used, as to the phenomenon that technical development, spurred on by prosperity, became so rapid that the human mind had no time to keep pace with it. In other words, those elements which might have transferred the tradition of craftsmanship to mechanical production, the independent masters of their apprentices, were eliminated from economic life before they had any chance of adapting themselves and the traditions of their craft to the new methods of production – all of a sudden there were too few experts in the industries rooted in the old traditions of craftsmanship'.[6]

A new method of teaching, based on team-work, could aim to reintroduce craftsmanship into industry, and thereby to salvage the values of the old artistic tradition – which had been expressed in history in this type of work – and to re-introduce them into the life cycle of modern society, while stripping from them all class characteristics, so that all society could partake of them.

This mode of teaching brought about a fundamental change in architectural thought. Concern with form was no longer a matter on its own, but became an integral part of productive activity. The aim of artistic work was not the invention of a form but the modification, by this form, of the course of everyday life, and it was valid in so far as it affected all production and the environment in which all men lived. For the first time Morris's formula, 'an art of the people for the people' took on a precise meaning, because the incisive 'if all people do not soon share it there will soon be none to share', suddenly acquired a real meaning.[7]

It is almost impossible to distinguish what portion of these aims was achieved by

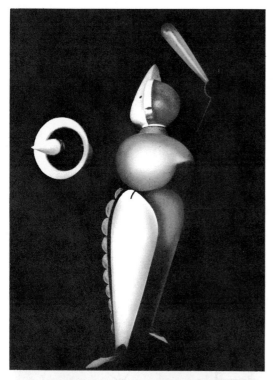

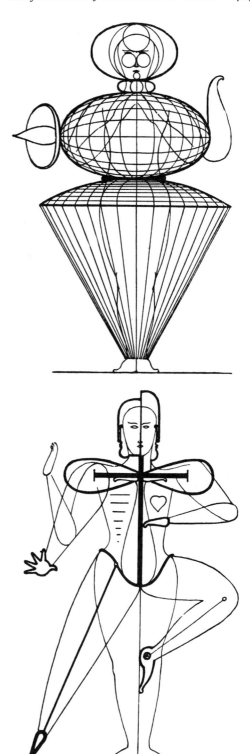

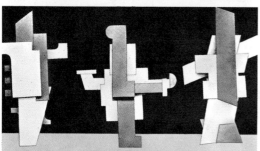

461, 462, 463 *O. Schlemmer, costumes for the Triadische Ballet (Stuttgart 1922, Weimar 1923; from O. S., Die Bühne im Bauhaus, 1925)*
464 *(below on left)   K. Schmidt, F. W. Bogler, G. Telscher, figures for the Mechanische Ballet, 1923 (op. cit.)*

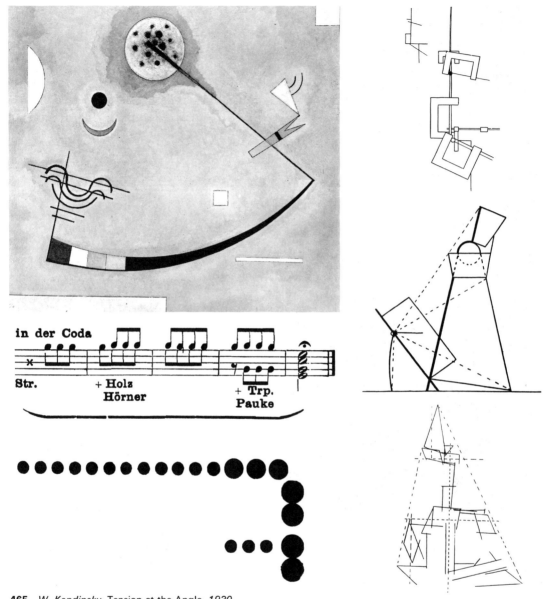

465 *W. Kandinsky,* Tension at the Angle, *1930*
466 *(below) W. Kandinsky,* Graphic transcription of a passage of Beethoven's Fifth Symphony *(from W. K.,* Punkt und Linie zu Fläche, *1926)*
467 *(right) An exercise from Kandinsky's course: the transformation of a material model into an abstract image*

468 *P. Klee,* Twittering Machine, *1922 (from W. Grohmann,* op. cit.*)*

Gropius himself, and what by his colleagues, precisely because the experiment was founded on the fusing of individual contributions. An open-minded attitude towards a variety of experiments was undoubtedly a psychological factor of Gropius' makeup; he writes:

'When I was a small boy, somebody asked me what my favourite colour was. For some years my family poked fun at me for saying, after some hesitation, "Bunt ist meine Lieblingsfarbe", meaning "Multicoloured is my favourite colour". The strong desire to *include* every vital component of life instead of excluding part of them for the sake of too narrow and dogmatic an approach has characterized my whole life'.[8]

Gropius' pre-war architecture was characterized by rigorous technical propriety and a certain lack of concern about using ready-made stylistic solutions which bordered on the eclectic. Nonetheless Gropius – except perhaps at the very beginning of his career – imagined that he could remain aloof from the particular currents of contemporary figurative culture. But there was a streak of curiosity in him which forced him to participate temporarily in a variety of current experiments, while not being in whole-hearted agreement with any of them. In this way, in the immediate post-war period he did not escape the wave of expressionism which affected so much German architecture, from Behrens to the younger artists, as can be seen in the Sommerfeld house at Dahlem (1921) and the Monument to the Fallen at Weimar (1922).

In the Bauhaus, too, during the early years, the contribution of expressionist tendencies was predominant, though not exclusive; Feininger, who came from the 'blaue Reiter' was in continual contact with Van Doesburg; Gropius had known Van Doesburg in Berlin in 1919, and the neo-plastic element was apparent in the students' work from the start. But Gropius' thesis,

that the school should remain open to the influences of all contemporary movements without falling within the exclusive orbit of any one of them, soon proved to be very difficult to maintain.

In 1922 Van Doesburg settled in Weimar and organized a section of the movement 'De Stijl', criticizing the Bauhaus teachers who did not accept its views; the students divided into two factions and a violent disagreement blew up, which calmed down only at the beginning of 1923, when Van Doesburg left for Paris.[9]

At this time inflation was weighing on the economic life of Germany and particularly on building activity; thus the energies within the Bauhaus were forced in upon themselves, in a tense atmosphere where quarrels quickly became intense; the inhabitants of Weimar regarded this group of individuals, engaged on an incomprehensible task, with suspicion, and the students reacted by behaving in the most unconventional fashion; a number of strange characters were connected with the Bauhaus, for instance the preacher W. Hauser, and on Saturday evenings the peace of the town was regularly shattered by the eccentric entertainments organized in the school.

Only Gropius' infinite patience succeeded in keeping all these heterogeneous and explosive forces united and directed towards a single goal. In 1922 the school's constitution was published, specifying its organizational structure,[10] and in 1923, at the request of the authorities of Thuringia, a first public report of its activities was produced; Gropius would have preferred to wait, but forced by circumstances, he encouraged the school to present the public with the fullest possible description of the movement and of its cultural attitudes.

The works of the school were exhibited in the halls of the Bauhaus and in the Weimar Museum, the programme of the 'Bauhauswoche' included lectures by Gropius, Kandinsky and Oud, a concert by H.

Scherchen with music by Hindemith, Busoni, Krenek and Stravinsky, film shows by C. Kock, parties with fireworks and jazz by the Bauhaus band, reflected light compositions by L. Hirshfeld-Mack; the stage of the municipal theatre of Jena, recently built by Gropius and Meyer, was used by O. Schlemmer for a ballet in which the dancers were hidden behind abstract forms. An album was published for the occasion with reproductions of the works of various masters and pupils.[11]

To sway the public, given the school's bias, emphasis was laid not only on plans and discussions but also on practical demonstration: a house designed and built entirely in the Bauhaus workshops, known as the 'Haus am Horn'.[12] The house was conceived as a single cell for a small district to be built round Van de Velde's building, and it was conceived so as to be easily repeated for mass-production, like the furniture for it by Breuer. But inflation was at its height and these plans remained on paper.

In the same year Gropius tried to condense the main points of the new teaching method into a pamphlet.[13] The integrated conception of technical and artistic work, already hinted at in the 1919 programme, was here expounded in these words:

'The dominant spirit of the epoch is already recognizable although its form is not yet clearly defined. The old dualistic world-concept which envisaged the ego in opposition to the universe is rapidly losing ground. In its place is rising the idea of a universal unity in which all opposing forces exist in a state of absolute balance. This dawning recognition of the essential oneness of all things and their appearances endows creative effort with a fundamental inner meaning. No longer can anything exist in isolation. We perceive every form as the embodiment of an idea, every piece of work as a manifestation of our inner selves. Only work which is the product of

inner compulsion can have spiritual meaning. Mechanized work is lifeless, proper only to the lifeless machine. So long, however, as machine-economy remains an end in itself rather than a means of freeing the intellect from the burden of mechanical labour, the individual will remain enslaved and society will remain disordered. The solution depends on a change in the individual's attitude towards his work, not on the betterment of his outward circumstances, and the acceptance of this new principle is of decisive importance for new creative work.'

He also attempted to describe the process of design:

'The objective of all creative effort in the visual arts is to give form to space. But what is space, how can it be understood and given a form?'

'Although we may achieve an awareness of the infinite we can give form to space only with finite means. We become aware of space through our undivided Ego, through the simultaneous activity of soul, mind and body. A like concentration of all our forces is necessary to give it form. Through his intuition, through his metaphysical powers, man discovers the immaterial space of inward vision and inspiration. This conception of space demands realization in the material world, a realization which is accompanied by the brain and the hands. The brain conceives of mathematical space in terms of numbers and dimensions . . . The hand masters matter through the crafts, and with the help of tools and machinery.

Conception and visualization are always simultaneous. Only the individual's capacity to feel, to know and to execute varies in degree and in speed. True creative work can be done only by the man whose knowledge and mastery of the physical laws of statics, dynamics, optics, acoustics equip him to give life and shape to his inner vision. In a work of art the laws of the physical world, the intellectual world and the world of the spirit function and are expressed simultaneously.'

The teaching method used in the Bauhaus is explained in this historical *excursus*:

'The tool of the spirit of yesterday was the "academy". It shut off the artist from the world of industry and handicraft and thus brought about his complete isolation from the community . . . Academic training, however, brought about the development of a great art-proletariat destined to social misery. For this art-proletariat, lulled into a dream of genius and enmeshed in artistic conceit, was being prepared for the "profession" of architecture, painting, sculpture or graphic art, without being given the equipment of a real education – which alone could have assured it of economic and aesthetic independence. Its abilities, in the final analysis, were confined to a sort of drawing – painting that had no relation to the realities of materials, techniques or economics. Lack of all vital connection led inevitably to barren aesthetic speculation. The fundamental pedagogic mistake of the academy arose from its preoccupation with the idea of the individual genius and its discounting the value of commendable achievement on a less exalted level. Since the academies trained a myriad of minor talents in drawing and painting, of whom scarcely one in a thousand became a genuine architect or painter, the great mass of these individuals, fed upon false hopes and trained as one-sided academicians, was condemned to a life of fruitless artistic activity. Unequipped to function successfully in the struggle for existence, they found themselves numbered among the social drones, useless, by virtue of their schooling, in the productive life of the nation.'

. . . The second half of the nineteenth century saw the beginning of a protest against the devitalizing influence of the academies. Ruskin and Morris in England, Van de Velde in Belgium, Olbrich, Behrens and others in Germany and, finally, the Deutscher Werkbund, all sought, and in the end discovered, the basis of a reunion between creative artists and the industrial world. In Germany, arts and crafts schools were founded for the purpose of developing, in a new generation, talented individuals trained in industry and handicraft. But the academy was too firmly established: practical training never advanced beyond dilettantism, and draughted and rendered design remained in the forefront. The foundation of this attempt was never wide enough nor deep enough to avail against the old *l'art pour l'art*, so alien to and so far removed from life. Meanwhile the crafts – and more especially the industries – began to cast about for artists. A demand arose for products, outwardly attractive as well as technically and economically acceptable. The technicians could not satisfy it. So manufacturers started to buy so-called "artistic designs". This was an ineffective substitute, for the artist was too much removed from the world about him and too little schooled in technical and handicraft to adjust his conception of form to the practical processes of production. At the same time, the merchants and technicians lacked the insight to realize that appearance, efficiency and expense could be simultaneously controlled only by planning and producing the industrial object with the careful co-operation of the artist responsible for its design. Since there was a dearth of artists adequately trained for such work, it was logical to establish the following basic requirements for the future training of all gifted individuals: a thorough practical manual training in workshops actively engaged in production, coupled with sound theoretical instruction in the laws of design.'

Lastly the need for links between the various fields of contemporary culture was expressed as follows:

'An organization based on new principles easily becomes isolated if it does not constantly maintain a thorough understanding of all the questions agitating the rest of the world. In spite of all the practical difficulties, the basis of the growing work of the Bauhaus can never be too broad. Its responsibility is to educate men and women to understand the world in which they live and to invent and create forms symbolizing that world. For that reason the educational field must be enlarged in all sides and extended into neighbouring fields, so that the effect of new experiments may be studied.

The education of children when they are young and still unspoiled is of great importance. The new types of schools, emphasizing practical exercise, such as the Montessori schools, provide an excellent preparation for the constructive program of the Bauhaus since they develop the entire human organism.'[14]

Many of these phrases were metaphors, through which a new strain of thought was struggling for expression, using the terms of the old culture. But they were to be interpreted literally by the majority and gave rise to a series of arguments, almost exclusively verbal, on mind and matter, man and the machine, brain and hand, which will be further examined in Chapter 14.

From 1924 onwards the general economic situation improved; the Bauhaus began to receive commissions from industry, while the fame of the movement grew, in Germany and abroad, with the publication of the *Bauhausbücher*.[15] But so did the harshness of reaction.

The Bauhaus received convergent attacks from right and left: traditionalists reproached

it with being a subversive movement, upsetting the bases of taste and not taking historical heritage[16] into account, while *avant-garde* artists reproached it with not being sufficiently consistent, with cultivating eclecticism and compromise.[17] There were, however, some critics who defended the school, for instance S. Giedion,[18] W. C. Behrendt,[19] B. Taut[20] and various eminent figures in European culture who recognized their own ideals in the work of Gropius and his colleagues.[21]

Inevitably, political themes entered the debate. Gropius made every effort to keep the Bauhaus out of the bitter party quarrels, and confirmed the apolitical nature of the institution on every possible occasion. But the very principles of the movement made this tactic difficult; once the unassailability connected with a purely contemplative position had been abandoned, and the fate of culture linked with economic and social reality, a political stand was inevitable. Furthermore this consequence, if modern architects hesitated to accept it, was immediately picked upon by their adversaries: the left accused Gropius of being an exponent of capitalism, the right of being a subversive, and each was partly right, because in the measure in which their conceptions were linked to the old culture, the modern movement was destined to become a real political adversary.

'Those who were no longer in a position, or no longer wanted, to change and accept the lesson [wrote H. Pflug in 1932] understood that the Bauhaus was aiming for a new life and a new style for new times; so they rebelled, and the animosity that they could not give vent to elsewhere was directed towards the practical incarnation of their fears'.[22]

When the battle became fiercer the Werkbund intervened to defend the Bauhaus and declared, through the mouth of its president H. Poelzig:

'The public controversy now raging around the Bauhaus of Weimar is no local matter; in more ways than one, it concerns all those interested in the growth and development of our art. It is always undesirable to confuse problems of art with political trends. The fury of political strife injected into all discussion of the work and purpose of the Bauhaus impedes any real consideration of the great and important experiment boldly going forward here. We trust that the officials and departments having jurisdiction over this matter will do their utmost to prevent political passions from destroying an undertaking which should not be measured by personal prejudices or by considerations foreign to art, but solely by its straightforwardness and its own unimpeachable objectives'. [23]

But the Weimar authorities could no long remain neutral and they created so many difficulties for Gropius that he decided to leave the city in 1924. On this occasion a number of eminent men, including Behrens, Oud, Mies, Poelzig, Hoffmann, Einstein, Hauptmann, Justi, Sudermann, Osborn, Hoffmannstahl, Kokoschka, Reinhardt, Schonberg, Strzygowsky, Werfel and Muthesius signed a protest addressed to the government of Thuringia. [24]

The school moved to Dessau at the beginning of 1925, at the invitation of the Mayor of Hesse. This step proved opportune, because Gropius and his colleagues were free of the tense, sophisticated atmosphere of Weimar and found a more peaceful and 'normal' atmosphere, which encouraged fruitful contact with German economic and productive reality.

The building of the new buildings at Dessau involved the school, for the first time, in an enormous practical task: Gropius was commissioned by the administration of Dessau to design not only the institute – with nearby accommodation for the teachers, a house for Gropius, and three double houses

for Kandinsky, Klee, Moholy-Nagy, Schlemmer, Scheper and Muche – but also a model district of working class dwellings in the suburb of Törten and the town's labour exchange.

The building for the Bauhaus was the only one in which Gropius did the architectural plan entirely himself – though calling in others to collaborate in its execution and interior décor – and it was also the building that revealed most clearly, beyond its basic desire to prove a point, and its formal severity, a warm movement of participation in the life that was to be lived within these walls.

The similarity between this building and certain designs of neo-plastic and constructivist artists has been noted more than once; Gropius showed that he had passed through the mesh of the most up-to-date pictorial movements, but contrary to what he had done in his earlier works, here he absorbed these experiments without trace and attained that unruffled coherence with which he had designed the Fagus works fifteen years before, though he was now moving in a much wider cultural scene.

It was a complex building, just as the life to be lived within it was complex: it included a block for the school and another for the workshops, joined by a suspended bridge housing the administrative offices, a low building with large rooms for communal life and a five-storey wing for the students (Figs. 469–76).

In Van Doesburg's plans the wall elements of the buildings were worked on in isolation and then juxtaposed according to definite relationships, so as to build up a new plasticity; there is nothing like that here where the volumes are enclosed and entire, but each geometrical element had a precise relationship with the others and each partial episode appeared tense and incomplete until one considered the whole, where opposing tensions cancel one another out, finding the 'balance' and 'rest' at which Van Doesburg

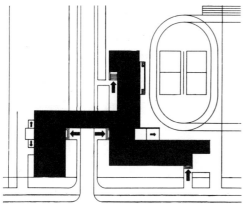

469, 470, 471 *Dessau, The Bauhaus building, 1926*

was aiming. The composition of the façades was never concluded at the edges of the expanses of wall but tended to be carried on to the adjacent façades, by means of some continuous element – the balconies running round the corners of the students' house – or by a studied asymmetry which was to be made up for somewhere else. The constructional elements seem to exist only by virtue of these mutual relations; for this reason Gropius avoided emphasizing their individual physical consistency and had recourse basically to only two materials: glass for the spaces, framed in metal, and white plaster

472, 473, 474   *Dessau, Details of the Bauhaus, today and in 1926*

for the walls.

The use of white plaster served to stress the geometrical relations, by temporarily renouncing the typical physical determination of the various materials; one may remember Brunelleschi's white plaster, equally necessary to underline the play of perspective and to erase references to the current constructional repertoire.

This type of finish emphasized problems of maintenance and, though cared for equally carefully, the Bauhaus building has certainly aged worse than the Fagus factory; but this consequence must be seen in relation to the new concept of architectural values. If architecture is not to restrict itself to representing the aspirations of society but is to contribute to realizing them, then architec-

475, 476 *Dessau, Details of the Bauhaus, today and in 1926*

tural products have value in relation to the life lived in them and do not last like natural objects, independently of men, but must be made to last with appropriate processes. For this reason, now that the original life of the place had been dispersed and that the work is reduced to a pathetic heap of shattered walls and door and window frames, to all intents and purposes the Bauhaus no longer exists; it is not a ruin, like the remains of

477, 478, 479   *Dessau, one of the double houses for Bauhaus teachers. In the plan: 1 kitchen; 2 dining room; 3 living room; 4 bedroom; 5 studio*

ancient buildings, and it has no physical fascination. The emotion that its sight arouses is historical and reflective in kind, like that one feels for some object which has belonged to a great man.

The 'new unity' between art and technical matters, which Gropius taught in his school, was put to the test in the Bauhaus building to an extent that could hardly be surpassed; he realized a building that was aesthetically impressive, even monumental in its own way, without moving away at all from the human scale and keeping rigorously to utilitarian needs. The character of the building was determined above all by the relation between the functional elements, and through the proportions of the lifeless blocks of masonry one can still catch a glimmer of the original fullness of life.

The teaching of the Bauhaus in the Dessau period grew and deepened, putting previous experience to good use. Five of its former ex-students, as well as Albers who taught the preliminary course, were chosen as heads of the workshops: Herbert Bayer (b. 1900) for typography, Marcel Breuer (b. 1902) for furniture, Gunta Stölzl (b. 1897) for weaving, Hinnerk Scheper (1897–1957) for painting and Joost Schmidt (1893–1948) for sculpture.

The most important innovations came from the metal and furniture workshops. In the first Moholy-Nagy abandoned the traditional working of precious metals and devoted himself mainly to electric lighting equipment in nickel or chrome-plated iron (Fig. 484); in the second Breuer invented and built the first steel tube furniture (Figs. 480–1). Similarly work in the typographical, textile and mural painting workshops became simpler and more rational. No more elaborate ornamental compositions but terse, legible pages (Fig. 483), fabrics and wallpaper of a single colour with varying grain and texture (Figs. 486–9).

Some of these models were accepted by industry, and patents provided the school with increasing and secure financial means. Meanwhile the fame of the Bauhaus was rapidly spreading; some schools, in Germany and elsewhere, adopted the new methods, and many former pupils occupied important posts in German industry.

In 1928, at the height of his success, Gropius gave over his post of director to the Swiss Hannes Meyer (1889–1954) and left the school, together with Breuer, Bayer and Moholy-Nagy. This decision was Gropius' master stroke in teaching: after having spent all his energies in the undertaking, throwing his authority and influence into the balance at crucial moments, but always avoiding personalizing his teaching beyond a certain

limit, he had the shrewdness and the courage to withdraw when he regarded the school's stability as established. On this occasion he declared:

'The Bauhaus, which I founded nine years ago, is now firmly established. This is indicated by the growing recognition it receives and the steady increase in the number of its students. It is therefore my conviction . . . that the time has come for me to turn over the direction of the Bauhaus to co-workers to whom I am united by close personal ties and common interests . . .'.[25]

But he also declared that he was retiring 'to exercise my capabilities more freely, in a sphere where they will not be hindered by official duties and considerations'. After designing the Törten district of Dessau in 1926 and winning the competition for the Dammerstock district of Karlsruhe in 1927, Gropius became involved in town-planning work and realized that it was not enough to supply society with perfect models but that it was necessary to be involved more directly, and in contact with the forces destined to utilize them. This task imposed stringent demands, particularly of time, and Gropius realized that he could not fulfil them except by devoting his whole working energies to them.

Before going any further one should consider carefully the meaning and implications of the experiment that took place within the Bauhaus.

Gropius' work has been aptly defined as 'the transcending of the *avant-garde*'.[26] *Avant-garde* artists had thought – and here lay their limitation – that the reform of modern architecture could be carried out within the cognitive sphere, i.e. by formulating a new style that was different from previous ones. Since contemporary reality did not usually offer suitable ground for this enterprise, they restricted their field of action artificially, or actually locked themselves into

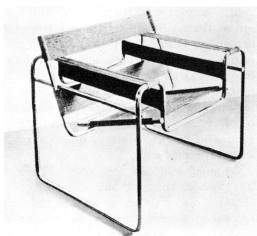

480 *(above)   A room in Gropius' house at the Weissenhof, 1927, with metal furniture by M. Breuer and a light by M. Brandt*
481, 482 *(below)   M. Breuer, Armchair in metal tubing and material, 1925 (from G. C. Argan, M.B., 1957);*
P. Klee, Linear perspective with open door, *1923 (from W. Grohmann, op. cit., 1929)*

INTERNATIONALE ARCHITEKTUR

HERAUSGEGEBEN
VON
WALTER GROPIUS

ALBERT LANGEN VERLAG MÜNCHEN

IM **ALBERT LANGEN VERLAG MÜNCHEN**
ERSCHEINEN SERIENWEISE DIE

BAUHAUSBÜCHER

Schriftleitung: GROPIUS und MOHOLY-NAGY

DIE ERSTE SERIE BESTEHT AUS 8 BÄNDEN

1 INTERNATIONALE ARCHITEKTUR von WALTER GROPIUS
2 PÄDAGOGISCHES SKIZZENBUCH von PAUL KLEE
3 EIN VERSUCHSHAUS DES BAUHAUSES
4 DIE BÜHNE IM BAUHAUS
5 NEUE GESTALTUNG von PIET MONDRIAN (Holland)
6 GRUNDBEGRIFFE DER NEUEN KUNST von THEO VAN DOESBURG (Holland)
7 NEUE ARBEITEN DER BAUHAUSWERKSTÄTTEN
8 MALEREI, PHOTOGRAPHIE, FILM von L. MOHOLY-NAGY

IN VORBEREITUNG:

KLEINWOHNUNGEN von DER ARCHITEKTURABTEILUNG DES BAUHAUSES
MERZ-BUCH von KURT SCHWITTERS
BILDERMAGAZIN DER ZEIT von OSKAR SCHLEMMER
SCHÖPFERISCHE MUSIKERZIEHUNG von HEINRICH JACOBY
AMERIKA? — EUROPA? von GEORG MUCHE
DIE ARBEIT DER STIJL-GRUPPE von THEO VAN DOESBURG
KONSTRUKTIVE BIOLOGIE von MARTIN SCHÄFER
DIE HOLLÄNDISCHE ARCHITEKTUR von J. J. P. OUD (Holland)
FUTURISMUS von F. T. MARINETTI und E. PRAMPOLINI (Italien)
DIE ARBEIT DER MA-GRUPPE von L. KASSAK und E. KÁLLAI (Ungarn)
PLASTIK DER GESTALTUNGEN von M. BURCHARTZ
PUNKT, LINIE, FLÄCHE von WASSILY KANDINSKY
RUSSLAND von ADOLF BEHNE
REKLAME UND TYPOGRAPHIE
NEUE ARCHITEKTURDARSTELLUNG von WALTER GROPIUS
BILDNERISCHE MECHANIK von PAUL KLEE
WERKARBEIT DER GESTALTUNGEN von L. MOHOLY-NAGY
ARCHITEKTUR, MALEREI, PLASTIK aus den WERKSTÄTTEN DES BAUHAUSES
DIE NEUEN MATERIALIEN von ADOLF MEYER
ARCHITEKTUR von LE CORBUSIER-SAUGNIER (Frankreich)
BILDERMAGAZIN DER ZEIT II von JOOST SCHMIDT
VIOLETT (BÜHNENSTÜCK MIT EINLEITUNG UND SZENERIE) von KANDINSKY

Jeder Band enthält zirka **16** bis **32** Seiten Text und **32** bis **96** ganzseitige Abbildungen oder **48** bis **60** Seiten Text ● Format **18 × 23** cm ●

483 *The first and last pages of the* Bauhausbuch *No. 1 (layout by L. Moholy-Nagy)*

their studies, devoted themselves to theoretical and demonstrational projects.

But the new movement came out into the open, taking as a field of action the whole environment and the whole scale of manufactured products which are of use to society at any given moment; at the same time it gave up the idea of gaining victory immediately, by instantly projecting a new system of forms into reality, and embarked on a patient and open work of improvement of current production. Its mode of procedure changed completely, because the objective of cultural action was not maximum modification but a degree of modification of the environment, and ready-made solutions could not be given, only methods to resolve problems step by step, taking continually changing circumstances into account.[27]

Gropius wrote: 'The solution depends on a change in the attitude of the individual towards his work, not on outward circumstances', and indeed the lesson of the Bauhaus affected what really counted in planning, the distribution of human energies rather than technical instruments or formal models.

It is now possible to describe some consequences of this decisive change in method.

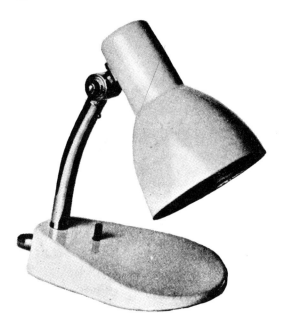

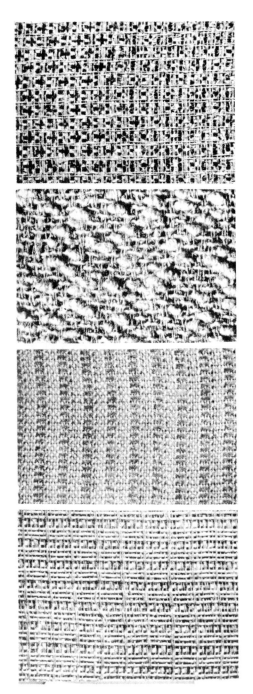

484, 485 *(left)   M. Brandt, Table lamp, 1924; A. Albers, Wool carpet, 1925 (from H. Bayer, W. & I.G. Gropius,* op. cit.*)*
486, 487, 488, 489   *A. Albers, Samples of materials made with the combination of two materials: paper fibre and cellophane, wool and rayon, cotton and rayon, cotton and cellophane* (ibid.)

1   Planning was no longer conceived of as a simple action, organizing reality from above according to an ideal rhythm and scale, but as a series of actions regulated according to the rhythm and scope of real phenomena, and therefore distributed over various scales and at various intervals.

In this way the relations between architecture, town-planning and interior decoration might be more precisely defined. These were not categories related to one another according to a fixed relationship, but historical and conventional partitions within a single activity, which in reality was divided into various stages because the necessary decisions for practical intervention must be taken at different times, in different fields and by different bodies of experts. The balance between the decisions on the various levels was never determined in advance, but was a question of degree to be solved afresh every time, by reconciling the various demands among themselves in a reasonable fashion.

2   Planning experiments were no longer considered as independent of each other, but formed a continuous sequence in the historical sense as well, and established a sort of permanent collaboration between all planners.

Every calculated action must aim to resolve a particular problem in a suitable manner, but at the same time it must be transferable and communicable to others and serve as a precedent for future action. The peculiarities of objective and subjective conditions – inspiration, sensibility – can never be invoked to arrive at a hasty conclusion, but every experiment must be left open and verifiable for all; furthermore a work should never be purely polemical and experimental, but should always be closely bound up with a practical aim. The balance between these two demands was another problem of degree that remained permanently open.

Thus the movement started by the Bauhaus was not just another style, set up in opposition to the previous ones, and it did not exhaust itself in the formal repertoire which it tended to utilize, but it was able to broaden its scope indefinitely, and took up an attitude of collaboration, not of preclusion, *vis-à-vis* other similar and parallel movements.

3   Architecture was not to be considered as either the mirror of the ideals of society, or as the mythical force capable of regenerating society on its own, but as one of the services necessary to communal life, which depended on the balance of the whole and which itself contributed to modifying this balance. One must not wait for society to be perfect before taking action, because its perfection depended partly on the architect's contribution, and on the other hand architecture alone could not claim to remedy all ills and resolve all problems itself, because architects did not act on society from the outside, and the modes of their action depended in part on the characteristics and tendencies of that society itself.[28]

Thus many extremist discussions on the relations between art and life lost their dramatic tone and changed accordingly. Art was one of the important things in the world but not the most important, and still less the only one: 'no work of art can be greater than its creator'.[29] Therefore the responsibility of the artist must not overshadow the more general responsibility of the man, and the modern artist, unlike the Romantic, must not sacrifice all his energies on the altar of art, but must devote to his profession a proportionate part of his strength and keep himself available, if necessary, for other more important and more urgent tasks

4   The concern of architecture was not only with quality, i.e. the visualizing of forms, nor merely quantity, i.e. the technical processes of execution and multiplication, but the mediation between quality and quantity.

Every working method contains within it

both qualitative and quantitative possibilities. The methods of industrial work, for instance, made it possible to produce a greater number of objects at a lower price than had been possible using manual methods; at the beginning, thinking that the transformation was purely quantitative men wanted industrial objects to be as like as possible to those produced by the old craftsmanship, but the original qualitative values inevitably disappeared with the processes of mechanical production. Hence a sterile battle between those who wanted the advantages of quantity, to the detriment of quality, and those who wanted better quality, at the expense of quantity.

Gropius was the first to state the question in modern terms. The conflict had arisen because of the warring possibilities of the quality of craftsmanship and the quantity made possible by industry; but what was necessary was to discover the new qualitative possibilities of industry, which were naturally compatible with its quantitative advantages. The number of objects of course increased with mass production, but, because of changes in organization, so did the time and money that could be devoted to perfecting the prototypes. Standardization had an extensive but also an intensive aspect, it meant the multiplication of the executive acts but also the concentration of those of the original devising, it produced both economy of capital and economy of thought.

In the productive cycle of the Bauhaus the quantitative pole was represented by industrial orders, the qualitative by the images conjured up in the painters' studios; they had the task of continually feeding and renewing the legacy of forms that workshops and industries could put into circulation and make available to everyone.

In this context it was vital that pictorial invention should not be restricted by preconceived rules such as the perpendicularity or uniformity of colours typical of neoplasticism, or the golden means of purism;

if this happened industrial designers would no longer receive inward stimuli but external prototypes and would fall back into the state of passive reception from which they were ideally to be aroused.

This was probably the origin of the conflict with Van Doesburg. Neo-plasticism, by aiming in an abstract way to perfect formal conception by means of a ready-made discipline, brought with it an unhealthy distribution of energies, because it was concerned with ensuring, in only one phase of the productive process, the integrity which could belong only to the whole; in this way everything would revert once more to being purely mechanical, and the old rivalry between art and technical matters would reappear.

Klee and Kandinsky on the other hand had meditated sufficiently on the spontaneity of conception at the time of the blaue Reiter to recognize that the artist alone cannot give life, in the workshop, to a new reality, but could draw out of the world of the imagination the initial seed, which could then go into circulation and multiply through the current productive processes; for this reason, unlike Van Doesburg and Mondrian, they adapted themselves to being part of a team and to considering their work not as an end in itself, but as an element in a vaster process which ended in the factory and in everyday life. Klee wrote in 1924:

'The artist does not attribute to the natural form of any phenomenon the obligatory meaning that many realists who act as critics do. He does not feel so bound up with this reality, because he tends to see the essence of creation less in these formal results, since he is more interested in the formative forces than formal results . . . He says to himself: this world used to be different, and will be different again. On other planets there may be quite other forms. This mobility along the natural ways of creation is a good formative school . . .

Our hearts drive us down, deep down, towards the first cause. Everything that is born of this impulse is to be considered with the greatest seriousness, if, linked with suitable figurative means, it reaches adequate formal fulfilment. Then these curiosities become realities of art which make life a little broader than it normally appears'.[30]

Klee was continually uttering warnings (not with words, but with his silent paintings) that the initial act of choice from which all planning proceeded could never come from the outside or be repeated passively, but must be renewed every time, involving the deepest resources of the personality. In this way artistic involvement became moral involvement; Giedion has told how Gropius used to call Klee 'the final moral arbiter of the Bauhaus'.[31]

Mediation between quality and quantity was possible in so far as there existed a common measure between the two spheres; here reason had a part to play, its task being clarified only in relation to these two poles.

From Durand to Labrouste, from Semper to Wagner, all reformers called on reason, defining it in many different ways. Gropius was not over eager to talk about reason; on this point, indeed, his thought was hesitant and his discussions of the subject are to be interpreted as specific reaction to controversies arising from the various definitions of 'rationalism', 'functionalism' etc.[32] But he was always firm on the need to find a ground for understanding where all particular demands and points of view could be objectively compared.

It did not occur to him to discuss whether calculation was more important than emotion, or deduction than intuition, but he was concerned that the various acts should remain compatible and comparable, because the integration or alienation of the contemporary consciousness was dependent on this possibility. The rationality he invoked was not an ideological programme but a method of working, or perhaps it was the minimal ideological premise compatible with the changes under way in contemporary society and with the multiplicity of opinions and tendencies to be safeguarded in this society.

In this way Gropius' thought had a deep and very real link with the heritage of humanistic thought. Rationality was the guarantee of that nucleus of permanent values which the modern movement chose to save from the collapse of traditional systems and attempted to safeguard, by purifying it, as Argan says, 'of all features of class, of all mythologizing, of every accent of authority, so that it should not be completely lost for the world of to-morrow'. Rationality meant humanity, as long as the Aristotelian definition of man as a rational animal was regarded as valid.

2 Le Corbusier's early career

To understand the work of Le Corbusier one must consider the economic and cultural situation in France during the years around the First World War. The population balance gave the French economy a special stability; there were no serious quantitative problems and even the internal movement from agriculture to industry and from the country to the town was less pressing than elsewhere; in their place there were mainly qualitative problems: the improvement of productive equipment, of dwellings and services. The political pattern reached in 1871, after such serious clashes, was apparently in a position to accommodate social progress and the gradual introduction of the working classes into the bourgeois State in an orderly fashion.

French culture as a whole, therefore, was not subject to violent upheavals. In the first decade of the twentieth century, while *art nouveau* was sweeping the rest of Europe, France participated in the international controversy with a bold movement of renewal actually within the lines of tradition:

Perret and Garnier made the last attempt at broadening the tenets of classicism by freeing it from academic formulae and bringing it to meet the needs of modern society. A further advance along these lines now seemed impossible; the splendid works of Perret and the *grands travaux* at Lyon marked a full stop and in a certain sense an end.

This situation could be broken out of only by individual initiative: in France the *avant-garde* was still a form necessary for the renewal of artistic culture and innovators had to know how to come into the open, attacking existing institutions from the outside.

Le Corbusier was able to take on this task and to attack the traditions of his country, without losing sight of the links with the international movement. If the collective experience of the Bauhaus was open to contributions from all parts of the world and acted as an ideal centre for the modern movement, the individual experience of Le Corbusier in its turn was open to influence by this potential unity. Thus he could act as a mediator between the modern movement and French traditions, and introduce into international culture some of the values inherent in this tradition.

Naturally his position was more exposed and in a certain sense weaker than that of the Germans or Dutch: he had no directly helpful background, he was not in a position to gather a real school around him, nor really to collaborate with others (Pierre Jeanneret and his other occasional 'partners' offered mainly moral support or acted as an ideal public). Thus the great mass of his undertakings and works was really based only on the consistence of his individual temperament, and the results were always to some degree one-sided.

Furthermore the influence of all his works – of his buildings and books and articles, even of his formulas and slogans – was always exceptional, and did not amount to a momentary triumph of publicity but continues unabated even today, and has a profound effect in the most far-flung places.

A part of this persuasive power certainly derived from the exceptional nature of his inventive ability. If there really is anything like artistic genius in the strict sense, as attributed to the great creators of the past, i.e. the complete mastery of form, Le Corbusier possessed this gift to a degree that has no equal in our time, and had few possible comparisons even in the past. Nonetheless, one cannot explain Le Corbusier as an artist in the old style, who acts by imposing the superior quality of his inventive temperament, and then look only at the works he built, interpreting his writings and justifications as polemical expedients to strengthen his actual works. The great merit of Le Corbusier was that he engaged his incomparable talent in the field of reason and general communication. He was never content for his inventions to be interesting and inspiring, they had also to be universally useful and applicable, and he never wanted to impose, but always to demonstrate his theses.

The mark of his personality was always visible in his works, but not at the expense of breadth of method. Thus personal values were always a point of arrival, not of departure, and they did not prevent his work from being generally persuasive, on the contrary they gave it extraordinary strength. This standpoint demanded unflagging inner tension, which Le Corbusier safeguarded with an exceptional spirit of sacrifice, and also with the susceptibilities and idiosyncrasies typical of his generation. It was his aim that was different: the 'patient research' aimed at building up not an individual but an objective perfection, offered to all and not connected to a personal guarantee, but capable of proving itself on its own and indeed of guaranteeing the work of the researcher.

This tension has still not slackened, and Le Corbusier is almost eighty years old; it has merely changed in emphasis and enriched itself with a sort of desire for recapitulation, as if to sum up a highly active life, as far as this is possible. It is in fact the lively presence of his last works that moves one to note the coherence of all his activities and to discern his true coin among the many counterfeit ones circulating in the twenties in *avant-garde* circles.

Born in Switzerland at La Chaux de Fond, C. E. Jeanneret left school early, worked in Perret's and Behrens' studios from 1908, and travelled in Europe and the East.

In 1919, together with the painter Ozenfant he founded the Purist movement and ran the review *L'Esprit nouveau.* Like neo-plasticism, Purism laid down certain formal rules – the use of simple forms, agreement between the processes of art and those of nature – which could be applied indifferently to painting, sculpture and architecture; but unlike the neo-plastic rules which led to the denial of the autonomy of the figurative arts and to their complete absorption within architecture, the Purist rules rather formed an *a priori* system, like 'design' in humanistic culture, on which the three major arts depended. Throughout his life Le Corbusier remained faithful to this habit and alternated painting, sculpture and architecture.

In 1922 he went into partnership with his cousin P. Jeanneret and opened the famous studio in rue de Sèvres; in 1923 he collected together his theoretical views in the slim volume *Vers une architecture,* which was soon widely read. Like Gropius, he too aimed to transcend the conflict between technical progress and artistic involution, between quantitative and qualitative results, but in accordance with French tradition he defined technique and art as two parallel values: 'The engineer, inspired by the laws of economy and led by calculation, puts us in agreement with the laws of the universe; the architect, by his arrangement of forms, produces an order that is the pure creation of his spirit.'[33]

Since this was so, the synthesis that was temporarily lacking must not be built up – therefore there was no problem of a new method of teaching or production – but must first be recognized by looking at natural and artificial objects with a mind freed from all bias and by seeing in them the immanent beginnings of a new architecture.

Here then are the subjects of the address Le Corbusier gives his readers:

Three reminders to architects:[34] simple masses, surfaces defined by means of the directing and generating lines of the mass, the plan as the generating principle;

Architecture must be subjected to the control of regulating geometrical lines;

The elements of the new architecture could already be recognized in industrial products: ships, aeroplanes, cars;

The means for the new architecture were: the relationships that ennoble raw materials, the exterior as a projection of the interior, profile (modénature) as pure spiritual creation;

The house must be mass-produced, like a machine;

Changes in economic and technical premises necessarily imply an architectural revolution.

In the successive volumes, *L'Art décoratif d'aujourd'hui* and *Urbanisme,* of 1925, Le Corbusier extended his reasoning very rigorously to the whole field of modern planning, from everyday utensils to the whole city. The two books are linked, more so than the earlier one, to specific controversies of the time, but they are admirable for the coherence of a line of thought which was to be borne out over a period of time. After having lightly discussed and set aside Le Corbusier's statements as they appeared, critics were destined to rediscover their more permanent meaning some time later.

One has only to think of the many protests aroused by the provocative definition of the house as a 'machine à habiter', of which it was recently written:

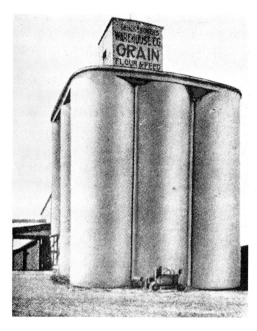

Silo à grain.

TROIS RAPPELS
A MESSIEURS LES ARCHITECTES

I

LE VOLUME

490   *A page from* Vers une Architecture, *1923*

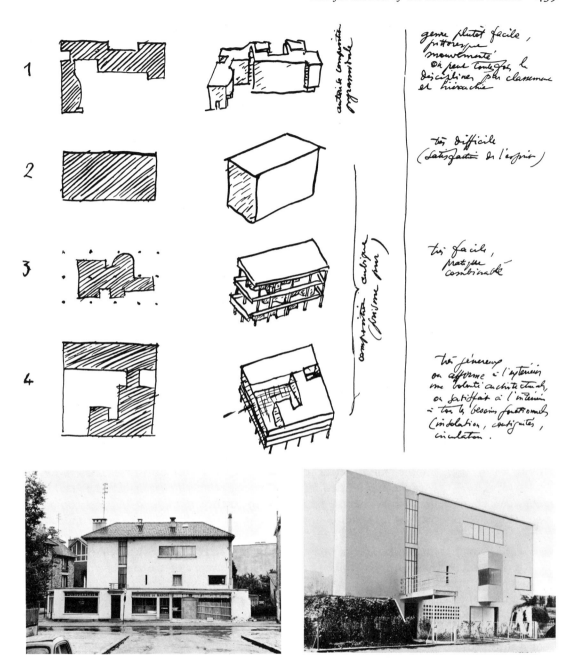

491 *Le Corbusier, Sketch from 1929 showing four types of composition for detached houses: Villa La Roche, 1923; house at Garches, 1927: house at the Weissenhof, 1927; house at Poissy, 1929*
492, 493 *The house at Vaucresson now and then (Le Corbusier and P. Jeanneret, 1922)*

'[Le Corbusier] offers the poetic solution, which is the only one that everyone seems to acknowledge in his work, but also the most practical and precise solution. I do not know of any more exact and civilized definition of the house in modern architecture than the one given by him: the house is a "machine à habiter". This definition is so precise that it still rouses the scorn of many critics; and it is certainly much more than a slogan. It is the most revolutionary definition in modern architecture'.[35]

Le Corbusier's crusade for mechanical exactitude and regularity was mistaken in its time for a one-sided theoretical vision, as happened with Gropius, while in fact it was precisely the reverse, a desire for rational control over an ever-growing field of stubborn material facts.

But true proof could come only from works, while until this time Le Corbusier's activity had been almost solely theoretical. From 1914 he worked on the mass-produced economic living cell: the Domino house of 1914, the house in *gros béton* of 1919, the Monol house of 1920, the Citrohan house of 1920 (perfected in 1922); but his practical activity was of quite another kind, detached houses (Fig. 491) and expensive houses for *avant-garde* clients: a house at Vaucresson in 1922 (Figs. 492–3), a Studio-house for Ozenfant at Paris in the same year (Fig. 494), the La Roche and Jeanneret houses of 1923, the Lipchitz and Miestschaninoff houses at Boulogne sur Seine of 1926. Only in 1925 did he have the opportunity of building a group of standardized houses at Pessac, for an enlightened Bordeaux industrialist, but with poor results because of a series of exceptional difficulties.

In 1922 Le Corbusier prepared the first plan for an ideal city: *une ville contemporaine* with three million inhabitants, exhibited that year at the *Salon d'Automne*. The buildings were of three types: large cruciform skyscrapers in the centre, six-storey houses *à*

redents in the intermediate zone and *immeuble-villas* on the outskirts. The plan was rigorously symmetrical, with orthogonal and diagonal streets, following academic models (Fig. 495).

The *immeuble-villas* (Fig. 496) were the most interesting type and contained the germ of the future *unités d'habitation*. This was a block of 120 apartments with terrace gardens, supplied with communal services: a co-operative food shop, where:

'provisions arrived directly from the provinces to the place of consumption . . .; on the roof . . . a track of 1000 m. where people could run in the open air and where sun-terraces made it possible to carry on summer sun-bathing . . .; six porters do three shifts of eight hours, day and night, looking after the house, announcing visitors by telephone and sending them up to the relevant floor by lift.'[36]

In 1925, in the international exhibition of decorative arts in Paris, Le Corbusier made use of the pavilion devoted to *L'Esprit nouveau* to build an element of the *immeuble-villas* and further to specify the overall organization. In the same exhibition Le Corbusier presented his first concrete town-planning proposal: the so-called *Plan Voisin* for the centre of Paris (Figs. 499–500).

The proposed layout–the superimposition on the traditional street system of a gigantic system of straight motorways; the demolition of a vast stretch of the *rive droite*, to be replaced with a symmetrical system of cruciform skyscrapers and linear buildings *à redents*, with the careful isolation and preservation only of historic monuments like the Palais Royal, the Madeleine etc. – may justly be criticized, because we today realize the enormous complexity of the problem, which cannot be solved so simply. Like the traditional plans for the transformations of French towns, from Vauban to Garnier, this too was basically an enormous *percement*, not unlike those of Haussmann.[37]

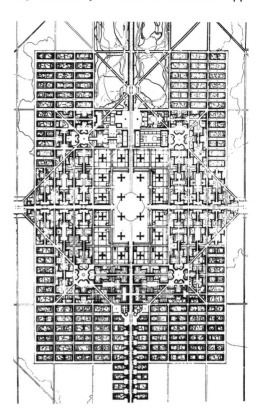

494 *(top left)   Studio-house in Paris for the painter Ozenfant (Le Corbusier and P. Jeanneret, 1922)*
495, 496 *Plan of the* ville contemporaine *(right) and view of an* immeuble-villa *(1922) from* Oeuvre Complète

497   *Interior of Ozenfant's studio*
498   *Sketch by Le Corbusier of an artist's studio (1922) from* Oeuvre Complète

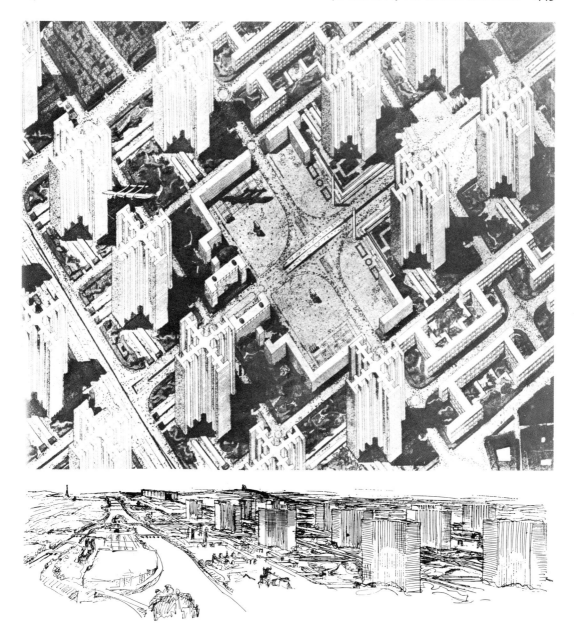

499, 500   *Views of the* Plan Voisin *by Le Corbusier (1925)*

Nonetheless this plan – lovingly perfected until 1946 – was always borne in mind by modern town-planning thought, and acquired interest gradually as the failure of moderate and partial provisions, or the abstract quality of alternatives so far proposed,

was felt. Commenting on recent plans for the decentralization of Paris, and reaffirming his own scheme after thirty years, Le Corbusier observed firmly: Paris is the centre of a wheel, and the centre of a wheel cannot be moved'.

The abstract logic of Le Corbusier's plan

has always been admired; roads were classified according to the types of traffic, buildings were rationally interconnected and set in green spaces, the needs of the pedestrian, car and aeroplane were accommodated within a single framework. The shaping of the component parts was generous and retained the best qualities of the French tradition: the grandiose scale boldly anticipating functional necessities, geometrical regularity and monumentality brilliantly combined with elegance.

Nowadays we are no longer certain that we can discount the *Plan Voisin* as an abstract exercise; the problem of reorganizing the great modern metropolises – on the scale of ten million inhabitants – is still to be solved, and is certainly not resolvable with the over-simple methods of decentralization, thought up and experimented with on a completely different scale. The most recent theoretical attempts – from Tange's plan from Tokyo to the Buchanan report – give glimpses of other trends, with regard to which Le Corbusier's designs of 1925 appear as amazing anticipations.

In 1926 Le Corbusier and P. Jeanneret published a document, where certain proposals elaborated in the previous years were systematically propounded, and were called 'the five points of a new architecture':

'1   "*Pilotis*"
Assiduous and dogged research has led to partial results which can be regarded as laboratory tested. These results open new perspectives to architects, perspectives which offer a great deal to town-planners who can find in them the means to cure the great sickness of our present day cities.

The house on "pilotis"! The house used to sink into the ground: rooms were dark and often damp. Reinforced concrete made "pilotis" possible. The house is in the air, away from the ground; the garden runs under the house, and it it also above the house, on the roof.

2   *Roof terraces*
For centuries a traditionally sloping roof has borne winter with its mantle of snow, while the house was warmed with stoves.

From the moment central heating was installed, the traditional roof was no longer suitable. The roof should no longer be sloping, but hollow in the centre; it must collect the water on the inside, no longer on the outside.

An incontestable truth: cold climates demand the abandoning of the sloping roof and necessitate the building of hollow roof terraces, to collect the water inside the house.

Reinforced concrete is the means which makes it possible to build all of one material. Reinforced concrete expands greatly; expansion causes the structure to crack when it suddenly contracts. Instead of trying to dispose of the rainwater rapidly, one should try to maintain a constant level of humidity on the concrete of the terrace, and therefore a regular temperature on the reinforced concrete. Special protective measure: sand covered with thick slabs of concrete, with widely spaced joints. The gaps are sown with grass. Sand and roots prevent water from seeping in fast. Roof terraces become lush: flowers, trees, bushes, lawns.

Technical, economic, functional and spiritual reasons advise us to adopt the roof terrace.

3   *The free plan*
Hitherto: load-bearing walls. Starting from the basement, they are placed on top of each other forming the ground floor and other floors, right to the top. The plan is the slave of load-bearing walls. Reinforced concrete brings the free plan into the house! Floors no longer have to stand simply one on top of the other. They are free. Great saving in volume, rigorous use of every centimetre. Great saving in money. Convenient rationality of the new plan!

4 *The "fenêtre en longueur"*
The window is one of the essential
elements of the house. Progress brings
liberation. Reinforced concrete
revolutionizes the history of the window.
Windows can run from one end of the
façade to the other. The window is the
standard mechanical element of the house;
for our villas, working-class houses,
apartment buildings . . . .

5 *The free façade*
Pillars set back from the façade, towards
the interior of the house. The floor continues
outwards, overhanging. Façades are simply
light membranes of isolating walls or
windows.

The façade is free; the windows, without
interruption, can run from one end of the
façade to the other.'[38]

This text gave rise to endless argument
between modernists and traditionalists, de-
fenders of the old types; critics never paid
much attention to it, or else branded it as a
contribution to the over-simple thought behind much modern architecture around
1930.

Today naturally we feel the narrow and
elementary character of a text written in
1926, in view of the enormous range of
problems we have before us now. All this
should not make us forget the revolutionary
value of such a pronouncement, which completely eliminated the literary and philosophical references which had hitherto been
de rigueur in any artistic manifesto (and
which had remained, from force of habit,
in the manifesto of the Bauhaus as well).

From 1890 onwards each trend put itself
forward as the fulfilment of the most daring
theories on man and the universe; in this
way *avant-garde* culture – apart from
obviously distorting the results of philosophical reflection – really confirmed the un-
committed character of artistic activity, to
which was attributed a universal and un-

limited field but no true autonomy or
precise responsibility.

In 1926, for the first time, Le Corbusier
no longer said that the new architecture
should be subjective or objective, immanent
or transcendent, but said that it must be such
and such a thing: it must have 'pilotis', a
free plan, free façade and even roof terraces
and lengthways windows.

Future experience was to decide whether
or not these standards were appropriate
ones. The basic fact remained that architects
were coming to the heart of the matter, that is,
they were recognizing that there existed an
autonomous and limited field, within which
precise choices must be made. Only in this
way could the new architecture find its
correct cultural position; its task was not to
provide a general backdrop but to carry out
one of the practical actions – that described
by Morris, i.e. the modification of the
physical scene – necessary to the organization
of modern society. The relationship between
this partial responsibility and general responsibility was still to be defined; but the
discussion on architecture became less tense,
judgment gave way to judgments of degree.

The tone of the debate, which the architect was now conducting on his own specific
ground, became peaceful and reasonable.
Over-simplification and stress on theory was
not avoided by abandoning these standards,
but by concentrating on evolving them
continually, as did Le Corbusier during the
forty years that followed.

In the house at Garches of 1927 (Figs. 501,
502) Le Corbusier could finally work with a
relative breadth of means, on a broad and
unrestricted terrain. The villa is a perfect
prism, proportioned according to the Golden
Rule, carried on slender regularly placed
pillars; within this elementary network
ground plans and prospects were freely
arranged, though their elements were, of
course, restricted by the regulating lines of
the ensemble. The relationship with the
surrounding park and views was established

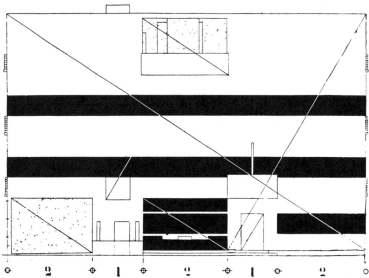

501, 502 *Le Corbusier and P. Jeanneret, Main façade of the house at Garches, 1927*

by the different treatment of the various parts and above all by the empty space of the covered garden which takes up a large part of the back façade, extending into the out-lying grounds along a long ramp. All the walls are plastered in white, while the metal frames are outlined in black, forming an abstract composition emphasizing their geometrical

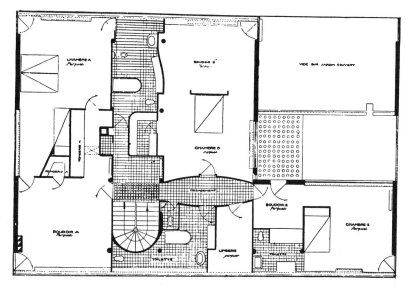

503, 504 *Plan of the second floor of the house at Garches (from* Oeuvre Complète*) and view of the main gate*

values. Here careful upkeep has prevented the premature decay of the building, but it has not managed to conceal numerous errors and difficulties of juncture, the inevitable consequence of the isolation in which Le Corbusier worked and of his sporadic contact with industry.

The house at Garches is, therefore, more valid as a manifesto than as a practical work of architecture; it does not bear comparison with the splendid contemporary works of Oud, Dudok or even the experimental building of Mies and Gropius; but it had a much greater influence and power, and not only because of its immediate comprehensibility or the fascinating comments made on it by Le Corbusier; while the interest of the architects of the previous generation had

505 *Façade of the house at Garches*

been concentrated mainly on details, on texture, on the use of materials, there now appeared a building where details did not count and where the attention was firmly directed towards the whole, the organism. The work itself suffered from this, but in this way the ideas behind it were freed from special circumstances and the incidental occasion and were given far broader implications.

The lesson of the Garches house was clearly independent of its specific purpose and of the technical means employed; it could be utilized in many other cases, for other subjects, with other instruments and other types of finish, to meet the needs that were emerging here and elsewhere, in relation to certain facts typical of our time.

3   The legacy of the German avant-garde

The German *avant-garde* scene, in the years immediately after the war, was rich in contradictory experiments, linked with the formation of the modern movement possibly only by a dialectical relationship of stimulus and comparison.

Gropius' position, in 1919, was already basically opposed to the *avant-garde* spirit dominant in artistic circles at that time. But it did happen that other protagonists in the German debate on art, after having accepted the working methods and principles of the *avant-garde* over a longer period, did then of their own accord discover a path that converged with that of Gropius; for some, participation in the *avant-garde* appeared to be more or less a matter of chance, and their further development was guided by the coherence of a stern individual temperament: this was the case with Mies van der Rohe; for others, participation in the *avant-garde* was crucial, and the margin of further development was more limited – as was the case with Mendelsohn and the Luckhardt brothers – so that the historical fruit of their work was the salvaging of the expressionist experiment,

purified and made communicable within the ambit of the modern movement.

As well as individual experiments, one should also consider the activities of certain technical and cultural institutions, like the Werkbund and the Reichsforchungsgesellschaft, where some of the best German architects were working, and where certain scientific contributions indispensible to the modern movement were worked out. Their activity has not yet been studied in relation to the general historical problem, and we can only make the briefest mention of it, and will return to the subject in the chapter devoted to it.

Soon after the war Mies took an active part in the artistic and social controversies in Berlin, worked within the Novembergruppe – the pugnacious group that was a rallying point for revolutionary artists – and ran the review *G* (initial of Gestaltung).

Mies prepared a number of theoretical projects between 1919 and 1923 for the exhibitions of the Novembergruppe; two glass skyscrapers (1919 and 1922, Figs. 506, 508), an office block in reinforced concrete (1922, Fig. 507) and two country houses in concrete and brick (1923).

It is difficult to pass judgment on these images, roughly sketched out in prospects and brief ground plans, but one can get an idea of their significance if one bears in mind Mies' later works. For instance there is the glass tower of 1922, of which the author writes: 'Skyscrapers reveal their powerful structure during construction; only then is the gigantic steel trunk truly expressive. When the panel walls are in position, the structural system at the basis of the composition is hidden behind a chaos of insignificant and trivial forms.'[39]

It is probable that Mies' plan aimed at expressing the intrinsic value of the multi-storey structure by abstracting it from all further finish and that the wavy or broken surround of the plan was intended precisely to avoid definition of the circumscribed

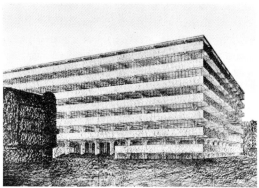

506, 507, 508, 509   *L. Mies van der Rohe, Designs for a glass skyscraper (1921); for an office block in reinforced concrete (1922); and for the Alexanderplatz in Berlin (1928)*

volume, to stress the original rhythmic significance of the superimposed storeys. The problem touched upon thirty years earlier by the masters of the Chicago school was here tackled boldly for the first time, even if only theoretically, and became an architectural reality in Chicago itself, through Mies' work, twenty years later.

Similarly, in the plan for a block in reinforced concrete and in the two houses in concrete and brick, Mies managed, by a striking effort at simplification, to pinpoint the essential root of the respective architectural problems. Furthermore his proposals were not at all abstract, because they did not give free reign to a taste for the geometrical plan, widespread at that time, but were based on an exact estimate of the characteristic features of the materials and building systems, grasped with unimpeachable technical expertise and swiftly transformed into the permanence of the architectural result.

Thus the plans made between 1919 and 1923, though they were born within the ambit of the German *avant-garde* and took various formal suggestions from the repertoire of expressionism – the curved or broken outlines of towers, the energetic drawing of perspectives – moved firmly away from the ambiguous realms of the dream, where Mies' contemporaries liked to roam, and made decisive moves towards reality. Mies kept apart from general discussion and did not wish to extend his activities so as to point the way to a general method, but offered his contemporaries the example of an individual commitment so rigorous and precise as to influence later experiments to no less an extent than the teaching of Gropius.

When given his first commissions he did not hesitate to defend these theoretical experiments to the letter and utilized them indirectly, to clarify the practical problems that he encountered.

In the popular houses of the Afrikanische Strasse in Berlin of 1925, in the house at Güben of 1926 and the one at Krefeld in 1928 (Fig. 510) there was no tendentious emphasis; these were simple brick buildings, elegantly and soberly articulated, where the traditional elements emerged purified by Mies' use of them, and the proportions bore the unmistakable mark of his genius –

particularly the frames of the rhythmical, elongated windows – without one being aware of any preconceived geometrical rules, as in the work of Le Corbusier.

In 1926 Mies built the monument to Karl Liebknecht and Rosa Luxemburg – a last inspiring image of the *avant-garde* movement, offered in honour of the fallen of January 1919 – and became Vice President of the Werkbund, initiating a vast organizational activity which we shall discuss in the next chapter. In this position, too, Mies was remote from theoretical commitment, and remained faithful to his individual commitment; sometimes – in his characteristic epigrammatic style – he tried to clarify his position by insisting on the decisive value of planning, to give sense and value to objective circumstances:

'Our age is a fact: it exists completely independently of our yea or nay, but it is neither better nor worse than any other. It is just a fact, which has no value in itself. For this reason I shall not persist in attempting to explain this new epoch, to point out its proportions or to lay bare its supporting structure. But let us not underestimate the matter of mechanization, typification and standardization. And let us accept the changed economic and social relationships as an accomplished fact.

All these things go their own way, which is blind to questions of value. What will be decisive is the way in which we manage to uphold our own values in the present situation; it is only here that spiritual problems begin. It is not a question of the "what" but purely and simply of the "how". Spiritually it means nothing that we produce goods, nor how we produce them, whether we build low or high buildings, in steel or in glass . . . whether we tend towards centralization or decentralization in building our cities. But what is decisive is the question of value. We must put forward new values, we must

510   *Krefeld, Lange house (Mies van der Rohe, 1928)*

511   Mies van der Rohe, Design for a building on the Leipziger Strasse (1928)

set ourselves ultimate goals, to conquer new standards.'[40]

This was an extremely personal way of thinking, which was very dangerous when taken literally (it may even have harmed Mies himself, for he remained in Germany under Nazism until 1937, deluding himself that he could distinguish between the 'how' and the 'what'). Here we should recognize the impatience of the architect, who does not

wish to be involved in discussions that are too general, and feels safe only within the limits of his actual work; in fact, however, Mies was far from indifferent to content, and his contribution was precise in all senses.

Mendelsohn's work, though much less important, should be mentioned because of the enormous influence it had at the time, greater at first than that of any other architect of his generation.

In 1919 Mendelsohn was already known

for his imaginary architectural sketches, exhibited that year at the Cassirer gallery and later collected into book form by the editor Wasmuth.

The first sketches of 1914 were inspired by the style of Wagner and Olbrich; those done during the war and immediately afterwards had an aggressive intensity and vaguely symbolist character which fitted in well with the contemporary expressionist movement.

Many other people at the time were drawing imaginary architectural sketches, sometimes in open defiance of any possibility of realization; Mendelsohn on the other hand worked with the definite aim of preparing a new architectural style that might be generally valid and searched methodically for its roots, trying to discover the initial intuitive germ from which all the rest could spring. From the trenches of the Russian front in 1917 he wrote to a friend:

'Until I am in a position to be able to realize my aims and thus give concrete proof of the usefulness of my work, all I can do is to express myself, so to speak, in terms of theoretical principles, and in this case I am forced to keep silent about subtleties, nuances, details and specific values. My sketches are only notes, the outlines of fleeting visions, though in their nature as buildings they immediately appear as actual entities. It is of vital importance to pin down these visions and catch them on paper as they appeared to me, because every new piece of creation carries within it the germ of its potential development and becomes a human being by the natural process of evolution'.[41]

In 1920 he was offered his first opportunity: Einstein's astronomical observatory tower at Potsdam (Figs. 512, 513). This was an attempt at transferring into reality, with the greatest possible immediacy, one of these 'fleeting visions', and Mendelsohn had in mind a form that would give the instan-

taneous impression of a fluid mass. In theory the most suitable material was reinforced concrete, whose plasticity seemed at this time to offer architects the best means of escape from the fetters of the right-angle and superimposed floors,[42] but there were no moulds available for curved and flowing forms, so that the tower had to be made with brick with a covering of cement. The work thus became the mere illustration of an abstract concept and remained, with the Dornach Goethaneum and various works by Poelzig, an attempt at a literal application, in the architectural field, of the post-war expressionist repertoire.

Shortly afterwards, in the factory at Luckenwalde in 1921, in the Gleiwitz house of 1922 and the building for the *Berliner Tageblatt* of 1923, Mendelsohn tried to apply his concept of composition to more usual subjects, exaggerating opportunities for plasticity and chiaroscuro, particularly with the decorative strips which underlined every protruding point and marked the sources of the curved elements.

After 1925, when inflation was over, Mendelsohn had great professional success and tackled very demanding works, gradually breaking away from his initial idiosyncrasies.

He built a series of exemplary stores for the firm of Schocken, at Nuremberg and Stuttgart in 1926 (Figs. 514–16) and at Chemnitz in 1928 (Figs. 517, 518). The organism was reduced to its most simple form, a block of many storeys emphasized on the outside by their continuous windows; these had the same function as the decorative strips in the early works, since they emphasized the basic shape of the volume, though this time the effect came from the internal organism.

In 1928 he built the 'Universum' cinema on the Kurfürstendamm in Berlin, and grasped the architectural consequences of this new theme with great broad-mindedness. Since the square of the screen was small and had to be viewed from directly in front, as far

512, 513   *Potsdam, The Einstein tower (E. Mendelsohn, 1920)*

as possible, the hall was long and narrow; since the hall lights play an important part by marking the rhythm of successive performances, they were to give the hall its particular character by their curved strips along wall and ceiling. From the outside the various different rooms, the curved mass of the hall, the lower and concentric one of the foyer, the prisms of the projection rooms and stage can be easily distinguished and firmly proclaimed the nature of the building (Figs. 519, 520).

Mendelsohn's career was sure, direct, apparently unfaltering, and his production was always characterized by the formal

514, 515, 516 *Stuttgart, The Schocken stores (Mendelsohn, 1926)*

preferences expressed in his youthful drawings, however complex the technical apparatus: the freshness of the original conception was retained in the finished building and gave every image a particular vigour. So that the inspiration of the Einstein tower was not fundamentally different from that of the Chemnitz stores or the 'Universum' cinema. But his first works were restricted experiments, almost incommunicable, whereas these were transmissible to and reconcilable with others under way in Germany and elsewhere.

4　The Dutch heritage: J. J. P. Oud and W. M. Dudok

Holland had a solid town-planning tradition based on the law of 1901, and it was the home of one of the most important post-Cubist movements, the neo-plasticism of Van Doesburg and Mondrian. Since it had not been involved in the World War, its building production continued in a normal fashion, undisturbed by sudden crises, and cultural research had time to affect current praxis, advancing in harmony with technical progress.

517, 518   *Chemnitz, The Schocken stores (Mendelsohn, 1928; from G.A. Platz,* op. cit.*)*

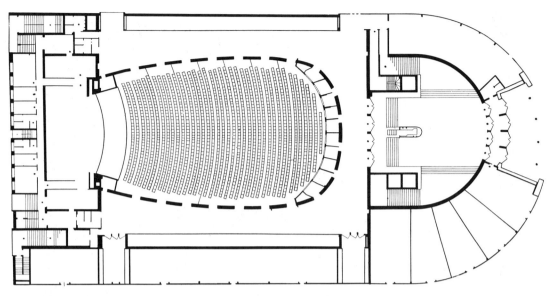

519, 520   *Berlin, The Universum cinema, now the Capitol (Mendelsohn, 1928)*

On the one hand Berlage and a group of young architects – M. De Klerk, P. L. Kramer, M. Staal-Kropholler, H. T. Vijdeveld, J. M. Van der Mey – were involved with the review *Wendingen* and worked on the plan of South Amsterdam, with the aim, based on Berlage's method, of reconciling traditional habits with the contributions of

521, 522 *Amsterdam, Two views of the Zuid district: houses on the Stalinaan (M. De Klerk, 1920–2) and on the Holendrechstraat (M. Staal-Kropholler, 1922)*

the *avant-garde* movements (particularly of German expressionism). On the other hand there was the rationalist and internationally-minded movement of neo-plasticism, led by Van Doesburg.

Remaining within the limits of current controversy, neo-plasticism represented the movement towards innovation, the Amsterdam school that towards conservatism; but today, some time later, we see that the two schools carried out complementary tasks and gave birth to homogeneous and compatible results. In fact, the most important results obtained in Holland after the war were produced outside the polemical battle which filled the pages of the reviews, indeed they brought together the two formal repertoires in a most unexpected way: Oud, after having belonged to the group 'De Stijl', worked after 1920 in very cramping conditions, and went straight from the neo-plastic repertoire to that of Berlage, though extremely selectively, with the rigour he had gained from his early experience. Dudok started off by combining the two conventional points of reference in an eclectic fashion, but had the perseverence to persist until he really integrated the two streams, managing to give technical consistence and meaning on a large scale to the geometrical combinations propounded by the neo-plasticists.

In 1918 Jacob Johannes Pieter Oud (1890–1963) was appointed chief architect for the city of Amsterdam. Although at this time he was taking an active part in the Stijl movement, his first groups of popular houses designed for the administration – Spangen in 1918 and Tusschendijken in 1919 – had only the slightest traces of neo-plastic ideas, as Van Doesburg did not fail reproachfully to point out.

The rectangular block of the Tusschendijken, (Figs. 523, 524) fitted into an unlovely peripheral system of lots, was plainly derived from Berlage's models. Oud took up his symmetry, the uniform repetition of columns of buildings, brick facing and the roof,

simplifying every structural element as far as possible and gleefully articulating the bevelled corners, where the neo-plastic desire to rearrange traditional volumes appeared at its most poignant.

The next complex, Oud Mathenesse of 1922 (Figs. 525, 526) was situated in an open area shaped like an isosceles triangle; Oud, like Berlage, found nothing in his cultural background that could be a valid help to him in its overall composition; he fell back on a highly formalized and absolutely symmetrical plan. The one- or two-storey houses are plastered in white, with brick bases and steeply sloping roofs, with large chimneys; the traditional elements were in a sense disjointed and the various materials used were juxtaposed with somewhat abstract colour effects, as in contemporary *collages*.

The ground plan acted as a purely external form of control, to limit the indefinite number of possible combinations, and it revealed its significance as an instrument quite clearly.

In 1924 came the first masterpiece: the twin rows of terrace houses at the Hook of Holland (Figs. 527–9). Here all reference to tradition was abandoned and at the same time the organism was once again enclosed and complete, with no further trace of the statutory decomposition required by neo-plasticism. The two identical blocks contained two rows of superimposed dwellings, so that the module as it appeared on the façade is fairly spacious and the rhythm slow and well-spaced; extremities were rounded so that the rhythm would not be broken but should turn the corner and come back upon itself. All walls were covered with uniform white plaster, as in the contemporary works of Gropius and Le Corbusier, but points of juncture and vulnerable points were resolved with more durable materials: the low base was of yellow brick, the doorsteps of red brick, the thresholds and doorposts of grey concrete; these elements, together with the doors and fences painted blue, the red-and-white striped curtains, grey pillars between the doors, metal lamps in red, black and yellow (Mondrian's colours) gave the buildings a liveliness of colour and emphasized the effects of light and shade. The upkeep of the plaster part proved easy, since the edges were protected by brick and concrete, and indeed after more than thirty years the two rows of houses are still in perfect condition.

The workers' village of Kiefhoek, of 1925 (Figs. 532–6) stands on an irregular patch of ground in the south part of Rotterdam, in a slight hollow between the banks of two canals. Oud tried to lessen the marks of these external restrictions by picking out certain axes of symmetry, as in Berlage's ground plans; the houses on the other hand are absolutely identical; the typical dwelling was a terrace house of two storeys, with an extremely small inter-axis (4·10 m.) but nonetheless able to house a family of five.

To mark the single element with too much emphasis would have tended to break up the composition; therefore the architect played down the divisions between the units, by treating the windows of the upper floors as one continuous strip. The blocks looked like single buildings, and great care was lavished on the terminal points, where continuity suddenly ceased; the acute and obtuse angles were rounded, with shops in the resulting spaces; elsewhere small semi-circular balconies, variously situated, marked the main lines of the composition, appearing in pairs so as to frame an axis of symmetry, or rotated over a right-angle to mark a rotation of a block.

The outer covering of the lower floor was almost entirely of durable materials: light bricks, which formed the low transversal divisions of the little gardens and the steps leading to the doors; the heads of the supporting partitions were plastered in grey cement, while the windows of the living rooms also had grey frames, forming a continuous band; the only obtrusive feature was the doors, painted in red gloss, with white frames. The upper floor was plastered

and treated as a strip, while the band of continuous windows, with yellow wood surrounds, extends up to the eaves, in galvanized sheet iron.

The Kiefhoek stands out as an architectural island in the outskirts of Rotterdam, a sea of brick houses with pointed roofs, but its upkeep, however careful, does not bear comparison with surrounding buildings. But in assessing the result one must bear in mind the economic basis on which it was built. Oud showed that it was possible to build a habitable district with much less than the usual expenditure, and he used the most threadbare resources of modern architecture to give dignity, by pure virtue of interplay of shape and colour, to very poor material.

The passion with which all the details were worked out went beyond pure technique and was a basic, one might almost say a moral, feature, if the word had not been so much abused, of Oud's architecture. Every element bears the imprint of energies expended during planning and acquired a special expressive intensity. Behind every choice one senses the figurative discipline of neo-plasticism; but the effort at simplification and lowering of costs led the architect to set aside any outlandish combinations, and therefore to accept certain typological restrictions, which would help to simplify his equation. Thus the thorough study of the various elements had as its counterpart the restriction of the field as a whole, and the weakness of overall composition.

But the certainty of the placing of the buildings was matched by the hesitancy of the town-planning. Oud felt the need to give order and structure to the communal spaces, to find links with the surroundings, but the means he employed were weak, even if as subtle and sophisticated as the spatial hints of the little balconies. Here lay the limit and also the danger of Oud's method; when town-planning commitment became absolutely vital, Oud was forced to choose isolation, and intentionally to harden traditional schemes

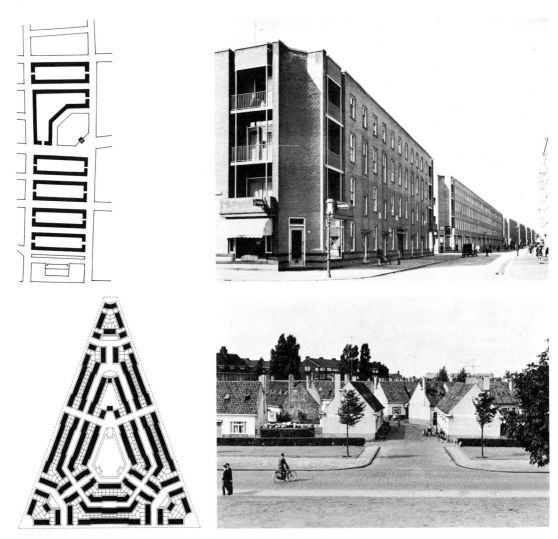

523, 524 *(above)* Rotterdam, Tusschendijken district (J.J.P. Oud, 1919)
525, 526 *(below)* Rotterdam, Oud Mathenesse district (J.J.P. Oud, 1922)

to the point of approaching an ambiguous classicism.

Thus after Oud's attempt, the problem of actually salvaging anything from neo-plasticism was still basically unsolved and was transmitted to the generation of young architects now beginning their careers, Brinkmann, Van der Vlugt and Van Tijen,

whom we shall discuss later on.

Willem Marinus Dudok at first chose a military career, specializing in engineering; at the age of thirty he left the army and was appointed municipal engineer in Leiden, then in 1915 in Hilversum.

Hilversum was a rapidly expanding centre, and Dudok had the opportunity of controlling

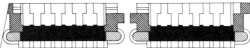

527, 528, 529   *Hook of Holland, Twin terrace-houses by J.J.P. Oud, 1924*

its development, designing the town-planning scheme in 1918 and, from then onwards, a long series of working-class districts and public buildings. With the exception of the Town Hall, none of these is of much distinction but the whole, where they all fit neatly together, was a contribution of singular importance for the history of town-planning. Dudok was able to translate into reality the theoretical dream of the garden city, doing away with the Romantic and Utopian aspects and taking account of relations with the outside world, particularly with nearby Amsterdam, no less than of internal ones.

At first Dudok followed the tradition of Berlage and De Bazel; the first residential quarters of Hilversum, the Rembrandt school (1920) (Fig. 537) and Oranje school (1922) repeat various features of the Amster-

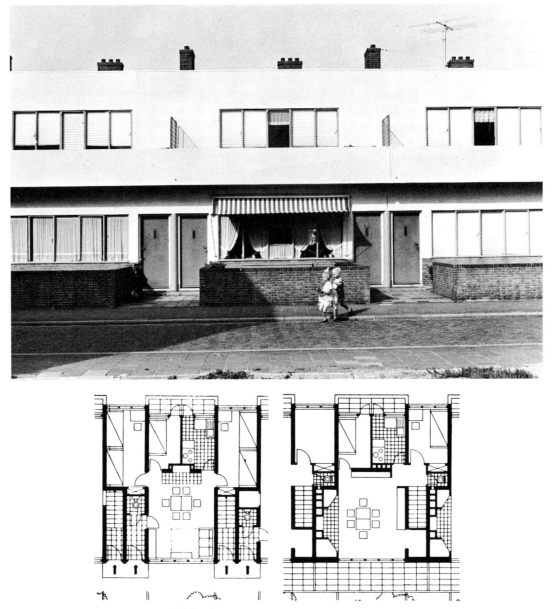

530, 531   *Housing at the Hook of Holland*

dam school, though without trace of the impassioned, Romantic involvement of De Klerk and Kramer, but almost eclectic in their moderation and detachment; indeed Dudok soon proved open to the contributions of the neo-plastic movement (the Bavinck school of 1921) and closely followed the most up-to-date European experiments.

With his subtle stylistic combinations Dudok certainly avoided some crucial problems about which the other masters of the modern movement were arguing at the same period, and rather utilized the formal results of the controversy. But his choices were never

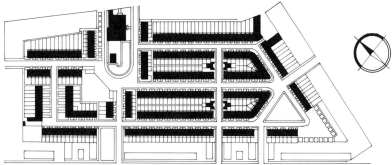

532, 533   *Rotterdam, The Kiefhoek district (J.J.P. Oud, 1925)*

completely exterior. In reality he followed a straight and consistent path, even if it was far from the beaten track, that of progressively purifying the values of recent Dutch tradition by putting them into contact with the European movement, while taking care not to break the continuity of experiment and avoiding over-rigorous and tendentious experiments.

In this way Dudok managed to retain the town-planning values accumulated by the previous generation, which had necessarily been lost in Oud's process of decomposition and recomposition. Continuity of experience

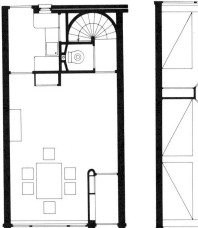

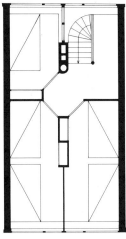

534, 535, 536   *Rotterdam, Housing in the Kiefhoek district*

was in fact the safeguard of continuity of general settings and surroundings; his buildings, with their formal sophistication and neo-plastic or Wrightian allusions, always had a balanced relationship with their surroundings, in fact the compositional elements were justified in the final analysis as a comment on the physical situation of the building, on the directions of the surrounding roads and on the open spaces (Fig. 538).

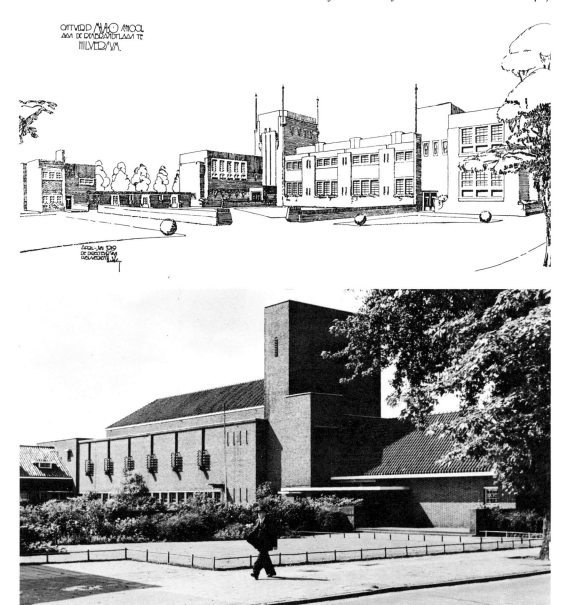

537, 538 *Hilversum, Rembrandtlaan school (W.M. Dudok, 1919; from the celebratory volume of 1954) and the Minchelers school (1925)*

Thus in Hilversum he managed gradually to translate Berlage's methods of overall planning into modern terms, passing from enclosed to open blocks, from symmetrical layouts, where the use of space was hampered by the need for exact mirror repetition, to asymmetrical groupings, scaled according to their different functions.

Dudok's *magnum opus*, where his empiricism was more exalted in tone, was the Town Hall of 1924 (Figs. 539–45). The reason for this may perhaps be connected with the

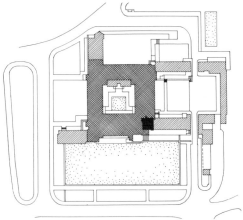

539, 540, 541   *Hilversum, Town Hall (W.M. Dudok, 1924–8)*

subject: the town hall is the emblem of the city, the summary of the whole urban organism, and here formal complications had a convincing, celebrative function. The traditional town hall was an enclosed block, a city within a city; this one, on the contrary, was an open organism, a singular element which stood out from the loose and tenuous fabric of the city without breaking its continuity. The elaborate setting, pools, gardens, lawns and groups of trees connect the building with its surroundings in every direction, and the tower, which has no two sides alike, sums up the varying spatial indications, even

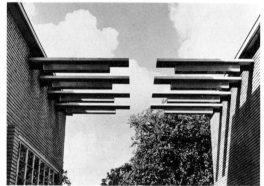

542, 543, 544, 545 *Details of the Hilversum Town Hall*

for the distant observer.

Dudok did not always remain at these heights in subsequent works. Nor were the repercussions of his architecture, in Holland and elsewhere, always very happy, because the traditionalists used his example to build up an artificial bridge between ancient and modern. Thus critics have been led to insist on the contrast between Dudok and the other masters of his time,[43] while today it is possible to recognize the complementary nature of his work and theirs.

Because of him, the heredity of Berlage and the much older one of domestic Dutch architecture have received an up-to-date formulation and have been successfully

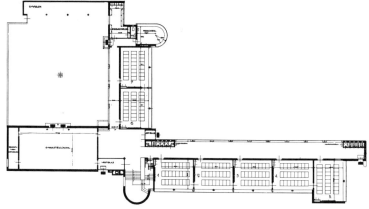

546, 547 *Hilversum, Valerius school (W.M. Dudok, 1930; plan from the celebratory volume of 1954)*

introduced into the modern movement; at the time of greatest theoretical intransigence and the most ferocious polemics against tradition, Dudok silently kept alive the necessary continuity between past and present, between architecture and town-planning, preparing a precedent indispensable to later developments.

For the first time for more than a century the most advanced experiments in European architectural culture were converging, rather than diverging.

The experiments of Mies, Mendelsohn, Le Corbusier, Oud and Dudok had their origins in different cultural environments and retained different stresses and styles, which nonetheless did not prevent the observer from sensing a basic unity of purpose. None of them came from the Bauhaus or was directly influenced by it, but all found there a point of reference, a common measure, a possible meeting point.

Gropius' lesson was validated precisely by what happened outside the school; with his eye on method, not on style, he discreetly but irresistibly invited the best architects from the various countries to look deeper into the rationale behind their experiments, their heritage. After sufficiently thorough investigation, differences weakened and the unity of intent, the common cultural root, emerged.

Reasonably enough, formal tendencies were manifold – even if certain less distinguished members of the younger generation were beginning to talk of an international style – but with a common character that laid them open to comparison, to integration and to a shared belief in certain principles: respect for the human scale, strict technical propriety, continuity between the various scales of planning (and hence the setting of practical questions within more general ones, and inversely the possibility of dividing larger difficulties into so many lesser ones).

While the artistic scene was still filled by the voluble and intolerant outpourings of the *avant-garde* groups – which already sounded out of place in relation to the new involvements that were emerging on the scene – the masters of the modern movement worked and spoke with a completely different tone: reasonable, modulated and concerned with a long-term task.

fourteen

Early relations with the public

The aims of the masters of the modern movement made their relations with the public somewhat delicate.

Aiming to influence building production, they had to spread their ideas well beyond the narrow worlds of their studios and put them before the general public, not only before a small circle of initiates. Also they had to avoid the idea that the new architecture was yet a different style, an alternative to those of the past. Gropius wrote: 'The object of the Bauhaus was not to propagate any "style", system or dogma, but simply to exert a revitalizing influence on design. A "Bauhaus style" would have been a confession of failure and a return to that devitalizing inertia . . . which I had called it into being to combat'[1] and even the dogmatic Le Corbusier:

'Let us abolish schools! (the Corbu school together with the Vignola, I beg of you!) No formulas, no expedients. We are at the beginning of the architectural discovery of modern times. Let frank proposals come in from all sides. In a hundred years' time we shall no longer talk of *a style*. This is no longer of any use to us, what we want is *style*, i.e. moral coherence in every created work'.[2]

For this reason those concerned did not waste much time demonstrating the excellence of the new principle with theoretical discussions and projects, but preferred to seek out every opportunity of showing that these principles could be applied successfully to concrete problems. The decisive argument was in fact that of experiment; people needed to be persuaded that the new architecture worked better than the old. Only in this way could the proof reach everyone, and the new architecture get a hold on general needs, not on the cultural attitude of a minority.

The search for opportunity was a constant feature of the masters of the modern movement; there was a positive haste to introduce thoughts into reality which sometimes led them beyond the limits of prudence. Le Corbusier would work for any client, from the Salvation Army to the Russians, without sufficient thought for the effect the client would have on the architectural product, and even Gropius and Mies, the most socially committed, at first made light of the political implications of their work, concentrating solely on making contact with economic forces.

The means regarded as most suitable to persuade the public were not exhibitions,

548   *Part of an illustrated letter where Le Corbusier described to Mme Meyer the plan of her villa (1925; from* Oeuvre Complète)

books, manifestos, but rather the buildings themselves. Competitions were particularly propitious occasions, allowing comparisons between various solutions of a single concrete subject. Even in exhibitions, rather than models and temporary pavilions, the protagonists of the modern movement preferred to exhibit objects industrially made for the normal market and permanent buildings, which would continue to be used afterwards.

549, 550 *Design (right) by Gropius and Meyer for the* Chicago Tribune *competition (1922) compared to current American building (from S. Giedion,* op. cit., *1954)*

1 Competitions

The first competition of world importance, in which several masters of the modern movement had an opportunity to test their skills, was that organized in 1922 by the *Chicago Tribune* newspaper, for its new offices, with a million dollars in prize money.

Among the competitors were Gropius and Meyer with a splendid work in steel, glass and terracotta (Fig. 550), Max Taut with a glass tower, the Dutchmen B. Bijvoet and J. Duiker with a building in the neo-plastic style, the Dane Londberg-Holm with a somewhat stiff functional organism and A. Loos

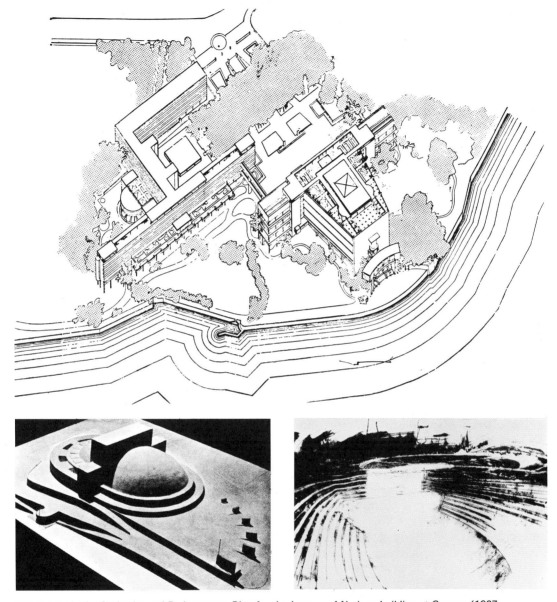

551 *(above)* *Le Corbusier and P. Jeanneret, Plan for the League of Nations building at Geneva (1927, from* Oeuvre Complète*)*
552, 553 *(below)* *E. Mendelsohn, Plan for the Palace of the Soviets, 1931 (from A. Whittick,* E.M., *1940)*

with a skyscraper in the shape of a Doric column. These projects were important for the history of the European movement, but they produced no proportionate effect on the public and jury; the prizewinners were all traditionalists and the modern plans were mistaken for the extravagances of an ump-teenth *avant-garde*.

The situation was quite different in 1927, when the League of Nations organized the competition for its headquarters in Geneva. Three hundred and seventy-seven plans were sent in from all parts of the world: among the competitors were H. Meyer and H. Wittwer, A. Fischer-Essen, the Dutch-man Vijdeveld and, with particular involve-ment, the Frenchmen Le Corbusier and Pierre Jeanneret. They were still a small minority in a sea of neo-classical projects, but the conditions of the struggle had changed, as had the possibilities of making a mark, since the jury included, as well as the academicians J. Burnet, C. Cato, C. Lemas-quier and A. Muggia, several masters of the earlier generation, Berlage, Hoffmann, Moser and Tengbom, capable of grasping the continuity between their experiments and those of the younger post-war masters. The chairman was Horta, the most sophisticated of *art nouveau* artists though the least suited to an understanding of the new course of European architecture.

Le Corbusier's project was the most important hitherto drawn up by this un-flagging master (Fig. 557). He submitted the exalted theme to the usual functional analysis: 'A Palace of the Nations houses four types of activity: a daily activity: the general Secretariat with the library; an intermittent activity: the small committee rooms without any public and the committee rooms with a public; a three-monthly activity: the Council of Nations; an annual activity: the General Assembly.'[3]

These activities should logically be accom-modated in different organisms: thus Le Corbusier designed an articulated system of well-spaced pavilions, set over an area of slightly sloping ground leading down to the shore of the lake. The rigorous functional analysis ('problem well-posed') gave him, among other things, considerable freedom in an area that the others regarded as too

limited, and a possibility of keeping the expenses within modest limits. The woody countryside, dominated by the horizontal stretch of lake, was well and intelligently utilized by avoiding enclosed courtyards and providing sweeping, restful views from each room.

The architectural solutions were not always successful, and certainly not com-parable to other contemporary works by the master; particularly detrimental was the desire to retain certain axes of symmetry in an organism that tended basically towards asymmetry, as in certain of Berlage's late works.[4] But the plan was particularly important for its immediate efficacy in proving its point; it showed the general public that the method of functional analysis could be successfully applied to an important work of prestige, that working space became more convenient, circulation easier and costs lower, that the infinite difficulties connected with the cramped setting – obstacles that would be insuperable with traditional com-positional criteria – could be overcome with the much more pliable criteria of the new architecture, indeed they could become opportunities for formal enrichment.

Of the jury Berlage, Hoffmann, Moser and Tengbom gave their support to this plan, while the four academicians were against it. It looked as though it might obtain first prize, but Horta's waverings prevented a definitive verdict and widely divergent plans including Le Corbusier's, were awarded equal prizes. Meanwhile, at the insistence of the academi-cians, a new area of ground was proposed, further upstream, and the competitors were invited to draw up new plans. Le Corbusier and Pierre Jeanneret adapted their original plan to the new area and spoiled it by break-ing up the original unity into three over-distinct pavilions (for the Secretariat, hall and library), each perfectly symmetrical.

In the end the academicians prevailed definitively and four[5] of the five prize-winners were commissioned to design the building.

Many of Le Corbusier's functional and distributive suggestions were accepted in the executive plan: the grouping of the small committee rooms within the organism of the Secretariat, and of the large ones along the side of the hall, the linear layout of the Secretariat, the roof garden above; even the definitive ground plan has an undeniable similarity with Le Corbusier's second plan, except that the direction was reversed. Le Corbusier fought fiercely against this[6] and even attempted legal action. Considered after a lapse of time, this incident is very instructive for the history of the relations between the modern movement and the public. The efficacy of Le Corbusier's statement, which derived its strength from functional advantages that were objective and controllable, was not lost even on his adversaries, but it was accepted only partially: the functional advantages gained approval, the new architectual language they entailed did not.

If the competition for the League of Nations ended, materially speaking, in a defeat for modern architects, it did, however, deliver the final blow, morally, to the prestige of the academy. Faced with a practical problem, with fairly narrow technical and economic restrictions, the academic architects had shown themselves incapable of resolving it satisfactorily. They had had to make a sharp distinction between technical and artistic values, making a show of defending the latter against the former, and they ended up with a borrowed functional organism dressed up in neo-classical garb; in this way, by isolating the real substance of their contribution, they demonstrated the vanity of it, since they had not managed to produce a beautiful or indeed even a passable building, but had simply raised the costs with dreary cornices and pointlessly thick masonry, which were completely unnecessary. They had won but without conviction, and the final building satisfied no-one.

In 1931 the Russian government organized an international competition for the Palace of the Soviets, which was to be the antithesis of the Geneva palace and was to prove the superiority of the Soviet world over the capitalist one. The government commissioned plans directly from the best-known modern masters, Gropius, Mendelsohn, Le Corbusier and Poelzig, as if to show that the Soviet Union eagerly welcomed the progressive forces defeated at Geneva.

Le Corbusier produced a complex organism where the articulation of the volumes analytically reproduced the distributive elements and their links, as at Geneva, but the supporting structures of the two big halls were left visible on the outside with a glee that was reminiscent of the Russian constructivist school. Gropius on the other hand set all the bodies of the building within a large circle, solving the problems of this unusually vast subject with this geometrical expedient. The best plan was certainly Mendelsohn's, and the only one that appeared capable of controlling the huge composition with sufficient energy and breadth of conception (Figs. 552 and 553).

The jury had praise for all the plans, especially for that of Le Corbusier which spoke a language more familiar to them, but gave the first prize to academicians: the first and third to the Russians B. M. Jofan and N. B. Joltowsky, the second to Hamilton. After a second competition in 1933, the commission was given to Jofan together with the traditionalists Schonko and Helfreich, and the final plan was a sort of skyscraper of gradually narrowing parts, topped by a statue of Lenin, about 100 m. high, and taller, altogether, than the Empire State Building which had been built in New York in the meantime.

2 The exhibitions

In 1927 the German Werkbund organized its second exhibition in Stuttgart; as well as the usual temporary pavilions, Mies, the vice president, obtained permission to lay out a district of permanent dwellings on some high

1 Mies van der Rohe	12 H. Poelzig
2 J. J. P. Oud	14 & 14 R. Döcker
3 V. Bourgeois	15 & 16 M. Taut
4 & 5 A. Schneck	17 A. Rading
6 & 7 Le Corbusier	18 J. Frank
8 & 9 W. Gropius	19 M. Stam
10 L. Hilberseimer	20 P. Behrens
11 B. Taut	21 H. Scharoun

554, 555   *Stuttgart, The Weissenhof, 1927 (from P. Johnson,* Mies van der Rohe, *1947)*

556, 557, 558   *Stuttgart, Block of houses by Mies on the Weissenhof*

ground on the outskirts of the city, the Weissenhof Siedlung. The plan was by Mies himself, putting into practice certain theoretically proven principles – the buildings' independence of the roadsides, separation of motor and pedestrian traffic – and following the suggestions of the sloping ground with sensitivity and moderation (Figs. 554 and 555); the best architects throughout Europe were commissioned to build the houses: the Germans P. Behrens, J. Frank, R. Döcker, W. Gropius, L. Hilbersheimer, H. Poelzig, A. Rading, H. Scharoun, A. Schneck, B. and M. Taut, as well as Mies himself, the Dutchmen J. J. P. Oud and M. Stam, the Frenchman Le Corbusier and the Belgian V. Bourgeois.

The district had an experimental character since it was not a unitary complex, formed of repeated building types, but a set of samples of different buildings, to be considered as so

559 *Stuttgart, Detail of Mies' houses on the Weissenhof*

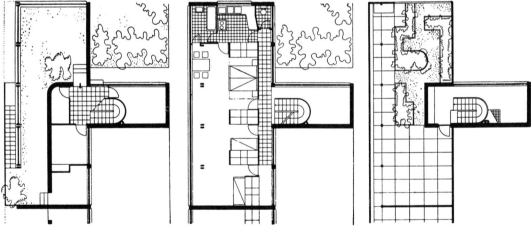

560, 561 *Stuttgart, The steel house by Le Corbusier on the Weissenhof*

many prototypes. The main building was a four-storey block of terraced houses with a steel structure, by Mies (Figs. 556–9). This was an eminently theoretical theme on which Gropius too was working at the same time: the open block, which was to replace the old building along the edges of the road and give all dwellings equally hygienic conditions, constituting a reasonable alternative to the detached one-family house. Three years later Gropius was to show that the open block was the more convenient the higher it was, compatibly with constructional and distributive limitations: without lifts it could be

562, 563   *Stuttgart, H. Scharoun's house on the Weissenhof*

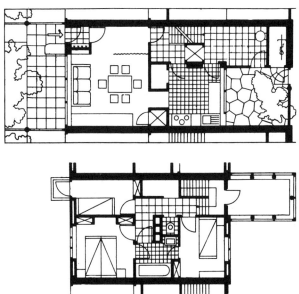

564, 565   *Stuttgart, Oud's terrace-houses on the Weissenhof*

566, 567   *Stuttgart, Terrace-houses by M. Stam on the Weissenhof*

568, 569 *Stuttgart, Interiors of houses by Gropius and Le Corbusier on the Weissenhof*

four storeys high, with lifts, ten.

Here Mies provided an unimpeachable architectural solution to the first alternative. Every additional or ornamental element was eliminated and the architect worked as usual by distributing the relations of the functional elements with inimitable confidence. Though the unusual system of building did not allow for an equally satisfactory degree of technical control, and though the state of preservation of the building is mediocre, the exquisite proportions of the design still shine through the poverty of the material.

Gropius used two detached houses to experiment with a system of prefabrication with metal supports and dividing walls in cork, finished on the outside with slabs of eternit; the dimensions of the slabs determined the module of the construction both in plan and elevation.

Le Corbusier built two other detached houses on 'pilotis', in reinforced concrete and iron, applying his usual five points and developing the basic idea of the Citrohan houses of seven years earlier (Figs. 560 and 561). These were the heart of the Weissenhof propaganda and polemic. The public was particularly shocked by the minimal dimensions of certain rooms, for instance the corridor of the house in iron, no wider than that of a railway train.

Oud designed a group of five terraced houses articulated more freely than those in Rotterdam and designed with equal care and sensitivity. One of the houses was exhibited with all its furnishings, so that every detail should be in harmony with the whole.

Behrens, the doyen of the German architects, built an animated organism full of hints and Romantic yearnings. Scharoun, one of the young architects, designed a house in which the elements of the new architecture were already being interpreted in a decorative way (Figs. 562 and 563): for the first time, encouraged by the partisan mood of the exhibition, modern mannerism made its appearance, i.e. the conscious transposition

of results hitherto achieved into the framework of the old eclecticism.

The Stuttgart exhibition presented a coherent review of the modern movement to the public for the first time. The direct comparison between works of many architects, of varying nationalities, emphasized their common aims rather than their differences and revealed the basic convergence between many activities with differing origins. There had been no overall planning and the buildings were simply juxtaposed, as usually happened in suburban areas. But if one remembers that the buildings were conceived as prototypes, suited for mass reproduction, and are in a certain sense the samples for so many districts, then the Weissenhof may be considered as an inspiriting representation of the modern city, and the basic harmony of the various contributions showed that a broader unity could be arrived at, in which the various methods of planning could balance one another.

In this way the Weissenhof, even if it made no definite contribution to the dawning problem of the uniform district, offered an interesting suggestion in connection with the town-planning problem potentially inherent in the activities of modern architects; to judge from contemporary comments, the public was aware, more or less confusedly, of this: this was not a collection of proposals for buildings, but a suggestion for a new concept of living, which set out to modify not only single dwellings but the whole of the urban scene.[7]

In the numerous exhibitions organized by modern architects between the end of the war and the economic crisis, the recurrent and almost exclusive theme was the modern house. In 1925 Le Corbusier, commissioned to build the pavilion of the Esprit Nouveau for the international exhibition of decorative arts in Paris, presented a perfectly furnished element of the 'immeuble-villas' worked on three years earlier. The views of Gropius and the modern German masters on the modern house were illustrated in 1928 with the exhibition Wohnen im Grünen in Berlin, in 1930 in Paris at the Werkbund exhibition and in 1931 in Berlin at the exhibition of German architecture.

The exhibition in 1930 at the Grand Palais in Paris was the most influential: Germany, officially invited, commissioned the Werkbund to take charge of the matter, and the Werkbund handed the responsibility over to Gropius, who made use of three old collaborators from the Bauhaus: Bayer, Breuer and Moholy-Nagy. Gropius aimed at presenting the flower of German production, already greatly influenced by Bauhaus models, and used the plan of a ten-floor apartment as an ideal setting. He designed the furnishings of the main room, using much mass-produced furniture, Breuer did the furniture for an apartment in the same house, Moholy-Nagy worked on the lighting fitments and Bayer on the textiles.

The reactions of the French public were mostly positive, and even amazed at the transformations the German movement had produced, in a few years, in German decorative art. Breuer's metal tubular furniture was particularly admired, being far superior to that exhibited a few months earlier in the *Salon d'Automne* by Le Corbusier and Charlotte Perriand; the lightness and impeccable execution of every object was much appreciated.

At this moment political circumstances favoured good cultural relations between Germany and France. Briand launched his proposal for a European union and serious efforts were made towards an economic entente between the various countries, as a possible way out of the imminent crisis. In fact the exhibitions, organized with rigid selective criteria, did not give at all an authentic image of German production as a whole, but was a generous anticipation of the harmony that the modern movement believed it could bring about in Germany and elsewhere if it was able to carry on its

work: it was for this reason that it was such an efficacious and inspiring influence.

Giedion reports several opinions from the Paris press, which fit well into the mood of hope for union, and faith in a better world to be attained through international co-operation; *Le Temps* wrote:

'The thing that impresses the French most about the German section of the exhibition is that they have found the emphasis laid upon just the opposite from what they expected – namely lightness . . . . In 1910 another exhibition was set up by German artists in the Grand Palais. How much has happened between then and now . . . . It is certainly not an exaggeration to say that the "section allemande" is not only a "salon" – a saloon among many others – but that it again, in very truth, shows us the face of young Germany'.[8]

And *Le Figaro*:

'Is this really an exhibition of decorative art, like so many others? No, it is rather a new conception of lines, surfaces, rooms for an abstract life, disciplined without restrictions and without concern for easing . . . life itself'.[9]

In 1931 much of the Paris material was exhibited once again at the Bauausstellung in Berlin (Figs. 571–3). This show took place at the very height of the economic crisis, and the evocation of a future world, functional and harmonious, took on quite another meaning, because events left no hope of carrying on the work undertaken with any degree of success. Germany had responded to moves for union with renewed manifestations of nationalism; in the spring of 1931 there was the catastrophe of the Reichsbank, while the delicate balance of German democracy was being rocked by the advance of the extreme right and the extreme left; the ruling class which had supported Gropius and his fellows, now closely threatened in its

570   *Common-room in the tall house at the Werkbund exhibition in Paris in 1930 (from Giedion,* Walter Gropius*)*

interests, promptly let fall its cultural ambitions. The German exhibition of 1931 thus acted as a summary of the work achieved, and the dogged attention given to general presentation revealed the poignant dis-appointment of the architects about the failure of their efforts.

Although they were concerned mainly with content, the above-mentioned exhibitions did also have a profound effect on the

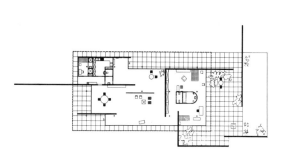

571, 572, 573   *Berlin, Bauausstellung 1931: (above) furniture by L. Reich; (below) plan and view of model house by Mies (from Johnson,* op. cit.*)*

traditional form of presenting exhibits to the public.

The aim of the method of presentation was not so much to exhibit as to demonstrate: the artists were aiming at explaining and making comprehensible to all an alternative to the traditional way of living. In this way the exhibition lost its original character of a showplace for goods and was conceived – ideally – as a mechanism for influencing the visitor, utilizing all the means of representation that the modern movement had elaborated in the meantime.

These means were described as follows by Moholy-Nagy in 1928:

'Movable walls lettered with new slogans, rotating colour filters, light projectors, signal demonstrations and reflectors: transparency, light and movement, all in the service of the public. Everything so arranged that it can be handled and understood by the simplest individual. Then also the exciting use of new materials: huge sheets of celluloid, lattice work, enlargements, small and large sheets of wire meshing, transparent displays with lettering suspended in space, everywhere clear and brilliant colours'.[10]

While modern architects were still kept at a distance from practical tasks and achievements, exhibitions often became opportunities for the practical realization of new spatial concepts, even if only temporarily.

As vice president of the Werkbund, Mies was commissioned to design the settings for exhibits: the pavilion for the glass industry at the Stuttgart exhibition in 1927, the German Pavilion at the international exhibition in Barcelona in 1929 and the model house at the Bauausstellung in Berlin in 1931.

In this subject – mid-way between a work of the imagination and a real building – he found an initial impulse for the realization of some of his finest images, whose value went far beyond their original starting point and stimulated much subsequent architectural thought.

Mies realized that an exhibition pavilion was not an ordinary building but something essentially different, which was to remain in existence only as long as it was going to be looked at and which was at the service of the public who was looking at it. For this reason he did not conceive of it as an enclosed building but as a collection of detached buildings, suited temporarily to defining a certain stretch of space (this was probably the link with earlier imaginative works, similarly

destined to stimulate a public of visitors or readers).

The temporary nature and the fact that he was building – in Berlin – under cover of a hangar, freed the artist from concern with any technical problems. In Barcelona the wealth of means enabled him to make use of precious materials such as marble, onyx, coloured glass: thus there was nothing to prevent perfect finish or the completeness of the architectural result. We can get an idea of these works only from photographs and the descriptions of contemporaries; like them, we are struck by the fact that there was apparently no wavering, in these buildings, between conception and execution, thought and reality.

Profiting from the subject, Mies offered a sort of theoretical demonstration of the modern method of architectural planning. By breaking the construction down into its primary elements he dispelled all echoes and residues of former building habits, and space was once again clean, uniform and blank, like the empty canvas of which Kandinsky speaks;[11] in this space simple geometrical prisms and pure materials gained extraordinary vibrance, like the elementary forms and colours which peopled Kandinsky's canvas; marble partitions, gleaming columns, delicately poised roof slabs were set with absolute firmness in their uncluttered surroundings, qualifying them with terseness and discretion yet never enclosing them, suggesting an unbounded field of possible developments.

The distinction between technical and artistic values could be maintained only as a critical expedient, since constructional elements were directly utilized as expressive elements, simply in the way they were used. Mies' handiwork was always recognizable, though not in any direct and particular way, since the extremely rigorous execution did not allow of any licence, any wavering; the forms he designed had the value of prototypes, ready for industrial reproduction.

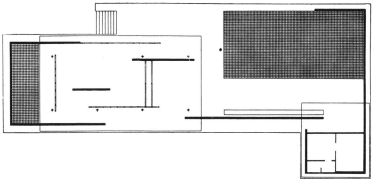

574, 575 *Barcelona, German Pavilion at the 1929 exhibition (Mies; from B. Zevi,* Storia dell'architettura moderna, *1950)*

3 The publications

After Gropius' short book *Internationale Architektur*, which came out in 1925, publications on the modern movement increased rapidly: a modest contribution by Hilbersheimer[12] in 1926, the large systematic volume by Platz[13] in 1927, the essays by Meyer[14] in 1928, Hitchcock[15] and B. Taut[16] in 1929, by Malkiel–Jirmounsky[17] and Cheney[18] in 1930; between 1929 and 1932 the four volumes of the *Wasmuth Lexicon der Baukunst* appeared and, in 1930, the first volume on the work of Le Corbusier from 1910 to 1929; in Italy, Fillia's anthology[19] was published in 1932 and A. Sartoris' book of illustrations in 1932.[20]

In these books modern architecture was presented not only as a future ideal but as a result to some degree already realized in the present, and therefore containing its own justifications in its very existence.

In the field of journals, too, the situation had changed: *avant-garde* publications vanished off the scene one by one: *L'Esprit nouveau* in 1925, *De Stijl* in 1928, the *Bauhaus Review* in 1929, and in their places various new periodicals with a broader critical outlook appeared. In 1929 there appeared *Die Form*, the organ of the Deutscher Werkbund, and *Das Neue Frankfurt* which dealt with the experiment of E. May; in 1930 *L'Architecture d'Aujourd'hui* appeared, and in Italy Pagano began to run *La Casa Bella*; articles and works of modern architecture began to appear in traditionalist publications such as *Moderne Bauformen*, *Wasmuth Menatshefte für Baukunst und Städtebau* and the *Architectural Review*.

It was not a question of advocating a new tendency but of documenting an already active movement, and those concerned tried to give simple, positive explanations, comprehensible to everyone, using mainly technical arguments and leaving aside formal justifications. Here are a few examples: in 1927 the editorial staff of *Moderne Bauformen*, commissioning Hilbersheimer to cover the Stuttgart exhibition, stated:

'We believe that we are doing a service to our members by presenting them with an anthology of the "new architecture" which the German Werkbund is now

presenting at Stuttgart at its international exhibitions of plans and models. Let us turn to its organizer, the Berlin architect, Ludwig Hilbersheimer, since it is only reasonable that the tendency struggling for recognition in the architecture of almost all countries, should be explained by one of its supporters. The following issues of *Moderne Bauformen* will once again be of a more usual character and will present modern furnishings and decor of the most varied kinds'.

Hilbersheimer wrote:

'The premises and bases of the new architecture are of various kinds. Utilitarian needs define the functional character of the building. Materials and statics are the means with which it is built. Distributive features and scientific and sociological factors exercise a considerable influence through constructional technique. But what dominates is the executive will of the architect. He defines the respective importance of the single elements and by means of their juxtaposition realizes the formal unity of the building. The procedure according to which the form is realized determines the character of the new architecture. It does not develop into a mere decorative exterior but is the expression of the vital interpenetration of all the elements. Thus the aesthetic factor is no longer dominant, an end in itself, as is the architecture of the façades which take no account of the architectural organism, but like all the other elements it plays its part within the whole and retains its value and its importance *vis-à-vis* this whole. The over-valuation of an element always produces disturbances. For this reason the new architecture aims at the balance of all the elements, at harmony. But this is not an external matter, or one that can be laid down dogmatically, it is different for each new undertaking. It does not involve any predetermined stylistic pattern, but is the expression of the mutual interpenetration of all the elements beneath the rule of the creative will. New architecture does not pose problems of style but problems of construction.

In this way, too, one can begin to understand the surprising harmony of formal appearance in the new international architecture. It is not a question of fashionable formal aspirations, as is often believed, but of the elementary expression of a new architectural concept. Although it is often differentiated according to local and national peculiarities and to the personality of the particular designer, nonetheless on the whole it is the product of unvarying premises; hence the unity of the formal results. This ideal unanimity goes beyond all frontiers'.[21]

In his book published in 1929 B. Taut summarized the character of the modern movement in these five points:

'1   The first requirement in every building is the achievement of the greatest possible utility.

2   The materials employed and the building system used must be completely subordinated to this primary need.

3   Beauty consists in the direct relationship between the building and its purpose, in the appropriate features of the materials and in the elegance of the constructional system.

4   The aesthetics of the new architecture do not recognize any separation between façade and ground plan, between street and courtyard, between front and back. No detail is valid on its own, but is a necessary part of the whole. Something that works well also looks good. We no longer believe that something can be ugly and yet work well at the same time.

5   The house too, like its component parts, is no longer an isolated and separate entity.

Just as the parts live within the unity of mutual relationships, so the house lives in relation to the surrounding buildings. The house is the product of a collective and social way of thinking. Repetition is no longer regarded as something to be avoided, but on the contrary as the most important means of artistic expression. For identical needs, identical buildings, while the anomaly is kept for cases where the needs are really special, i.e. particularly for buildings of general and social importance.'[22]

These views, like those of Gropius in the previous chapter, are comprehensible only if one bears in mind their metaphorical nature. The modern movement shifted the significance of the terms of architectural discussion, as we tried to explain in the section devoted to the Bauhaus, but it is almost impossible to give this explanation directly, since every word had a scope and reference different from its usual ones. Architects themselves often retained old habits, because the modern movement was an operative choice which became a theory only later, and then only partially.

Discussions, therefore, were always somewhat forced and allusive. When talking to the general public, architects had to choose between precision and simplification; precise discussions were always complex, simple ones ambiguous and approximative.

The various labels which supporters and adversaries applied, at this time, to the modern movement, were comprehensible only in relation to this difficulty. They were formulae in which certain traditional terms were used to stress certain aspects of the movement by allusion; but the words could also be interpreted literally, and produced a series of misunderstandings.

The formula 'neue Sachlichkeit' was borrowed from literary discussion and was used to emphasize the relation between the architectural movement and similar experiments in other fields. The new architecture, like Brecht's theatre, aimed at affecting people's practical behaviour, at 'getting decisions' rather than at 'encouraging emotions'.[23] Here architects had the advantage over writers; the latter were forced to put their proposals before the public indirectly, by modifying the traditional forms of entertainment destined to occupy free time – and therefore by addressing the public just when it was hoping for an escape from everyday responsibilities – while architecture involved men every moment of the day and affected them just when they were thinking of their practical interests.

The comparison with literature helps to explain the meaning of the other labels. The formula 'rational architecture' can be interpreted with the words of Piscator: the new architecture 'must no longer influence the spectator by purely sentimental means, no longer speculate on his emotional availability, but must address itself quite consciously to his reason; it must no longer communicate excitement, enthusiasm, ecstasy, but clarity, knowledge, understanding;'[24] a rational state of mind, in fact, was a vital condition for ideas to gain a hold on the world of reality:

> *Nur belehrt von der Wirklichkeit, können wir*
> *Die Wirklichkeit ändern.*[25]

The formula 'functional architecture' was closely related to the preceding one. The new architecture (to use Brecht's words) was 'the affair of the technician rather than of the connoisseur'[26] and aroused feelings of mathematical calculation and objective evaluation in its beholder rather than a subjective rush of admiration. It was considered preferable to concentrate on functional advantages, which could be demonstrated rationally, rather than on matters of taste; only thus could demonstration be basically free of the degree of the public's culture and reach them directly, not through the medium of a sophisticated élite: i.e. it could escape the hierarchical organization which had always

dominated traditional culture.

The formula 'international architecture', clinched by the title of Gropius' book, referred to the first two formulae. Gropius gave this explanation:

'It is wrong to put the stress on the individual at all costs. On the contrary, the desire to develop a unitary view of the world, which is a feature of our time, underlines the need to free the values of spirit from individual restrictions and to raise them to the heights of objective validity . . . . In modern architecture the objectivization of what is personal and national is quite clearly noticeable. A modern unifying tendency, conditioned by world communications and world techniques, is making headway in every field of culture, going beyond the national boundaries to which individuals and peoples are still bound. Architecture is always national, it is also always individual, but of the three concentric circles – individual, people, humanity – the third and largest embraces the other two: hence the title: international architecture!'[27]

In 1934 Persico wrote: 'If one wants to consider the new architecture apart from aesthetic formulae, then rather than talking of internationalism one should go back to the concept of a world that is completely rational, intelligent.'[28]

These concepts could be understood within the ambit of a new thought, which was now emerging amid the new experiments; but the verbal formulae used to express it could be understood only in terms of traditional habits, and could be referred only to the old system of values.

Thus the 'new objectivity' could be interpreted as a mechanical adherence to circumstances, 'rationality' as exaltation of deduction over induction, the idea of 'functionality' could be restricted to material facts – i.e. the distinction between material and spiritual requirements could be maintained in the old terms – and 'internationality' could be understood in a literal sense, as if the new architecture were to be identical in each country and independent of local traditions.

Faced with these accusations modern architects sometimes defended themselves, but usually they implicitly accepted the traditional meanings of the words and became bogged down in sterile discussions, which they had no hope of winning. For instance they insisted on stating that they were concerned not only with techniques and material commodities, but also with spiritual and artistic values, indeed they said that spiritual satisfaction was more important than material, and feelings more important than convenience (still using the vocabulary of their adversaries). They hastened to justify the forms they used on aesthetic grounds and once again brought into circulation summary interpretations of neoplasticism, Cubism, Purism and other *avant-garde* movements.

At this point the positions were reversed: modern architects appealed to high-flown esoteric theories, sometimes incomprehensible, while their adversaries noted with sarcasm that these theories were leading them to overlook certain elementary practical and economic criteria; and they were often right, because in the heat of the discussion modern architects adopted technically dubious systems that were not yet sufficiently tested. Examples of this were the discussions about the horizontal window advocated by Le Corbusier and the efforts of the traditionalists to prove scientifically that the vertical window lit the room more efficiently, the arguments about the flat terraces which allowed water to leak in or on the abolition of cornices, which protected the façade from the weather.[29]

These idle arguments were still being echoed until very recently, and they have not completely died down even today. They did the modern movement a serious disservice, because they prevented its basic and important argument from being developed and hindered the simultaneous evolution of theory and practice, and when the social and political situation became really serious they served as an excuse for an escape from real responsibilities and difficult choices.

We shall use the expressions 'rational', 'functional' and 'international' architecture only when referring to the above-mentioned discussions, and we shall avoid using them to indicate the movement as a whole. This will complicate the exposition a little, but it will enable us to avoid many commonplaces which weigh heavily on the history of modern architecture, and not to confuse historical reality with the polemical and restrictive interpretation that was put upon it at one stage.

4 The foundation of the C.I.A.M.

In 1927 the competition for the League of Nations and the Stuttgart exhibition proved that a large number of architects in various European countries were working with similar methods, and that their contributions were in fact reconcilable among themselves.

In 1928 the need arose to translate this hypothetical unity into association, and the opportunity was offered by Mme de Mandrot, who offered the castle of La Sarraz for a congress of modern architects.

Le Corbusier did a coloured diagram of the six points to be discussed, which was put up in the hall:

Modern technical knowledge and its
consequences
Standardization
Economy
Town-planning
Education of the young
Realization: architecture and the State[30]

The discussions at La Sarraz, as was usually the case on such occasions, were not of much importance; most of those attending[31] were certainly in basic agreement as

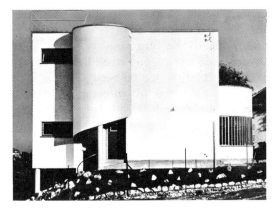

576, 577, 578 *(left)   The rational style. F. Molnar, house in Budapest (1932); L. De Konnick, Claes house in Anderghem (1931); J. Fischer, house in Budapest (1932)*
579, 580, 581 *(right)   Cornell and Ward, house in Grayswood, England (1932); S. Papadaki, house at Glyfada (1933); M. Jancu, house at Bucharest (1933); (all from A. Sartoris,* Gli elementi dell'architettura razionale*)*

far as facts were concerned; but it was far more difficult to put this agreement into reality, since those able to simplify discussions, sailing over these difficulties, naturally had the advantage over those who saw the problems in their complex entirety and were hindered from talking by this awareness.

The final statement is in the style of Le Corbusier:

'The undersigned architects, representatives of national groups of modern architects, affirm their identity of views on the basic concepts of architecture and on their professional duties. Above all they insist on the fact that "building" is an elementary human activity closely bound up with the development of life. The destiny of architecture is to express the spirit of an age. They affirm the need, today, for a new concept of architecture, which will satisfy the material, spiritual and emotional needs of contemporary life. Aware of the profound upheavals produced by the machine age, they recognize that the transformation of the social and economic structure demands a corresponding change in architecture. They have come together to seek for the harmonizing of the elements present in the modern world and to put architecture back in its true sphere, which is economic, sociological and altogether at the service of humanity. In this way architecture will escape the sterile influence of the academies. Strengthened by this conviction, they proclaim their association for the attainment of these ends.

To be of use to a country, architecture must be closely bound up with the general economy. The notion of "profit", introduced as an axiom in modern life, does not imply maximum commercial profit but a production sufficient to meet human requirements fully. Real profit would be the fruit of rationalization and standardization flexibly applied to architectural plans as to industrial models. It is important that architecture, instead of having recourse almost exclusively to anaemic craftsmanship, should utilize the immense resources of industrial technique, different from those which were responsible for its past glories.

Town-planning is the design of the different settings for the development of material, emotional and spiritual life in all its manifestations, individual and collective, and it includes both town and country. Town-planning cannot be submitted exclusively to the rules of an arbitrary aestheticism, it is essentially functional. The three basic functions with which town-planning must concern itself are: (1) living; (2) working; (3) recreation. Its objectives are: (a) the use of the land; (b) the organization of transport; (c) legislation. These three functions are not made any easier by the pattern of existing settlements. The relations between the various places in which they take place must be re-calculated, to establish a correct proportion between built-up space and open space. The chaotic division of the land, the result of its division into lots, of selling and speculation, must be replaced by a rational system of regrouping. This reorganization, the basis of all town-planning answering modern needs, will guarantee landowners and the community at large a fair division of the increase in value that will come from works of public interest.

It is vital that architects should exercise an influence on public opinion, to make the means and resources of modern architecture known. Academic teaching has perverted public taste and usually the real problems of the house are not even posed. The public is ill-informed and the users themselves are usually very poor at formulating their desires in connection with their houses. So that housing has for some time been foreign to the architect's main concerns. A body of elementary ideas, taught in primary schools, could form the basis of a domestic education. This teaching could form new generations equipped with sensible ideas about housing, and they, the architect's future clientèle, could force him to solve the problem of the house, which he has neglected for too long.

Architects, with the firm desire to work in the real interests of modern society, believe that the academies, conservers of the past, hinder social progress by ignoring the problem of housing to the advantage of public architecture. By their influence on teaching they distort the architect's vocation from the start and since it is they almost exclusively who obtain public commissions, they prevent the spread of the new spirit, which is the only thing that can breathe new life into the art of building'.[32]

It is particularly interesting to consider the discussions on the means of realization, which defined the action of the C.I.A.M. towards contemporary society.

The sixth of the points put forward by Le Corbusier was: 'Realization: Architecture and the State'. Various lines of thought converged in this formula: Le Corbusier cultivated the idea of a demiurgic architecture, where the behaviour of the many should be regulated by the enlightened action of the few. In 1923 he wrote: 'The art of our time is performing its proper functions when it addresses itself to the chosen few. Art is not a popular thing . . . art is not an essential pabulum except for the chosen few who have need of meditation in order that they may lead. Art is in its essence arrogant.'[33] and it was natural that he should want to carry out this task of guidance at the highest level, through the State.

Gropius saw that the current *élites* could continue to serve a purpose in modern society only by giving up their superior power to assume a task of cultural mediation:

to ensure the transference of the old legacy of values from the old to the new social structure (in technical terms, from craftsmanship to industry);[34] they must, one might say, not 'meditate in order that they may lead', but lead only long enough to formulate, by meditating, an appropriate system of values that may be left to others in the future unified society. And since the point where everyone's interests emerge and where the means of intervention are concentrated ever more intensively, was the State (one need only think of the increasing importance of subsidized building in the building industry as a whole), Gropius and his colleagues, too, set their sights on the State as the new means to translate their ideas into action.

The decisive difference was this: Le Corbusier had no experience of dealings with the State, while Gropius, Mies and the others had been fostering such relations for some time; both the Werkbund and the Bauhaus were state institutions, and the Stuttgart Weissenhof – like the Dessau buildings – had been paid for by public money. The Dutch had had a similar experience, for they had been working for public administrations for thirty years; Berlage, an old man by now, arrived to make his contribution to the sixth point, with a report entitled: *Relations between the State and Architecture*.

Le Corbusier, like the French intellectuals of the eighteenth century mentioned by de Tocqueville, had a formal conception of power, as the possession of the financial and legal means necessary to carry out certain programmes, and thought that he could use public power to execute his intentions without giving up the detached position which he occupied as an intellectual.

Gropius, Oud and Berlage knew that to stake their cards on the State meant giving up their privileged position of *avant-garde* artists and accepting political struggle on an equal footing with other men. If architects believed that they could influence the living conditions of all men, the least that could be asked of them was that they put forward their proposals according to current rules, valid for all.

This step was very important: even those who, from lack of experience, thought they could give birth to a new academy or could dabble in pure ivory-tower culture, were implicitly accepting the rules of the game by asking for help from the state: the democratic game or the totalitarian game. And those who thought that they could keep ends distinct from means, that they could offer their work to those in power, whoever they might be, while keeping the field of design at least free from concessions, were soon to be disappointed: dictatorships did not want modern architecture, but arches and columns, and were much more consistent than architects because they refused to acknowledge any distinction between the 'how' and the 'what'.

These problems were in the air at the castle of La Sarraz; the talk was optimistic in tone though the participants were aware of the gravity of the problems touched on and the alternatives open to them. For this reason, wisely, the organizational structure was left fairly elastic and the initials adopted (Congrès Internationaux d'Architecture Moderne) referred only to the opportunity of meeting periodically to compare the various experiments carried out. Gropius wrote:

'The most important thing was the fact that in a world full of confusion, of piece-meal efforts, a small, supra-national group of architects felt the need to rally in an effort to see the many-sided problems that confronted them as a totality'.[35]

In reality there were two distinct tasks: to compare experiments periodically so as to come closer to an understanding of un-resolved problems, or to decide how to present the public with the solutions that were gradually being worked out. The first

requirement would lead to a narrowing of the field of agreement between the various trends, stressing the basic difficulties, the second to broadening it by obscuring controversial arguments with temporary formulae so as to gain in clarity of exposition.

The two tasks were not always carried out at the same rate and cultural investigation was sometimes sacrificed to propagandist presentation; despite the sincerity of involve-ment, discussions were in danger of being divided into two types, for internal and for external use, and the modern movement, by presenting itself in official dress and agreeing to specify its theses in a simple, schematic form, sometimes the fruit of verbal compro-mise, implicitly authorized the public to judge it in an equally simple and schematic way.

In the years around 1930 modern architec-ture reached a peak of prestige and popularity, particularly in Germany and to a lesser extent in other countries.

This was the moment when the attraction of the formal repertoire elaborated by modern architects led many other designers who had undergone quite different formal influences, sometimes even positively aca-demic – to modernize their language more or less sincerely. The spirit of modern architec-ture also spread to other fields; in 1930 Hindemith wrote his cantata 'Wir bauen ein Haus', performed by a choir of boys imitating the gestures of builders, while the words extolled teamwork.

In this climate, between 1929 and 1931, three remarkable works were built almost simultaneously; all three were soon to be-come famous and acted as points of reference for arguments for and against the modern movement: the Savoye house at Poissy by Le Corbusier, the Tugendhat house at Brno by Mies and the Columbushaus in Berlin by Mendelsohn.

Conceived in a strikingly polemical climate, these very different buildings had in common an unusual clarity of layout,

582, 583 *Poissy, Villa Savoye (Le Corbusier and P. Jeanneret, 1929–31)*

showing that their authors were involved in an exceptional effort of demonstration. The result was a little stiff, and indeed the passage from these prototypes to mechanical and banal imitation was only too easy. These were three suggestive, rather facile images, on the verge of becoming commonplaces.

The Villa Savoye (Figs. 582–6) was a luxury villa about thirty kilometres from Paris, in a setting which offered very few possibilities of inspiration as far as general outlook and fruitful functional limitations were concerned: a large, slightly hollow field, surrounded by thick woods. For this reason the house was conceived with almost no incidental bonds with its surroundings and

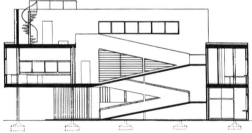

584, 585, 586 *Poissy, Villa Savoye (section and original view; from* Oeuvre Complète*)*

might become the faithful representation of an abstract concept, like Palladio's Rotunda.

The building did not merge with its natural setting but was placed at its centre without modifying it, resuming the features of the landscape with its equally symmetrical form: it was a parallelepiped on a square base, raised on *pilotis*, with four identical façades facing the four points of the compass: 'Grass is a wonderful thing and so is the forest; we

shall interfere with them as little as possible, and the house will stand on the grass like an object, without spoiling anything.'[36]

The relationship between house and site was therefore one of contemplation (Le Corbusier utilized only a very slight functional starting point: the curve of the car as it turned amid the *pilotis*, determining the outer limits of the ground floor rooms and the area of the basic square); since the view was identical in all directions, the natural surroundings could be identified with the cosmic surroundings and indeed the sole asymmetrical principle introduced *a priori* into the composition was the path of the sun, which regulated the layout of the living rooms inside.

Having established the outer limit, Le Corbusier concentrated on an ingenious distribution of all the functional elements in its interior. The continuity between the three floors was obtained by a gently sloping ramp from the ground floor to the roof garden and then to the sun terrace: 'It is an architectural stroll, offering constantly varied, unexpected and sometimes even surprising aspects. It is interesting to obtain so much diversity when, for instance, one has taken as one's constructional system an absolutely unbending cagework of uprights and girders.'[37]

The comparison of successive stages of the plan is very revealing:[38] the structural framework, the references to position, the design of the façades and functional programme were the same, while the distributional solutions and incidents of the architectural 'stroll' were very different and could presumably have been further elaborated, since the distinction between variable and invariable aspects was very clear-cut.

The execution was not on a par with the conception, as often happened with Le Corbusier around this time, and technical defects marred the architectural effect by introducing a margin of hesitation between image and reality; today, now that the house is abandoned, these weaknesses come to light, no longer being masked by the décor, and the visitor has the impression of moving on a theatre stage, where the props and stays of the scenery are visible.

Even on this occasion Le Corbusier insisted on considering his building as a prototype to be mass-produced, in a series of lots near Buenos Aires. Since this house was plainly conceived as a unique example, to be set within a virgin and ideally un-

bounded landscape, this surprising intention can be explained only as a further process of abstraction, which the artist took in homage to another theoretical principle (that of mass-production).

The Tugendhat house too (Figs. 587–92) was no normal building: it was a sumptuous residence built on sloping ground and approached from the uphill side. The building stood near the road, breaking the view between this and the garden.

Mies carefully adapted his architecture to the limitations of the position: it was a simple volume, clearly articulated according to distributive needs. The rooms facing the road were closed off, with the exception of the domestic services, and open towards the garden: functional links were well studied though without Le Corbusier's complex dove-tailing, and without the effort at accommodating several functions within the smallest possible spaces; the rooms were grouped in compact blocks, well-spaced and conveniently arranged within the uniform network of the metallic structure. With geometrical links reduced to a minimum and distributive ones suitably flexible, Mies was moving decisively towards concentration on constructional technique, and since the client had imposed no economic limits, the architect could choose the materials and processes he thought best.

An enterprise of this kind could not be completed in a single building, because the opposite technical solutions could be found only after many experiments. But Mies was counting primarily on the quality of the materials (the cruciform metal pillars were chrome-covered, the dividing walls of the living room of onyx and ebony) and exceptional mechanical devices (the large window in the same room could run vertically into the floor, by means of an electrical device) making direct communication possible between interior and exterior.

Mies' architecture too, like Le Corbusier's, was based on rigid control of the relation-

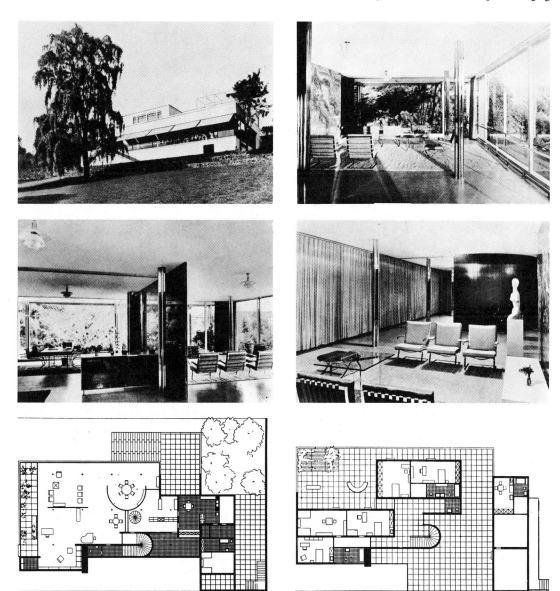

587–92 *Brno, Tugendhat house (Mies; from Johnson, op. cit.)*

ships between the functional elements; but Mies, unlike Le Corbusier, realized that to transform surfaces and masses into architectural realities, dogged technical diligence was vital, proportionate to that which had gone into the original design. The attention here was directed towards proving his point, because of lack of time and experience, but it was a taste of the attitude that Mies was to maintain unflinchingly from now on, until his masterpieces in America.

This work soon became very well known and appeared in all the reviews accompanied by admiring commentaries, mainly generic

593   *Berlin, Columbushaus (Mendelsohn, 1931; from A. Whittick, op. cit.)*

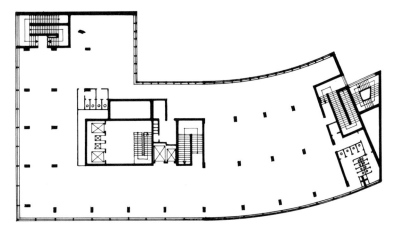

594   *Berlin, Columbushaus, plan (from Whittick)*

in tone, partly because few of the commentators had actually managed to see it, while the photographs conveyed only the external aspects (the architect's plans were much more informative). Persico touched upon this basic point when he wrote:

'Someone, in connection with this house, mentioned a "spirit of technique". Undoubtedly this means that Mies has finally created not only a "rational" building but, above all, a building expressive of the modern state of mind, of a "civilization" which laid down its bounds without any link with earlier ideas. It is not true that the freedom with which it was built was the result of caprice made possible by modern technical progress; the reverse is true: we are here faced with a work which lays down a law with regard to new feelings. In it technique and art have reached inevitable agreement, as in the past.'[39]

The Columbushaus (Figs. 593 and 594) was a commercial building on the Potsdamerplatz in Berlin: the ground floor was to be occupied by shops, the first floor and semi-basement by restaurants, the seven intermediate floors by offices and the top floor by a panoramic restaurant. Unlike the Schocken shops and the building for the

Union of metal-workers, here the actual nature of the activity to be carried on in the offices was not specified in advance and therefore the maximum flexibility was needed, since the various rooms would be divided up in unforeseeable and varying ways.

The building was supported by a steel skeleton; the pillars were set back about 1·5 metres in the façade in the first two storeys, so that the display windows of the shops and the great glass windows of the restaurant could run unbroken for its whole length; on the ceiling of the first floor, by means of corbels, pillars carried a huge girder on which stood the supporting structure of the offices, flush with the façade and formed of slender closely-set uprights (1·80 m. apart); thus the office partitions could be placed in almost any position, corresponding to the external uprights, and the whole façade was built as a huge frame, supporting itself and the floors of the various storeys. The parapets were covered with polished stone, and formed unbroken horizontal strips between the various rows of windows.[40]

The expressionistic tension typical of Mendelsohn's architecture was at its lowest in this building and at last made possible a smooth, serene style. The reticular structure could be clearly seen on the façade, despite the partial covering of stone, and it prevented the graphic effects of the horizontal strips of dark and light from being too emphatic; only the end of the shorter side with the solid glass window of the staircase, and the slight curve of the long side gave movement of the composition, and retained a faint echo of the whirling compositions of his youth.

But apart from its stylistic excellence, this work made a more substantial contribution to modern architecture than the suburban villas of Le Corbusier or Mies. It demonstrated to the public, in the most persuasive way, that only modern architecture was in a position to resolve certain functional problems typical of a modern business centre. The impossibility of knowing their exact destinations in advance made it impossible to define rooms and façades in the traditional fashion; it would, therefore, have been absurd to think of applying the traditional

stylistic finish. On the other hand the ideal flexibility inherent in the new style made it possible to realize the necessary distributive flexibility and the possibility of spreading planning decisions over a period of time made it possible to be specific about the economic programme when the final purpose of the various rooms was still unspecified, as was necessarily the case with this kind of building.

In this case it was proved that the new architecture was relevant not only for the building of the eccentric homes of a few unusual clients, but that it was an indispensable condition for the regeneration of city centres, and thus concerned everybody; the man in the street might believe that the Villa Savoye was no concern of his but he could not help accepting the Columbushaus, since certain functions that involved his everyday life were for the first time to find a satisfactory solution in this building.

fifteen

Approach to town-planning problems

1 Post-war town-planning legislation and experiment

In the post-war period the housing problem suddenly became acute in many European countries. The shortage of accommodation was due not so much to war damage – which was really serious only in France, where about 350,000 dwellings had been destroyed – as to the pause in building activity during the war, in the countries involved and in many of the neutral ones. Furthermore, building costs rose faster than the cost of living, partly because of the rise in the cost of materials, labour and sites, and partly because of the constant desire for better-finished types of building. For this reason state intervention for the housing of the poorer classes was now even more necessary.

State intervention could be exercised in two ways: with credit and with the concessions made to private associations, or with the building of houses through the direct initiative of public bodies.

The first system was adopted mainly in England; as a result of laws introduced by Addison (1919), Chamberlain (1923), Wheatley (1924) and Greenwood (1930), the state undertook to subsidize by up to 75 per cent public and private building enterprises which agreed to observe certain

pre-determined rules of distribution and hygiene; in 1936, when the various laws were consolidated in the Housing Act, about 1,100,000 dwellings had been built with these subsidies, i.e. about a third of the whole of English building production; Welwyn too, Howard's second garden city, profited from Addison's law. In Sweden the state guaranteed the loan interest to private undertakings, particularly co-operatives; this period therefore saw the formation of several important building co-operatives, for instance the H. S. B. of Stockholm (1924) which was a vital factor in the realization of town-planning schemes in the Swedish capital. In Belgium in 1920 the Société Nationale des habitations bon marché was founded; this did not itself build, but financed other societies. France had the old Siegfried law of 1894, improved in 1928 by the Loucheur law, but private building activity marked time, and in places where there was urgent need for more dwellings, as in Paris, the state had to intervene.

The second system was better adapted to coping with emergencies. In France a law of 1912 empowered the communal administrations to build popular houses; the Paris Office municipale des habitations bon marché was founded in 1914 in conformity

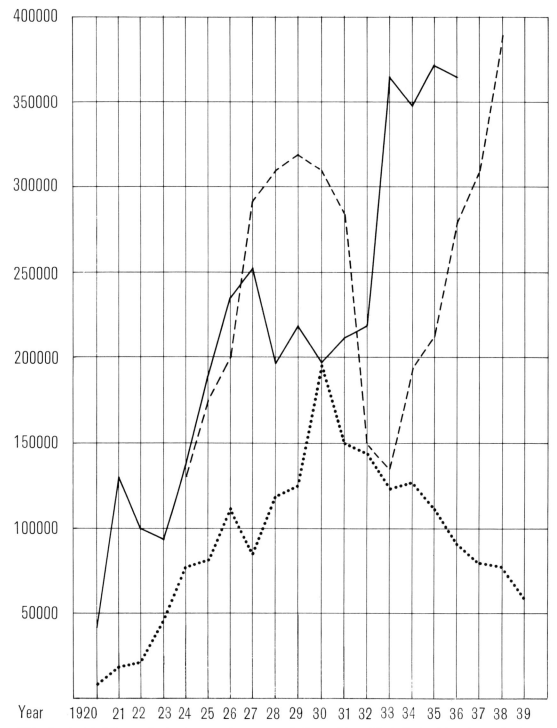

595 *Graph of building production between the two wars in France (dotted line), England (continuous line), Germany (broken line); on the ordinates, the number of buildings built every year*

with this law, and became active in 1920. In 1915 another similar office was added, dealing with the department of the Seine, and built a number of satellite districts in the Parisian suburbs after the war (including the tower houses by Beaudouin and Lods at Drancy), in all 18,000 dwellings. In England, public bodies too could profit from government subsidies. The most important was the L.C.C., which from 1920 to 1936 built more than 70,000 dwellings, of which 25,000 were at Becontree in Essex, so far the largest complex of subsidized building in the world. These were mostly one-family houses, set in extensive green spaces; nonetheless the great size of the undertaking, which artificially created a town of 125,000 inhabitants, raised serious organizational problems which were only partly solved. In Germany one of the last laws promulgated under the Empire, in 1918, required Prussian cities to create municipal offices for building; the system became general in the Weimar republic, and it has been estimated that almost half of all building production, between the inflation and the crisis, was done by public bodies (including the Stuttgart Weissenhof). The Dutch cities, too, set up technical offices and realized the first municipal districts, using first-rate architects such as Oud and Dudok. In Italy the Institutes for Popular Housing intensified their activity and built about 80,000 dwellings between the two wars.

The most instructive case of an extensive programme of municipal building, carried out without any concern for the balance between investment and return, was that implemented by the Socialist administration of Vienna from 1920 onwards. The Austrian republic, shut in within the new frontiers laid down by the treaty of Versailles, had a population out of all proportion with her natural resources, and could survive only by exporting industrial products; it was therefore vital for her to cut production costs by restricting wages, and she could do this only by keeping rents low. For this reason in Vienna – and to a lesser extent in the other cities – the Administration embarked on a colossal programme of building, financed *à fonds perdu* by special graduated taxes, in such a way that the burden would fall mainly on the more wealthy classes; tenants could therefore be asked to pay rents which corresponded to the expense of administration and upkeep. In Vienna alone, about 60,000 dwellings were built on this system, grouped together in large uniform architectural units, often around courtyards, and provided with numerous amenities; one of these, the Karl Marx Hof (Figs. 596 and 597) held 1,300 dwellings, with playing fields, day nurseries, laundries, a surgery, library, post-office and shops; another, the Sandleitenhof, with nearly 1,600 dwellings, had a theatre. The best Austrian architects worked on these building programmes, for instance Hoffmann, Holzmeister and Frank, and the architecture often bore the mark of Wagnerian monumentality.

This brief summary is enough to give some idea of the scope of the building programmes under way in the various countries of Europe, some significant because of the number of the people housed, like Becontree, others for their actual architecture, like Drancy and the Viennese courts. But this concern for the quality of the building was not matched by adequate concern for the town-planning aspect; in fact while the internal organization of the single districts was given careful consideration, and often with satisfactory results, the placing of the districts within the city was almost always a matter of chance, in the least expensive areas; adequate street links were lacking and the integration of the new districts into the life of the city was often very difficult.

There were none of the necessary legal instruments for an effective town-planning framework. While the laws on subsidized building had been quickly perfected through numerous experiments and were based on absolutely efficacious financial arrangements,

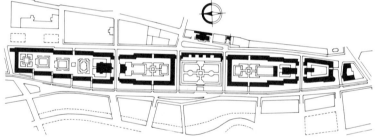

596, 597 *Vienna, Residential complex Karl Marx Hof by C. Ehn*

laws concerning town-planning programmes, having stopped short at theoretical pronouncements which had not yet received decisive corroboration through experiment, were largely dependent, for their implementation, on the discretion of the single administrations and included no proportionate financial means.

In England the town-planning law of 1909 was completed by that of 1919 – which made plans for extensions of the major cities compulsory and authorized the drawing up of regional plans – and by the law of 1925, authorizing the county councils to promote town-planning schemes in their own areas, and finally by the law of 1932, which brought together previous rulings and extended the obligation to plan to all building land, whether urban or not (and therefore also to old centres, provided that their transformation appeared at all probable). But these rulings were still optional, in the majority of cases, and entailed no obligation of fulfilment.

'The preparation of a plan [said the official instructions] does not by any means imply the intention of actually building on the land under consideration, immediately or in the near future. The aim is to regulate and guide the transformation, when it happens, by laying down the general norms to be applied and by safeguarding existing values'.[1]

In the other European countries town-planning legislation was usually late in coming; a general law was passed in Sweden and in Finland in 1931, in Denmark in 1939, in Italy in 1942 and in France only after the Second World War.

The planning of the major cities therefore proceeded amid difficulties of all kinds. In France in 1919 the Prefect of the Seine organized a competition for a town-planning scheme for Paris, but only in 1932, after the institution of the region of Paris, was any practical work begun. The plan, known as the Prost plan, was approved only on the eve of war, in 1939. In 1927 a similar undertaking was begun for London, but here too planning continued almost until the outbreak of war and the plan remained inoperative. The plan for Berlin, on the other hand, fared better; it was begun in 1920 and was partially realized during the short period between inflation and the crisis. In Rome, the authoritarian régime rushed through a general plan in 1931, but its application was not equally prompt and the plan was soon by-passed by events.

The only important centre where a large-scale planning programme was successfully carried out – apart from the Dutch cities – was Frankfurt-am-Main; here the Commune implemented a rational development scheme, concentrating subsidized building mainly in a single area, to the north of the city, and during the short period between the stabilization of the currency (1925) and the crisis (1931) about 15,000 dwellings, grouped in organic districts provided with collective amenities (Figs. 598–602) were built. The programme's coherence was the work of E. May, who was both an engineer employed by the Commune, and president of the two main building societies that the Commune controlled.

The weakness of the laws depended, not only on the considerable economic and political interests at stake, but also on the traditional analytical attitude of town-planning thought, which took into consideration particular problems before general ones, and believed it could resolve difficulties one at a time, ignoring the connections which bound them together.

It is interesting to see that the modern movement, in the immediate post-war period, was by no means immune from this limitation; indeed, by involving itself in the effort at going beyond the empiricism of *avant-garde* culture, for some time it set aside the legacy of the town-planning experiences accumulated between 1870 and 1914.

Gropius saw the need to begin again from scratch and to break down architecture into its component parts, so as to be able to view the problem of composition in as general a way as possible. In this way the house was broken up ideally into a series of elementary manufactured items and planning was done in stages: first the various parts were worked out, then their combinations were studied; in the same way a district would be broken up into a series of component parts (residential units, roads, public buildings) and the city was conceived of as an aggregate of districts, gathered together in groups, or in groups of groups, according to the scale of functions. This methodology could be used to obtain economy of means in the realization, since it answered to the criteria of industrial production, but it could also obtain economy of thought in the planning, because it made it possible to distribute intellectual efforts in the most profitable way, putting every decision in its opportune time and place. In this way the nature of town-planning activity

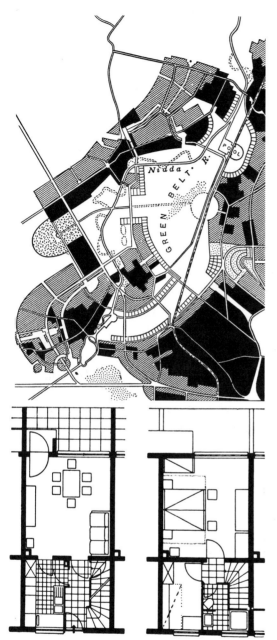

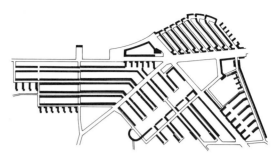

598–602 *Frankfurt-am-Main, Ground-plan of the new residential districts beyond the Nidda (the black shows the part built before the crisis, the shaded the projected part; from C. Bauer,* Modern Housing, *1934); plan of the Riedhof-West district, two views of the Römerstadt district and one of the unified building types.*

and its relationship with architecture was defined in a satisfactory way; in fact it became plain that it was no longer possible to take in the whole field of planning with individual control, but that decisions would have to be staggered, moving from the general to the particular, and the responsi-bilities divided between the various planners, at different times and on different scales.

But since the first step consisted in gaining a clear picture of the various elements and entailed an enormous effort – since it was a question of breaking up the associations inherited from the old culture – the modern

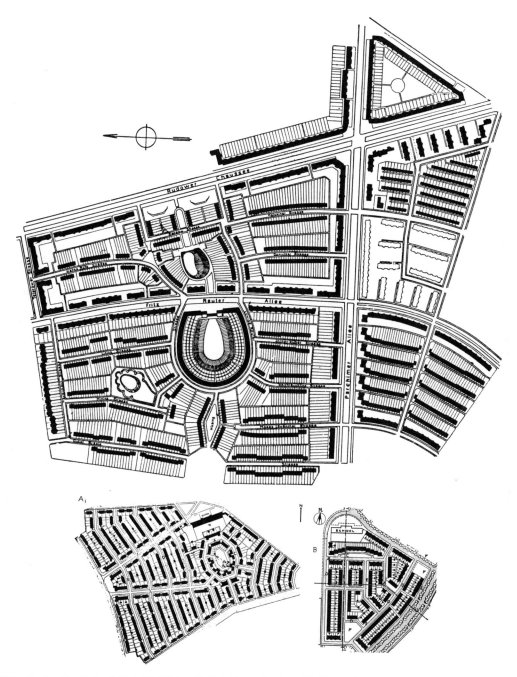

603 *Berlin, The Britz district (H. Häring, R. Salvisberg, B. Taut, M. Wagner)*
604, 605 *Amsterdam, The Buiksloterham district (1928) and Het Blauwe Zand (1931)*

movement had at first to play down problems of overall composition, regarded as an almost deductive process of assemblage; in this way, the district was studied as the largest unit, and the problem of the urban organism was not tackled, except by transposing it into abstract terms and imagining ideal cities formed of aggregates of hierarchically arranged districts.

This was a failing due to lack of experience, and indeed it was corrected when those concerned came face to face with facts; but meanwhile the modern movement failed to influence the field of town-planning just while tremendous activity was under way, changing the faces of the cities of Europe.

The process that had taken place during the industrial revolution was now repeated, at a much greater rate. At first the single elements of the industrial city were studied, and only later, when the city was already formed, and the inconveniences resulting from the faulty co-ordination were felt, did experts begin to work upon remedies; but meanwhile problems had been dealt with in so dilatory a fashion that it was very difficult to catch up again, because the transformations were ever more rapid and always preceded efforts at tackling them in a broader context.

In the crucial post-war years the masters of the modern movement were slow to develop the town-planning implications contained in their beliefs and, with the exception of Dudok, underestimated the activities begun in this connection by the previous generation (Garnier, Wagner, Berlage).

Still, the logic of facts forced them progressively to widen their field of action; but the accumulated delay, however slight, proved decisive, because the economic crisis and then the political crisis no longer allowed any time for experiments to mature. And when, about 1930, the modern movement concerned itself seriously with town-planning problems, building production was already declining because of the economic

crisis, and the political chaos that was shortly to lead to the Second World War was already in the air. In this way the effort foundered just when it was about to produce results, and an imbalance was created between architecture and town-planning involvement which lies heavy on our culture even today.

The graph in Fig. 595 shows the course of building production in France, Germany and England between the two world wars, and the reader should constantly compare these three curves with the developments of architectural culture in these three countries. Many facts that cannot be adequately explained in terms of the history of forms, become clear if one takes into account the relationship between culture and industry, between the quantitative and qualitative aspects of architectural reality.

2 Gropius and town-planning

The methodology of the Bauhaus affected the whole cycle of design, from furnishing to territorial planning. For this reason every building always contained a potential town-planning implication; private dwellings in particular were conceived of as building types that could be reproduced as the elements of a district.

At first this aim remained inoperative because of economic difficulties (so that the 'am Horn' house was the prototype of a colony of one-family houses that was never realized). The first practical experiments took place in Dessau, in the houses for teachers at the Bauhaus and in the Törten district built for the Reichsforschungsgesellschaft in three stages, between 1926 and 1928 (Figs. 606–8).

The district was made up of two-storey terraced houses. The three types of building had been studied with great care; the supporting structures were transversal partitions in masonry, linked by concrete girders, and in the houses built in 1927 they were painted in different colours from the frontal panel walls, accentuating the inter-play of protruding and receding bodies because all the walls running parallel to the terrace were light and all those set perpendicularly were dark. In the centre of the district was a four-storey building which contained the smallest flats and the consumers' co-operative. The furnishings were made in the Bauhaus workshops, so that the sizes of the rooms could be gauged in relation to the furniture.

While the types of building had received careful consideration, the overall composition was somewhat indecisive. The plan – terrace houses with separate gardens – made it more or less necessary to retrace the original land boundaries and, furthermore, represented a half-measure between town and country ill-suited, at this moment, to the inspiration of a clear architectural image. The district was organized centrifugally: it spread in concentric rings into the surrounding countryside and was concentrated in a small square near the centre, where the tall co-operative building was situated.

Gropius was probably aware of these faults and of the impossibility of remedying them while remaining within the ambit of the Bauhaus. In fact didactic commitment, which necessarily proceeded slowly and analytically, was not easily reconcilable with town-planning commitment, which demanded perfect timing and promptness so as to synthesize the various factors at stake.

Furthermore, the difficulties of the Bauhaus echoed those of European culture in general. While work on the composition of building types went ahead successfully and moved towards results of general importance (this period saw the publication of the fundamental works of Alexander Klein,[2] Fig. 616), there was still extraordinary confusion over the criteria for the composition of the various districts: solutions ranged from the one-family houses scattered over garden-districts of Berlin to the monumental Viennese courts and Dutch blocks,

without the difference being justified by a proportionate difference in ways of life.

To provide any definitive clarification of the housing problem, Gropius realized that he would have to face professional competition in the open, by making direct contact with the economic and political forces at work on building production. Thus in 1928 he gave up the school and settled in Berlin as a freelance architect.

In 1927 he won the competition for the Dammerstock district of Karlsruhe, and enlisted the help of nine other architects for the building of the houses.[3] The overall plan was very simple: all the blocks were orientated from north to south, so as to distribute the sunlight symmetrically over the two façades, and were served by pedestrian roadways, since those for motor vehicles ran perpendicularly from east to west (Figs. 611 and 612). The variety which seemed lacking in the general plan was re-established by the actual architecture, since the blocks were of varying heights (from two to six floors), variously spaced and treated in different ways by the nine architects. It is immediately noticeable that the district has no central space and is not at all enclosed, but closely linked to the surrounding spaces; public buildings and any usual building elements were placed at the edges of the area, at the points best suited to drawing the tissue of the new district into that of the town, while the least regular points, for instance the edges of the lots towards the Heidelbergerstrasse, were carefully dealt with by arrangements at ground level.

If Gropius' town-planning vision was objectively defective, because it actually looked no further than the single district, it should however be noted that the concept of district had changed greatly: it was no longer an independent composition but an act of intervention in the shapeless mass of the city outskirts, a calculated and ordered modification of a casual and disordered setting; the problem was to link these two

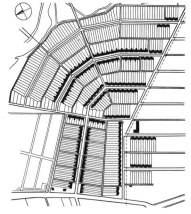

606–608 *Dessau, The Törten district today and in 1926 (Gropius, 1926–8)*

different realities, which affected and balanced one another mutually.

A certain light on the composition of Dammerstock and the other districts planned by Gropius may be given by contemporary explorations by Klee, expressed in pictures that could well be called urbanistic. We do not wish to point to a formal similarity between paintings and ground plans – which in any case did not exist – but a similarity of mental procedure and a probable related origin. As an example one could take a drawing of 1928, with the title *Mechanics of an Urban District* (Fig. 609) (Dammer-

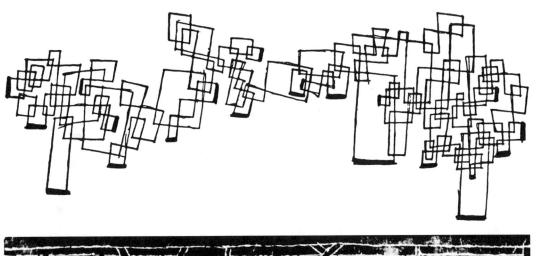

609, 610 *P. Klee,* Mechanics of an Urban District, *1928;* Castle to be Built in the Forest, *1926 (from W. Grohmann,* op. cit.*)*

stock and many districts of the time were based on the recurring right-angle): Klee showed the qualitative variety that could come from the repeated application of this principle, provided it was not purely mechanical, but bore in mind, at every step, the infinite range of possible decisions and faced every choice with renewed spontaneity, emphasized in the drawing with the branching of the line and calculated slant away

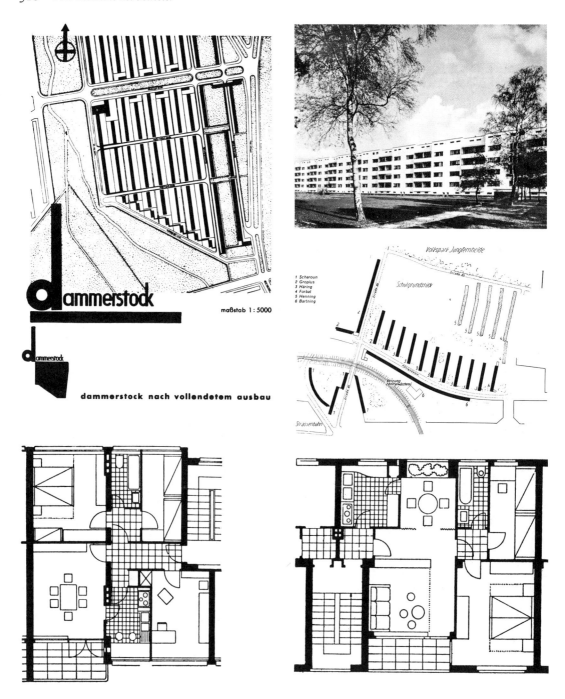

611, 612 *(left)   W. Gropius, Dammerstock district in Karlsruhe (1928) and building type (from 'Stein, Holz, Eisen', 1929)*
613–615 *(right)   W. Gropius. Siemensstadt district, Berlin (1930); building type by H. Scharoun (from Giedion, op. cit.)*

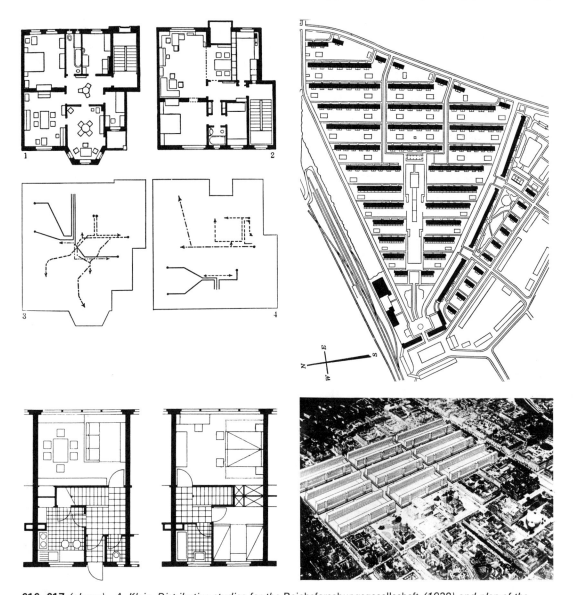

616, 617 *(above)   A. Klein, Distributive studies for the* Reichsforschungsgesellschaft *(1928) and plan of the Bad Durrenberg district (Berlin, 1930; from C. Bauer, op. cit.)*
618, 619 *(below)   The building type 'Existenzminimum' discussed at the C.I.A.M. of 1929 and a study by Hilbersheimer for the city of Berlin (1930)*

from the square.

In the picture *Castle to be Built in the Forest* of 1926 (Fig. 610) Klee studied the effects created by introducing a regularly

orientated form into an irregular background, crowded with lines going variously at a tangent. The form disturbed the background, found a way for itself and gripped

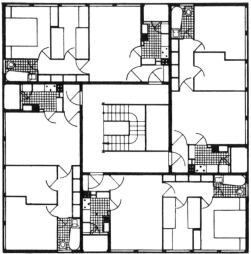

620, 621   *District with tower-houses designed by the Luckhardt brothers in 1927*

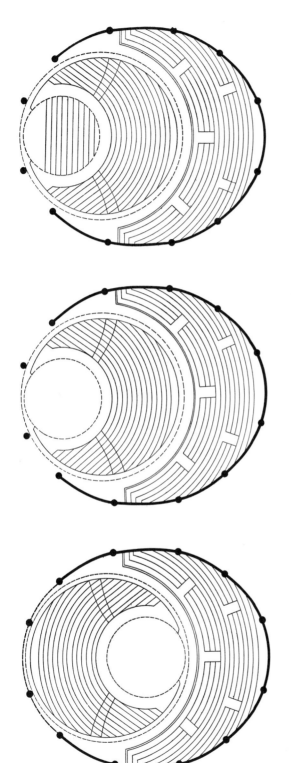

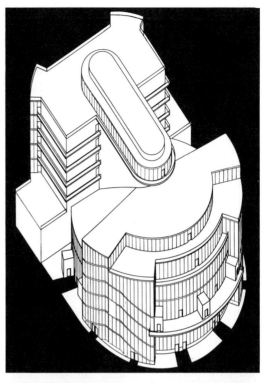

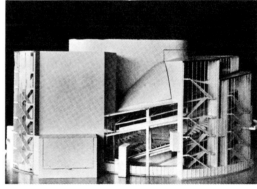

622–624 *W. Gropius, The 'Totaltheater' worked on in 1926 for Piscator (from Giedion, op. cit.)*

the surrounding elements with its own dynamic law; in the form of a metaphor, Klee was tackling the same problems as were the architects: that of breaking through the complex and disordered fabric of the towns with a uniform building or district, while bearing in mind the probable repercussions on the surrounding districts and trying to reconcile the two heterogeneous realities.

It was therefore natural that in the later Siemensstadt district,[4] cut through by a railway line and curving road, Gropius should subordinate composition to these pre-existing elements: the long block by Bartung, with apartments facing south, ran along the road going from east to west; on the other side were Häring's perpendicular blocks with apartments facing both sides, while to the south of the railway Scharoun's buildings converged, framing the subway. Gropius himself designed the three blocks of houses near the main crossroads, which was the district's potential centre, though barely accentuated (Figs. 613–15).

Here too, public buildings stood on the outskirts and were utilized to solve the problem of introducing the ends of the residential blocks into the surrounding districts. There was no longer any trace of the minute and laborious compositions which complicated the distribution of contemporary districts, including the two by Taut at Britz and Zehlendorf,[5] just completed.

The street system for vehicles was very much reduced, the hierarchy of functions immediately simple and evident, the uniformity of sanitary arrangements in every dwelling was ensured by regularity of layout, while every particular detail was made use of to vary and enrich the composition. In short, every feature was logically justified and had the same sincere and persuasive character as the surrounding industrial structures; for the first time a working-class district had a uniform plan and the substantiality it

needed so as not to suffer by comparison with the factory, though it respected the human scale in every aspect and the needs, so very delicate, of domestic intimacy.

The plans for public buildings which Gropius was drawing up from 1926 to 1931 – and particularly the theatres, from the theoretical one made in 1926 for Piscator (Figs. 622–4) to the competition for the Kharkov theatre in 1931 – were closely related to town-planning experiments. The expressive element of these buildings, with their oblique, complicated structures, rotating elements and façades encumbered with stairs and ramps, was undoubtedly complementary to the rigour and simplicity of residential building, which amounted to the repetition of a few uniformly orientated building types. Public buildings were in fact the focal points of urban arrangements, where particular prestige values were concentrated, having been driven out of the residential fabric during the process of standardization. For the moment the accent was on housing, but later the problems of the civic centre – or core, as it was later to be called – were to come to the fore.

Between 1929 and 1931 Gropius gave theoretical form to his town-planning experience and specified the lines along which research could profitably be carried out. He did not think that the minimum dwelling was an abstract entity that could be defined *a priori,* and therefore did not aim at an absolute definition of the best form of such a dwelling:

'The problem of the minimum dwelling is that of establishing the elementary minimum of space, air, light and heat required by man in order that he be able to fully develop his life functions without experiencing limitations due to his dwelling, i.e. a minimum *modus vivendi* in place of a *modus non moriendi*'.[6]

It was a question of examining the relation between a physical form and a set of vital requirements 'not only economic' – he noted two years later – 'but mainly physical and sociological'.[7] Furthermore this relation could not be deduced *a priori*, but had to be found through experiment; research must start from difficulties experienced in ways of living which were typical of a particular time and place.

Starting from these principles Gropius compared the two traditional solutions used in our time, the detached one-family house and the collective dwelling, and refused to give his support, in abstract, to either one or the other, as Wright and Le Corbusier had done. Each had its own advantages and disadvantages: the one-family house made possible direct contact between house and garden, greater independence and flexibility, but was more expensive to build and to run; also, by lowering the density of residential districts, it meant that workers had to travel further to work.

The collective house lessened the independence of each family and complicated life a little, particularly for the children, but it encouraged the community spirit and was in line with modern social tendencies, which were gradually taking certain functions from the family and reorganizing them in the form of collective services; furthermore it was more economic, and made greater density possible, which meant that workers did not have so far to go to work and could have more free time.

The solution he preferred varied, according to the weight that such advantages and disadvantages had, in relation to the economic resources, and the occupations and psychological attitudes of the various classes; in the Germany of the time the one-family house was convenient only for the middle classes, while the collective house seemed the most suitable form for popular building since in this case economy (to distribute the benefits of public intervention to the greatest number), and density (to lessen journeys for workers, mainly clerks and labourers) be-

came the dominant needs, to which seclusion and spatial freedom had to be sacrificed. But after this sacrifice, considerable and unbiased thought had to go into discovering what type of collective house would enable such advantages to be enjoyed to their fullest extent, and it was seen that by increasing the number of storeys:

a Building density increased on a par with the spacing between the various buildings and therefore with conditions of hygiene; or, the denser they were, the more widely spaced the buildings could be;

b Certain costs diminished, i.e. those of the site itself (because of the increased density mentioned above) and of communal amenities, installations, roads; the cost of the actual building, however, increased, because of the importance of the supporting structure and the lifts.

In Germany, bearing all these factors in mind, the optimum was between ten and twelve storeys: this height made possible the desired co-existence of ample spacing and high building density, therefore a satisfactory concentration of amenities without building costs rising prohibitively. The usual buildings with three to four storeys on the other hand must be regarded as an irrational compromise, because they offered neither the advantages of the one-family house nor those of the tall blocks.

Two lines of research emerged from this reasoning. Since tall blocks were a new type of building, town-planning arguments must be adduced to show that they could advantageously replace the usual three- to five-storey blocks. But in the case of one-family houses the problem was strictly technical: the limitations on their use depended largely on the cost, and it was therefore necessary to reduce it by making the house up with elements that could be mass-produced industrially, a fact which led to an interest in prefabrication.

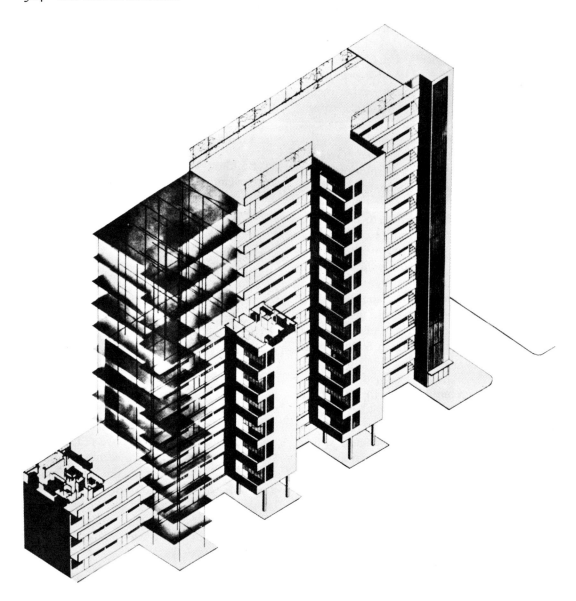

625   *W. Gropius, Tall building worked on for the Spandau district in 1929 (from Giedion,* op. cit.*)*

The first line of thought produced, for instance, the plans for the experimental district of Spandau-Haselhorst (Fig. 625) and the models exhibited at the exhibitions in Paris in 1930 and in Berlin in 1931. However, Gropius did not manage to build any of his tall houses in Germany, either because of the hesitations of the authorities or because of the resistance of the technical experts, and particularly because of the reluctance to install lifts in popular houses. The first ten-storey residential unit along the lines of Gropius' thought was built in Holland in 1934 and will be mentioned in the next chapter.

The second line of thought, that concerning prefabrication, extended further back into history; as early as 1909, when working

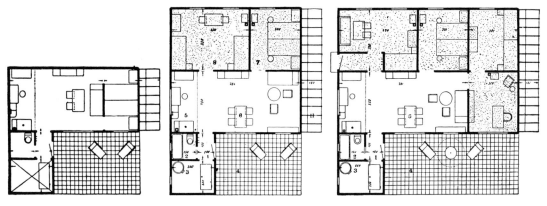

626   *W. Gropius, Extendible prefabricated house worked on for Hirsch Kupker und Messingwerke A. G. in 1931 (from Giedion,* op. cit.*)*

with Behrens, Gropius submitted to E. Rathenau, president of the A. E. G., a *Programme for the establishment of a company for the provision of housing on aesthetically consistent principles.* During the years immediately after the war, while he was running the Bauhaus, he continued to study the subject theoretically and in 1924 propounded the basic principle which he was later to confirm several times:

'The majority of citizens of a specific country have similar dwelling and living requirements; it is therefore hard to understand why the dwellings we build should not show a similar unification as, say, our clothes, shoes or automobiles . . . . However, the danger of too rigid a standardization . . . must be avoided . . . . Dwellings must be designed in such a way that justified individual requirements derived from the family size or the type of profession of the family head can be suitably and flexibly fulfilled. The organization must therefore aim first of all at standardizing and mass-producing not entire houses, but only their component parts which can then be assembled into various types of houses'.[8]

Partial prefabrication was realized in the Törten district at Dessau, in 1926; another attempt was made in 1927 at the Stuttgart Weissenhof where two one-family houses were built with metal skeletons, panel walls in cork and outer walls in Eternit. In 1931 Gropius invented a type of minimum, extendible house (Fig. 626) for the Hirsch Kupker und Messingwerke A. G.; but in the same year the experiment was cut short by the economic crisis, and soon afterwards the coming to power of the Nazis interrupted both fields of activity.

Gropius' failure in both lines of action was certainly due to the headlong course taken by external events, but the brief episode is of great cultural importance, since it reproduced in miniature the central difficulty of the modern movement vis-à-vis contemporary society.

During the years of his frenzied activity as a freelance in Berlin, German building production first stagnated, then collapsed completely, struck by the general economic crisis (Fig. 595); there were an enormous number of unemployed and of underemployed, which posed a serious social problem and made nonsense of any attempt at increasing productivity in building or any other field, since on the contrary what was needed was to distribute what work there was to the largest possible number of workers. Unemployment was also a source of political concern, recalling to mind the Spartacist

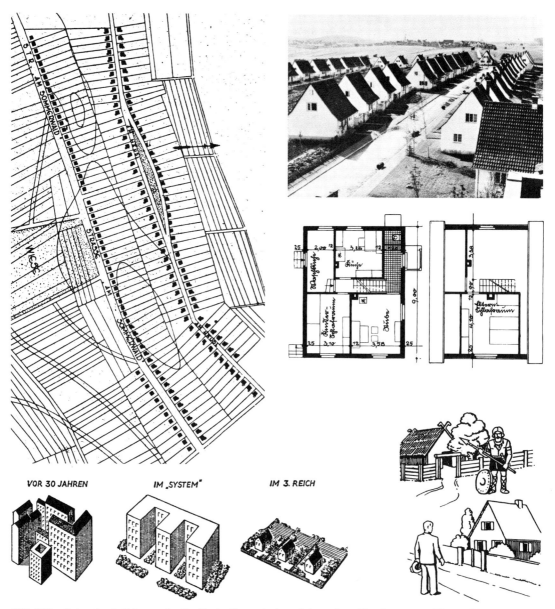

627–631 *Extensive building under the Nazis. Ground-plan of the colony 'Am Sommerwald' near Pirmasens (from* Architettura, *1937); building type of the 'Auf die Brücke' colony near Rottweil (P. Schäffer 1937–40, from* Der Baumeister, *1941) and a series of propagandist sketches*

revolt of 1919 and the Austrian Socialist uprisings; hence the fear that densely built up and organically conceived working-class districts, integrated into the fabric of the town, would provide the working classes with a support to organize themselves politically and would even become strongholds of sedition (Persico remembers 'the amazement felt by journalists throughout Europe when the inhabitants of the popular housing blocks in Vienna shot from the windows as if from loopholes and barricaded themselves in the Siedlungen as in so many fortresses'.[9] A way of avoiding this double difficulty, economic and political, was the rural colony, which was realized by democratic governments after 1931 and which became the favourite type of settlement under the Nazis after 1933 (Figs. 627–31).

These colonies were the exact opposite of the districts planned by Gropius; they were situated right in the countryside for the unemployed and in the outermost suburbs for the under-employed (who had to go to work periodically), and they were always separated, at a proper distance one from the other. Each family had a plot of land big enough to support it totally or partially, so that it would be obliged to stay in one place; almost any industralization was excluded from the start, because the building of the houses had to absorb as much labour as possible and often the future occupant was required to work on his own house.

Traditionalist architects soon solved the problem of design by providing rustic or vaguely medieval forms. Economists expressed doubt about the vaunted self-sufficiency and possibility of supporting the inhabitants with the produce of the plots of land, which were often very small,[10] but economic reasoning was based, in the last analysis, on a political choice; architects, by choosing between the modern scheme of tall blocks or the traditional cottages, were virtually passing their own judgment on the integration of the working classes into the modern city.

Thus the pressure of events, at the moment when it made impossible the work of modern architects and indeed their very presence on German soil, was also decisively clarifying a cultural issue, and revealed the values at stake in an apparently academic discussion on the shape of a district.

Gropius and his colleagues believed at first that it would be enough to perfect technical and formal processes, the means of action in the building field (Mies' 'how') and lie in wait on this terrain for the political and economic forces. In 1928 Gropius first realized that this was not enough and he put himself into personal contact with economic reality, convinced that he had the time to parley with those forces and to channel them in the direction he wanted; but time was short, and the economic and political forces moved stealthily off in the opposite direction, crashing through the frail apparatus of architectural culture and sweeping it away.

The attempt at putting the analytical procedure examined at the Bauhaus into reality, with the same orderly process, and at controlling the whole by starting from control of the various elements had proved a failure, since there had been a miscalculation of the importance of the organizational problems arising from the vastness of the interests at stake and the speed of transformations. The speed of events had proved much too rapid for the rhythm of men's thoughts.

At this point a doubt arose, logically enough, about the method of work, and indeed here the anti-rationalist polemic found its place, upheld now not only by the older generation but also by the younger, who regarded the experiments of the twenties as proven, but preferred to label them with one of the current dialectical terms – rationalism, functionalism – and countered rational values with meta-rational ones, in the spirit of eternal oscillation which characterized *avant-garde* debate.

This doubt thus became the touchstone of the commitment of the modern architects; while a vast majority – including first-class architects such as Oud – preferred to blame the difficulties of the moment on to the rigidness of rational methods, Gropius once again gave a decisive example, by avoiding an opposition which would have put the problem on a metaphysical level, and by doggedly seeking specific solutions for the

632, 633 *(above)   Paris, Two views of the house at the Porte Molitor (Le Corbusier and P. Jeanneret, 1933)*
634, 635 *(below)   Geneva, Façade and section of the Clarté apartment building (Le Corbusier and P. Jeanneret, 1930; from* Oeuvre Complète*)*

difficulties he encountered.

This method of activity implied the confirmation of the rational method, but demanded that it be exercised in a more realistic and thorough manner: that it should take not only space but also time into account, not only single elements but the whole, every aspect and every theme of reality, because, if one wanted to take practical action one had only to ignore one aspect to find the whole action jeopardized. If the initial effort had not prevented a new gulf between culture and reality, culture now had to quicken its pace and broaden its outlook, involving itself on the same scale and with the same rhythm as the processes it was intending to control.

3   Le Corbusier's town-planning activities

In the second volume of his *Oeuvre Complète* Le Corbusier wrote:

'Chance has had it that the first volume ended with 1929. In a sense this year marked the ending of a long period of research. 1930 opened up a cycle of new interests: the *grands travaux*, great events in architecture and town-planning, the miraculous era of the creation of a new machine-orientated civilization . . . . From now on I shall no longer talk of the architectural revolution, which is over; town-planning is now the main concern'.[11]

Indeed between 1930 and 1933 – while France was suffering from the effects of the building crisis, though less intensely and less severely than other countries – Le Corbusier had the opportunity of building three considerable buildings where town-planning involvement was present not only potentially but actually, in that the buildings were brought into effective contact with the surrounding city: these were the Swiss pavilion at the Cité Universitaire in Paris (Figs. 637–9), the Clarté apartment house in Geneva (Figs. 634–6) and the *Cité du Refuge* (Figs. 640–2) for the Salvation Army.

A communal house, for tenants who were unknown quantities, was quite a different problem from that of a house for a predetermined owner; the functional needs could not be defined through direct relations with the client; here the general trends of the market had to be considered, as did the problem of the changing of tenants and those arising from their contacts with one another; maintenance became an important problem and had to be taken into account from the start. It is perhaps for these reasons that the Geneva Clarté building has a technical correctness, density and proportion superior to all Le Corbusier's other previous works; it was an exceptionally deep nine-storey block, with forty-three duplex apartments and several shops; the structure was of steel, based on an unvarying module, and the outer coverings were of durable materials: stone, metal, glass; the two internal staircases, lit only from above, were entirely of glass and metal, so that the light filtered down through the floors to the ground floor. The arrangement of each apartment over two floors enabled it to have some rooms that were the equivalent of two storeys in height and to vary the level of the rooms; from the outside it made it possible to vary the uniform super-imposition of one storey on another, since the continuous balconies occurred every other floor, introducing a more peaceful rhythm and leaving large intermediate spaces free, in transparent or opaque glass (Fig. 636).

The Swiss pavilion at the Cité Universitaire also had to be an impressive building; Le Corbusier resolved this problem by using a variety of materials, and by the stress put on certain functional elements, like the great detached pillars supporting the dormitory block; also in front of the entrance to the communal rooms was a pleasant, airy portico, which immediately introduced the visitor into the constructional reality of the building proper and mediated successfully between exterior and interior. For the first time Le Corbusier rejected the expedient of uniform white plaster, and had every surface characterized by the materials used; reinforced concrete was left bare, with the lining left by the moulds; the walls were covered with

636   *Geneva, Detail of the Clarté apartment building*

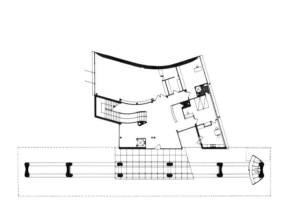

637, 638, 639 *Paris, Swiss pavilion at the Cité Universitaire (Le Corbusier and P. Jeanneret, 1930; from Oeuvre Complète)*

strips of rough cement and the end wall of the communal hall was of natural stone. The building acquired a surprising density and hinted, with a considerable advance in time, at a trend that was shortly to become widespread in European architecture.

The problem of the *Cité du Refuge* was somewhat different: here a rather irregular and uninspiring area, with only two short façades to the east and south, posed first of all a serious distributive problem. Le Corbusier showed that, by taking as his starting point not the volume allowed by the regulations but the distributive programme, and by articulating the various elements in separate blocks, it was possible to place all

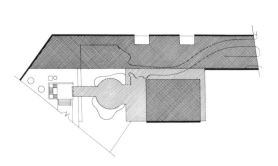

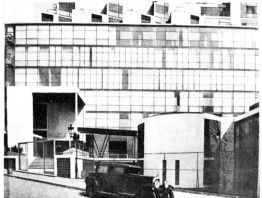

640, 641, 642 *Paris, Cité du Refuge (Le Corbusier and P. Jeanneret, 1932; original photo from* Oeuvre Complète*)*

the rooms in convenient positions according to their functions, and that it was possible to turn to account the difficulties of the site to obtain singular expressive effects. The building was characterized above all by the tense interplay of volumes, which made up a sort of abstract scenery above and in front of the great unbroken expanse of glass of the south façade (Fig. 642). The consideration of materials played a secondary part (the walls were plastered in white or covered with white majolica) and the building had various technical faults due to Le Corbusier's desire to tackle new problems with limited experi-

643, 644 *Le Corbusier's town-planning: a view of the A plan for Algiers (1930) and of the clearance plan for the îlot insalubre in Paris (from* Oeuvre Complète*)*

ence and meagre financial resources; for instance the hermetically sealed windows proved incompatible with air-conditioning, and had to be shielded with a *brise-soleil.*

All three buildings discussed were forced violently into the surrounding urban fabric,

though this was less noticeable in the case of the Swiss dormitory block because of the vastness of the surrounding spaces.

In fact the three works were three pieces of a new type of city which, being introduced into practical reality, inevitably stretched its

645, 646 *Sketches by Le Corbusier for a town-planning scheme for Rio (1936; from* Oeuvre Complète)
*Le Corbusier's captions: 1 adopt the most profitable type of house; 2 situate it in the most suitable place;
3 situate business activities and industry; 4 create main traffic communications (here in Rio the proposed
solution is prodigious; it provides for a fantastic* cube à logis *and creates immense municipal resources;
splendour will be upon the city)*

tissue; Le Corbusier was well aware of this, and looked for every opportunity of extending concern from the building to the surrounding terrain, to place it in an appropriate setting; meanwhile he continued to examine further new applications for the town-planning principles put forward for the first time in 1922: the substitution of well-spaced skyscrapers for normal buildings in business centres, the grouping of dwellings in vertical units with communal amenities for residential districts, the classification of types of traffic. In 1929 he reverted to the old plan for the centre of Paris and proposed similar solutions for the cities of South America, Rio, Sao Paulo and Buenos Aires; in 1930 he worked on a scheme for the district around the Porte Maillot, profiting from the placing there of a monument to Foch; in 1933 he took part in the competition for the new district of Antwerp beyond the Schelde, repeating his suggestion of skyscrapers for offices and of linear buildings *à redents* for houses, and drew up a plan for the development of Geneva; from 1930 to 1934 he put forward various solutions for the development scheme for Algiers (Fig. 643), with two motorways running above the city, one parallel and one perpendicular to the coast, hinging upon an administrative centre consisting of skyscrapers; in 1934 he worked on a plan for a model factory and the town-planning scheme for Nemours, also in Africa; in 1935 he published his book *La Ville Radieuse*, where he once again gave fascinating expression to his theory of town-planning, and it was promptly applied the same year to the schemes for Hellocourt and the Zlin valley for the Bat'a organization, in 1936 to the plan for Rio de Janeiro and the *îlot insalubre* in Paris (Fig. 644), in 1938 to the scheme for the bridgehead of St Cloud and the plan for Buenos Aires. Significantly Le Corbusier's new review, which came out from 1930 to 1933, was called *Plans*.

All these plans were also architectural images on an urban or general scale. Le Corbusier skipped all problems of realization, with its difficulties of timing, spheres of competence and levels of planning, which so concerned the Germans of the time; but perhaps for this reason he was the only person who, at this time, had a clear idea of the modern city as a complete alternative to the old. From his drawings the unified, specific quality of the future reality of our towns leapt to the eye, emerging far more clearly than in the repetitive schemes suggested by Hilbersheimer, for instance; works like the *Cité du Refuge*, with their distributive plan energetically projected towards the surrounding spaces, afforded architectural proof of this new quality; nonetheless the proof was given at an inappropriate moment, like that of Gropius, indeed it did not find the slightest echo in the French situation between the wars, and was charged with a polemical resentment which further limited its effectiveness.

4   The town-planning of the C.I.A.M.

The meetings of the C.I.A.M. from 1929 to 1933 hinged on town-planning problems, and the series of subjects dealt with indicated the progressive broadening of the fields of study.

The second Congress in 1929 at Frankfurt dealt with defining the concept of the minimal dwelling as the point of departure for discussions on subsidized building. This meeting, like the next one, was influenced mainly by the German groups and by the experiments under way in various German cities, the most important being that by E. May in Frankfurt. The features of the minimum dwelling were laid down by reference to the sociology of the time, founded on statistical observations or on embryonic theories of evolution (Gropius referred to the works of F. Müller-Leyer). It was noted that the area of the apartments, in accordance with the sanitary experts' opinions, could be considerably reduced while lighting, ventilation and possibilities of sunlight should be further increased; it was shown that the growing emancipation of the individual within the family made it advisable to provide a room, no matter how small, for every adult member of the family, while it was recognized that current tendencies towards solidarity showed that communal blocks were more suitable than single houses, at least in industrial centres.

Once the standards had been laid down, the economic problem arose. The fact that the poorer classes were not in a position to afford a tolerable house, and that State intervention was necessary, made the problem of housing one of finding the lowest common denominator, since any wastage would develop into a greater injustice. The same consideration demanded that general costs, too, be reduced to a minimum; those of the site, roads etc.; thus the problem of the type of building necessarily led to the problem of the district, which was dealt with in 1930 at the third Brussels Congress.

Gropius posed the question in the form already mentioned: low houses, medium or tall? Böhm and Kaufmann of Frankfurt analysed the costs, R. Neutra described the American regulations for tall houses, the Bohemian K. Teige summarized the facts about subsidized building in the .various countries. Le Corbusier made one of the most important contributions, with his discussion of two related general problems: that of the city and that of the authority charged with implementing the solutions agreed upon.

The simple way in which Le Corbusier expressed himself put the basic questions of contemporary town-planning thought very effectively. He wrote:

'Is the big city something good or something bad? What should be its limits? one, two, five, ten million inhabitants? We must not answer these questions here; the problem of big cities exists and represents, at

certain moments, a hierarchical problem that is qualitative, not quantitative; the big city becomes a centre of attraction which receives and sends off spiritual effects born of such intense concentration. The big cities are, in fact, control posts'.[12]

In this Le Corbusier grasped the essential relationship between town-planning problems above a given scale, and social and political ones. But here he stopped and uttered a warning:

'Let us keep abreast, personally, of the forms of current development, but I beg of you, do not let us concern ourselves here with politics and sociology. These two phenomena are too infinitely complex; there is also the economic aspect, and we are not qualified to discuss these daunting problems before a public gathering. I repeat, we must remain architects and town-planners, and on this professional terrain must make known to those concerned the possibilities and needs of an architectural and urbanistic order'.[13]

When he came to list these needs: vertical garden-cities, roads within buildings, flat roofs, buildings independent of roads, he arrived at a consequence which was no longer of a technical nature: the availability of land independently of private ownership. How could this be arrived at? 'Before the incontestable, incontrovertible claims of the modern schemes, appropriate authorities will emerge. But let us repeat the chronology of events: when the technicians formulate what they must, then the authorities will appear.'[14]

The exhortation not to discuss politics and sociology was probably directed at Germans like Taut and May. But they themselves, outside the controversy, had nothing to suggest that was really very different from what Le Corbusier himself proposed; they had their own abstract model, deduced from theoretical considerations – logical, bio-logical, economic – and from average general statistics, not from historical reasoning and an exact assessment of the forces involved; they also had a specific political bias, but they had learned not to link general choices to particular ones.

In this way, at the threshold of the crucial thirties, the C.I.A.M. of Brussels was in no position to throw out the problem of the district, nor to draw on past experience for a general conclusion that would be valid for the future, but only to order this experience technically.

In the pages of the volume published the following year by the C.I.A.M.[15] European building production of the previous decade was diligently reviewed and judged according to uniform criteria; there was no echo of the grave basic problems raised by the economic situation in the various countries during those very years.

Official conclusions mirrored the unease of this situation; certain obstacles were noted which had to be got rid of: the lack of regulations for the dividing of land into lots, the persistence of buildings in the form of enclosed blocks, distrust of new building methods, the harmfulness of period buildings in old centres, the economic difficulties, lack of interest on the part of the authorities, in the less developed countries, in the studies carried out and the results obtained abroad.

Nor did the question posed by Gropius, low, medium or tall houses, receive a clear-cut reply:

'Experimentation in the field of low and medium houses [four to eight floors] is already sufficient for one to judge of their convenience, while for tall houses we can go by American experience, but only for luxury dwellings. The Congress notes that this form of building may offer a solution to the problem of the minimal dwelling, though plainly it cannot prove that this is the only form desirable. It is therefore necessary to continue to examine all the possibilities of the tall house and to study

its effectiveness in actual examples, even if there are financial and emotional problems, and others arising from building regulations'.[16]

The fourth Congress took place in 1933, on a boat going from Marseilles to Athens. It considered the problem of the city, examining thirty-three examples,[17] and this time no official report was made; only in 1941 was an anonymous document (edited by Le Corbusier) published in Paris, with a preface by Jean Giraudoux, and was known as the *Charte d'Athènes*.

It was significant that studies of thirty-three cities were carried out, rather than summaries of thirty-three actual planning experiments. In fact the protagonists of the modern movement were cut off from the town-planning experiments of this period; they could only note the chaos of the towns, contrast it with the characteristics of order and functionality which should have typified the modern city, and hint fleetingly at the means necessary for obtaining them.

The partial experiments in Berlin and Frankfurt had been interrupted by the economic crisis, the programme of popular housing considered by the commune of Vienna was dropped soon after the fall of the Kredit-Anstalt in 1931, elsewhere either the modern movement had no effective cultural influence, or else legislation was too far behind to allow decisive experiments. Not even after 1933 could the members of the C.I.A.M. extend their activities from the district to the whole city, except in Holland, as we shall describe further on. The examination of what was happening in thirty-three cities throughout the world could not make up for experience that had never been gained.

It was therefore natural that the C.I.A.M. should fall back on theory, and propose a code of general principles which sounded abstract and almost ironical in a troubled world, where the very rules of human co-existence were in jeopardy. But precisely in relation to these circumstances the theoretical nature of the document acquired a precise significance and a pregnant political value. It would have been easy for a member of the 1933 Congress, and even more so for Le Corbusier in 1941, to be technically specific in their treatment of the subject, and to attempt a rationalization of current methods and models, offering the operators of their time exact and more advanced information; this was done, in France, two years later, by the architects of the town-planning law of 11 June 1943, and a year later in Italy by those responsible for the law of 1942.

But the aims of the C.I.A.M. and of Le Corbusier were almost the opposite: the new type of town-planning could not become merely a technical improvement on the current version, but it was a real alternative which demanded above all a different political and moral inspiration. If circumstances made this alternative impossible, then it had to be formulated in a manner that was Utopian but terse, not blurred into a compromise acceptable to those in power.

The object of the discussion was not a city that would work better, but a city that would work for everyone, and distribute equally among its citizens the benefits of possible improvements; it was Morris' ideal 'art for all' all over again, and this, in contact with authoritarian regimes, became a definite political objective.

Thus, at the crucial moment, the choice of the C.I.A.M. was exactly contrary to the technically inclined one which is usually regarded as being implicit in rationalist leanings.

This choice appears absolutely clearly, twenty years after the event, in the concluding paragraphs of the *Charte d'Athènes*:

'Today, most cities are in a state of total chaos. These cities do not come anywhere near achieving their aim, which is to satisfy the biological and psychological needs of their inhabitants.

From the beginnings of the machine age, this situation bespeaks the proliferation of private interests.

The pressure of such interests causes a disastrous break in the balance between the force of economic circumstances on one side and the weakness of administrative control and the impotence of social solidarity on the other . . . .

On a spiritual and material level, the city should ensure individual freedom and the benefits of collective action.

Reorganization within the urban pattern must be regulated on the human scale only.

The key points in town planning lie in the four functions: living, working, recreation (in free time), circulating.

Plans will determine the structure of each of the sectors attributed to the four key-functions and will fix their respective positions within the whole.

The cycle of the daily functions: living, working, recreation (recuperation) will be regulated by town-planning with the most rigorous economy of time, considering housing at the centre of town-planning concern and as the point of departure for every assessment . . . .

It is necessary and urgent for each city to draw up its own plan by making laws which will make its implementation possible.

The plan must be based on rigorous analysis by specialists, it must anticipate stages in time and space, it must link the natural resources of men, the general topography, economic data, sociological needs and spiritual values in productive partnership . . . .

The basic nucleus of town-planning is a living cell (a dwelling) and its introduction into a group constitutes a unit of habitation of suitable size.

Starting from this unit, the relations between living place, place of work and place of recreation can be worked out.

To solve this serious problem it is vital to utilize the resources of modern technical progress which, with the help of its various specialists, will give support to the art of building with all the safeguards of science and will enrich it with the inventions and resources of the age . . . .

There exist two warring realities. On the one hand the extent of the works needed to begin reorganizing the city, on the other the conditions of extreme fragmentation of building land.

This serious and obvious contradiction poses one of the most difficult problems of our time: the urgency of finding a legal instrument to regulate the availability of building land to correspond to the vital needs of the individual in complete agreement with collective needs.

Private interest will be subordinated to public interest'.[18]

sixteen

Political compromise and the struggle with the authoritarian régimes

In 1925, during the controversy about the transference of the Bauhaus to Dessau from Weimar, Gropius had supported the idea of the independence of the new architecture of all political trends.

Gropius realized that the aims of the movement, and therefore also the phases of the collective work begun in 1919, could hardly be in accord with the aims and expectations of the political parties in conflict in Weimar Germany. But behind the minor events of the everyday political struggle a profound historical upheaval was maturing, which was to lead Germany and many other European countries to dictatorships, and then to the Second World War. Even if the problems of modern architecture could be regarded as independent of the contingencies of political thought, it had necessarily to come face to face with the ideal terms of the conflict between democracy and dictatorship, which emerged so dramatically between 1930 and 1940.

Already the development of the town-planning proposals elaborated by German architects around 1930 – standardization of housing, concentration of accommodation in tall, well-spaced blocks, industrialization of constructional elements – led to an inevitable clash with politicians, as we said in the previous chapter.

We must now extend the discussion, and examine the course this political compromise took in the various countries – in Germany, Italy, Russia and in certain ways in France – where the causes and circumstances were undoubtedly different; in any case there did exist certain circumstances common to all, which make a comparison between the various events relevant.

1   Germany and Austria

In Germany and Austria the modern movement found the most favourable conditions: the representatives of the pre-war *avant-garde* trends who were now the most eminent figures, were favourably disposed towards the most daring attempts of the younger generation; among the young there was a group of really important figures, to whom the institutions in power offered many opportunities of work and chances of contact with bodies of political power.

Nonetheless the modern movement not only remained in a minority position, but it did not manage to become a closely-knit body. There was a short period, from 1922 to 1931, in which this seemed about to

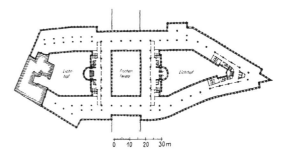

647, 648, 649 *Hamburg, The Chilehaus (F. Höger, 1923)*

happen and in which a single style seemed on the verge of being formed, capable of attracting all professionals who were culturally at all modern in outlook; meanwhile the same repertoire was spreading to all countries, levelling out national difference and almost bringing to life the ideal expressed five years before by Gropius, with the formula 'international architecture'.

This was the moment when its adversaries were really forced to acknowledge the modern movement, classifying it as yet another 'functional' or 'rational' style. But the apparent harmony soon revealed deep conflicts; the modern movement was not like the traditional styles, because it did not

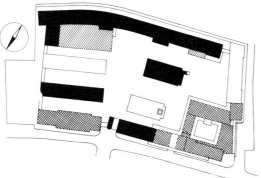

650, 651   *Linz, The tobacco factory (P. Behrens and A. Popp, 1930–4; the industrial buildings are shown in black, the administrative in cross-hatching)*

provide ready-made solutions but methodical suggestions for the implementation of a variety of various and unpredictable solutions, which consisted essentially in assessments of degree. In this way planners could not escape from responsibilities deriving from the single concrete problems by professions of faith in certain principles, indeed they were well aware that they were without any ideological cover when faced

with this responsibility.

Consensus on a certain repertoire of forms or a certain system of theoretical concepts was therefore not enough to guarantee unity of approach, indeed it led to the proposing, in a more serious and decisive form, of alternatives on practical behaviour. Nor were acquired habits valid, because faced with certain basic alternatives each generation and each group remained divided.

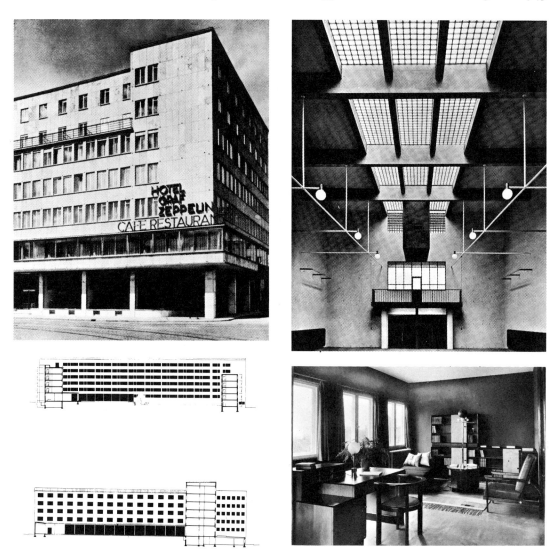

652, 653 *(left)   Stuttgart, Zeppelinbau (P. Bonatz, 1929–31); façades of an apartment block designed by R. Kressler, a pupil of Bonatz (from* P.B. *und seine Schüler)*
654, 655 *(right)   Celle, School by O. Haesler, 1927 (from A. Sartoris,* op. cit.*); Stuttgart, Furnishing of H. Poelzig's house*

German architects found themselves undergoing this trial in particularly difficult circumstances, in the brief interval between the end of the inflation (1924) and Hitler's coming to power (1933); the cultural debate took place first against the background of the defeat and allied occupation, then of the economic crisis, and was finally violently broken off by Nazism which denied modern architects the possibility of working and even of living in the country, forcibly imposing a return to a dreary neo-classicism which was

656, 657 *(left)   Mohren pharmacy at Breslau (A. Rading, 1925); house with workshop by K. Schneider (from G.A. Platz,* op. cit.*)*
658, 659 *(right)   Berlin, Plan of building on the Potsdamerplatz (H. & W. Luckhardt, 1931) and town-planning scheme near the Jaegerstrasse (H. Scharoun, 1927)*

accepted, in good faith or bad, by the majority of German architects.

The experiment begun by Gropius in 1919 ended in a check, which did however produce a conclusive clarification of the basic nature of the modern movement. In this way the chain of events in Germany was to some extent the paradigm of what happened all over Europe and must be considered first of all, since it sets the tone for all the rest.

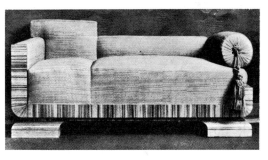

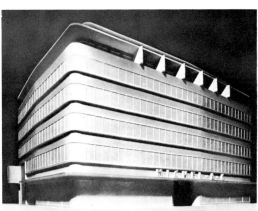

660, 661 *(left)* *E. Fahrenkampf, Church at Mühlheim (1928) and stores at Elberfeld, 1929 (from* Moderne Bauformen*)*

662–665 *(right)* *L. Ruff, Design for the Lechbrücke near Hochzoll (1927; from* Moderne Bauformen*); furniture for the Zilling house in Leipzig, by H. Straub (from* Moderne Bauformen*) and Dr Seipel – Dr Dollfuss Gedächtnis in Vienna, 1933 (from C. Holzmeister,* Bauten, Entwürfe und Handzeichnungen, *1937)*

The picture of German architectural thought, in the immediate post-war period, was, roughly speaking, the following:

The masters who had waged the *avant-garde* battles at the beginning of the century were now the most important figures in the professional and academic field: Behrens, the Artistic Adviser to the A.E.G. and professor at the Academy of Art in Vienna, Hans Poelzig (1869–1936) professor at the Technische Hochschule of Charlottenburg and president of the Werkbund, Fritz Schumacher, Oberbaudirektor at Hamburg; Austria, after Wagner's death, was dominated by the figure of Hoffmann, professor at the Kunstgewerbeschule and at the Oberbaurat in Vienna.

The four were almost contemporaries (Behrens was born in 1868, Poelzig and Schumacher in 1869 and Hoffmann in 1870). At the time of the foundation of the Bauhaus they were all about fifty and at the height of their activity; their formation in the ranks of the *avant-garde* made them sensitive to the aggressive mood of the post-war period and inclined to accept the contributions of the new trends. So Poelzig and Behrens designed several buildings of expressionistic inspiration, among the most daring and fascinating (see Poelzig's designs of 1919 for the Salzburg theatre and the offices for the Höchster Farbwerke at Frankfurt-am-Main, built by Behrens between 1920 and 1924); but afterwards they were willing to follow the young architects of the modern movement, accepting their methods of activity as far as was possible. Both took part in 1927 in the building of the Stuttgart Weissenhof, and Behrens ended his career with a simple, spacious industrial building, almost the antithesis of the massive factories of the early years: the tobacco factory at Linz, built between 1930 and 1934 (Figs. 650 and 651).

Between their generation and that of Gropius (he was born in 1883) there was a group of professionals who were already established in the pre-war period: Paul Bonatz (1877–1951), Bruno Taut (1880–1938), Dominikus Böhm (1880–1955), Hugo Häring (1882–1958) – all pupils of Theodor Fischer (1862–1938) and the first two also his collaborators, at the beginning of their careers – Fritz Höger (1877–1949) who worked in Hamburg in Schumacher's wake, Otto Haesler of Munich (b. 1880) and the Swiss Otto Salvisberg (b. 1882), also brought up in Munich.

These men, having grown up in the lull between the cultural battle of 1900 and that now under way after the war, were generally unsympathetic to extreme positions and worked to introduce the contributions of *avant-garde* movements into a broader eclecticism; they were concerned mainly not to lose contact with constructional processes and with the traditional stylistic repertoire. This was not only a professional interest, since faithfulness to tradition made it possible to maintain a constant high technical standard and accept constructional innovations only after a suitable period of trial; they had inherited the almost craftsmanlike care and competence typical of German architecture of the late nineteenth century.

As far as non-technical matters were concerned they were fluent and highly imaginative. They welcomed the contributions of Expressionism, appropriately toned down (Höger in the Chilehaus in Hamburg, 1923), they involved themselves in complicated formal combinations (Taut in the Ledigennheim at Schönenberg in 1919) or in a subtle transcription of rustic forms (Bonatz in the country houses along the Rhine, Salvisberg in the first workers' district). They reacted in various ways to the modern movement: some, already deeply involved in eclecticism were not in a position to take part in the new development of experiments, while others were attracted in various ways to the path of Gropius and Mies: Taut arrived there via theoretical considerations and became one of the propagandists of the new architecture, Haesler – adviser of the Reichsforschungs-gesellschaft on building economy – through his experience in the field of popular building in Celle (Fig. 654), Häring with a frankly formal choice. They all retained the mark of their original eclecticism, with their formal restlessness and sophistication; one needs consider only Taut's popular districts in the Berlin suburbs of Britz (1926–7), where the composition is subordinated with obvious contrivance to various dramatic overall expedients, for instance the double horseshoe in the middle of the first district.

Then there were the young men who were beginning their careers immediately before and after the war. Some of these were attracted to the modern movement early on: Max Taut (b. 1884), Ludwig Hilbersheimer (b. 1885), Ernst May (b. 1887), Adolf Rading (b. 1888), Karl Schneider (b. 1892), then the Luckhardt brothers – Hans (1890–1954) and Wassili (b. 1889) – Hans Scharoun (b. 1893), who were at first influenced by Expressionism. With the exception of May, none of them made substantial contributions to the investigation of their common problems; indeed it is interesting to see that the youngest, for instance Schneider and Scharoun, tended to indulge in a literal and formalistic interpretation of the modern style (Figs. 656–9); they took the experiments of their masters as a ready-made repertoire and their work sometimes justified the accusation of blank over-simplicity levelled at the modern movement, just as the writings of Taut and Hilbersheimer justified the conventional qualifications of 'rationalism and functionalism'.

Other young people, contemporaries of the rationalists, worked from the first in the line of traditional eclecticism: the most successful in Germany were Emil Fahrenkampf (b. 1885) and in Austria Clemens Holzmeister (b. 1886). Their professional success had the same explanation as that of architects such as Bonatz or Böhm, because they coincided

with the inclinations of the majority; further-more, having a very marked facility for imitation, they were always up-to-date with cultural innovations, ready to absorb the contributions of any trend, providing it was modern, and adapted their style to suit the circumstances.

Thus between 1927 and 1930, when the modern movement was, so to speak, at its most modern, and was filling books and reviews, many eclectic architects of the younger generation temporarily absorbed the linguistic elements of their rationalist contemporaries and created a watered down version of modern architecture which was extraordinarily successful in Germany and elsewhere, putting themselves forward as mediators between old and new.

Fahrenkampf was inspired at first by a bland neo-classicism – in the office block at Düsseldorf and the Otto house at Aachen of 1923 – which gradually became more allusive and sophisticated, with its culmination in the Stadthalle of 1926 at Mühlheim. In the Breidenbacher Hof hotel at Düsseldorf of 1927, the stamp of historicism was no longer distinguishable: the masonry casing was finished in an intentionally generic way and classical references were reduced to barely perceptible allusions, for instance the im-probably elongated arches of the façade, while there were various Mendelsohnian reminiscences, the horizontal strips, the flat coping, the contrast between the base and the main floors. In the church of St Mary's at Mühlheim, of 1928, (Fig. 660) some reference to traditional forms was obligatory, in the ground plan and façade with their three identical arches, but the later hotels Monopol at Cologne (1928) and Haus Rechen at Bochum (1929) were simple, smoothed out blocks, in the rationalist manner, and the big Michel stores at Elberfeld (1929) were more or less a transcription of the similar works by Mendelsohn (Fig. 661). Fahren-kampf passed for a modern architect[1] but the difference in inspiration was easily grasped by his adversaries, who contrasted Fahrenkampf and his 'diluted modernism' with Gropius and Mies, because they saw in his example a method of accepting new formal contributions without involving oneself in any of the basic problems.

In the same way, Holzmeister passed from early works laden with medieval allusions – the church of Bregenz of 1924 and the Vienna crematorium of 1925 – to the unadorned blocks of the Viennese school buildings of 1928–1930; he then designed a large number of prestige buildings in Turkey, in the same terse style, and had no difficulty – when necessary – in turning to a bloodless modern classicism, for instance in the State Bank of 1931.

It is revealing to examine the distortions the modern repertoire underwent in this process of transcription. A constant characteristic was for example the use of smooth, white walls; this expedient served to reduce the wall to the simple function of a geometrical field, on which the proportional relations of the constructional elements could be made to stand out, so that the plaster was always smooth and uniform. Imitators accepted this suggestion, but were concerned not to let the wall surface lose its physical consistency, treating it in such a way that it retained a perceptible texture: this explained the widespread use of coverings of slabs of stone, reminiscent of Wagner (Fig. 652) which formed a regular order around doors and windows, where the slight differences of plane and colour introduced a subdued chiaroscuro, though still allowing the façade to appear as a single chromatic plane (for instance in the above-mentioned hotels by Fahrenkampf at Düsseldorf and Bochum); or sgraffito work on the plaster which made it possible at least to establish a graphic relationship between the angles of the windows (as in the Böhmische Union-Bank at Brünn, by E. Wiesner). When plain plaster was used, it was preferably rough-grained, so that it would be affected by the

light, and often the surrounds of the windows were made to protrude, so that light should project rhythmical shadows on to the wall (as in the schools in Vienna by Holzmeister and in the work of the Austrian masters generally).

This attitude could also be seen in the taste in design – in the charcoal drawings of elevations – and in the style of the photographs, which were taken in very indirect light and with marked foreshortening; one has only to examine the plates of this chapter and to compare them with the photographs by Lucia Moholy-Nagy, for instance with Fig. 607 of the previous chapter, where the buildings are photographed almost frontally and with direct light.

Similar processes of dilution occurred in furnishings as well. Various items of furniture and fittings designed at the Bauhaus were mass-produced industrially and certain technical or formal expedients became commonplace: for instance in the 1931 Berlin exhibition other designers exhibited furniture in metal tubing, sometimes transforming Breuer's exact framework into decorative arabesques along the lines of Thonet (A. Lorenz and the Luckhardt brothers); in wooden furniture simple square forms were accepted, but care was taken to destroy their geometrical severity with variegated veneer, preferably arranged in transversal lines; thus the rough materials designed by Anni Albers and Gunta Stolzl were used to accentuate the pronounced fullness of the upholstery, as in the furniture of H. Straub[2] (Figs. 663 and 664) (some French decorators went as far as to apply a varied covering of wood to furniture in metal tubing, for instance M. Champion in 1923).[3]

The masters of the Kunstgewerbeschule – Hoffmann and Strnad – and the young men whom they taught, deserve special attention.[4]

It has already been noted in Chapter 9 that one of the possible ways of developing the Wagnerian tradition was to eliminate all secondary plasticity and reduce the buildings to bare walls, provided they kept the reference – in their symmetry of layout, in the spacing and grading of doors and windows – to the original proportional values, reduced to relationships between expanses of light and shade; this was the line taken by Loos in the Villa at Montreux and by Hoffmann in the Purkersdorf sanatorium.

This method, which helped to destroy the eclectic tradition, by paving the way for the modern movement – hence the polemical forcefulness of the buildings of Hoffmann and Loos in the immediate post-war period – could, later, assimilate the formal contributions of the modern method and introduce them into the mainstream of tradition.

In some works Hoffmann and his pupils came very close to the rationalists – Hoffmann in his popular houses built between 1925 and 1930 – but they kept their traditional tone with the studied elegance of the sections, the prompt utilization of every accessory – a drainpipe, an inscription or sign – as a linear arabesque in black on white. When E. Kaufman suggested the neo-classicists Boullée and Ledoux[5] as the precursors of the modern movement, he was plainly thinking of the Viennese school, of Hoffmann, Loos, Strnad.

The influence of the Viennese was widespread throughout Europe, because of the authority they had gained during the first decade of the twentieth century and because of the possibilities of escape they offered to moderates everywhere. In all the countries formerly part of the Hapsburg empire, Czechoslovakia, Hungary, Yugoslavia, the spread of the modern repertoire took place mainly through the mediation of Austria. Hoffmann continued to dictate to European taste as far as furnishings were concerned until the Wiener Werkstätte, still organized along the traditional lines of craftsmanship, collapsed in 1933 because of the economic crisis.

A significant confirmation of the position of the Viennese with regard to the international movement was offered in Vienna by the Werkbund exhibition in 1932. On this occasion, as at Stuttgart, a model district of two- and three-storey houses was built (Figs. 666–75) designed by Hoffmann, Loos, Strnad and twenty-two Austrians,[6] with A. Lurçat and G. Guevrekian from France, G. Rietveld from Holland, R. Neutra and A. Grünberger from America and H. Häring from Germany. The list of participants alone indicates the cultural bias: flat roofs, white walls and plain rooms, as at the Weissenhof, but a somewhat different spirit, more formalist and escapist. This experiment made no important contribution to the solution of the technical and economic problems of popular building, but only spoke in favour of low houses and extensive districts, as opposed to the intensive blocks built in the previous decade by the Viennese administration; this bias, in 1932, and on German soil, had obvious social significance, that of the abandoning of the idea of integration of the workers' quarters into the city and of escape towards semi-rural suburbia.

The rapid spread of the new architectural repertoire and its more or less superficial imitations posed a serious difficulty for the theoreticians and protagonists of the modern movements. It had been shown that the use of certain forms did not guarantee the acceptance of certain principles, but could be turned to various ends, contradictory among themselves. Some, identifying the 'modern movement' with this repertoire, announced that the new architecture was an accomplished fact, because certain formal rules were broadly observed, and regarded problems as solved from the moment the way of formulating them in conformity with these rules was found. Their adversaries were quick to agree, because they concluded that the movement was a style like all the others, which would soon be out of date or would be absorbed into the traditional repertoire of eclecticism, as an alternative to be used in

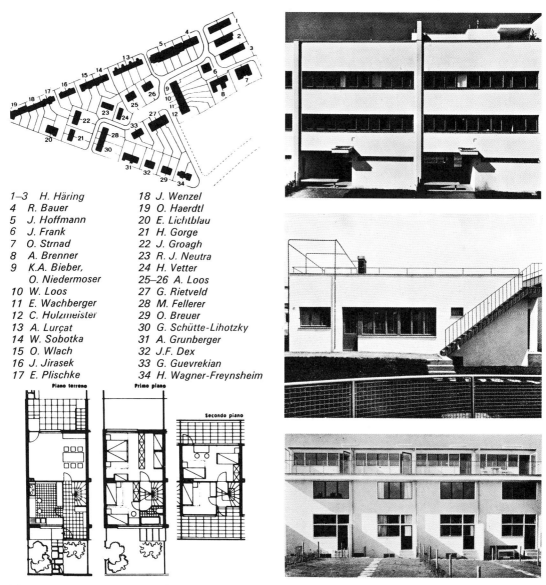

1–3   H. Häring
4   R. Bauer
5   J. Hoffmann
6   J. Frank
7   O. Strnad
8   A. Brenner
9   K.A. Bieber,
      O. Niedermoser
10   W. Loos
11   E. Wachberger
12   C. Holzmeister
13   A. Lurçat
14   W. Sobotka
15   O. Wlach
16   J. Jirasek
17   E. Plischke

18   J. Wenzel
19   O. Haerdtl
20   E. Lichtblau
21   H. Gorge
22   J. Groagh
23   R. J. Neutra
24   H. Vetter
25–26 A. Loos
27   G. Rietveld
28   M. Fellerer
29   O. Breuer
30   G. Schütte-Lihotzky
31   A. Grunberger
32   J.F. Dex
33   G. Guevrekian
34   H. Wagner-Freynsheim

666–670   *Vienna, Werkbundsiedlung of 1932: general ground-plan and houses by A. Lurçat, R. Neutra and G. Rietveld (from A. Sartoris, op. cit.)*

marginal circumstances: for industrial buildings, popular housing etc. Others began to give consideration to the relationship between form and substance, and realized that they must elaborate new methods of exposition and polemic which would make it possible to distinguish sincere involvement from conformism within the confusingly uniform scene of so-called modern production.

This situation dampened the enthusiasm and bite of the polemic for and against the new architecture and offered a glimpse of

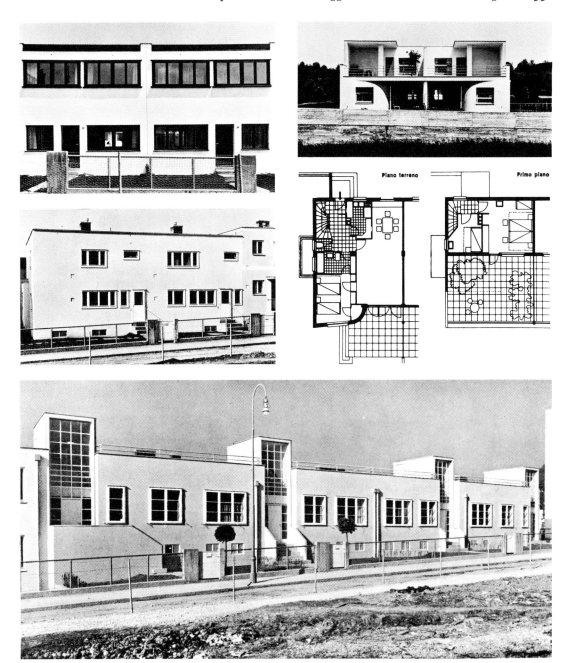

Plano terreno

Primo plano

671–675 *Vienna, Houses by J. F. Dex, W. Sobotka, O. Strnad and J. Hoffman at the Werkbundsiedlung of 1932 (from Sartoris, op. cit.)*

another order of choices, which threw most architects off course.

At this point the critics, if they accepted the narrow version of, say, Taut or Sartoris, talked of a crisis of rationalism. They reinforced an interpretation which was in fact widespread, between 1930 and 1933, particularly among the younger critics: now that the modern movement had been reduced to a system of formal precepts, it was assumed that the origin of its present uneasiness lay in the narrowness and schematic nature of these rules, and it was believed that the remedy still lay in a change of formal direction, in a lessening of the stress on technical features and regularity, in the return to a more human architecture, warmer, freer and inevitably more closely attached to traditional values.

The economic crisis meant that this debate was compressed into a very short space of time; the Nazi dictatorship that followed saw to it that it was cut short once and for all and at the same time acted as a touchstone, openly revealing what choices had been concealed beneath the stylistic controversy.

In 1932, when the Nazis came to power at Dessau, the Bauhaus had to move to Berlin and the following year, when Hitler became Chancellor, Mies had to close it down altogether, while the buildings at Dessau were turned into a school for government officials.

Of the former teachers, Albers emigrated to America; Klee and Schlemmer, who had left in 1929, and had been teaching at Düsseldorf and Berlin, retired in 1933; Gropius and Breuer settled in England in 1934 and Moholy-Nagy in 1935, after having tried to work as a typographer and stage manager in Berlin. Many of them eventually went to America: Feininger in 1935, Gropius, Breuer and Moholy-Nagy in 1937, Bayer in 1938.[7]

Mendelsohn was forced to leave Germany in 1933; Hilbersheimer, B. Taut and May emigrated to Russia as planning experts; of the older men Schlemmer and Poelzig remained more or less inactive, while Behrens settled in Austria.

The person who stayed longest in Germany, hoping to salvage what could be saved, was Mies; in 1933 he was still invited, together with another thirty architects, to take part in the competition for the Berlin State Bank, and was one of the six to gain a prize, but since he was no longer managing to build anything he devoted himself to the theoretical plans of his courtyard houses, until the situation became absolutely untenable and he was forced to emigrate to America in 1938.

In the same way Haesler, Rading and Max Taut had to cease their activities. Only a few designers of the younger generation, for instance Scharoun and the Luckhardt brothers, were able to escape the ideological conflict because of the more personal and evasive character of their activities, and they still had a few opportunities for work; Scharoun, for instance, designed the Schminke at Lobau in 1933.

The professional position of modern architects was linked, in Germany, mainly with public commissions and work on subsidized building. This was the modern movement's point of strength between 1925 and 1933, enabling Gropius and May to make profitable contact with the economic realities of the country; but now it was the cause of its paralysis, because it had made architecture directly dependent on political power. In comparison, moderates like Bonatz,[8] Böhm and Fahrenkampf fared better, able to count on a large private clientèle, and they continued to build important works for some time.

The most at a loss, in this predicament, were the young people who were just starting their professional careers. In 1936 J. Posener described their situations very well, for he shared many of their thoughts.[9] This generation, 'fed on Nietzsche and Stefan George', was restless and sentimental. The battle fought by Gropius, Mies and May against the traditionalists lost all attraction for them when it lost its adventurous, pioneering character of the young against the old, i.e. when it went beyond the limits of an *avant-garde* movement. The protagonists of that battle, who were now over forty and had established themselves through their many works, appeared as old men in their turn and the young attacked them in the name of contrary principles.

'For them pure reason was suspect *a priori* . . . . They tried to close the profession within clearly visible limits, when it was on the point of losing itself in the abstract, to reforge the links which had formerly bound it to craftsmanship, to begin to value habit as an important factor in the designing of dwellings, rather than re-casting them according to the image of a new way of life. The "natural" became their watchword, as opposed to the sensational novelty of modern creations'.[10]

They found inspiration in the work of old teachers such as W. Kreis, H. Tessenow and P. Schmitthenner, who continued to draw subtle and elegant inspiration from the period styles; Tessenow, who defended craftsmanship against industry, handiwork against that of the machine, with Romantic obstinacy, appeared as the bearer of a new ideology which satisfied their uncertain aspirations. Hoffmann echoes him in Austria, coining the formula *Befreits Handwerk*.[11]

But Nazism had very precise requirements: it wanted a celebratory, traditionalist architecture, strictly German. The older people had what was needed: neo-Medievalism for residential buildings, with pointed roofs, carved woodwork and Gothic inscriptions, for public buildings a Greco-German neo-Classicism, with fluted Doric columns, marble, flights of steps and allegorical statues, eagles and swastikas all over the place. Older men like W. Kreis, P. Schultze-Naumburg and P. L. Troost (a former naval ship-fitter, personal friend of the Führer and responsible for the Brown House in Munich, Fig. 676) came to the fore, occupied the important posts in public administration and in the professional associations, thus imposing their directives from on high.

The young remained disorientated and refused to believe that anyone could arrive at these consequences after having started with their original aspirations. In this way the great majority, not wanting to enter into the spirit of official directives, were excluded from the building activity of the State and administrations, and carried out modest commissions for private clients. Some – H. Volkart, G. Harbers, E. Kruger – obstinately tried to take a third way, from both the rigours of rationalism and official eclecticism, but it became ever harder to maintain the double distinction and the results were ambiguous; examples were Volkart's suburban houses, where stylistic references were restricted to a very subtle play of allusions and omissions, or the hill house by Kruger, of 1935 – built on the top of a high pillar in a wood near Stuttgart – where the exceptional expedient acted as a substitute for architectural commitment.

Posener ended his article as follows:

'They had taken the older men as allies against the generation of forty-year-olds, but their as yet immature opinions had been crushed by the drearier though more clear-cut opinions of their professors . . . . Now it seems that they are gradually emerging from this muddle, and it is possible that they may be becoming conscious of what it is that separates them from their allies. The works of the best of them seem to us less imitative and less mannered than those of their leaders. They have evident freshness, naturalness, simplicity, details that are solid, pure and pleasing, a considerable degree of intimacy. These are the qualities that we look for in vain in the works of the moderns but which we find, for instance, in Austria and the Scandinavian countries. Certainly, it is not much to come out of a great movement. A serious question has been posed too timidly by the young and has received too brutal an answer. The question remains open and we must await the future'.[12]

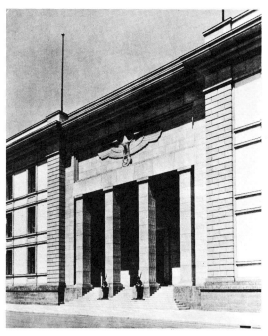

676, 677, 678 *Munich, The Brown House (P.L. Troost, 1936); Berlin, the new Chancellery (A. Speer, 1938; from A. Speer,* Neue Baukunst, *1940) and a design for the new university clinic (H. Distel, 1941);*

Posener realized that the fate of German architectural culture was linked to the development of the political régime; he noted for example that the revaluation of craftsmanship had become a constant thesis of Nazi propaganda, so much so that 'when Hitler had his country house built, the papers announced that no machine had been used'; but he saw that the Nazi society and propaganda were based on an unscrupulous application of mechanization and mass organization. The question of architecture was therefore conditioned by the more general one of the political experiment under way: 'The movement wavered between the medieval Guild and the Trust, between craftsmanship and big industry, between individual effort and a terrible degree of organization, and no-one could yet presume to define its true character.'[13]

Unfortunately the answer to the true character of Nazism was to come a few years later and sweep away Posener's timid optimism; the tightening-up of the régime soon restricted and annulled the small margin of independence in which the young people just mentioned had moved. At this point a small group, led by a very young pupil of Tessenow, Albert Speer (b. 1905) threw themselves into the arena, intent on gaining control of official architecture.

Speer became director of the Nazi party Kraft durch Freude und Schönheit der Arbeit, and in 1937 he was appointed director of building in the German capital: he built the Zeppelin stadium at Nuremberg, the new Chancellery in Berlin (Fig. 677), the German Pavilion at the 1937 Paris exhibition. His responsibilities did not stop at building but extended into the political field, as emerged from the Nuremberg trials where Speer was tried together with Nazi political leaders.

If one could talk of cultural conviction for Kreis and the other older men, because late in life circumstances offered them the opportunity to practice an architecture in which they had always believed, for Speer and his contemporaries it was a question only of cynicism and fanaticism; it was a *reductio ad absurdum* of the link, now ineluctable, between architectural decisions and moral ones.

Thus the course of German architecture between the two world wars wound up with an unfortunate epilogue; after having made a decisive contribution to modern architectural culture, Germany was temporarily cut off from this culture, deprived of her best men, and became the theatre of the most grotesque experiment in stylistic disinterment.

It is unpleasant to note, in the work pro-duced according to Nazi directives, the names of E. Fahrenkampf (Hermann Goering-Meisterschule in Kronenburg, 1939) and J. Hoffmann (house for German officers in Vienna, 1940); the traditionalist tone of the first and the classical allusions of the second formed a perfect background for eagles and swastikas, while in the works of Speer and Troost many horribly distorted motifs of the Viennese school reappeared, of Behrens for instance, and even of the youthful works of Gropius. The historical lesson, however painful, was eloquent, showing that forms had no cathartic power and that artistic tradition could be emptied of meaning from within, when its moral propositions changed.

2 The Soviet Union

The period from the 1917 Revolution to the first Soviet Constitution of the USSR at the end of 1922, was one of continual disturbance: the war against the White armies supported by the French and English, the conflict with Poland in the summer of 1920, the famine of that year and the follow-ing, and the exceptional measures taken to cope with it.

Building production was almost com-pletely suspended, but the state of emergency was propitious, as in the immediate post-war period in Germany, to lively ideological debate. As the leaders of Soviet politics came from groups that had opposed the old régime, so the tendencies which clashed in this controversy were inspired by pre-war movements, with the logical prevalence of 'left-wing' tendencies: cubism, construc-tivism, symbolism etc.

But just as the politicians had to build up a new society as well as destroying the old, so artists set themselves to conceive new forms as well as repudiating the old ones, and then arose the problem that was to concern all Russian architects from now on: what should the new architecture be in order to deserve the description Socialist and Soviet?

One first difference was connected with the fact that the *avant-garde* movement of before the war had an individualist and aristocratic character, while Soviet society was collectivist and popular. The group 'Proletcult' tried to deduce from the principles of collectivism a completely new art of the proletariat, in contrast to the bourgeois, but the artificiality of this attempt was soon apparent, because the so-called collective and proletarian forms were selected by certain individuals in a plainly arbitrary manner.

A second difficulty arose from the conflict between the technical and ideological aspects of architecture. The stress on technique and functionality, in the modern movement, was just the first step towards establishing a new relationship between architecture and society. But everywhere, and in Russia too, the movement was presented as a programme to reduce architecture to a matter of pure utility. It could be said that this programme was quite in line with Marxist materialism, because it showed that cultural values had their roots in production relations, or that it was a dangerous deviation from Marxism since it gave architecture an autonomous and objective worth, removing it from political and ideological control. The two arguments were developed by the supporters and adversaries of modern architecture, but the argument, invalidated by the common restrictive concept, achieved nothing and only prevented the understanding of the cultural contributions that came from Europe.

Even in the main current of the Russian *avant-garde* constructivism, there was an insoluble antagonism between technical matters and ideology. The work of architecture should respond fully to material utility and at the same time should express the new political ideas in emotional terms: the concrete results were heavily contrived, spectacular designs, like Tatlin's famous plan for the monument to the Third International of 1919 (Fig. 679).

The first free association of progressive Russian architects, the A.S.N.O.V.A., set up in 1923, inherited the constructivist antagonism but organized it into something less dramatic. Technical and ideological factors had to be dialectically united, according to an objective hierarchy, but within this hierarchy ideological values ended by becoming identified with the values of traditional aesthetics. Another group (S.A.S.S.) was formed in protest against this interpretation, preaching intransigent functionalism and in 1929 a third group (V.O.P.R.A.) was formed in protest, putting the emphasis on formal values.

In the absence of current theoretical premises the conflict could never be settled, and the formula officially adopted to define Marxist architecture, 'dialectical unity between technique and ideology', limited itself to naming the two terms without indicating any way of linking them. It was also generally admitted that this unity could not be established immediately and automatically, but that it must emerge from a long process of elaboration. In 1931 an official theorist wrote, *à propos* of the Russian designs for the Palace of the Soviets:

'It has been shown that in respect to unity of technique and ideology a great deal of work remains yet to be done. The utmost subjectivism and the instability of the presented and exhibited projects proves that the Soviet architects have not yet shown a distinct type of proletarian architecture . . . . This is comprehensible and explicable, as ideological superstructures usually are late in history. They are always lagging behind social and economic changes'.[14]

In practice the attitude of the political authorities was decisive, and they, having to make the practical decisions, could not content themselves with pronouncements on

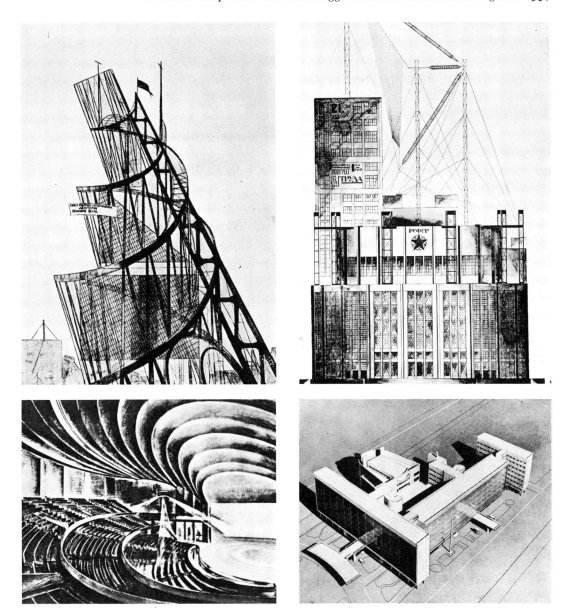

679, 680 *(above)   Designs for the monument to the Third International (V. E. Tatlin, 1920) and the Palace of Work in Moscow (A. L. and V. Vesmin, 1923; from* L'Architecture Vivante*)*
681, 682 *(below)   V. Gherassimov, Design for the theatre at Kharkov, 1930* (op. cit.)*; Le Corbusier and P. Jeanneret, the Centrosoyus building in Moscow, 1928 (from* Oeuvre Complète*)*

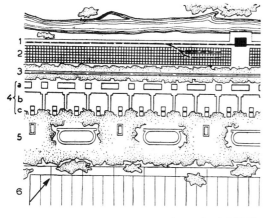

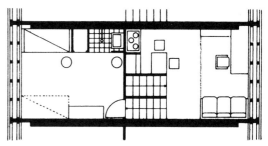

Piano superiore

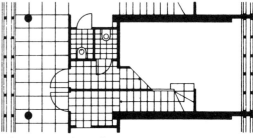

Piano del ballatolo

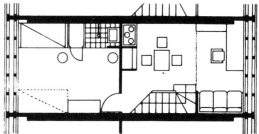

Piano inferiore

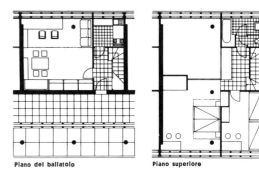

Piano del ballatolo   Piano superiore

683 *(above on left)   Scheme for the linear city of Miljutin. 1 railway; 2 industries; 3 motorway; 4 dwellings; 5 green spaces; 6 agricultural land*
684, 685, 686   *House for employees of the Commissariat of finances (Ginzburg and Milinis, 1928)*

dialectical unity. The basic reasoning was formulated as follows by Lenin, in 1920:

'It is impossible for us to solve the question of proletarian culture without a clear understanding and exact knowledge of that culture which was created in the course of humanity's development; it is only by remaking this that proletarian culture is possible'.[15]

But most of the political leaders were

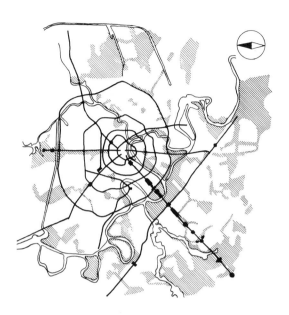

687, 688 *(left)   Moscow, development plan of 1935 (green spaces in cross natching) and view of the university on the Lenin hills*
689, 690 *(right)   Moscow, Two underground stations*

suspicious of modern artists, either from habit or for fear of not being able to control their unpredictable activity. Kamenev wrote in 1919:

'The workers' government must decisively stop the support which it has given to all kinds of Futurists, Cubists and Imagists – all those contortionists – they are not proletarian artists and their art is not ours. They are the product of bourgeois corruption and bourgeois degeneration'.[16]

Thus Kamenev's argument was superimposed upon Lenin's and limited its range: since a link with recent experiments had been excluded – the only one that would have made possible a real and fruitful link up with past tradition – the only alternative was eclecticism, i.e. the utilization of the styles corresponding to the various periods of the distant past, according to their suitability and associations.

Of the period styles classicism was certainly the most advantageous: it symbolized the civic virtues of ancient civilization, was normally associated with revolutions and had been the official style of the Tsarist Empire in the eighteenth and nineteenth centuries. Thus the path of Soviet architecture was clear and in fact neo-classicism gradually became the official style for public buildings.

This process took place gradually. Between 1925 and 1932 there was still a relative variety of tendencies, and dignified works inspired by the international movement were built; these included the *Isvestia* building by G. Barchin (1925–7), the Mostorg stores in Moscow by the brothers Vesmin (1928), the *Pravda* building by P. Golosov (1934) and a certain number of industrial buildings. Particularly worthy of attention are the collective housing blocks worked on by designers from the S.A.S.S., one of the most important being the house for the employees of the Commissariat of Finance in Moscow, by Ginzburg and Milinis (1929). Contact with the outside world, too, was relatively free: in 1925 Mendelsohn built a large factory in Leningrad, in 1928 the President of the Union of Co-operatives, M. Lubinov, obtained the commission to build the organization's new headquarters for Le Corbusier (Fig. 682) and in 1931 the Russian government invited the chief masters of the modern movement to take part in the competition for the Palace of the Soviets. Soon afterwards, however, stylistic conformity became more noticeable, a fact which was related not so much to the

nationalistic policies of Stalin as to increasing organizational demands: with the fulfilment of the first Five Year Plan begun in 1928, with the decision of the Party Central Committee in 1931 to begin territorial planning and with the beginning of the second Five Year Plan in 1933.

1930 was the crucial year, when the illusions of the Russian *avant-garde* faded once and for all and 'the boat of love was shattered against the rock of everyday life'; in the same year the architectural free associations were federated into V.A.N.O. and were dissolved in 1932; their members were incorporated into a State federation, the S.A.S.S., which ran the building activities of the whole country. In 1933 the competition for the Palace of the Soviets concluded with the triumph of the traditionalists Jofan, Schouko and Helfreich, as mentioned in Chapter 14, and from this moment onwards Russia was dotted with vast colonnades and pinnacled skyscrapers, and even the most modest buildings were covered with anachronistic decoration (Figs. 688–90).

During the first Five Year Plan the members of the S.A.S.S. made an important contribution to town-planning by making a model of a continuous, linear city, with the declared intention of overcoming the contrast between town and country and of building over the whole countryside. This scheme envisaged the total collectivization of domestic life, both for workers and peasants.

Together with the theoreticians of the S.A.S.S. worked German left-wing town-planners – May, Meyer, Hilbersheimer, Bruno Taut – who afterwards settled in Russia to escape the Nazi régime. The plans of several new cities emerged from this collaboration, for instance those of Stalingrad (by Miljutin), Magnitogorsk and Elektrovoz.

In town-planning the conflict between innovators and traditionalists was translated into an argument as to whether to apply new schemes of settlement or to base themselves on existing schemes, with a few modifications of detail.

In 1930 the political authorities clarified the official point of view on this controversy:

'It is impossible suddenly to overcome obstacles that are centuries old, the fruit of the cultural and economic backwardness of society. Yet this is the system implicit in these unrealizable and Utopian plans for the reconstruction, at State expense, of new cities based on the total collectivization of living, including collective provisioning, collective care of children, the prohibition of private kitchens. The hasty realization of such schemes, Utopian and doctrinaire, which take no account of the material resources of our country and of the limits within which the people, with their set habits and preferences, can be prepared for them, could easily result in considerable losses and could also discredit the basic principles of the Socialist reconstruction of society. Architects must avoid the danger of being slaves to their imaginations, because an appropriate solution of the problem must come from an architect who understands life and the social conditions of the masses. During the period of the family's change from a basis of individual family economy to a collective basis, all mechanical, administrative solutions are self-defeating; the process must be gradual, it must be cherished and encouraged, adequate organization must be brought into existence to highlight the advantages to and increased well-being of the workers inherent in the programme of collectivization'.[17]

Thus, while granting a certain margin for experimentation with linear schemes, the authorities were gradually going back to their approval of the ordinary centralized city. There were attempts, it is true, at limiting the size of existing and of new cities, but the logic of centralization made its demands, and town-planners could do nothing except regulate it with the traditional criteria of zoning and geometrical street-layout.

In 1935 the town-planning scheme for Moscow was approved; it was technically praiseworthy for the clever zoning and abundance of green spaces, but weighed down with academic formalism – a monumental axis of over twenty kilometres, dotted with squares and immense palaces, ran from Red Square to the Lenin hills (Fig. 687).

Official building was run, as in Germany, by elderly survivors of the old régime or by young opportunists, and it is interesting to note the almost incredible unscrupulousness with which some of the most famous architects followed official directives, even in their most subtle variations.

A typical example was that of A. V. Schoussev: he had been active in the time of the Tsars, producing eclectic buildings such as the Kazan railway station (1913); in 1926 he built the Lenin mausoleum in Red Square, with its simple and dignified forms, but soon afterwards he designed the highly ornate Meyerhold theatre in Moscow (1932); he moved closer to the European movement with the building for the Commissariat for Agriculture (1933), a poor copy of a work by Mendelsohn, but soon afterwards he was lavishing columns and ornaments of all sorts on the Hotel Moscow (1935) and received the Stalin Prize in 1941 for the Marx-Engels Institute at Tiflis, where the façade was completely screened by enormous Corinthian columns.[18]

3   Italy

When the modern movement began in Italy, the Fascist dictatorship was already established, with its intention of regulating every aspect of national life from on high, and therefore, of course architecture as well. But the pressure Fascism exerted on architecture was sporadic and variable, according to the various successive trends, and therefore never as heavy as that of Nazism; furthermore, Italian rationalism would never have been associated with the earlier democratic régime, as happened in Germany, and indeed many architects and politicians tried to present it as the 'Fascist style' as in Russia, where a 'Soviet style' was similarly spoken of. In the end Fascism too, like the other totalitarian régimes, enforced a return to neo-Classicism and forcibly impeded the development of the modern movement, but the process was slow and passed through many shades of emphasis.

Immediately after the war Italian culture in its turn became aware of the alternative of the rejection of all current rules, and a renewed desire for regularity and stability, but it did not have sufficient energy to carry this dilemma to its logical conclusion. The remaining futurists repeated their revolutionary declarations without much conviction and soon swerved towards pointless and escapist experiments. In 1921 Marinetti launched the 'tactilist'[19] manifesto and ended his career in 1938 with the manifesto for an 'imperial culinary art',[20] while the younger generation no longer felt any affinity at all with these formulae and turned to the past, where they hoped to find constant rules and certain and permanent values. This was a tendency shared by the *Ronda* by A. Casella and the *Return to Bach*, and by the painters who in 1922 founded the *novecento* (Twentieth Century): A. Bucci, A. Funi, P. Marussig, M. Sironi, L. Dudreville, E. Malerba, U. Oppi.

In this period many former futurists suddenly changed their allegiances, from Funi, Sironi and Carrà who moved towards the *novecento* to Soffici and Papini who became men of order and ultra conservative. 'Classicism' was talked of constantly and in 1923 Soffici explained:

'The spiritual movement which we support could be described as classical provided that one dissociates this word from all connotations of rhetorical reaction and the restoration of out-dated fashions and ideas . . . in so far as it supports certain fundamental norms, respects a certain political and moral order, and certain principles which wisely unite, rather than divide in the anarchist fashion, all men living in a single national community'.[21]

Everywhere reason and tradition were invoked, in Gentile's actualist manifesto of 1924 and in Croce's counter-manifesto. Garin, recalling this cultural mood, observed that 'the finest proof of a triumph of irrationalism was to be found precisely in this general, ambiguous lack of direction, in these sudden conversions, in this loss of the meaning of words, in this blind and uncertain wrangling'.[22]

Futurism, after Sant'Elia's death in the war, lost all hold on the architectural field, and produced only the futile but spectacular designs of Marchi and Depero. On the other hand the traditionalist attitude bore consistent fruit: a group corresponding to the *novecento* painters was that of neo-classical Milanese architects: G. Muzio, P. Portaluppi, E. Lancia, P. Ponti, O. Cabiati, A. Alpago-Novello, who were inspired by the early Lombard nineteenth century, the last overtly European architectural experiment attempted in Italy. Writing the history of the movement, Muzio (b. 1893) commented:

'There was a spontaneous and absolute break (after the great war) with the various currents which continued their peaceful existence, thanks to the activities of the older professionals. It seemed necessary to replace the exaggerated and arbitrary individualism, which gauged the talent and fame of a designer by the singularity of his solutions, by a system of rules; only discipline and communal feeling could lead, shortly, to a new architecture'.[23]

Shrewdly, Muzio linked this desire for regularity with the need for town-planning:

'A medley of heterogeneous and jarring buildings could never give rise to a new stylistic epoch; concern must be concentrated on complexes of buildings rather than on the single one. It was therefore natural to study the art of building cities, an art hitherto neglected in this country. The best and most original examples of the past were certainly those of classical derivation, and in particular, those of early nineteenth-century Milan . . . . It was necessary for these architects, generically called "town-planners", to turn once again to these illustrious examples, convinced of the basic excellence of their method. For architecture, as for town-planning, a return to classicism seemed necessary, and the same thing occurred in the plastic arts and in literature. This happened because of a profound conviction that the essential schemes and universal and necessary elements of the architecture of the classical periods were always applicable, and the proof lay in their continued survival in ever changing stylistic expressions, from Rome to the present day.[24]

This could be mistaken for a strange anomaly, the result of a provincial deafness while all Europe was in convulsions and eager for extreme novelty . . . but in fact it was an original and deeply-rooted movement. [Extremist tendencies had proved inconclusive, since] after all links with the past had been done away with . . . the doors had been opened to all manner of eccentricities and exoticism. In Italy the cycle was run even faster, and in fact it was here that, after the war, these architects, by reviewing the past, could produce this new classical spirit. Are we not perhaps anticipating a movement whose imminent birth is announced throughout Europe by hesitant but widespread symptoms?'[25]

Muzio's analysis is accurate on many points. The need for a new regularity, which would also help to define relations with the past, was felt throughout European culture. But while Gropius found a fairly penetrating method of transcending the usual conflict between historicism and the *avant-garde*, the *novecentisti* remained prisoners of the old dilemma – past or future – and could suggest only a return to certain models of the past. In this way they were really anticipating a European movement, though one very different from the one they were expecting: it was state neo-Classicism, which was already in sight as early as 1931, and which made progress everywhere during the next few years, sweeping away both the modern movement and the aristocratic dream of the *novecento* on its wave of rhetorical dreariness.

Other similar experiments were taking place in various parts of Italy. Within the enclosed, conformist atmosphere of the capital, while the tradition of G. Koch and L. Carmini was fizzling out into the vogue for *barocchetto*, P. Aschieri and A. Limongelli were advocating a return to a simplified neo-classicism, and Marcello Piacentini (1881–1950), following this line of thought, came upon the Viennese repertoire. Their works, particularly Piacentini's Corso Cinema, were considered very daring by the most orthodox traditionalists, and provoked quite disproportionate arguments, whose lively exterior concealed a basic ultra-conservatism.

To understand the development of the Italian controversy of the decade between 1920 and 1930 one must bear in mind her isolation and scarcity of contacts with Europe, accentuated by the protectionism of the régime. No-one before Persico had even the slightest idea of what was going on in Germany; even information was scarce, and soon translated into the conventional terms of local debate.

In 1930 Piacentini described the German situation in these surprising words: 'In Germany no dominant and precise character has as yet emerged: the struggle between the vertical and horizontal line is still going on, in a sea of uncertainties';[26] and in 1931 a photograph of the Bauhaus was published in *Architettura* with this caption: 'Headquarters of the Bauhaus building contractors at Dessau',[27] while a few pages later the reader was informed that 'the small houses by Meis van der Rohe (sic) are more or less identical to those of the Swiss Le Corbusier or the Frenchman Mallet-Stevens'.[28]

In this lazy and ill-prepared atmosphere the group of the '7' appeared in 1926 – consisting of G. Figini, G. Frette, S. Larco, G. Pollini, C. E. Rava, G. Terragni and U. Castagnola, replaced the following year by A. Libera – which drew explicitly upon the theses of the modern movement.

The '7' presented themselves to the public with a series of articles in *Rassegna Italiana*[29] affirming, among other things, that:

'The new architecture . . . must be the result of a close adherence to logic and rationality . . . . We do not claim to create *a style*, but from the constant application of rationality, the perfect correspondence of the building to its aims, in fact by selection, *style* must inevitably result . . . . It is important to be convinced of the need to create types, a few basic types . . . it is important to see that, for the moment at least, architecture must consist partly of renunciation . . .'.[30]

These theses were expounded with great circumspection, in an attempt to forestall possible objections and to stress the moderate, not extreme, character of the new trend; and the '7' offered their assurance that:

a   They did not want to break with tradition: 'In Italy there is such a pronounced classical substratum, and the spirit of tradition – not the forms it takes, which is something quite different – is so deep that, obviously and almost mechanically, the new architecture could not fail to retain a typical national character'.

b   They did not share the extremist tendencies of part of the European movement: 'This architecture, in so far as it frequently makes the mistake of pushing rationalism beyond the limits that a sense of aesthetic measure would impose, is remote from our own spirit'.

c   That the new architecture could be compared with that of the distant past.

The young members of the '7' started, as had the *novecentisti*, from 'a desire for sincerity, for logic, and order', but they ended up with something very different. The *novecentisti* sought the principle of regularity from the outside, in a repertoire of forms from the past, while the '7' thought that a new rule could be found in the practice of architecture itself, and this led to a decisive shifting of the relations between life and culture. Seen in this perspective, all the terms – 'tradition', 'style', 'rationality', 'beauty' – were given a new meaning.

But the '7' avoided going more deeply into this distinction, which would logically have led to a break with current habits, and borrowed words and phrases familiar to the public to show that they accepted – with some unspecified modifications – the corresponding conceptions. They were particularly concerned, with the comparison with archaism, to make their position known to ordinary people, who tended to judge all tendencies through retrospective comparison.

In this way they managed to keep the tone of the controversy subdued and reasonable, realizing that they had nothing to gain from the heated atmosphere of the old *avant-garde* debates, but they accepted a certain ambiguity in discussion which was ultimately to be paid for dearly.

It was practical experiment that clarified matters. The first works by Terragni (the Novocomum apartment house at Como), of Lingeri (the headquarters of the nautical club Amila at Tremezzo) and Pagano (the Gualino office block at Turin) all completed in 1929, showed that it was not just the formal repertoire that was involved, but a whole way of understanding architecture. Now argument flared up fiercely and while in 1928 the first exhibition of rational architecture, in the Palazzo delle esposizioni in Rome, did not arouse much interest, the second, organized in 1931 at the gallery of P. M. Bardi in via Veneto, gave rise to serious controversy.

The young people exhibited within the framework of a national organization, the Movimento Italiano per L'Architettura Razionale (M.I.A.R.) which had forty-seven members, divided into regional sectors; the exhibition was presented under the patronage of the national union of architects, and Bardi, by publishing the *Report to Mussolini on Architecture*, gave the debate a political meaning, declaring that traditionalist architecture belonged to the old bourgeois world, while the new architecture was suited to expressing the revolutionary ideas of Fascism. A declaration of the M.I.A.R., printed for the opening of the exhibition, pointed in the same direction: 'Our movement has no other moral aim than that of serving the [Fascist] Revolution in the prevailing harsh climate. We call upon Mussolini's good faith to enable us to achieve this'.[31]

The battle ended negatively on organizational grounds, because the Union withdrew its support from the show and promoted a rival one, the Raggruppamento Architetti Moderni Italiani, which exhibited to the public with a proclamation condemning both traditional eclecticism and 'the tendencies which aim to discount entirely the magnificent experience and architectural glories of the past and which, enslaved by new materials, produce utilitarian solutions which are not in keeping with our people's way of life.'[32] Most of the members of the M.I.A.R. went over to the other group and the organization broke up.

This failure was due only partly to political

and organizational reasons and could not be fully explained even in terms of the economic interests that were concealed beneath cultural matters. By declaring that the modern movement interpreted the Fascist spirit, indeed was the only movement to interpret it legitimately, and by making the 'call to order' in specifically political terms, the architects of the M.I.A.R. found themselves in an unfavourable position for arguing with those who likewise claimed allegiance with Fascism, claiming to interpret its needs through traditionalist architecture. In fact, these conflicts of ideas were masked by declaration of loyalty to the régime; the only thing left to be discussed was the actual forms, whether ancient or modern, and the traditionalists had really triumphed from the start because the argument was taking place on their cultural ground.

So the debate split into so many idle problems: decorations or smooth walls, arches and columns or pillars and architraves, vertical or horizontal lines, Nordic or Mediterranean tradition. Particularly pointless was the debate on 'rationality': the traditionalists assiduously pointed out the technical inconveniences arising from smooth plaster, the lack of cornices etc.[33] and the modernists gave evasive answers.[34]

Art criticism offered little help in clarifying these problems. The critics of the younger generation, fed on Crocian thought – G. C. Argan, R. Giolli, C. L. Ragghianti – inclined towards an artistic liberalism which led them to support the modern movement, but also prevented them from fully understanding the problems the movement raised.

Croce taught that the distinction between artistic and logical, economic and ethical values was primary and categorical, and that their joint presence in individuals and actual situations was secondary and conventional. Formerly, this teaching had given new vigour to other fields of Italian culture, helping people to recognize the specific and irreducible character of the interests proper to each field and sweeping away various types of confusion and interference between interests of different orders, but now it was mainly a hindrance to efforts for further innovation, inspiring a false sense of superiority in the face of each new tendency, which because it was assimilated into one or other of the prejudices criticized by Croce, was regarded from the start as invalidated.

In architecture Crocianism – coming as it did from a line of thought completely different to that which had led to the modern movement – actually prevented people from seeing the novelty inherent in the rationalist theses, and immobilized the efforts made in this direction by the best and most open-minded sector of Italian culture. The reasonings of Le Corbusier, for instance, or Gropius, were regarded as specious justifications, hindrances to the direct enjoyment of their works, and each was regarded preferably as an 'artist' in the old style.

Thus, because of their haste to establish themselves on the organizational level and because of the lack of any suitable response from contemporary culture, the attempts of the '7' and the M.I.A.R. faded away before they could form themselves into a real movement. From now on the best architects worked on their own or in small groups, and managed, even in the uncertain situation that had grown up, to win certain individual battles.

In 1932 P. Aschieri, G. Capponi, G. Michelucci, G. Pagano, G. Ponti and G. Rapisardi were asked by Piacentini to collaborate on the building of the new 'Città Universitaria' in Rome. Piacentini was responsible for the general plan and designed the public parts – the Propylaea and offices of the Vice Chancellor – Capponi and Ponti built two aggressively modern buildings, the Botany and Mathematics institutes, while Giovanni Michelucci (b. 1891) and above all Giuseppe Pagano (1896–1945), with the Institute of Physics, finally gave up any attempt at making a mark on the whole and

tried to escape from the general rhetorical layout. Pagano's building accepted the volumetric condition of symmetry of volume with Aschieri's Institute of Chemistry and of uniform finish in yellow clinker and travertine, and it passed almost unnoticed near Piacentini's dull blocks; only when looked at from close to could it be distinguished by the generous and varied spacing of the windows, the ingenious care taken over the distribution, the successful characterization of the rooms inside, with their standardized furniture. It was the first Italian building that could be called modern not just in intent but also because of the real novelty of the method of planning, and the actual result (Figs. 691–3).

The following year the competition for Florence station was won by the group Baroni, Berardi, Gamberini, Guarnieri, Lusanna and Michelucci. This judgment was due to a singular combination of circumstances: to the presence on the jury of Marinetti, to the disagreement between the academicians and above all to Piacentini's desire to act as arbiter between traditionalists and modernists, as in the team for the Rome Città Universitaria. But there was also a less marginal reason, which is very significant for this discussion: since the site of the station was in a very exacting position, behind the apse of S. Maria Novella, none of the traditional architects felt certain of being able to to solve the problem with the usual stylistic adulteration, and none of the judges had the courage frankly to hope for such a solution. But the plan of Michelucci and his colleagues showed that the subject could be interpreted with the necessary discretion precisely by the use of the 'rational' style (Figs. 694 and 695). The situation of the Geneva competition had been repeated with exactly the opposite result.

From 1933 onwards modern architects obtained an increasing number of commissions (already in that same year Giuseppe Samonà (b. 1898), Adalberto Libera (1903–

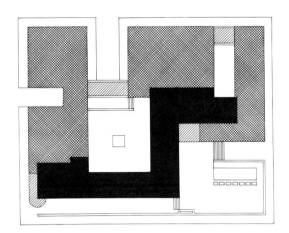

691, 692, 693 *Rome, Institute of Physics in the Città Universitaria (G. Pagano, 1932)*

63) and Mario Ridolfi (b. 1904) had won three of the four competitions for the Rome post offices; Luigi Piccinato (b. 1899) with G. Cancellotti, E. Montuori and A. Scalpelli were drawing up the plan of Sabaudia, interrupting the thread of monumentality in the design of towns for areas of reclaimed land) while many other architects who normally composed in period styles – A. Foschini, V. Morpurgo, E. Del Debbio – began to adopt simplified forms, smooth walls, full balconies and flattened cornices.

694, 695   *Florence, Railway station (Baroni, Berardi, Gamberini, Guarnieri, Lusanna, Michelucci, 1933)*

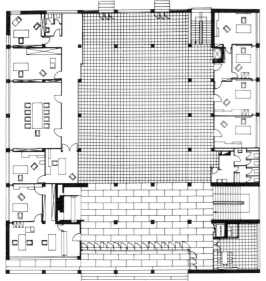

696, 697   *Como, Casa del Fascio (G. Terragni, 1934)*

In this process of outward modernization the original qualities of many traditionalist architects were lost – since these were connected with the use of period styles as parametres of composition – and since after all they gained most public commissions, the level of official building fell conspicuously.

Also, the supporters of this middle way no longer felt isolated and looked to similar experiments abroad, reassessing Fahrenkampf, Holzmeister, Böhm against Le Corbusier, Gropius and Mies.

It is interesting to note the confusion of the 'novecentisti' at this point. With the 1934 manifesto they too placed themselves in a mid-way position and defended 'the classical concept of the arts, tending to create the unity of purpose and of achievement which leads to the formation of the style of an age. This hoped-for unity is threatened by the tenacious, infectious and academic pictoricism on the one hand, and by a Calvinist rationalism on the other, which is the repudiator and destroyer of images.'[35] Despite this, they tried to keep themselves apart from Piacentini and his supporters with their simplifying tendencies, but in the end the movement broke up. Of the architects, some were attracted by the dominant taste of the time (Lancia in the offices on Piazza S. Babila

698 *Detail of the Como Casa del Fascio*

in Milan) while others were attracted by rationalism (Ponti in the Montecatini headquarters in Milan).

This general uncertainty deprived the best architects of the younger generation of the opportunity of fully exercising their talents, and the most important victim was Giuseppe Terragni (1904–42) who was certainly the most gifted. Terragni did not tend to restrict himself of his own accord, as did Pagano, and he gradually began to concentrate his forces in the only direction that still seemed to be open to him, i.e. in a dogged exploration of formal problems. The Como Casa del Fascio (Figs. 696–8) was a typical result of this effort; it was as if he had set himself to realize the polemic declaration of the M.I.A.R., modern architecture equals Fascist architecture; thus the subject became a myth, depriving the architecture of the support of a precise functional relationship. Terragni's intentions could thus become realities only in an emblematic way, in a serried and masterly interplay of volumes which nonetheless came to formalism, as Pagano did not hesitate to point out to him, reproachfully.[36]

The thinking of Edoardo Persico, in this confused situation, was the main settled point which gave support and coherence to the modern movement. As editor of *Belvedere*, then writer for and co-editor of *Casabella* from 1930 to 1936, he continually compared the Italian movement with the European one, shrewdly noting the complication and confusion of the process which had begun in Germany and France in 1933. He was one of the first to recognize the importance of Gropius, Mies and May *vis-à-vis* the more widely praised and recognized Mendelsohn and Fahrenkampf, to note the new trends of the Dutch movement,[37] the decline of Hoffmann,[38] and the real nature of the Hitlerian movement.[39]

Though his literary upbringing led him to misunderstand the reasonings of the European masters (he often attacked Le Corbusier

and Taut) Persico understood perfectly what a deep conflict of ideals lay beneath the controversy for and against the modern movement and what the real stake was: the shape of the imminent mass society, for which architects were partly responsible.

If the hardness of the times forced everyone to restrict their own action to a specific field, the vastness of what was at stake could not, however, be lost sight of; for this reason Persico ended by loading all the cultural themes in which he believed – the aim for greater justice, belief in spiritual freedom – on to the notion of 'style', which became the symbol of a general faith, beyond architecture. Stylistic consistence seemed to him a vital condition to maintain moral consistence too and the only means of handing his own convictions down to future generations, even if only symbolically:

'Today, artists must tackle the thorniest problem of Italian life: the capacity to believe in specific ideologies and the will to pursue the struggle against the claims of an "anti-modernist" majority. These demands, ignored by our perverse polemicists, constitute the ideal heritage that we shall leave to generations to come, after having frittered away our lives pointlessly on problems of style; the highest and most unavoidable problem of culture in this obscure period of the history of the world'.[40]

After Persico's death, in 1936, the political difficulties facing Italian architecture increased rapidly. Pagano still tried, with characteristic tenacity, to remain in contact with official circles, thinking that initial compromises could be compensated for by personal commitment.

In 1937, together with Piccinato, Rossi and Vietti, Pagano collaborated once again with Piacentini for the plan of the Rome Universal Exhibition, but this experiment ended very differently from that of the Città Universitaria. He thought that this time the younger

699   *Brescia, M. Piacentini's buildings in the old centre*
700, 701   *Rome, Clearance round the Augusteo (V. Ballio-Morpugno, 1937) and the church of SS. Pietro e Paolo at E 42 (A. Foschini, 1939)*

architects, since they were four out of a total of five, could run the whole affair efficiently, and thoroughly committed himself by praising the first results of the work in *Casabella*.

'As far as practical work was concerned, the authority of Piacentini, a member of the Accademia d'Italia, was immediately fused with the enthusiasm of his colleagues, and

702   *Rome, a view of E 42*

collaboration was truly effective'; Pagano also avoided being too precise about the personal contribution of each one, since this was 'a real work of collaboration, which by putting no stress at all on individual contributions, allowed the communal inspiration, the product of all and yet of none, to make itself felt.'[41]

The definitive plan of the exhibition was published contemporaneously in *Architettura* and *Casabella* in June 1937 and commented on with almost identical words:

'The architects have aimed at giving this monumental complex new and modern values, though with an ideal link with the examples of the great Italian and Roman compositions'.[42]

'This complex has been conceived with a new spirit and aim, though ideally it is linked to the example of our glorious past and particularly to the great art of Rome'.[43]

In reality the plan was the fruit of an unstable compromise. In the definitive version Piacentini's monumental concepts easily prevailed, and rhetorical and academic plans were the result of the competitions for the main buildings. Pagano was indignant, protested, published the unsuccessful plan in *Casabella*,[44] but it was probably not the outcome of the competition that concerned him so much as the fact that the unsuccessful and successful plans, by old architects and by young ones, were alarmingly alike: those of Libera, Minucci, Figini and Pollini had a few less columns, the buildings of Brasini a few more, but they all resembled one another: symmetrical, rigid ground plans, enclosed and 'Mediterranean' volumes, coverings in marble, rhythmic porticoes (Fig 702). It is also interesting to note how the youngest architects – Muratori, Quaroni, Fariello, Moretti – deprived of an effective cultural influence, moved of their own accord towards an extreme neo-classicism, which they regarded as a further transcending of the old debate between the tendencies, and which they were anxious to distinguish firmly from that of the old guard.

The compromise attempted by Pagano was thus untenable: by following 'ideal links' back to Roman times architects would arrive at one result only, neo-classical conformism; the differences of tone between Brasini's applied archaeology and Foschini's measured simplification, between the sophisticated elegance of the young Romans and the calculated rhythms of the young Milanese, which seemed important in the plans, dis-

appeared entirely in the execution. What had happened in Germany, Russia and France was repeated here too: this was the *internationale des pompiers*.[45]

During the war, Pagano's obstinate nature led him to go back to the origins of the conflict between the régime and modern architecture. He made Morris's spiritual journey all over again:

'I realized that the causes of the vulgar appearance of the present day city were deeper than I had thought, and gradually I was drawn to the conclusion that all these ills were simply the outward expression of a basic lack of moral roots, into which we had been driven by the present organization of society, and that it was pointless to try and remedy this from the outside'.[46]

For this reason after having believed in Fascism and having tried to improve it from the inside, Pagano became an anti-Fascist and, as usual, was active from a dangerously exposed position, until he was arrested, deported to Germany and died in Mauthausen in 1945.

His history was in a way the reverse of that of the *avant-garde* artists who had fretted in Paris during the First World War: these lived and died for their art, abstracting themselves from their duties as men, while Pagano forgot that he was an architect, when this was necessary, and took up his position among men, artists or non-artists, by fighting for a better world where everyone could once more practice their professions with dignity.

Why were the totalitarian régimes hostile to the modern movement and why did they finally adopt neo-classicism as their official style?

Many accusations were levelled at the modern movement, some of which were justified by the failings of the type of 'functionalism' and 'rationalism' in vogue around 1930. The new architecture was coldly utilitarian, and at the same time it obeyed preconceived formal rules; it allowed any caprice, and at the same time claimed to level out the architecture of all countries with these same canons; it did not fulfil either the utilitarian purposes or the psychological hopes of individuals and society. But the summary tone of the accusations and the facility with which one line of criticism alternated with an opposite one (too functional or not functional enough; too arbitrary or too uniform) showed that the real motive was quite different: the fear of the ideal implications which was confusedly sensed beyond the forms and conventional phrases, and which sounded a threat to the established order or at least constituted an unknown quantity, which those in power preferred not to put into circulation because they did not know how to control it.

Gropius made this conflict inevitable when he deprived artists of their privileged ivory tower position, and forced them into practical involvement with society; first political decisions were associated with artistic ones, now artistic decisions implicitly contained a political charge, even if indirect and not necessarily coinciding with the positions of the parties struggling for power.

It could not be said that the modern movement demanded a particular pattern of society, and even less so that it could actually produce it, but it was not indifferent to the type of society in which it existed, and it contained a hint, a 'prophecy' as Persico said, of a society more just and more humane than the present one. Giunta, protesting in the Chamber of Deputies about Florence station, produced the best of the many definitions of modern architecture on 20 May 1934: 'the egalitarian style'.[47] The modern movement led to the distribution of the products of art beyond the boundaries of class or group while the régimes, in so far as it was in their interest to preserve these limits, saw the modern movement as an obstacle and regarded it as inspired by their adversaries. Thus modern architecture was considered 'Bolshevik' in Geneva, Fascist by *Humanité*

and petit bourgeois in Moscow.[48]

The choice of neo-classicism was justified by a variety of arguments concerning form and content:

'The classical [wrote Giovannoni] is dignity, a serene feeling of harmony. Perhaps because of the anthropomorphism of its proportions, or because of the consciousness with which it has grown into the soul of our cities and generations, it is the point of reference for taste and public art, it is the supreme expression found by man . . . whenever he has wanted to raise himself from material contingencies to the pure expression of the life of the spirit.[49]

Soviet architecture [says Lunaciarsky] should be inspired by Greek architecture because those democracies "were favourably characterized by Marx because of the freedom and the many-sided accomplishments of the republics' citizenry." There are many reasons for the impossibility and incongruity of wholesale transplantation of the Hellenic architectural forms into the U.S.S.R. . . . but in that "cradle of civilization and art" there is much that is of value and that could serve as a guide for the development of the architecture of Russia.[50]

Classicism [wrote Speer] again regenerates the form and content of architecture, because it goes back to Greek forms, which have forced themselves upon us ever since the great Attic times'.[51]

These were the old arguments of ideological neo-classicism. But can we believe that these artists were speaking with the conviction of a David, and that the concerns of the ruling classes, in this respect, were the same as those of Jefferson?

The political régimes in power in Italy, Russia and Germany were certainly not of the same character, nor did they have the same aims; how, then, did they come to regard as desirable the same categories of forms?

Whatever the reasons, Fascism, Nazism and the Stalinist régime all needed to be able to keep close control on every aspect of national life and habits, and also to cover their frequent changes of directive with certain invariable formalities. For its part the neo-classical repertoire, well-worn by continual repetition, had lost any intrinsic ideological significance it had ever had, and was valued precisely because it had become an empty form into which any content could be poured.

By adopting columns, pediments, symmetry and the focal-point, the state authorities had at their disposal a very convenient system of rules which offered no resistance and no surprises, and which was therefore excellently suited to giving a predictable character to state building and town-planning, avoiding any conflict with official directives and their variations.

France

France did not have an authoritarian régime like that of the Nazis, Fascists or Stalin, which would have inevitably come into conflict with modern architecture; after 1934 there was a radicalization of political struggle and increasing economic unease, reflected in building production – which dropped continually, as we noted in Chapter 15 – and in the conditions of cultural debate, so that modern architects were cut off almost entirely from any opportunity of work.

But it is not possible to accept the thesis – put forward by Zevi, among others – that this crisis was caused by the intrinsic weakness of the 'rationalist' theses; the architects certainly behaved mistakenly and hesitantly, but there was also a heavy political and economic conditioning – more open in the totalitarian countries, concealed in the France of the thirties – which systematically thwarted even the best contributions, for instance that of Le Corbusier, which was already bearing fruit in many other countries.

It is also noteworthy that the most important works of Le Corbusier – the Swiss pavilion, the Cité du refuge – of André Lurçat (b. 1892) – the school at Villejuif – and those produced in the studio of Beaudouin and Lods – the Cité de la Muette – were executed between 1930 and 1933, and coincided with the moment of comparative political balance dominated by the figure of Herriot (Garnier's employer at Lyon).

At this point *avant-garde* artists even tried to form a united front. In 1929 the Union des Artistes Modernes was founded, and in 1930 the review *L'Architecture d'Aujourd'hui*.

The Union included painters, sculptors, and architects, including R. Mallet-Stevens, P. Barbe, P. Chareau, R. Herbst, F. Jourdain, and C. Perriand, and its aim was to organize an international exhibition each year; in 1931 it was joined by Le Corbusier, Bourgeois, Dudok, Gropius, in 1932 by Lurçat and Sartoris. In 1934 the Union published a manifesto with the literary collaboration of I. Cheronnet called *Pour l'art moderne, cadre de la vie contemporaine*, where accusations currently levelled at modern architecture were refuted (of being of foreign inspiration, the slave of the machine, harmful to the interests of French production, too poor and bare to give aesthetic satisfaction) and the usual futurist,[52] purist[53] and rationalist[54] arguments were employed.

L'Architecture d'Aujourd'hui, edited by A. Bloc, for the first time offered *avant-garde* artists a widespread outlet in print, something quite different from the partisan reviews which circulated among the initiated. But the habits of the French, rather than the wishes of the editors, meant that this wider circulation could take place in one way only: by showing an impartial sympathy for a variety of tendencies, from Perret to Le Corbusier, and by classing them together as formalistic variations on a single whole.

Abroad, the preference was for Austria and the countries influenced by the Viennese school.[55] During the course of the controversies, the editors did not declare their support for any existing tendency, but took refuge, predictably, in the field of first principles. When for instance the first number of *Quadrante* came out in Italy – with its declarations reminiscent of all the most intransigent tendencies of modern architecture, of Le Corbusier, Gropius, Mies – *L'Architecture d'Aujourd'hui* commented in a decidedly unfavourable way, claiming that the time of *avant-garde* tendencies was over, and that today architects should go beyond all tendencies: 'we are attempting to bring out the truth – truth in form as in spirit – by examining all contemporary architecture produced in the light of the eternal principles of architecture.'[56]

As we said before of Le Corbusier, the methods of the *avant-garde* seem second nature to the French spirit, and the positions adopted remained at all clear-cut only when the initiative came from individuals or small groups; but when the circumstances demanded any mediation between various ideas and various individuals, mediation became compromise and the positions became generic.

Furthermore the distance between the general public and the élites had now grown so much that it was not possible to carry the debate outside *avant-garde* circles, or to carry practical undertakings into the field of current production, while hoping to maintain a minimum of rigour and coherence.

In this way the most committed artists preferred to work for an élite already convinced of their own principles, or indeed for each other. Le Corbusier built houses for Ozenfant, and for Lipchitz; Lipchitz, Léger and Gris decorated Le Corbusier's houses, etc.

During the Athens congress of the C.I.A.M., in 1933, Léger expressed this unease clearly in a speech to the architects from all over the world, but to the French in particular:

'You have discovered a new raw material for architecture, which is "air and light". The ornamental materials and elements which were stifling earlier architecture, are disappearing; weight, volume, solidity are vanishing into air. The revolution has come. An élite has followed your heroic epoch. This is quite normal. You have built houses for people who were already won over to your radical formulae. We painters know this minority; our works are in the possession of various initiates scattered all over the world . . . . But your formula should expand. The word "town-planning" should dominate the aesthetic problem. Town-planning and the social conscience. You are entering a completely different world, one in which your pure, radical formulae will have to fight. Your drama is just beginning: this is the cold period, I think I can claim that there is a break, an absolute gulf, between your aesthetic conception as achieved and admitted by the minority and your conception of town-planning which is in difficulties everywhere, faced with the incomprehension of the "average man" . . . and then in this gap, in this split between these two conceptions of yours, modern architects appear, make the hoped-for concession and thus clinch the deal'.[57]

A minority of modern French architects was in fact locked in this impasse. The 'cold period' coincided, in France, with the building crisis (see graph in Fig. 595) and with an intensification of political struggle, which led the left into power from 1936 to 1938 and increased fear of all novelty among the conservatives, in the cultural field as well.

While Le Corbusier and Lurçat were almost without work, the 'new modern architects' were making progress and found success by proffering a watered-down version of the modern style or a compromise version of Perret-modern. Their works were comparable to those of Fahrenkampf and

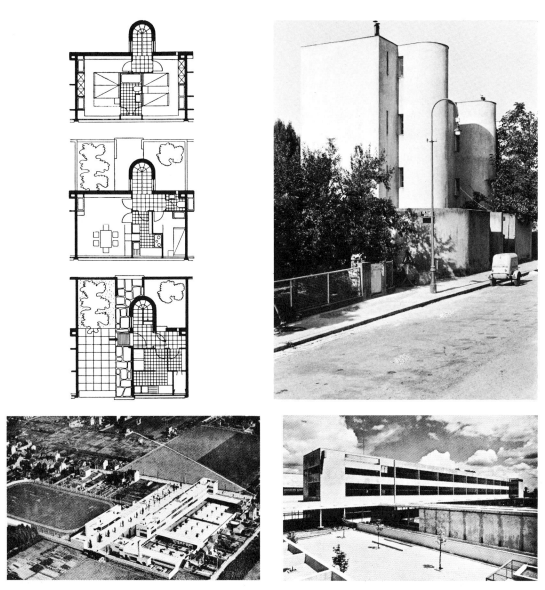

703, 704 *(above)* *Vienna, Houses by A. Lurçat at the Werkbundsiedlung, 1932*
705, 706 *(below)* *Villejuif, School by A. Lurçat, 1932 (from A. Sartoris,* op. cit.*)*

Holzmeister in Germany, but of a far lower quality; the most significant examples were to be seen in certain intensive building enterprises such as the Immobilière du parc des expositions at the Porte de Versailles (Lucas et Beaufils, 1933) or the Villeurbaine district, near Lyon (M. L. Leroux, 1934) (Figs. 707 and 708). Architects uncritically accepted the implications concerning volume which derived from the maximum exploitation of sites and the traditional expedients to make these volumes acceptable, with the attempt at partial symmetry, blunted corners etc.; whether architecture should be ancient or modern, with walls smooth or undecorated, was really a question of pure taste, so that

707, 708   *Villeurbaine, New district by M. L. Leroux (from* L'Architecture d'Aujourd'hui*) and the Town Hall by M. R. Giroux, 1934*

when M. R. Giroux, Prix de Rome, built the Villeurbaine Hotel de Ville in the neo-classical style, it fitted in in the most natural way possible.

From 1934 onwards reviews and even the general press endlessly discussed the new Universal Exposition planned for 1937; it is interesting to read the quantity of historical reminiscences about the nineteenth-century exhibitions and about the French art of the

709, 710, 711 *Paris, Museum of Public Works by Perret (1937)*

past, which did not seem to have taken any note of the change of times and the pressing new problems.

The site chosen was the Champ de Mars, with the corresponding area on the other bank of the Seine, below the Chaillot hill. While there was no question of dismantling

the Eiffel Tower, there was the problem of what to do with the Palais du Trocadéro. At first a scheme was considered to mask the exterior with new architecture, then to leave it intact and build an intermediate building at the head of the Pont de Iena to 'introduce' the old building to people coming from the

712, 713 *J.J.P. Oud, The Shell building at the Hague, 1938*

Champ de Mars, then finally to demolish Davioud's building and build a new one in its place, making use of a part of its foundations. The competitions organized for these various solutions offered traditionalists an opportunity to dream up dull and dutiful imitations of the old '*grand goût*' and all kinds of stylistic hodge-podges. In 1936 the decision to have a new building was made: J. Carlu, L. A. Boileau, and L. Azéma designed a neo-classical building 'whose sober and dignified character should be worthy of the monumental character of French art.'[58] Artists and men of letters addressed a protest to the authorities 'considering the solution adopted as a real waste of public money and a serious mistake'; signatories included J. Cocteau, F. Mauriac, H. Focillon, G. Marcel, P. Picasso, H. Matisse, G. Rouault, R. Dufy, M. Chagall, J. Lipchitz, and O. Zadkine.[59]

In 1936 the announcement of a neo-

LE PLAN

1

Nous ouvrons une rubrique permanente : « 1937 ». Nous avions, en 1924, institué déjà, au cours de douze numéros, une rubrique « 1925 : Expo. Art. Dec. Mod » (1). Ici, encore, nous nous plaçons hors de toutes personnalités et de toute polémique. Nous nous mettons au service de l'idée. Nous cherchons à servir. Nous nous abstenons de nous consacrer au cas des arts purs qui ont aujourd'hui, à leur disposition, dans le débat intellectuel, tous les moyens d'expression, d'exposition, d'attaque et de défense. Nous nous consacrons au cas poignant des centaines et des centaines de milliers d'individus qui mènent une existence morne, tragique et sans espoir dans l'indifférence cruelle d'une vie urbaine demeurée sans plan. De ce point de vue hautement social, à l'occasion de l'Exposition internationale des Arts Modernes, prévue pour 1937, nous soumettons à l'opinion publique un plan.

NOTRE PLAN :

Nous proposons un autre titre à l'exposition annoncée :

1937
EXPOSITION INTERNATIONALE
DE L'HABITATION

714 *First page of a brochure containing Le Corbusier's proposal for the Paris exhibition of 1937 (from* Oeuvre Complète*)*

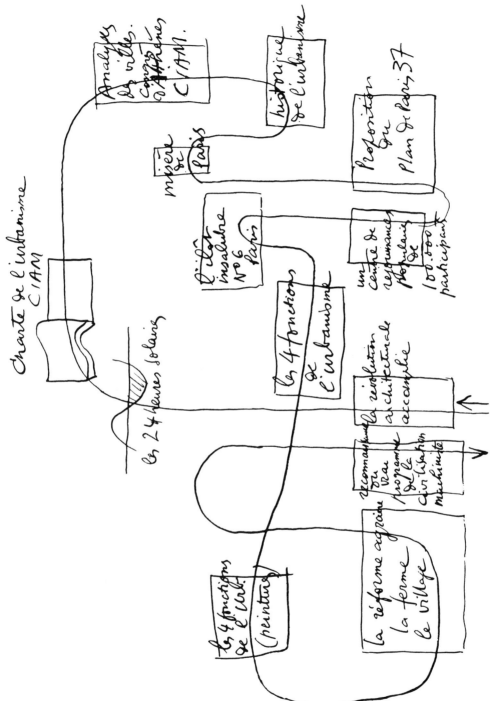

715 *Le Corbusier, Plan for the layout of the pavilion at the universal exhibition of 1937 (from Oeuvre Complète)*

716   *Paris, Museum of Modern Art (J.C. Dondel, A. Aubert, P. Viard, M. Dastuge, 1937)*
717   *Pablo Picasso,* Guernica, *painting in the Spanish pavilion at the Paris universal exhibition of 1937*

classical building still aroused a great deal of protest, but the following year works of this kind – temporary or permanent – multiplied in the French capital. Near the new Palais de Chaillot, J. C. Dondel, A. Aubert, P. Viard and M. Dastuge built the new Musée d'Art Moderne, with its dreary colonnades (Fig. 716); in the nearby Museum of Public Works Perret revealed his usual technical mastery, but now he frankly identified his round pillars with columns and his beams with cornices; within the exhibition itself Speer's German pavilion and Jofan's Russian one competed in archaeological rhetoricism; in this climate even former functionalists inclined towards the monumental, as can be seen in the pavilions of Mallet-Stevens.

This classicist regression, in fact, was by now an international phenomenon; in the same year, 1937, Oud built the Shell building at the Hague, where he went back not only to the rigid, symmetrical ground plan, but also to a decoration underlining the focal elements of the composition, as in the past.

Le Corbusier, with his usual confident energy, tried to bring up his views on this occasion as well. After having suggested in 1932 that the forthcoming exhibition should be transformed into an international exhibition of building and should be set in the Bois de Vincennes – and that advantage should be taken of this to realize the first stretch of the new east-west motorway, as means of access to the exhibition – he managed to have the fifth C.I.A.M. convened

in Paris for 1937 and arranged for the Paris authorities to make the site of the Kellermann bastion available for him, where a model unité d'habitation for 4,000 inhabitants was to be built. But when the opposition of the administrators caused the enterprise to founder at the last minute, all he could do was to concentrate on the exhibition pavilions, and he attempted to realize a first nucleus of his expandable museum near the Porte d'Italie. When this too failed, he did at last realize a pavilion to house information about modern town-planning, near the Porte Maillot, where he illustrated the principles of the *Charte d'Athènes* and presented his plans for the redevelopment of Paris.[60]

Le Corbusier clashed with not only this or that academic or political faction, but met with the 'wrath of the idiots' mentioned by Bernanos in 1937. His proposals fell on empty ears, and he found himself forced to take refuge in theory.

At the 1937 exposition Picasso's great composition illustrating the bombing of Guernica in the Spanish pavilion – one of the best, prefabricated, and with paintings by Miró and a fountain by Calder – revealed the true face of the forces which were preparing to unleash a new war, and warned educated men that it was necessary to commit themselves beyond the boundaries of their special limits, with all the others, so as to be able, later, to carry on working in their respective fields (Fig. 717).

seventeen

Progress in European architecture between 1930 and 1940

The conflict between the modern movement and the authoritarian régimes was the salient fact of the 1930s. But precisely because of the nature of the movement, the problem of the new architecture could not be reduced to a question of principle, and had to take practical shape, as a series of partial experiments and results.

In relation to the political conflict, the work of the architects who were isolating themselves to pursue specific lines of activity acquired definite value with regard to the cause for which they were fighting: symbolic rhetoric was replaced by the reality of everyday needs, the prestige requirements of power by the needs of ordinary people. This was architecture 'for the man in the tram', as Persico had said in 1932.[1]

From 1935 onwards, the radical nature of the political conflict eliminated the space vital to these experiments, which survived only marginally in Italy and in France, were completely cut out in Germany and Russia, but found fertile ground in England and the small countries of northern Europe. Beside the masters of the twenties – driven from their native countries, or kept in peripheral positions as was Le Corbusier – a new generation of planners was active, born after 1900, who were in a position to put into practice many of the theoretical proposals formulated in the previous decade.

1 The German masters in England, and the rebirth of English architecture

Of the German architects in opposition to Nazism after 1933, some reacted by accentuating their political radicalism – for instance Meyer, May and Taut; they concentrated on town-planning and found a new field of activity in Russia, where they soon came into conflict with the Stalinist régime. Others reacted in an almost diametrically opposed way, for instance Mies, who cut out all external references from his architecture and arrived at the threshold of formalism.

The activity of the former was more or less lost to posterity, because of the events described in the last chapter; Mies' work, as long as he stayed in Germany, remained closed in within itself, and bore fruit only after 1938, in Chicago, a phase to be described in a later chapter. The case of Gropius was entirely different. The former head of the Bauhaus was still remote from both these extreme positions and moved cautiously, trying primarily to make his entry into a new

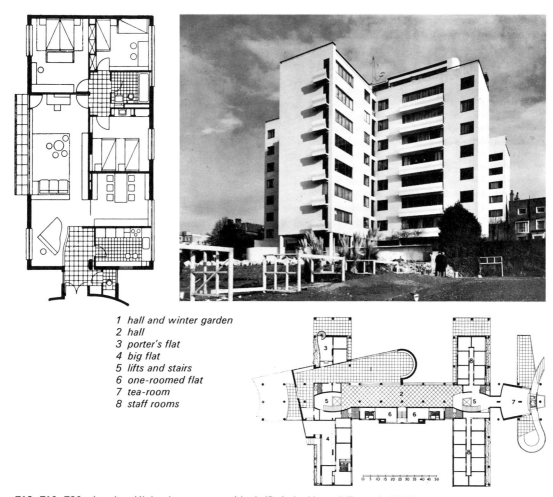

1 hall and winter garden
2 hall
3 porter's flat
4 big flat
5 lifts and stairs
6 one-roomed flat
7 tea-room
8 staff rooms

718, 719, 720   *London, Highpoint apartment block (B. Lubetkin and 'Tecton', 1933)*

professional circle; he began to associate with Edwin Maxwell-Fry and settled in England, where he was soon joined by Breuer. In England current practice was still closely linked to traditional models, but there was still a lively theoretical interest in innovations from the continent.

In 1923 Mendelsohn was presented to the English with a translation of a monograph on his sketches and actual building;[2] in 1924 the *Architectural Review* published a study on the work of Gropius;[3] in 1926 Mendelsohn's book on America was published

simultaneously in English and German;[4] in 1927 the English translation of Le Corbusier's *Vers une Architecture*[5] appeared, and in 1929 that of *Urbanisme*.[6]

Meanwhile several foreign architects had had occasion to work in England: in 1925 Behrens built a controversial villa, a solid unornamented square of masonry near Northampton. The Russian Berthold Lubetkin (b. 1901), who worked with several young Englishmen, connected with the Tecton group, built the first tall block of flats, standing in isolation in green surroundings, in 1933 – Highpoint, in Highgate (Figs. 718–20). Between 1934 and 1935 Mendelsohn collaborated with Serge Chermayeff (b. 1900), a Russian brought up in England, and built a house in Chelsea, the De La Warr pavilion at Bexhill-on-sea and a house at Chalfont St Giles.

These architects, and a handful of English designers – Cornell and Ward, J. Emberton, E. Owen Williams – introduced the modern European repertoire into England amid much controversy, but their work (with the exception of Highpoint, which contained the germ of a completely new idea for the residential house) did not move far from the wave of formalist modernism which was spreading everywhere at this time.

Gropius' contribution was less obvious, but more important in the long run. He began very cautiously in England, without attempting to impose his personality or to repeat the experiments that had been broken off in Germany, but by attempting methodically to assimilate and elaborate the characteristics of the British environment. His working relations with Edwin Maxwell-Fry (b. 1899) were closer than those of Mendelsohn with Chermayeff, both because of the superiority of his English partner and because Gropius demanded much more: not only the exploitation of certain specific opportunities but an integration of two cultural heritages, emphasizing their common themes which went back to Morris and Cole.

Maxwell-Fry describes as follows his first meeting with Gropius, at a meeting organized by the Design and Industries Association:

'I can remember exactly the overcrowded room and he standing among us, speaking with the utmost clarity in broken English of how we could mend the disunity of our machine civilization, and what moved us was the mixture of humility and authority with which he addressed us. He gave us in that moment an unexpected accession of strength and assurance. The theme was

already familiar, but not the depth of purpose with which he invested it'.[7]

In the Levy house in Chelsea and the Donaldson house in Sussex, Gropius tackled the theme, new to him, of the wealthy man's private residence, from which he excluded any idea of mass-production, while the values of intimacy and individuality were predominant.

At Impington village college (Figs. 721–2 and 724) Gropius and Fry gave thorough consideration to one of the most important aspects of the modern English city. The building, set in generous green spaces, included a completely glassed-in block of classrooms facing south-east, an assembly hall, a complex of laboratories, recreation and games rooms, set round a large space on to which the centralized services also faced. As in the Bauhaus, the architecture gave simple form to rooms performing various complementary functions, and eagerly took into account the technical and psychological leads offered by the kind of activity that was to take place in them, but the tension and concentration of the Dessau building were here replaced by tones that were more subdued and discrete. The highly articulated plan, the slight height of the buildings as compared with their length, the porticos, the slight curve of the wing containing the recreation rooms and the brick covering, fused the building with the surrounding tree-filled spaces, made it approachable and welcoming, as a building for children should be. At the same time the absolute clarity of the plan and the tremendous skill of the architect in interpreting all the functions with appropriate means, gave the building a controlled yet irrepressible energy, which extended from the school into the surrounding space and the fabric of the whole town; thus the college has tended to become the element which orders and orientates the composition of the whole town.

M. Breuer, who lived in England from

721, 722   *Impington village college (W. Gropius and E. Maxwell-Fry, 1936)*

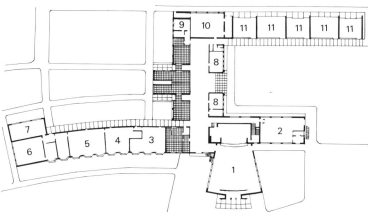

1 lecture hall
2 wood and metal workshop
3 staff common room
4 table tennis
5 billiards
6 reading room
7 library
8 entrance
9 surgery
10 laboratory
11 classrooms

723 *Isokon wooden armchair (M. Breuer, 1936)*
724 *Plan of Impington village college*

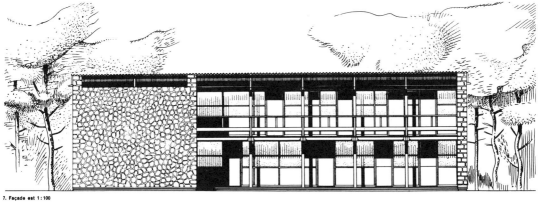

7. Façade est 1 : 100

728, 729   *Main façade of the house at Mathes (from* Oeuvre Complète*)*

2   The results of peripheral research in France and Italy

During the thirties Le Corbusier was the main protagonist in the polemics on modern architecture in France, and he was one of the first to suffer from the tightening up of the régime, which cut off modern architects from public appointments and from much private building activity.

After 1933 he designed only small buildings, for a limited clientèle, as in the 1920s; but these were not repetitions of those earlier experiments, on the contrary they were treated as opportunities to explore new constructional systems and new functional standards, in surprising anticipation of European architecture in the next decade.

As early as 1930, when he had to build a house for M. Errazuris on the Chilean coast, Le Corbusier used walls in stone and timber from barely dressed trunks: 'the rusticity of the materials in no way hinders a clear scheme and modern aesthetic from being felt'[10] and in fact the composition did not aim at any traditional effect, but gained a character of unusual solidity from these materials. In 1935 he built two country houses – on the outskirts of Paris and on the Atlantic coast – very different to one another but both making use of modest and traditional building processes. In the first the stone walls supported very low arches in reinforced concrete, covered on the outside with loam and on the inside with plywood; in the second, because of the impossibility of supervising the building directly, the construction was firmly broken up into three parts: a stone framework, joinery in wood and a series of prefabricated non load-bearing walls, consisting of wooden frames surrounding glass, plywood and asbestos-cement. Commenting on the house in Paris in the *Oeuvre Complète*, Le Corbusier notes:

'One of the serious problems of modern architecture (which in many ways has an international character) is the judicious establishing of the use of materials. In fact, together with the new architectural volumes determined by the resources of new techniques, and by a new aesthetic of forms, the intrinsic virtue of the materials can give a precise and original character to the work'.[11]

This research is connected with the idea of the *brise-soleil*, which Le Corbusier was elaborating during these years; at first this was merely a technical device, i.e., a screen against the sun's rays placed in front of the *pan de verre* in the plans for Algeria made from 1933 onwards; later it became a fairly spacious loggia – in the design for the Algiers *Cité d'affaires* of 1939 – and led to the outward projection of the structure in reinforced concrete, leaving the panel walls and windows standing underneath. This in turn led to the elimination of any finish that would alter the natural appearance of the concrete, such as resulted from the contact between it and the walls of the mould; in this way the building lost the abstract geometrical character deriving from glass and plaster, and was able to weather the marks of time and to merge with the natural countryside.

At this point Le Corbusier's *recherche patiente* diverged from that of the other French *avant-garde* artists, Lurçat, Mallet-Stevens and Chareau, who in fact were unable to contribute anything after 1933. But the work of the younger men was gaining in importance, for instance that of Eugène Beaudouin (b. 1898) and Marcel Lods (b. 1891) and it was they who represented the most advanced sector of French building production at this time.

As both were working in the 'Office public d'habitation' of the department of the Seine and for the 'Société des logements économiques pour familles nombreuses', they realized that the introduction of modern distributive concepts into the field of popular building must be achieved by a corresponding exploration of constructional matters.

In the Cité de la Muette at Drancy, built in 1933, which included several four-storey blocks and five sixteen-storey towers, the supporting framework was in metal, while the roofs and vertical non-load-bearing walls were of pre-fabricated elements in reinforced concrete; the outer coverings, the stairs, the balcony balustrades and many other details were also of concrete panels, making rigorous qualitative control possible within the pre-established economic limits, and simplifying subsequent maintenance. In this way the architecture which, when seen from a distance was aggressively dogmatic in appearance, had a convincing and realistic character when seen from close to (Figs. 730–4). A similar system of prefabrication was used in the open air school at Suresnes near Paris in 1935, skilfully laid out over the slope of a hillside.

In Italy, as we have said, modern architects attempted from the very beginning to follow the directives of the Fascist régime; as long as this attempt lasted, and looked as though it might be successful, almost all the works, even the best ones, had a doctrinaire character which distorted their appearance and which today, with the passing of time, makes them look definitely old-fashioned; this is true of the modern buildings of Rome University (with the partial exception of Pagano's Istituto di Fisica), of Florence station and the Como Casa del Fascio. In other cases the effects of political compromise were more serious: architects aimed at absurd monumental effects, there was confusion between the smooth masses of the rationalist style and the heavy masonry typical of Piacentini, as in Terragni's plan for the Palazzo del Littorio in the via dell'Impero, or in many of the rationalist plans submitted for E 42.

Only after 1936, when the illusion of occupying important public posts faded, the better architects sought more limited offers of work, and in this context produced the best works of pre-war Italian architecture:

two houses and a library in Rome, by M. Ridolfi, the buildings for the Università Bocconi in Milan, by Pagano and G. Predaval, some exhibition architecture by Franco Albini (b. 1905), the intensive housing at the mouth of the Bisagno in Genoa, by Luigi Carlo Daneri (b. 1900); the dispensary at Alessandria by Ignazio Gardella (b. 1905) (Figs. 735–42), the hangars at Orbeletto by Pier Luigi Nervi (b. 1891).

Behind each of these works lay patient and fervent personal research – for instance Ridolfi's studies on the joins of door and window frames and fitted furniture – which stopped short at a certain scale, beyond which it became pure theory: the district 'Milano verde' by Albini, Gardella, Minoletti, Pagano, Palanti, Predaval and Romano; the horizontal city by Pagano, Diotallevi and Marescotti, the Rebbio district by Terragni and Lingeri were simply didactic proposals, made with the knowledge that the possibilities of realization were very remote.

Nothing similar happened in Germany, because political control, from 1933 onwards, was so rigid as to cut off the few modern architects who remained in the country from almost every opportunity. There were very few exceptions to official conformism: two or three by R. Schwarz and J. Krahn, some of the industrial building for the Rimpl organization, and several bridges designed by Bonatz for the German autobahns.

In Russia even these exceptions were lacking, because there were no building concerns independent of public powers. Our incomplete knowledge of events prevents us from commenting on the extent of the controversies that accompanied the academic bias demanded by Stalin. In fact, there is no concrete evidence of any resistance to official directives.

3 The Low Countries

After the crisis of the German movement, the

730   *Detail of external staircase in tall building of la Muette district in Drancy*

731–734　*Drancy, Muette district (Beaudouin & Lods, 1933)*

main contributions to the progress of modern European architecture came from Holland.

In Holland, as elsewhere, there were heated controversies between the masters of the pre-war *avant-garde* and the successive generations of rationalists; in this case, between the school of Berlage and the group of neo-plasticists. But the distance between Berlage and the modern movement was undoubtedly less than that between Horta and the young Functionalists like V. Bourgeois, or in France between Perret and Le Corbusier. Dudok's experience showed that this gulf could in fact be bridged. Furthermore Berlage – like

735 *Rome, Library in via Veneto (M. Ridolfi, 1940)*
736 *Genoa, Houses at the Foce (L.C. Daneri, 1934–40)*
737 *Milan, Università Bocconi (G. Pagano and G. Predaval, 1938)*

Behrens and Poelzig in Germany – renewed his repertoire to some degree towards the end of his life, moving in the direction of recent tendencies, in so far as this was compatible with his principles.[12] His

Gemeente Museum in the Hague, left unfinished in 1934, was still based, as were the ground plans of the southern district of Amsterdam, on the linking up of two systems of symmetry, directed towards the two main

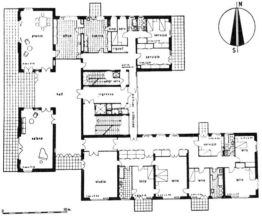

738-741 *Rome, House in via S. Valentino (M. Ridolfi, 1938; plan from* Architettura)

roads leading to the museum; but the size and limited height of the various blocks meant that this remained a mere guide-line to give order to the composition and could not easily be grasped by the observer, who saw a lively, articulated whole, skilfully set in the surrounding district. In this way

monumental implications were reduced to a minimum and the enclosed composition moved towards openness in so far as this was possible without going against the basic plan.

Of the artists of the following generation, Dudok continued his logical activity, Oud underwent the process of academic regres-

742   *Milan, Fiera campionaria 1935, I.N.A. pavilion (F. Albini)*

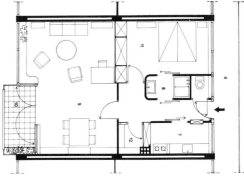

748–750   *Rotterdam, The Plaslaan (Van Tijen and Maaskant, 1938)*

productive process were rigorously analysed and faithfully expressed in the articulation of the building, including the pipes carrying the product to warehouses along the canal, which were openly set into the glass façade. The precision of the plan, rather than accentuating the oppressive effect of the industrial installations, gave them a warm, human appearance, cutting out all Romantic emphasis and any dramatic pandering to the myth of the factory's mechanism. The open form of the building also made it possible to incorporate successive additions, made necessary by the changed requirements of a modern industry without spoiling the harmony of the architecture (Fig. 744), as happened for similar reasons in Gropius' Fagus.

751   *Rotterdam, The Plaslaan*

752, 753 *Town-planning scheme for Amsterdam of 1935 and part of the execution of it (green zones in black, new districts in cross-hatching)*

After this Brinkmann and Van der Vlugt applied the same method of functional analysis to other public and industrial buildings (a silo in the port of Rotterdam, the Van Nelle buildings in Leiden, the Mees en Zoonen bank, the buildings of the Theosophical Union in Amsterdam) and many private houses; continuing along the same lines, in 1932, in collaboration with Van Tijen, they built the first high popular apartment house as conceived of by Gropius, the Bergpolder (Figs. 745–7).[13]

This building stands in a working-class district of Rotterdam, closely built up with three- or four-storey houses; the accommodation is concentrated in a ten-storey linear block, leaving much of the terrain free as a green space. The main structure is of steel, while the horizontal partitions, and door and window frames, are of wood. The apartments, all identical, for families of four, are distributed according to rigidly economical criteria. The eastern façade is balanced by the open staircase, while the rows of balconies open on to the west façade, with netting parapets and blinds. Here for the first time a lift was installed in a popular apartment; the cabin was spacious, had no doors and stopped every two floors.

This unusual building proved to have several shortcomings: the extreme elasticity of the steel structure, the difficulty of giving periodical coats of paint to extensive metal surfaces and the proximity which resulted from the continuous balconies. These faults were partly corrected in a suburban building by Van Tijen and Maaskant, the Plaslaan (Figs. 748–51) built in 1938 in a better-class district. The structure in reinforced concrete was left visible, the apartments, which varied in size and were distributed less rigidly, were each provided with a loggia that was smaller but deeper, the simplification of the exterior reduced the problem of upkeep. The area covered by the Plaslaan was less than that of the other building, but it stood in a more open site, on the edge of a lake surrounded by gardens.

According to Gropius' theory, ten-storey residential blocks were to be used mainly for the sake of certain town-planning advantages, better use of the land, a better distribution of services, economy of roads and sewers etc. These problems could not be tackled in the Bergpolder and Plaslaan, because the two blocks had been fitted into a ready-made urban context; however, the prejudices against this type of building were shown to be illogical, the use of the life had produced no problems, certain types of family had shown that they approved of this kind of accommodation, and the economic suitability of ten- or twelve-floor structures with this kind of framework was established.

Even today the contrast of the two buildings with the surrounding fabric – particularly of the Bergpolder, which stands in a district of ribbon development – is striking for its potential import in town-planning terms: it showed that another type of city was possible, where architecture could be used not only to modulate mere outer walls, but to place building masses freely in space, and where buildings came into direct relationship with empty spaces, like the Bergpolder with the field surrounding it, where children could play completely protected from road traffic.

The constructional details of the two blocks confirmed this impression, being defined with exceptional frankness and simplicity. In fact they did not count on their own, but only in relation to the composition as a whole, which rigorously defined the degree of individual importance of each one.

But meanwhile the new city did not remain a mere theoretical aim. During these same years a group of town-planners was working on the new town-planning scheme for Amsterdam, where for the first time the principles of the *Charte d'Athènes* were applied to reality, and strengthened by the architects' solid grounding in town-planning experience.

In 1928 an independent town-planning office was set up in the department of public works in the Commune of Amsterdam, run by L. S. P. Scheffer. Soon afterwards the planning of the general scheme began, directed by Van Eesteren, a former member of 'De Stijl' and a collaborator of Van Doesburg's.

The ground needed for the expansion of the city already belonged to the Commune, thanks to the far-sighted policy of compulsory acquisition of outlying areas. Since the main obstacle mentioned in the La Sarraz declaration and later documents was absent, planning could proceed in accordance with the theoretical principles which had been elaborated during the same period.[14] The main innovations of the plan with regard to earlier ones, were:

a Minute statistical enquiries, preceding decisions on the general plan and detailed plans; these made possible an estimation of the movement of the population for about fifty years, and the measures to be taken were shaped accordingly: district by district the number of houses of all sizes, the distribution of the social classes and the whereabouts of the basic services were ascertained.

b The subdivision of the suburbs into districts of about 10,000 inhabitants each, provided with the necessary amenities and separated by strips of green; each new quarter necessitated a new detailed plan, which was elaborated only when it was actually about to be realized.

c The gradual replacement of Berlage's enclosed blocks with open ones orientated from north to south, or less commonly from east to west, following the example of the German districts (Fig. 752).

The plan of Amsterdam offered a new alternative to the theory of the garden city, which had cropped up in almost every discussion on town-planning since the turn of the century. The idea of the garden city had been born as a contrast to the town, not for the reorganization of the town, and by stressing the need to articulate the fabric of the towns into self-sufficient nuclei, it placed an unfortunate emphasis on the concept of self-sufficiency, which recurs in the thought of all advocates both of the horizontal city and the vertical, like Le Corbusier.

In Amsterdam the concentration of economic and business activities around the port, amid the seventeenth-century fan-shaped centre, the high cost of land and the consideration of the bicycle as the main means of transport made the idea of development by separate centres an irrelevance. Thus the stress was not on the single districts but on their unity and interconnections, and it was shown that a city could be well run even when its density was kept high and its growth compact.

Architectural design was guided by consideration of a minute system of controls, each district was divided into lesser units and each was put into the hands of a supervising architect, whose task was to harmonize the individual plans. The supervisors made up a permanent planning committee, presided over by Van Eesteren who occupied the position of general supervisor.

The Amsterdam town-planning scheme, passed in 1935, is still in force and is continually up-dated: the validity of the experiment is proved by its ability to adapt itself to changes in circumstances, while maintaining the continuity and coherence of the initial ideal.

4 The Scandinavian countries

The modern movement arrived in the Scandinavian countries about 1930, without meeting the strong resistance it had done elsewhere; and soon afterwards, considerably before anywhere else, a revising and broadening of the international repertoire took place there, enabling it to incorporate some of the values inherited from tradition. Since these experiments were to have a widespread influence on other countries, it is important to trace the causes which worked on Scandinavian architecture in this way.

In these countries where a learned architectural tradition had always come from the outside, and been superimposed upon a modest, popular one, the passage from classical to neo-classical was not as marked as elsewhere and nineteenth-century revivals were expounded with genuine feeling.

This explains the high quality of the neo-classical architecture of G. F. Hetsch and G. Bindesboll in Denmark, of J. L. Desprez in Sweden, of G. L. Engel in Finland and C. Grosh in Norway in the first half of the nineteenth century, the mildness of the battle between classicism and medievalism and the vitality of eclecticism until the First World War and indeed afterwards.

The movement of *art nouveau* passed without leaving any real trace, or was taken up as a stimulus to the search for more unusual forms, for instance in the Danish neo-baroque movement and the early activities of Saarinen in Finland. After the war the general aspiration towards regularity once again produced an architecture disciplined by period styles, and transfigured by a persistent and excited Romantic spirit: the architecture of R. Ostberg and I. Tengbom in Sweden, C. Peterson in Denmark, M. Poulsson in Norway and J. S. Sirén in Finland.

This late eclecticism gave way with surprising suddenness to the modern movement, sometimes through the work of these same architects. Persico wrote: 'In this Olympian climate rationalism, or *funkis* as it is called in Swedish, was not a polemical attitude or a new set of dogmas, but the unwavering aspiration of a whole people towards ideal beauty, almost towards intellectual beauty.'[15]

What remains a puzzle is why the noble and illustrious models of the past should have been replaced by the more modern, and poorer, models of Functionalism as principles of beauty. To understand this one must bear in mind the social and political changes, the growth of Christian democracy and the rapid levelling out of standards of living, which led to the practical fusion of the various social classes. In the Swedish catalogue of the Paris exhibition of 1935 one reads:

'The synthesis of art and industry has different meanings in France and Sweden. While in France current habits, in the working and middle classes, are extremely stable, in the latter they are undergoing radical changes. Here the two classes are tending to draw even closer to one another. As far as the working class is concerned, this appears in a noticeable rise in the standard of living while, at the same time, the bourgeoisie has felt its economic situation becoming less advantageous . . . . While an impartial observer gets the impression that in France, for instance, the new developments in the domestic arts depend economically and morally on the upper classes in the large towns, he will observe that in Sweden this development is the work of the intellectuals and middle classes and the upper strata of the working classes. This means that the decorative arts in Sweden are unconsciously regulated by the needs of these two classes, and have not had an opportunity to develop in the direction of luxury production. On the one hand the improvement of the standard of working-class life and its lively concern with intellectual needs made it possible to improve articles of current use and to produce them at less cost; on the other hand, these two cases have necessitated the standardization of utensils and houses. Considerable and, we believe, successful work has been done since the war on the standardization of economic family dwellings and furniture. In this way one can feel the close link which joins economic

754, 755, 756 *E.G. Asplund, Detail of the Stockholm library (1927), one of the pavilions at the Stockholm exhibition of 1930 (from Sartoris,* op. cit.*) and the extension of the Göteborg Law Courts (1934–7)*

757   *Stockholm, The crematorium in the southern cemetery (E.G. Asplund, 1939)*

and aesthetic needs, since both have simplicity as their ideal'.[16]

The aims of Functionalism were precisely the new ideals well-suited to mass-production and the changed structure of the market. The relative continuity of the process of social change made it possible to spread the habits and aims of the old ruling classes throughout vast sectors of the population; modern architecture was thus the direct heir of the old Romantic inspiration, the love for a rich and fanciful outward appearance, for traditional materials, for quiet, picturesque surroundings.

Therefore, while the support of Scandinavian architects for the modern movement was motivated by precise social demands, conditions did exist which made it possible to broaden the international repertoire, retaining some of the values of traditional architecture.

Scandinavian architecture embarked on this road about 1933, just when in Germany and the rest of Europe rationalist ideas were meeting with the first strong resistance. However, it would be unwise to draw any direct parallel between the two facts, and to claim that this tendency was the right solution for the difficulties which were emerging elsewhere.

It is necessary in fact to bear in mind that the European crisis was due to the inadequacy of methods of cultural control regarding the timing and scale of economic and political processes under way. The Scandinavian countries and small nations in general escaped this conflict largely because their social changes were less rapid and less extensive.

For this reason the inspiring results of Scandinavian architecture could rarely be utilized profitably elsewhere, especially where the scale of the problems was greater and where greater disparities between groups and classes had to be overcome.

In Sweden the theses of the modern movement were at first polemically introduced by

a group of young architects: S. Markelius who built a much-talked-of house for himself in 1928 and the Hälsingborg concert hall in 1932, U. Ahren who built the Ford factory in 1929 and P. Hedquist who built the Eskilstuna indoor swimming pool in 1931. This work aroused the usual reactions from the public and the masters of the Romantic school, such as Ostberg.

Controversy died down when custom softened the raw novelty of the bare forms of Markelius and others and allowed the subtle references to tradition to re-emerge; in fact they had never been completely lacking, not even in those works that were closest to the international tone, and their reappearance was particularly marked when one of the masters of the Romantic school, Erik Gunnar Asplund (1885–1940) went over to the modern movement.

In the earlier part of his activity Asplund had been inspired by a chaste neo-classicism which became increasingly reticent, concentrating stylistic allusions into a few highly refined details (Fig. 754) and simplifying the volumes of his buildings proportionately. When appointed to design the pavilions of the Stockholm exhibition in 1930, he frankly accepted the international repertoire and invested the geometry of pillars, panels, tie-beams and curtains with an exceptional elegance, which shines forth even from the faded photographs of this ephemeral decor (Fig. 755).

In his later activity Asplund managed to keep faith with tradition, while remaining in contact with the international movement; in this way he gave form to certain recurrent facts of Swedish culture in such a way as to make them lose their local limitations and so as to make a valuable contribution, however peripheral, to the modern movement.

The studies for the extension of the law courts of Göteborg were begun in the immediate post-war period but fortunately the work was not actually built before 1937; in fact Asplund rejected various solutions in

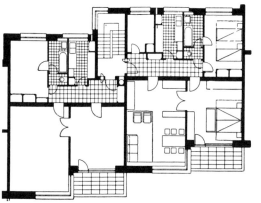

758, 759, 760   *Copenhagen, Bellavista housing estate (A. Jacobsen, 1934)*

period styles one after the other and had the new wing built in a decidedly modern style. Standing at the side of a small neo-classical building and looking on to an old square, the building fitted perfectly into its surroundings: it was centred around a covered courtyard, which communicated with the old open one by means of a glass door and

included it in a vast articulated composition, where the communicating spaces of the whole organism could be taken in simultaneously. But from the exterior the whole new block appeared as ancillary to the old and accepted its main graphic features (Fig. 756).

This was the first example of a modern

building being introduced into an old setting without intentionally and polemically breaking its unity, indeed intentionally respecting its continuity. The success of the experiment was assured by the consummate skill of the old architect, but this intention was soon to exert a widespread influence and this building became the model for many others built in the old quarters of European cities, particularly after the damage caused by the Second World War.

The Danish movement was influenced by the Swedish one. Here too, in a mood dominated by a bland neo-classicism, there was a short period of controversy aroused by the review *Kritisk Revy* which came out between 1926 and 1928 in support of an orthodox rationalism.

Of the young architects, the most important was Arne Jacobsen (1902-71) who with F. Lassen, was the author of a 'house of the future' which won a prize at an exhibition of the Akademisk Arkitektforening of 1929. Jacobsen alternated buildings in the traditional spirit (the Steensen house, 1932) with others which were strictly rationalist (the Rothenborg house, 1931) until in 1934 he created a work of surprising originality: the Bellavista housing estate in a seaside resort to the north of Copenhagen (Figs. 758–60).

Jacobsen had worked on a complete plan for this area as early as 1932, to include a restaurant, a theatre – built in 1935 – and a panoramic tower, never built because it would have interfered with the general countryside. While each of these buildings constituted an independent episode, in each of them – particularly in the residential complex – the single elements are fused with extraordinary skill. The brilliant staggered layout, the gradation of the number of floors, the shape of the terminal elements concealed the uniformity of the building types and made it possible for the building to merge with the woody countryside and the presence of the sea without the architect having to have recourse to traditional disguises.

Here for the first time Jacobsen achieved a result which was to be typical of his production: the rigid and enclosed composition of the elements was compensated for by careful chromatic control, which was largely responsible for the compositional unity of the whole and for its merging with the countryside. In this case, notable features are the perfect combination of light and shade between the 'fenêtres en longueur' and the solid balconies, which tempers the staggered effect of the actual building, and the placing of glass screens in the continuation of the masonry planes, which extends the tense interplay of masses into the surrounding space. Like Aalto in Finland, but by subtler and more rigorous means, Jacobsen here shows that the international style makes possible a range of effects wide enough to fulfil every need, even those of the picturesque and the *charme* dear to Nordic tradition.

Jacobsen's later activity was strongly influenced by Asplund and by the new course of Swedish architecture; in 1939 with E. Moller, he won the competition for the new town hall of Aarhus, which was plainly reminiscent of the similar building in Göteborg, completed two years earlier (Figs. 761–2). The economic difficulties caused by the war and disagreements with those commissioning the building endangered the coherence of the work at the planning stage; here too, the unity of the composition depended largely on the unerring harmony of light and shade, particularly from the outside where the concrete, grey stone facing and white paint of the door and window frames had an almost monochrome effect. These difficulties were more successfully overcome in the later town hall of Sollerod, completed in 1942, and the most balanced result of the first part of Jacobsen's activity; then the German occupation forced him to emigrate to Sweden, where he remained until the end of the war.

In the immediate post-war period Finland lost her greatest architect, Eliel Saarinen

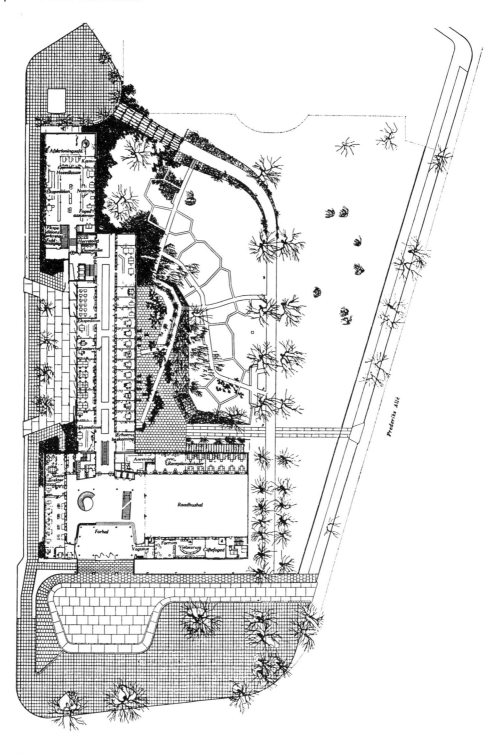

761   *Aarhus, Plan of the Town Hall (A. Jacobsen and E. Moller, 1939; from J. Pedersen, A.J., 1957)*

762   *Aarhus, Town Hall*

(1873–1950), who settled in America in 1923. Immediately afterwards there was the usual controversy with regard to the introduction of rationalism, but the course of events was dominated by the exceptional personality of their protagonist, Alvar Aalto (b. 1898).

Aalto entered the profession at Turku, about 1925; he was soon known in Finland and abroad for his building for the newspaper *Turun Sanomat*, built between 1928 and 1930 in correct and rigorous international forms; in 1929 he took part in the second congress of the C.I.A.M., in Frankfurt; soon afterwards he won first prize in the competition for the Paimio Sanatorium and created his first masterpiece (Figs. 763–9).

The elements were the usual ones: plastered walls, dark base, continuous horizontal windows, identical and rhythmically repeated bedrooms, but they took on a new meaning with the brilliant angle of rotation of the various buildings and the obliquity of the angles of juncture, used to attenuate the geometrical stiffness of the volumes and to link them with the countryside. In the first modern buildings the constancy of the right angle served mainly to generalize the compositional process by instituting *a priori* a geometrical relationship between all the elements, which meant that all conflicts could be resolved geometrically, with the balancing of lines, surfaces and volumes. The use of the oblique pointed the way towards a contrary process, that of making the forms more individual and precise, allowing imbalance and tension to exist and to be balanced by the physical consistency of the elements and surroundings. Such architecture lost in didactic rigour but gained in warmth, richness and feeling, and ultimately extended its field of action, because the process of individualization was based on the already recognized generalizing method and indeed presupposed it.

In marked anticipation of the whole European movement, this building expressed a tendency which five or six years later was felt in many places, and indeed in Gropius' work from the time he came to England.

In the Viipuri library (1932–5) (Figs. 771–3) Aalto tackled another complicated distributive organism and resolved it in an equally original way, continually varying the size and heights of the rooms and inter-connecting them with all the glee of a man solving a puzzle (here the constant use of the right-angle was indispensable for the achieving of so taut a system of linkages). The rooms were enlivened by the variety of their detailed finish, always most elegant: the undulating wooden ceiling of the lecture room, the frame-like structure for opening the main door, the great moulded wooden handrail along the stairs, the circular openings for the lighting in the reading room. At this time Aalto was also making his own furniture in curved plywood, where the static characteristics of the piece of wood were utilized to eliminate the usual framework (Fig. 770); often he also worked on the furnishing of his buildings, from the Paimio sanatorium onwards.

It was perhaps in domestic building that Aalto's architecture attained its most assured results; in 1937 he built his own house in Helsinki, in 1938 a large house for the industrialist Gullischen, known as Mairea, and some working-class districts. The organisms were geometrically simple and relaxed but enlivened by the variety of the finishing touches, by the materials, often used in contrast to one another, by the disparity in level and by the extraordinary harmony between architecture and décor. Often he attempted partial breaks with the orthogonal texture of the building by means of obliquely placed accessories – in Mairea, for instance, the wide-wall of the kitchen adjacent with the office or the wall between the living room and the hall. The control of so complex a layout was not always easy, even for someone as skilled as Aalto, and often he did not attempt to solve a compositional difficulty but left it visible, simply juxtaposing

  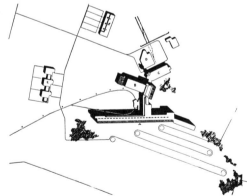

763, 764, 765   *Paimio, The Sanatorium (A. Aalto, 1929–31)*

heterogeneous elements, with effects of extraordinary directness.

Unlike other modern masters, Aalto was not concerned about justifying work with technical discussions, and indeed he did not write willingly at all.[17] Almost always his

incomparable talent makes up for incomplete rational control, but sometimes this tendency exposed sudden weaknesses, particularly when he happened to be working in the face of problems of another scale.

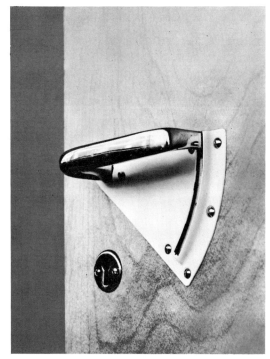

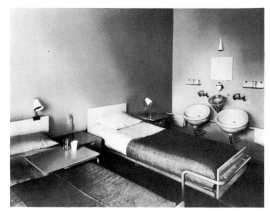

766–769   *Paimio, Details of Aalto's sanatorium*

8   Switzerland

The spread of the modern movement to Switzerland was due mainly to the presence and teaching activity there of an old master, Karl Moser (1860–1936).

He had studied in Paris and settled in Karlsruhe in 1888, where he went into partnership with R. Curjel; from 1915 he was in Zurich, a professor at the University, and as a result of his teaching, a group of young architects came into being there: his son Werner M. Moser (b. 1896), the brothers Emil (b. 1893) and Alfred Roth (1903), Max Ernst Haefeli (b. 1901), Carl Hubacher (b. 1897), and Rudolf Steiger (b. 1900). Almost all of these, after having studied at the University of Zurich, completed their education abroad: W. M. Moser in Holland

and America with Frank Lloyd Wright, A. Roth in Paris with Le Corbusier (working on the two Stuttgart houses in 1927) and then in Sweden, Haefeli in Berlin with O. Bartnung, Steiger in Belgium and Germany. In 1930 they came together again in Zurich and were asked to build a model residential district for the Swiss Werkbund, together with P. Artaria and H. Schmidt of Basel; this was the origin of the Neubühl, where the views elaborated at Frankfurt and Brussels on popular building were consistently applied; the concept of one-family dwellings grouped in terrace houses was implemented more perfectly here than in any other district built before that time (Figs. 774–7).

The Neubühl was situated on undulating ground forming a sort of promontory facing north, with two abutting slopes facing east and west; the rows of houses ran downwards over the slopes, so that the houses were arranged in tiers, breaking up the uniformity of the blocks; the ground plan was relatively simple while the types of building were designed with great care; the perfection of the details gave the dwellings intimacy and precision, and the repetition of the types did not produce monotony, since it was quite plainly made up for by the high standard of finish in each one.

Until 1933 the modern movement in Switzerland was closely linked with that of Germany (in fact the Swiss Werkbund was a section of the German one); but when the Nazis came to power this link was broken, and the Swiss movement became more independent. In the subsequent works of Haefeli (the country houses at Goldbach of 1931–4) of Roth (the houses at Doldertal built in 1936 for S. Giedion, with M. Breuer) and in the joint works of Moser, Haefeli and Steiger after 1937, the architectural tone was always firmly based on technological necessity, which meant that it could absorb many different contributions without succumbing to the stylistic confusion which affected

France, Italy and Germany at this time.

At this period the works of Robert Maillart (1872–1940) were held very much in regard. In many ways Maillart's position was similar to that of the great nineteenth-century pioneers in iron and reinforced concrete (Eiffel, Hennebique) or to that of his contemporary Perret, for whom architecture was closely linked with technical processes; if anything Maillart seemed to have fewer architectural ambitions than Perret and emerged almost as a pure technician and calculator, often planning the structures of other people's buildings. But he was unique in that his works were not only technically correct but also endowed with absolute stylistic severity which extended to the final details and accessories, in fact his involvement as a technician was so intense that it amounted to total architectural involvement.

Maillart began his independent activity in 1902 and, like Perret, was both a designer and a contractor. Reflecting on the construction of bridges in reinforced concrete he observed that the various parts, the supporting arch, the platform supporting the trafficway and the linking elements, were usually conceived as being separate and superimposed, a lazy piece of reasoning made in the past for bridges in masonry. But since the main feature of buildings in reinforced concrete was continuity between the elements, he realized that it would be more economical to consider arch, linking elements and road surface as a single system.

In 1938 he explained his reasoning as follows:

'Here for the most part the arch, derived from the masonry form, is still the main feature: whether it be reduced into flanges or hollowed out into flanges it remains basically the same. Upon this, steel or wood structures are "set up" and it is always preferable to reinforced concrete columns dressed to resemble masonry walls.

770 *Armchair in plywood,
made by Aalto for Artek*
771–773 *Viipuri, The library (A. Aalto,
1932; plans from A. Roth, op. cit.)*

Ground floor
1   *entrance*
2   *double door*
3   *hall*
4   *cloakroom*
5   *kitchen*
6   *lecture room*
7   *entrance to reading room*
8   *stairs to lending section*
9   *stores*

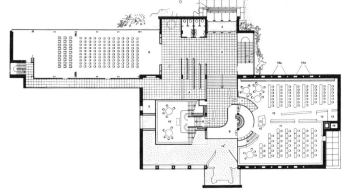

10 control desk
11 reading room
12 periodicals room
13 private rooms
14 children's reading room
15 Swedish and foreign literature

First floor
16 lending section
17 control
18 wastepaper basket
19 air conditioning
20 research room
21 ladies' lavatory
22 staff room
23 head librarian
24 store
25 rest rooms
26 binding shop
27 terrace

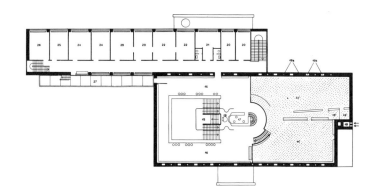

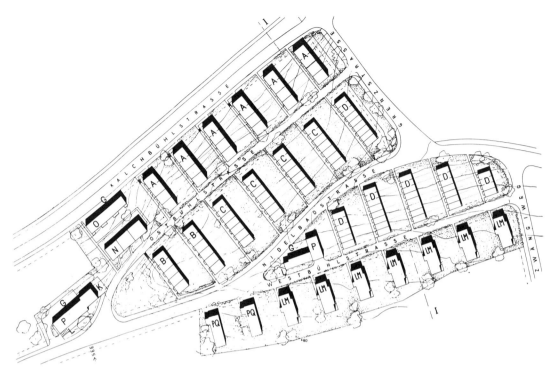

774, 775   *Zurich, Neubühl district (P. Artaria, M. E. Haefeli, C. Hubacher, W. M. Moser, E. Roth, H. Schmidt, R. Steiger, 1930)*

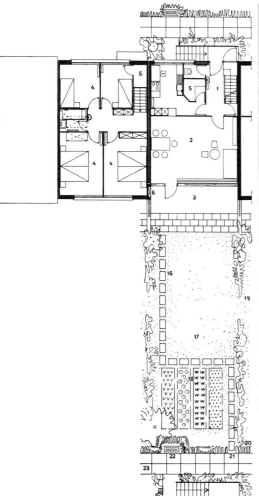

1   entrance
2   living room
3   portico
4   bedrooms
5   box room
6   garden equipment
16 path of cement slabs
17 grass
18 kitchen garden
19 small bushes
20 hedge
21 garden entrance
22 footpath

776, 777 *Zurich, A view and one of the building types of the Neubühl (from A. Roth,* op. cit.)

The traffic way rests on pillars and columns. It is known from numerous experiments that the most exact calculations for the design of the arch no longer prove to be correct, and because the stresses occurring in the arch are smaller, one is satisfied without further investigation that this over-estimation corresponds to the increased loading of the superstructure.

These heterogeneous structures assembled from forms stolen from the language of older materials cannot possibly give any aesthetic satisfaction. They are also less economical than any type of structure between and above the abutments, that is co-ordinated as a whole, and is constructed in the most practical and appropriate way. Only then can a clear construction evolve with the minimum waste of material.

The engineer should then free himself from the forms dictated by the tradition of the older building materials, so that in complete freedom and by conceiving the problem as a whole, it would be possible to use the material to its ultimate. Perhaps then we should also arrive at a new style as in automobile and aircraft construction, as beautiful, and in the same way determined by the structure of the material. Then perhaps taste will begin

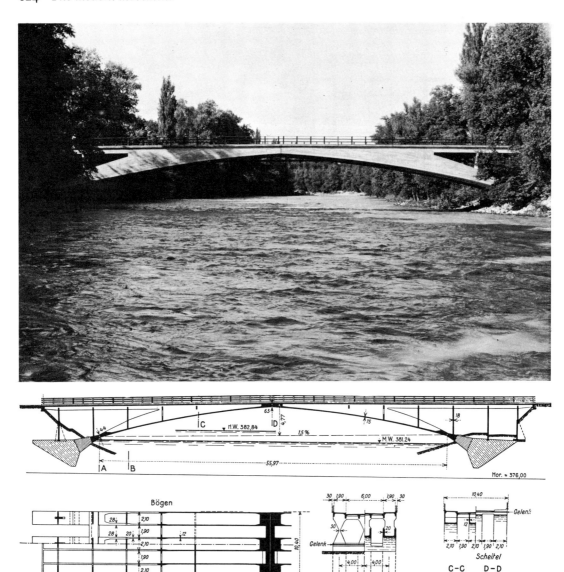

Bögen

Gelenk

Kämpfer

Scheitel

C – C   D – D

778–779   *Geneva, Bridge over the Arve (R. Maillart, 1936; drawings from M. Bill, R. M., 1949)*

to be rectified, so that the public judge the traditional form of reinforced concrete bridges in the same way as they judge the automobiles of the turn of the century, whose prototype was still the horse-drawn carriage'.[18]

This reasoning was at the origin of the box-section bridge, over the Inn near Zuoz in the Engadine; Maillart won several contracts with this system and built various important works, for instance the bridge over the Rhine at Tavanas, in 1905.

780–781   *Geneva, Bridge over the Arve (R. Maillart, 1936; drawings from M. Bill, R.M., 1949)*

Similarly, he noticed that the structure of reinforced concrete ceilings was conceived of along the same lines as wooden structures, by considering pillars, beams and the actual ceilings themselves as independent and super-imposed elements, each to be calculated separately. Reflecting on the possibility of regarding this structure too as a continuous whole he managed, in 1908, after a long series of experiments, to patent his mushroom ceiling, applied for the first time to a ceiling in a Zurich warehouse in 1910. In 1912 he settled in Russia, where he was caught by the revolution and lost his possessions. In 1919 he went back to Geneva and opened an engineering office; his system of planning and calculation, moving ever further from current concepts, aroused the suspicions of his clients and he had to be content, particularly at first, with minor works, often in remote Alpine valleys.

His first work of some importance was the bridge over the Salgina near Schiers, of 1929; then followed the bridge on the Rossgraben near Schwarzenburg of 1931, over the Thur near Felsegg of 1933 and over the Arve near Geneva of 1936 (Figs. 778–81). This last was made up of three identical box arches – enabling the same mould to be used three times – while the roadway at the two abutments was held up by special supports formed of double centrally-articulated triangles.

The device of the concrete slabs was visually so tense, and also logical, that it led Giedion to compare Maillart's structures with the products of contemporary abstract art. Formal comparisons are naturally inconclusive, but there was a similarity in method: like the painters, Maillart gave up the idea of subordinating his processes to the traditional canons of perspective, and virtually put paid to the old association between engineering and classicism.

The science of constructions and current practice had remained firmly though unconsciously faithful to the classical assumptions of symmetry and gradation, and calculations too had developed according to the same criteria. In this way the structures took form according to a previous conditioning of perspective and revealed a basic propensity towards certain classical models, as can be seen in Perret and many great modern builders, not excluding P. L. Nervi and F. Candela. This fact was currently interpreted by the postulating of the existence of certain natural laws, valid in the scientific and technical field as in the aesthetic one, while it could be shown that the association between classicism and engineering was above all a legacy from the past, which had gradually become a habit and was therefore all the more tenacious.

Maillart's merit was to break this parallelism decisively for the first time and to tackle problems of statics without preconceived notions; he was thus in a position to resolve certain concrete problems with absolute faithfulness to particular conditions, orientating his works from the start so as to take account of the particular nature of the subject, even if this led him towards solutions which were judged as 'irregular'. In this context two bridges in particular are significant, the bridge over the Schwandbach of 1933, which follows the elliptical movement of the road, and that over the Engstligen of 1931, which crosses the river diagonally, and has two twin arched ribs – staggered – so that the linking elements are all inclined in a different way.

The year of Maillart's death, 1940, A. Roth published a book entitled *La nouvelle architecture présentée en 20 exemples* (with texts in French, English and German) which appeared to be purely documentary in character, since it illustrated analytically certain little known buildings of the decade 1930–40, but the method of exposition and the choice of examples offered a clue as to the views of its author and was a fair guide to the situation of the modern movement on the eve of the Second World War. In the preface Roth wrote:

'This book is a contribution towards establishing the present state of the development of the New Architecture. Its intention is to be able to test from the numerous practical results of different countries its general validity, and to gain an outlook into possible future developments . . . .

The meaning and purpose of the book require a clearly determined method of research. Consequently only finished buildings will be considered . . . . The first object was to make a suitable selection of examples characteristic and informative in their problems and practical execution for the present state of the New Architecture.[19]

The selected examples show that the New Architecture has made the greatest advances in the small countries of Finland, Holland, Sweden and Switzerland. The explanation is partly to be found in the unanimity of certain principles, of which the possibility of the free development of the individual and of society stands in the foreground. In addition, the social, economic and political equilibrium of these countries is comparatively stable. At the same time they can profit by highly developed techniques. Although architecture owes its renewal only in a slight degree to the small states, it being due rather to the big intellectual centres of Vienna, Berlin and Paris, it has found favourable premises for its development in these small countries. To this must be added a not unimportant factor, viz. the lack of a big historical and architectural tradition such as exists with the big nations and hampers the advance of the new endeavours. Italy, however, forms the exception; she is beginning to loosen the bonds of tradition by her strong consciousness of reality. Hence it is the task of the small states to bear the New

Architecture far into the future till the big nations are in a position to perform their own great tasks on the basis of experiences gathered elsewhere'.[20]

The arguments used to define the new architecture and to defend it from its detractors were the usual well known ones, but put forward with unusual clarity and with a precise sense of the historical exactness of the problems:

'Frankness and imagination form the source of living architectural wealth. The honesty with which all questions are treated is expressed in the clear spatial structure, the clear constructive execution and the proper application of the materials. Spatial and constructive clarity are the immediate premises for the beauty of the building'.[21]

The work also contains very interesting considerations on tradition and on history, where the rationalist controversy appears truly resolved:

'The renewal of architecture at the turn of the century started with a superstructure doomed to destruction from the outset, of the most varied styles of architecture, thus representing a break in the continuity of stylistic tradition. A living tradition can only come into being if an epoch nearing its end hands over certain worked out knowledge to its successor, and this successor makes this inheritance the foundation for its own further development. At that time these premises were no longer present. In addition, this important historical event coincided with a number of known occurrences lying outside of architecture. Apart from the enormous innovations in techniques and the change in social conditions, the awakening of the consciousness of one's own time stands in the foreground. The New Architecture in its present form is the immediate and clear expression of the expanded consciousness of the times we live in. The task of living history can only be to arouse in mankind a sense of the present to be created and not for the already completed past.

History will thus become an indispensable element of practical life in as far as it contributes to affirm and extend the consciousness of one's own time'.[22]

eighteen

Modern architecture in America

Discussions of modern architecture in America are hampered by a pointless controversy about the European or American origins of the movement, which must be dealt with first of all.

When tracing the history of architectural forms one can come to two contradictory conclusions: if one looks at the basic repertoire one can say that American architecture is basically dependent upon European, since the stylistic elements utilized in the various periods have usually been imported from Europe; if one looks at the character of the forms and the intentions with which they are used, one can say that American architecture is basically autonomous, because from the very beginning European contributions were interpreted in an original manner.

The modern movement shifted the terms of the problem, because it aimed at a general method, which went from Owen to Ruskin, Morris, Van de Velde and Gropius; however, one could rightly say that the modern movement was born in Europe – even, to be more exact still, in Weimar Germany – just as the Renaissance is said to have been born in Tuscany because its underlying principles were formulated there for the first time by a group of Florentine artists in the second decade of the fifteenth century. But just as these principles made possible a large number of different experiments, and the confines of the movement broadened beyond the initial formulations, so the contribution of the European masters was not limited to the place and circumstances of its origins, but on the contrary allowed European culture to shed some of its historical limitations and to open itself towards an international movement.

The result of this process was not therefore a superimposition nor a contamination of European with American culture, but the clarifying of specifically American experiences and problems in an international setting.

We have already noted the strange contrast between the dynamism of the American scene – where many of the consequences of industrialism in building came to light earlier than elsewhere, and were tackled with great open-mindedness – and the persistence of certain initial conventions, all the more tenacious because they were not seen as conventions, but accepted as facts.

The tone of H. Greenough, when arguing in favour of a new architecture in conformity with the dictates of reason, was much more like that of Durand or Ledoux than that of

782–785   *New York, Examples of pre-war building (from J. Gréber,* L'Architecture aux États Unis, *1920)*

his contemporaries Cole and Ruskin. He used abstract concepts such as nature, function and beauty with an eighteenth-century confidence and never seemed to wonder what problems or difficulties lay behind each one.

The influence of Ruskin, which was very great in the United States, was mainly that of partial aspects of his work – his medievalism and his anti-classicism, i.e., the external results – while the facet that was seized upon by Morris in Europe was ignored. Even now, as in Jefferson's time, Americans do not import problems but solutions, which they

786 *New York, Detail of the Telegraph building on Broadway*

787　*New York, Detail of the Equitable building*

788 *New York, Daily News building (R. Hood and J. Mead Howells, 1930)*
789 *Philadelphia, Savings Fund Society building (G. Howe and W. Lescaze, 1932)*

adapt to their own needs in a precarious way.

Thus between the nineteenth and twentieth centuries, when the problem of centralized control of building production arose – because the scale of economic and social processes was growing, and demanding commensurate planning – while in Europe the rebirth of architectural culture was beginning, the Americans were not able to apply any rules other than the ready-made ones of the historical styles and fell back upon eclecticism.

The attempts of the *avant-garde* did not survive the particular circumstances in which they were born, and they were cut short by this last wave of conformism; the Chicago school lost its distinctive physiognomy after the exposition of 1893 and the legacy of the Californian school was dispersed in the same way, after the San Diego exposition of 1915.

On the other hand American eclecticism was endowed with singular coherence and its results were often valuable, at least as long as confidence in the stylistic rules was still fairly widespread. Just as Richardson's neo-romanesque was partly superior to the European models from which it derived, so the neo-classicism of Mackim, Mead and White or the neo-gothicism of R. Hood had a rigour and breadth greater than those of similar European experiments.

The Frenchman Gréber, who worked in America during the first years of the century, was amazed at the 'over absolute application that American pupils have made of the classical principles they learned in Paris',[1] at 'the desire for perfection that American architects have always shown in the conception and execution of every tiny detail of their works'[2] and concluded:

'After one has lived only a few months in the United States, if one chooses to open one's eyes, one is struck by the qualities of order, logic and clarity in the plans, the purity in the study of the details (sometimes copied a little too closely from the classical examples of the past) and . . . one is really amazed by the perfection that the Americans almost always achieve along these lines'.[3]

Le Corbusier, visiting America in 1936, wrote:

'The skyscrapers of Wall Street – the older of them – repeat from top to bottom the superimposed orders of Bramante, with a terseness in the form and modulation that enchant me. Here there is an acquired perfection . . . that is typically American'.[4] (Figs. 782 and 784)

This perfection faded, obviously, in the face of the increasing demands of modern life, just as – for similar reasons – the regularity of the chess-board system of town-planning was blurred, though hitherto it had proved capable of coping in an orderly way with changing demands of American cities for over a century.

The change took place about 1930 and coincided, not by chance, with the economic circumstances, when it was realized that the formal rules of liberalism were no longer adequate to tackle the problems of contemporary society, which were more widespread and more complex.

At this point the modern movement made its contribution felt. The American economic crisis coincided with the European political crisis and many first-rate artists moved from Europe to the United States. But the penetration of the modern movement into America was neither easy nor continuous; often the international style was received just as another European style and the Americans imitated the new models just as their ancestors had imitated those of the Parisian *beaux-arts*, or else they expostulated against it, countering it with a specifically American style and tradition.

Nothing could be more idle than these arguments as to what was American and what was European. From the first European masters were concerned to overcome social and national peculiarities and to establish a general plane or culture in which local traditions should not be abolished, but should be determined afresh. America in her turn offered far more than a clear-cut tradition: she offered a vast, composite setting, where many races and traditions coexisted and where real international discussion could be born, far from the narrow European confines.

We shall not therefore draw any preconceived distinction between European and American architects, and we shall try to give a coherent picture of architecture in the United States between the First World War and the present day. The picture will necessarily be partial, because the U.S. is a whole continent and it is almost impossible to make statements that would be valid for all American building production; whole sectors of this production are still unexplored, and it would be impossible to fill this gap in a general work like this one.

By describing American experiments after the Second World War before describing European experiments, we hope that the European reader will become aware of the reversal of the relations between Europe and America. Today American architecture acts rather as a precedent for European, and one cannot understand the directions taken by European building without first having some idea of its models from the other side of the Atlantic.

1 The Roaring Years

During the period of prosperity between the First World War and the crisis of 1929, building production was very intense and the American cities changed a great deal; meanwhile architectural thought had stopped short at eclecticism and architects used the norms of the historical styles to give order, at least external order, to this feverish activity.

There were two main changes, apparently contradictory: the further concentration of business activities in the centres of the cities and the extending of the residential quarters into the suburbs, because of the spread of the motor-car as an individual means of transport.

In the business centres skyscrapers proliferated; these buildings were derived from the old commercial building types (whose history we traced in Chicago during the last decades of the nineteenth century) with an increase in size and a subjection to a more rigid stylistic treatment. In 1920 Gréber saw the problem in these terms:

'The primitive idea of the outward appearance of a commercial building was that of the simple block, occupied by the cells of the offices and topped by a very elaborate cornice; the exterior was therefore so to speak an exaggeration of the use made of the interior. The defect of this intentional lack of architectural consideration was made worse by the appearance on the roof of numerous utilitarian fixtures: reservoirs, lift-cabins, air-shafts etc., which were supposed to be "out of sight" but which unfortunately could not be sufficiently concealed; these mechanical parts were sometimes in naïve contrast to the Florentine façade.

The great step subsequently taken by commercial architecture was that of taking architectural advantage of the distributive plan, by treating these great commercial buildings as "towers", and by utilizing the tops of the towers to house and to conceal the utilitarian volumes, to the great advantages of the outward appearance of the building.

The difficulty deriving from the great number of windows, which always made these buildings look like huge beehives from a distance, was happily resolved by grouping the windows vertically, by means of strongly marked ribs which accentuated the verticalism and therefore the impressive appearance of the towers'.[5]

It is easy to see a similarity between this description and Sullivan's description, quoted in Chapter 8. The need to give a multi-storey utilitarian building some kind of overall unity naturally led towards vertical gradation, as in an ancient tower; Sullivan, however, stopped half-way and tried to satisfy these demands without falling into stylistic imitation, while the architects of the following generation, more consistent and harassed by the ever-larger scale of the buildings erected, had recourse to formal rules already proven by period styles: particularly in skyscrapers in the Gothic style, which made possible the desired vertical emphasis.

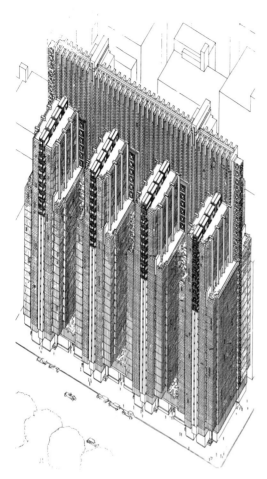

790 *(left)   Frank Lloyd Wright, Plan for offices of the International Life Insurance Co., Chicago (1920–5; from E. Kaufmann,* Frank Lloyd Wright*)*

791, 792 *(right)   New York, Rockefeller Center (Reinhard and Hofmeister, Corbett, Harrison, and Macmurray, Hood and Fouilloux, 1932)*

The greatest builder of skyscrapers in New York was Raymond M. Hood (1881–1934), and in Chicago, Holabird and Root. The technical advances in structures in steel made it possible to put up increasingly tall buildings. The Chrysler building, by W. Van Alen, was over 300 metres, the Empire State building, by Shreven, Lamb and Harmon, over 400 metres.

The rapid growth of suburban districts of one-family houses posed a similar architectural problem. During the last decade of the nineteenth century the theme of the detached house gave Richardson, Sullivan and Wright inspiration for some of the most daring and original research: but these were the houses

Be sure to visit ROCKEFELLER CENTER *in New York*

1 Observation Roof, and U. S. Weather Radome, RCA Building, 70th Floor

2 Rainbow Room, RCA Building, 65th Floor

3 RCA Building, 30 Rockefeller Plaza

4 U. S. Rubber Company Building, 1230 Avenue of the Americas

5 The Forum of The Twelve Caesars, 57 West 48th Street

6 Rockefeller Center Parking Garage

7 Armstrong World of Interior Design, 60 West 49th Street

8 NBC Studios, RCA Building

9 Eastern Air Lines Building, 10 Rockefeller Plaza

10 Holland House Taverne, 10 Rockefeller Plaza

11 General Dynamics Building, 9 Rockefeller Plaza

12 Sinclair Oil Building and Touring Service, 600 Fifth Avenue

13 La Maison Française, 610 Fifth Avenue

14 Lower Plaza with Prometheus Fountain of Lights; Promenade Café in Summer, Skating Pond in Winter Café Français, English Grill

15 Channel Gardens

16 British Empire Building, 620 Fifth Avenue

17 International Building, 630 Fifth Avenue; Atlas statue in forecourt

18 Brass Rail Restaurants and Cafeteria, International Building, 630 Fifth Avenue

19 The Rockefeller Center Visitors Information Booth, 630 Fifth Avenue

20 Associated Press Building, 50 Rockefeller Plaza

21 Guild Theatre, 33 West 50th Street

22 Chase-Manhattan Bank Money Museum, 1254 Avenue of the Americas

23 Esso Building and Touring Service, 15 West 51st Street and 22 West 52nd Street

24 Radio City Music Hall, 1260 Avenue of the Americas at 50th Street

25 American Metal Climax Building, 1270 Avenue of the Americas

26 Time & Life Building, 1271 Avenue of the Americas

27 The Tower Suite, Time & Life Building, 48th Floor

28 La Fonda del Sol, 123 West 50th Street

29 Sperry-Rand Building, 1290 Avenue of the Americas

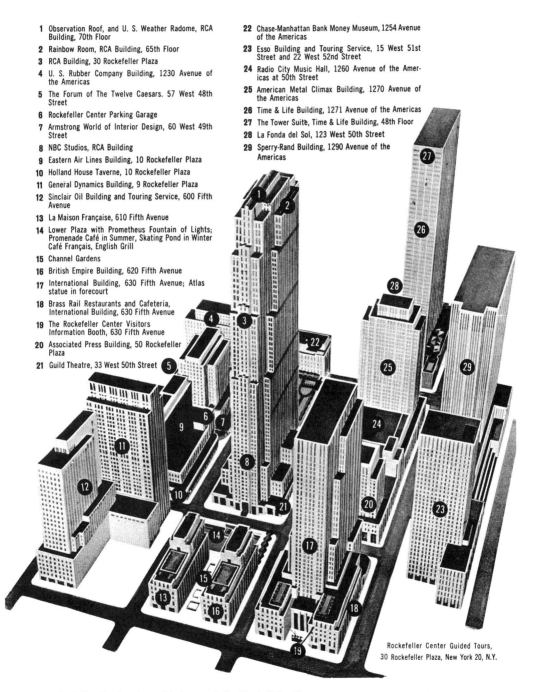

Rockefeller Center Guided Tours,
30 Rockefeller Plaza, New York 20, N.Y.

793 *New York, Leaflet for the guided tour of the Rockefeller Center*

of a very limited class, on the outskirts of the city proper, each conceived as a unique creation not to be repeated. But now it was a question of building vast districts, which formed the body of the new city, for a much broader class of people; the old planning criteria were no longer suited to the new scale of problems, and once again architectural control could be guaranteed only by the already known rules of the historical styles. Industry promptly took over the problem and began to produce little prefabricated houses in the colonial style, or houses with interchangeable décor in the style the client preferred (Figs. 816 and 817).

This was the climate, energetic and confident of its own technical and artistic means, of the post-war period onwards, into which the modern movement let fall its contributions.

In 1922, as has already been mentioned, the newspaper *Chicago Tribune* put out an international competition for the building of its new headquarters. The most important European masters, from Gropius to Loos and M. Taut, took part, unsuccessfully; the first prize was won by Hood with a design in the Gothic style and the second by the Finn Eliel Saarinen with a Romantic tiered tower.

Encouraged by his success Saarinen settled in Chicago the following year, bringing to America the rich experience of Nordic Romanticism and a lively awareness of problems of town-planning; he designed the layout of the lake front in Chicago and was then appointed to teach in the University of Michigan and the Cranbrook academy, whose various buildings he designed in 1925 – the boys' school, the art school, the scientific institute, the museum and library. The formal features of Saarinen's architecture – the discreet reference to medieval styles, the careful craftsmanship, the feeling for constructional honesty – were congenial to the American climate and brought him rapid success; meanwhile he continued his teach-ing, inspired by Berlage, and did not stagnate at his starting point but began a patient work of purification and clarification of his style, at first alone and then with his son Eero who was studying at Yale with Albers and was absorbing the teaching of the most modern European trends.

The international style was controversially introduced into the east coast cities by the Swiss William Lescaze (b. 1896) who worked first with the American George Howe (1886–1955). The two of them built private houses, where the rationalist repertoire was inflexibly applied and, in 1931, an important work: the skyscraper of the Philadelphia Savings Fund Society (Fig. 789). The rigour of the modern method worked a notable clarification in the traditional organization of the skyscraper; in this way an exemplary result was immediately obtained, and the work remained a persuasive argument in favour of the new architecture, more effective than endless discussion.

About 1930 the modern repertoire began to spread more widely: Hood's last skyscrapers – the *Daily News* building of 1930, the McGraw Hill building of 1931 and the Rockefeller Center begun in 1932[6] – had smooth walls, horizontal copings and vaguely Cubist juxtapositions of volume. In 1932 the New York Museum of Modern Art organized a memorable exhibition with the title the 'International Style', which provided fuel for many discussions; but this was not the vehicle for any real penetration of the theses of the modern movement into American society. The international style was soon drawn into the ambit of eclecticism and was regarded as one of the many possible styles, leaving earlier habits unchanged but lessening faith in the usual stylistic repertoire and destroying the 'acquired perfection' which had hitherto characterized American architecture.

Production now lost its former compactness and broke up into many parallel and watertight styles: some of the connoisseurs and clients wanted modern objects, and the artists who wished to remain up-to-date followed the new tendencies that came from Europe; the majority was content with the objects in period styles which industry continued to mass produce, though now without the consolation of a quality production and therefore of an ever lower standard. Many older designers felt it their duty to simplify the external appearance of their buildings or their décor, and gave rise to an intermediate production, neither old nor modern, and even drearier than its European counterpart.

2   The work of Richard Neutra

Richard Neutra (1892–1970) was an exception among the European masters who had gone to America during the twenties; in fact he succeeded in achieving a first, real introduction of the modern method into practical American life, even though he was working in a limited field.

Neutra was Viennese, he had studied at the Technische Hochschule where he had graduated in 1912; then he had worked in Loos' studio until the outbreak of war. After the war he had settled in Berlin, collaborated with Mendelsohn from 1921 to 1923 and taken part in the violent arguments which had marked the beginning of the modern movement, though remaining aloof and concerning himself with technical problems. In 1923 he moved to Chicago, worked in the offices of Holabird and Root and met Sullivan, in the last year of his life; in 1924 he spent a short time with Wright at Taliesin and in 1925 he opened a studio in Los Angeles, began his charmed career as a European designer in an American setting, in the years of prosperity which preceded the financial crisis.

From his earliest works – the apartment house in Los Angeles of 1926, the Lovell house of 1927 (Figs. 794–7) – Neutra made no concessions to current taste but neither did he put polemical emphasis on the repertoire of the international style, as did Lescaze by implicitly accepting the traditional terms of the conflict between the two styles. He was more concerned with building with unimpeachable technical correctness, with moving the public's attention from the form to the functioning of buildings, keeping their outward appearance intentionally unpretentious.

Neutra's production was very various; he built economic houses, moderately-priced ones and luxury ones, public and industrial buildings, but his success was undoubtedly due to his wealthy clientèle, and particularly to the film world of Hollywood.

It is not easy to explain why so rigorous and controlled an architecture should have appealed so much to such people. Perhaps it had a certain snob appeal, particularly at the beginning because of the cultural prestige accruing confusedly in America to anything of European origin; but this would explain a short vogue, not a lasting success. It is more likely that the Functionalist thesis, not being linked to any particular degree of figurative culture, met with real approval in these circles and that the cinema tycoons were struck by the practical arguments in its favour, noting that Neutra's houses, designed with such technical rigour, worked better and lasted longer than those in the various period styles.

The Moorish or neo-gothic castles in which the inhabitants of Hollywood lived did in fact contain an overt contradiction: they claimed to offer their inhabitants the advantages of modern industrial technique and at the same time the feeling of individuality which derived from a certain stylistic atmosphere, to offset the equalizing tendencies inherent in this very technique. This prevented industrial processes from being used in their true capacity and emerged in terms of a technological restriction, i.e. in greater cost, poor finish and rapid deterioration of the buildings. Neutra wrote:

Lower floor
1   entrance
2   study
3   living room
4   bedrooms
5   terrace

Upper floor
6   living room
7   dining room
8   veranda
9   kitchen
10 guest room
11 library

794–797   *Los Angeles, Dr Lovell's nursing home (R. Neutra; plans from the volume by Girsberger)*

'Design resisted the trend to standardization in the name of so-called individualism. But the individual interpretations of architectural beauty, which are assembled along the streets of Hollywood and elsewhere, the curious jumble of French chateaux, English half-timbered Tudor, Spanish, Moorish, Mediterranean homes, apartments and bungalow courts were not built according to individual background or the respective historical standards of craftsmanship; they were merely mimicked . . . . What modern industry contributed was mainly milled, second-grade, shrinking and warping timber, and black paper and chicken wire to cover the roughly nailed carpentry frame and serve as a thin base for the cracking stucco. (Cracks seemed only to add to the charm of this quick-turnover traditional architecture, which aspires to look venerably antique). Galloping depreciation and what may be called "obsolescence praecox" kept this type of enterprising construction in ever-new demand'.[7]

Neutra started from this contradiction and thought he could overcome it by a rigorous and logical application of technical processes, and on this basis tried to institute a franker and more direct relationship between planner and public; it was not a question of offering the public a new architectural style and persuading them that it was better than the previous ones, but of approaching them in another way, offering them a service which would cater adequately for a whole sector of their interests. Not being a theoretician, Neutra did not waste time on general discussions and used facts to show the advantages that could be gained by using industrial elements according to their true nature; he shows that the modern architecture worked better than the old, produced less expensive houses that were easier to maintain, windows that closed well, installations that did not easily go wrong; furthermore it made possible, by distributing the functional elements appropriately, to provide for the most divergent emotional, psychological and environmental needs.

With great perceptiveness, Neutra saw that the first and second groups of requirements need not be separate, since the designer, by concerning himself sincerely with technical matters, was establishing a human as well as a functional relationship with clients and executors. This gave rise to a broadly-based process of collaboration which was ultimately to involve those people who were going to live in the finished building.

He wrote:

'Human beings must be served and they are reached by design not only as ultimate consumers; in the process they must be won over as co-performers and working crew. Every step must be acceptable, understandable, convincing, so as to enlist the necessary co-operation, and the final solution must be appealing, both rationally and emotionally'.[8]

This observation of Neutra's has direct links with the thought of Ruskin and the emphasis on craftsmanship of Neutra's master Loos. Ruskin wrote in 1849: 'Ornament, as I have often observed has two entirely distinct sources of agreeableness: one, that of the abstract beauty of its forms, the same whether they come from the hand or the machine; the other, the sense of human labour and care spent on it.'[9] Neutra repeated, with modern words: 'If aesthetics is a matter of brains and nerves, the finished product and its mode of production – perceived or remembered – are closely linked.'[10]

However, he did not share the condemnation of mechanical production that Ruskin deduced from his principle, nor did he think he could always narrow the relations between architect and executor to one of direct contact, as Loos had hoped. He realized that mechanical production complicated matters, but he firmly believed that the human mind could successfully dominate these new instruments as well, and that a human contact could be established, even if remotely, between designer and executor, by conventional means such as site plans. Neutra explained this by describing a personal experience:

'During the construction of San Francisco's Golden Gate bridge, the chief engineer

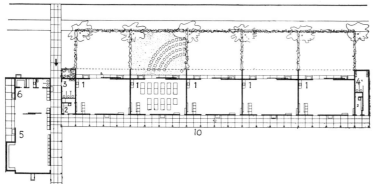

1   classrooms
2   cloakrooms for teachers
3   girls' cloakroom
4   boys' cloakroom
5 & 6   kindergarten
10   covered passage way

798, 799   *Los Angeles, Experimental school (R. Neutra, 1935; plan from A. Roth,* op. cit.*)*

took me up to the south bridge tower, then already soaring some 183 metres above the waters of the bay. We donned steel helmets, which were scant enough protection against the red hot rivets that, occasionally missing their destination, came swishing down like bullets. Two workingmen, blueprints in hand, made the ascent with us in the dangling, doorless wire mesh cage of the construction elevator. At sea level, the weather was rather calm, but we seemed to be climbing slowly into a raging storm as our little cage, swinging to and fro, rose ever-higher through the red-painted steelwork of the tower, and the foam-capped waves below became tiny and insignificant.

At a height of 150 metres the elevator reached a heavy diagonal bracing of the gig structure and made an intermediate stop. Here our two companions got off; they were riveters and had a four hour job ahead of them at this hazardous station. There were other men at work on the slanting brace in front of us. They shoved out a heavy board, cantilevering it towards the elevator cage, which seemed to me to sway more violently than ever in the high wind.

I clutched the wire mesh enclosure with both hands as the two riveters jumped on to the plank. I saw them, blueprints always faithfully in hand, crawl up the steel girder to the isolated foot-hold where they would have to work for long hours, all alone between sky and sea. There would be nobody to ask questions of; their only link with the world would be their crumpled rolls of drawings. I saw them looking at those as the elevator moved upwards. I hope that in those documents the designing engineer was speaking to them with a voice that was comforting and reassuring in the storm and the danger'.[11]

This faith was at the root of the coherence of his production, from the earlier buildings to the Bell Experimental School of 1935, the Von Sternberg house of 1936, the village of workers' houses, Chanel Heights, of 1942, the Tremaine house of 1947 and other more recent works.

Many of Neutra's buildings stand in the open countryside, often in really sensational settings, for instance the rocky Californian desert, yet they make no naturalistic con-

cessions to their surroundings. There are no walls of massive stone, no roughly-hewn masses inside the houses, no tree-trunks or waterfalls.

In fact, the house cannot merge with the countryside because its elements have come from far away, from storehouses and work-shops often hundreds of miles away, and it is not intended to last for nearly as long as the masses that people the desert. Therefore it is advisable that it should appear for what it is: a work of man, artificial and temporary. This is what is natural to it, and by being juxtaposed to nature without artifice it can legitimately bear comparison with the trees, rocks and mountains.

The limits of Neutra's experience derive from the narrowness of his field and the insufficient attention he paid to problems of town-planning. He tended to see architecture as a service to man and thought of man as an isolated person, 'Man the Unknown' in the fashion of Alexis Carrel, to be studied with the scientific methods of physiology and psychology.

The exploration of social motives, which characterized the European movement after 1930, was partly foreign to him. Perhaps this limitation was the armour he needed to keep the coherence of his method intact, without yielding to outside temptations. In the hectic environment of the American West, Neutra tenderly nurtured the delicate plant of modern architecture, almost always in the shelter of the walls of a detached building; in this way he achieved results that were modest, but perfectly clear and communic-able, and exercised a discreet but widespread influence on American domestic architecture.

3 Wright's example

The work of Frank Lloyd Wright still continued without pause, indeed it gained a new vigour from 1930 onwards, when the European Rationalist repertoire was spreading.

1   living room
2   dining room
3   kitchen
4   study
5   guest room
6   bedroom
7   dressing room
8   garage
9   patio

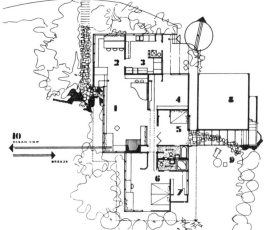

800, 801   *Palos Verdes, Beckstrand house (R. Neutra, 1937)*

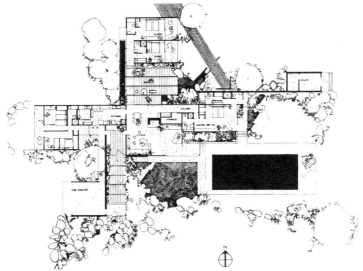

802, 803 *House in the Colorado desert (R. Neutra, 1946)*

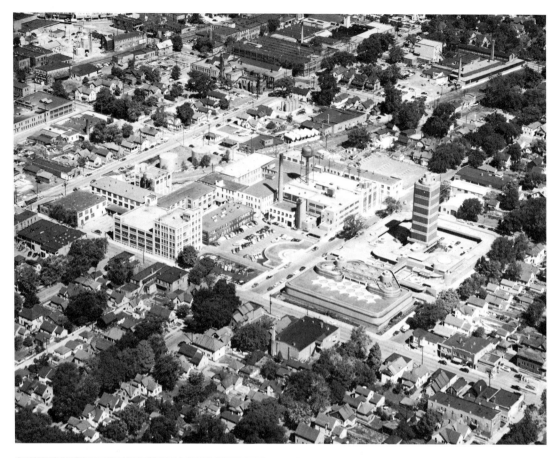

804, 805, 806   *Racine, Wisconsin, Johnson works, with office building by Frank Lloyd Wright (1936)*

It has been suggested on several occasions that Wright was influenced by the European movement, and the signs of this influence

have been pointed out in the square volumes of the plan for the Noble apartments in Los Angeles (1929), the great flat roof-surfaces of

807, 808   *Two views of D. Wright's house in Arizona (Frank Lloyd Wright, 1952)*

the Mesa river house (1931), in the use of reinforced concrete and the pale surfaces of Falling Water (1936). But these formal similarities appeared only sporadically, without any continuity, and alternated with other quite different episodes. If Wright had taken

809 *(above)   D. Wright's house in Arizona*

810   *New York, Design for the Guggenheim museum (Frank Lloyd Wright, 1946, finished 1960; from E. Kaufmann, op. cit.)*

up any suggestions from Europe – as he had absorbed Japanese influence during the previous decades – he modified them very considerably and made them elements of his own highly personal vision.

It is therefore more reasonable to consider Wright's activities, from beginning to end, as an independent experience, all his experiments being explained as coherent developments of the position he had adopted from the beginning, when he began to work as an independent architect. Once and for all, he broke the link between his architecture and contemporary society, between the phases of his work and those of the economic, social and cultural processes which were going on at the same time. He decided to work in the United States but to live in Usonia, and to accept only that portion of reality that he needed, as the occasion arose, to translate a part of his ideal world into reality.

In this way not only did Wright escape Sullivan's fate, and the wave of conformism which threatened the Chicago school, but he avoided remaining tied to any definite historical movement and was safe from the danger of appearing outdated, because his past was not comparable to anybody else's.

Running parallel to the modern movement, and precisely because of the detachment here described, his architecture exerted an exceptionally valuable and insistent influence. We have already talked of the decisive contribution he made to the birth of the modern movement with his journey to Europe, the exhibition and Wasmuth publication of 1910. From 1936 – when he designed the Johnson Offices in Racine (Figs. 804–6) and the Kaufmann house in Pennsylvania – he began to arouse great interest in America and throughout the world; the two above-mentioned buildings, the school of Taliesin west in Arizona (1938), and the houses belonging to the series of the 'Usonian' houses were illustrated in publications everywhere; in 1938 the most important American review, *Architectural Forum*, devoted a

special number to him and in 1942 the best known critic, H. R. Hitchcock, published a lengthy documentation of his works.[12]

Part of this interest, particularly in America, derived from the desire to counter European architecture with 'American' architecture; but, irrespective of this pointless debate, Wright's architecture continued to exert a suggestive power which was widely reflected in the statements of the European masters, from Mendelsohn to Oud, and Mies.[13]

While the numerous variables which modern architecture had to take into account did continually disturb the coherence of its results with their mutual movement, upset timing and continuity and made difficult compromises necessary, Wright's architecture, free from all these bonds, emerged as honest, compact and unfaltering, and it therefore re-established an exemplary goal, helped architects to regard their own difficulties as already resolved and encouraged them to look ahead, beyond circumstantial difficulties.

Of course, Wright's detachment from historical circumstances was not complete, and his capacity for renewal was not inexhaustible. Perhaps a deeper study would show a considerable disparity in importance between the works completed before the First World War, and those that followed it. The first show greater confidence with technical processes, closer attention, within the limits already mentioned, to the interests of the clients. In the more recent works technical solutions were often faulty, the movement of the volumes was often realized with visible constructional effort – for instance the fitting together of the various buildings of the Johnson offices – while his desire to differentiate between the various parts of the building implied such a variety of articulations and joins that they could hardly all be resolved correctly. Agreement with the client, too, became more difficult; while the 'prairie' houses were designed for a definite social class, whose needs they could interpret precisely, the 'Usonian' houses were intended for a somewhat abstract category, or rather for a series of individuals taken out of their social context.

In the last decade his spontaneity dwindled even further, to be replaced by a sense of over-intellectual strain and a ferocious concern for propagating his views; his self-regeneration had become almost a myth, of which Wright himself was a prisoner, and it led him to formulate irrational projects, like a sky-scraper a mile high.

The best demonstration of the merits and limits of Wright's experience is that of his ideas on town-planning. In 1932 he wrote *The Disappearing City*, in which he reveals his lack of faith in the survival of the present city, and in 1934 he put forward his plan for the ideal city, Broadacre, whose charac-teristic feature was to grant an acre to each inhabitant, and wherefore to isolate each ʿamily within a green zone sufficiently extensive for neighbours not to bother one another at all.

The traditional city would become just a workplace, 'invaded at ten and deserted at four, three days a week',[14] while communal life would take place in special centres, more numerous than at present and scattered throughout the countryside; travel would be by car and a large number of contacts and entertainments would take place long dis-tance, by the modern means of telecommuni-cation; 'by these gifts of science we shall try to come together more intelligently, and therefore ever less frequently'.[15]

Wright did not see that what the inhabi-tants of Broadacre city would gain in freedom of space, they would lose in restriction in time; he said: 'between the lift and the motor-car, I choose the motor-car', which made it possible for people to move where they wanted to, but not when they wanted to; he condemned Le Corbusier's vertical city because it fixed the place of every human activity, even of rest and entertainment, without seeing that Broadacre led to the equally rigid fixing of the time of every activity, including entertainment.

The reason for this choice lies in the fact that Broadacre was not a true design for a town, but the illustration of a principle; this was the type of city compatible with Wright's architecture, i.e., with an architecture which has precise needs in space, while living in a mythical, imaginary sphere of time.

If Broadacre were to be taken for a practical scheme, it could produce only confusion and feed a rhetorical programme of escapism into nature, directly opposed to the tasks of modern town-planning; if recognized as an abstract allegory, it has an important value as a stimulus, because it was the one-sided expression of a real town-planning need.

4 The 'New Deal' and the contribution of former masters of the Bauhaus

The United States, where the economic crisis began in 1929, was also the country where the crisis had its most serious and prolonged effects and produced a decisive change in political and cultural customs.

When the ineffectiveness of the measures taken by the Hoover administration had made itself felt, Roosevelt was elected President for the first time on 8 November 1932; he promptly set about implementing his programme of radical political and economic reforms; in April 1933 he devalued the dollar; in May, with the Agricultural Adjustment Act, he began his policy of state intervention in agriculture and, in June with the National Industrial Recovery Act, in industry; in the same year the Tennessee Valley Authority was set up to plan for a vast stretch of depressed land involving various states; in 1934, when the currency had been stabilized, the National Housing Act was passed, giving new impetus to subsidized building; in 1935 the National Resources Committee was set up, and in 1939 the National Resources Planning Board, which

outlined the planning of resources throughout the whole country with great theoretical
zeal; in 1937, with a new law on subsidized
building, a new central organ of control was
set up, the U.S. Housing Authority, and the
Farm Security Administration was set up
within the Department of Agriculture, to
co-ordinate rural building.

These measures radically changed the
conditions in which architectural planning
was carried out, and in this way the theses
of the modern movement were able to penetrate deep into the realities of American life,
far more intimately than through controversies of the *avant-garde* and the formal propaganda of the Museum of Modern Art. The
need to link activities within the framework
of a single plan, the inflexible limits set by
time and economy, and the desirability of
getting specialists in various fields to work
together in groups, posed new problems
which could be resolved only by the methods
of the modern movement. A new class of
technicians was growing up, aware of the
demands of collaboration and used to
contact with political and administrative
authorities, while the architect became ever
less an independent technician and ever more
a co-ordinator of the works of other technicians.

At this time a specific professional organization for Industrial Design was formed.
W. D. Teague began his activities in 1926,
N. B. Geddes and R. Loewy in 1927; in 1932
the model gas stove designed by Geddes for
the S.G.E. appeared based on a careful study
of proportion and absolutely without ornament.

After 1930 the first large-scale experiments
in prefabricated building began. In America
prefabrication had a long history, and was
therefore linked from the beginning with
certain particular characteristics of local
industry. In the first years of the twentieth
century there was a series of theoretical
studies and experiments, based on the use of
concrete panels; G. Atterbury built an

experimental house in 1907 and put up a
first series of buildings in Forest Hills in
1910; in 1908 T. A. Edison had been preparing a patent, which never came to anything. After the First World War other
experiments were made, using steel; the
dizzy growth of suburbs, with the detached
and often identical houses, and the disturbances caused by the economic crisis in the
traditional systems of building led many
industries to concern themselves with the
problem, adapting the usual methods of
wooden joinery for mass production, or
using the new materials, concrete and iron.

From 1933 onwards the contribution of
the European masters who had come to
teach in American universities was grafted
on to this new reality; by influencing the new
generation of planners in their practical
education, they gave them a whole legacy of
methods and ideas, not only the example of
a new formal repertoire, and had a decisive
influence on American culture, even if it was
not always immediately noticeable because
the new forms were nothing like the European
ones.

Of the former teachers of the Bauhaus,
Albers settled in America in 1933 and began
his formal teaching in Black Mountain
College; A. Schawinsky carried on with
Schlemmer's work on theatrical scenery;
L. Feininger, American by birth, went back
to New York in 1936; in 1937 Moholy-Nagy
founded the New Bauhaus in Chicago, with
the explicit intention of carrying on with the
European experiment; at the same time
Gropius and Breuer settled in Harvard, Mies
and Hilbersheimer in Chicago, Bayer, Ozenfant and later Mondrian in New York.

After the war A. Aalto too spent some time
in the United States, while E. Mendelsohn
lived in California until his death in 1935.
In 1938 the New York Museum of Modern
Art organized an exhibition of the Bauhaus
from 1919 to 1928, with material brought by
Gropius and Breuer, and published a volume
on the same subject,[16] which for a long time

remained the best source of information on the German school. The director of the museum, A. H. Barr, wrote in the preface:

'It is hard to recall when and how we in America first began to hear of the Bauhaus. In the years just after the war we thought of German art in terms of Expressionism, of Mendelsohn's streamlined Einstein tower, Toller's *Masse Mensch*, Wiene's *Cabinet of Doctor Caligari* .... It may not have been until after the great Bauhaus exhibition of 1923 that reports reached America of a new kind of art school in Germany where famous Expressionist painters such as Kandinsky were combining forces with craftsmen and industrial designers under the general direction of the architect, Gropius. A little later we began to see some of the Bauhaus books, notably Schlemmer's amazing volume on the theatre and Moholy-Nagy's *Malerei, Photographie, Film*.

Some of the younger of us had just left colleges where courses in modern art began with Rubens and ended with a few superficial and often hostile remarks about Van Gogh and Matisse; where the last word in imitation Gothic dormitories had windows with one carefully cracked pane to each picturesque casement. Others of us, in architectural schools, were beginning our courses with gigantic renderings of Doric columns and ending them with projects for colonial gymnasiums and Romanesque skyscrapers .... It is no wonder, then, that young Americans began to turn their eyes towards the Bauhaus as the one school in the world where modern problems of design were approached realistically in a modern atmosphere. A few American pilgrims had visited Dessau before Gropius left in 1928; in the five years thereafter many went to stay as students. During this time Bauhaus materials, typography, paintings, prints, theatre-art, architecture, industrial objects, had been included in

American exhibitions .... In America, Bauhaus lighting fixtures and tubular-steel chairs were imported or the designs pirated. American Bauhaus students began to return; and they were followed, after the Revolution of 1933, by Bauhaus and ex-Bauhaus masters who suffered from the new government's illusion that modern furniture, flat-roofed architecture and abstract paintings were degenerate and Bolshevistic. In this way, with the help of the Fatherland, Bauhaus designs, Bauhaus men, Bauhaus ideas, which taken together form one of the chief cultural contributions of modern Germany, have been spread throughout the world'.[17]

But the spread of the results and methods of the Bauhaus was merely the most superficial contribution that its former masters had brought to America. It is interesting to see that Gropius would not take any part in any of the attempts at directly reviving the Dessau school in America; when appointed to teach at Harvard he embarked upon a completely new experiment in teaching, and as a designer he made no effort to impose either the architectural repertoire, the town-planning schemes or European professional habits upon his new surroundings.

He never tired of pointing out that the European Modern Movement had never had any fixed repertoire, any set schemes or habits. For instance in 1938, when there was a discussion, during the exhibition at the Museum of Modern Art, as to what was contemporary and what outdated among the objects on show, Gropius pointed out that 'the inevitable process of aging was even more active in the Bauhaus itself when it was still in existence, because ... the idea of a Bauhaus style or a Bauhaus dogma, as something fixed and permanent, had always come from the hasty conclusions of superficial observers'.[18] At the beginning of his teaching career at Harvard he stated:

'My intention is not to introduce a, so to

speak, cut and dried 'Modern Style' from Europe, but rather to introduce a method of approach which allows one to tackle a problem according to its peculiar conditions. I want a young architect to be able to find his way in whatever circumstances; I want him independently to create true, genuine forms out of the technical, economic and social conditions in which he finds himself instead of imposing a learned formula on to surroundings which may call for an entirely different solution. It is not so much a ready-made dogma that I want to teach, but an attitude towards the problems of our generation which is unbiased, original and elastic. It would be an absolute horror to me if any appointment were to result in the multiplication of a fixed idea of 'Gropius architecture'. What I want is to make young people realize how inexhaustible the means of creation are if they make use of the innumerable modern products of our age and to encourage these young people in finding their own solutions'.[19]

The first building by Gropius in America – a house for his family – was a rather different work from all his earlier ones, and it was largely influenced by its setting. But it is also probable that, after careful consideration of his experience, particularly that acquired in Berlin between 1928 and 1934, he was led to a broader understanding of the tasks of the modern designer.

At the time of the Bauhaus all the work was concentrated on elaborating a new method of planning capable of breaking down the contradictions of eclectic culture. Since this step absorbed an enormous amount of energy, the conviction arose that the main bulk of the difficulties had actually been solved, and that the effort of thinking up solutions was greater than that of their application, which was conceived of almost as an inevitable executive consequence.

One of the motives which led Gropius to leave the Bauhaus in 1928 was certainly the need to go deeper into this second point and to establish more direct contacts with the forces able to translate the ideas elaborated by the Bauhaus into reality. The experience of the six years from 1928 to 1934 showed that the contact with these forces was more difficult than had been believed, that the rate and scale of the applications were not just quantitative circumstances but basic problems.

The architect, therefore, must face the problems of conception and execution together at every stage; he must gauge time factors as well as those of space and must be more cautious in his attitude to overall schemes, because it had been noted that to discount any one of the aspects of a concrete problem, even with the aim of demonstration, introduced a defect into the result which was invariably paid for at the practical stage. If Gropius' European experience contained the germ of these conclusions, it is certain that his American experience confirmed them; the vastness of the scale, the urgency of the rhythm of economic development, the variety of the settings and the presence in a single place of many conflicting factors showed that it was necessary to maintain extreme flexibility, to gain a hold on so complex a reality, and to bear in mind, at every moment, the totality of the component factors.

To indicate this need for completeness Gropius reverted, particularly in his last years, to the terms 'art' and 'beauty':

'In a long life I have become increasingly aware of the fact that the creation and love of beauty not only enrich man with a great measure of happiness but also bring forth ethical powers. An age which does not give this love for beauty sufficient room remains visually undeveloped; its image remains blurred; and its isolated artistic manifestations find only such limited response that they remain uncharacteristic of the general development'.[20]

It would be a definite over-simplification to regard this line of thought as a retreat towards a new aestheticism in relation to the rationalism of the German period. We have already noted that Gropius uses the words of contemporary language to express new thoughts, so much so that his thought processes are always somewhat sibylline; this time it is as though he were by-passing the modern accepted meaning of the word 'art', were restoring to it the meaning it had in remote tradition: *recta ratio factibilium*.

Gropius gives a great deal of importance, in his later writings, to problems of education and interprets the didactic formula developed in the Bauhaus almost as a system of exercises in experimental psychology. Here he was influenced by the psychological leanings of a part of American educational theory, but his aims were more far-reaching; he had in mind the balance between the aesthetic, logical and moral needs of all society and in the lives of all men, not only in the education of designers.

Sketching a plan for the teaching of architecture, Gropius wrote in 1939:

'If we investigate the vague feelings of the average man towards the arts, we find that he is timid and that he has developed a humble belief that art is something which has been invented centuries ago in countries like Greece or Italy and that all we can do about it is study it carefully and apply it. There is no natural, eager response to the works of modern artists who try to solve contemporary problems in a contemporary way, but, rather, a great uneasiness and a strong disbelief that they can turn out something worthy of the great works of their forefathers. This surprising sterility is in my opinion due not so much to inborn lack of ability or interest, but it is a result of the fact that we are today separated into two groups of beings – the "public" and the "expert". Each person feels that he is an "expert" in one or two fields and just the "public" in all the others. But you know, probably, from experience that no-one is really able to appreciate any display of ability in any field if he, himself, has not to a certain degree taken part in its problems and difficulties at some time'.[21]

The formal subtleties of an Albers or a Moholy-Nagy were basically exercises for initiates, but for the cultural balance of modern society, and to justify the very existence of professional artists, everyone's intuitive capacities needed educating, to some degree, since the artist's intensive experiences were the stimuli intended to elevate and enrich everyone's everyday experiences. Teaching methods must therefore rid themselves of all intellectualist complacency, of all pointless complications, and this aim necessarily had connections with work done by psychologists on basic education.

In the first four years after his arrival in America Gropius was still working with his former pupil Breuer.

The buildings they built together – their own houses and the Ford house at Lincoln, the Fischer house at Newton, the arts centre at Wheaton College (1938), the Frank house at Pittsburg, Black Mountain College (1939), the Chamberlain house at Weyland (1940) (Fig. 812), the group of workers' houses at New Kensington (1941) and the arts centre at the Sarah Lawrence College in Bronxville (1951) – were very different and at first sight it does not seem probable that they could have been built by the same people. This may be explained by the alternating preponderance of one or other of the personalities concerned, or more probably by Breuer's ability each time to adhere closely to the particular requirements of the subject, to invent a new form to resolve each new problem (Breuer's production as an independent architect, too, is marked by this apparent lack of coherence) while Gropius exercised a mainly intellectual control, ensuring that

1 existing roads
2 projected roads
3 one-family houses
4 public buildings
5 multi-family houses
6 central administration
7 local administration

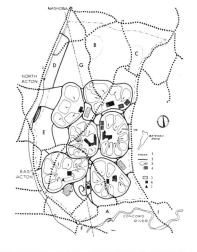

811 *Design for a new settlement at Concord, Mass. (produced in 1946 by students at Harvard under W. Gropius, J.C. Harkness, M. Wagner; from Giedion, op. cit.)*
812 *Weyland, Chamberlain house (W. Gropius and M. Breuer, 1940)*

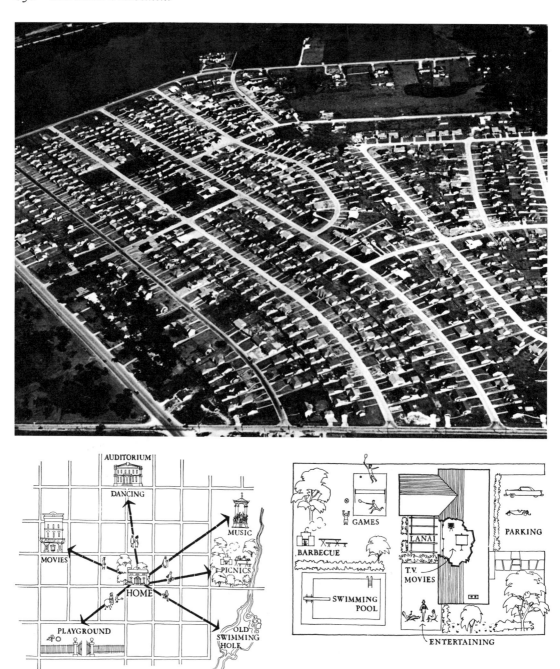

813   *Suburban housing at Houston, Texas*
814, 815   *The American house yesterday and today (sketch from* House Beautiful*)*

816, 817 *Two types of American prefabricated houses: the 'colonial cottage' produced by the American Houses Inc. at $7,500 and the 'Catalina' house produced by the U.S. Steel Houses Inc. at $11,500*

every experiment would be conducted with the utmost thoroughness; even the points of inspiration drawn from the American tradition of domestic and local building habits were developed in an almost academic fashion, as though Gropius and Breuer wanted to try out this tradition, by applying to it the analytical methods elaborated in Europe.

Each of these buildings appears as an

818 *Model of a tubular structure by Wachsmann*

object in itself, as the logical solution of an individual problem (and here one might remember one of Wright's precepts: that there are as many styles of architecture as there are of people); this attitude indicated – at least on Gropius' part – a certain caution in penetrating a new world, which he wanted to know primarily in its individual manifestations, suspending general judgments, but it was also justified by the different situation in town-planning, which meant that the problem of the individual house was posed in a very different way from the similar problem in Europe.

In Europe Gropius had as his starting point the consideration of the traditional city, with its concentration and its chaotic superimposition of functions; the aim was to restore order, to distinguish the functions rationally and to localize them precisely in different parts of the city. The function of residence was reduced to the minimum compatible with a certain level of life (the so-called Existenzminimum) and the residential districts consisted of the repetition of standardized cells; the uniformity and incomplete quality of this fabric was compensated for by the public buildings, destined for collective functions, where the life of the individual once again found its

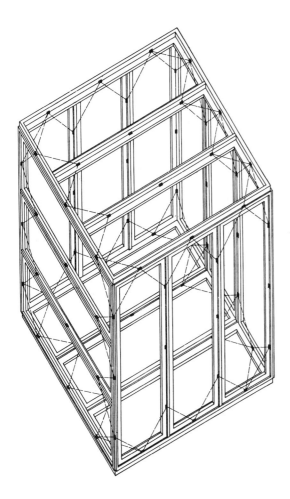

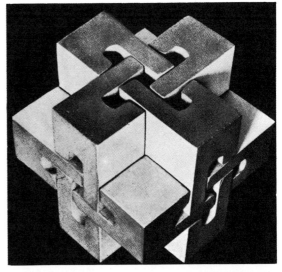

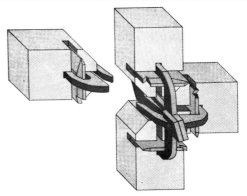

819–822 *Details of the packaged house system worked on by Gropius and Wachsmann in 1942 for the General Panel Corp. (from K.W.,* The Turning-point of Building*)*

823, 824   *Two works by T.A.C., the high school of Attleboro, Mass. (1948) and the Harvard Graduate Centre*

original integrity and complexity through the interplay of social relationships.

In America the situation was completely different; ever since the appearance of the motor-car the decentralization and dispersal of residences in the suburbs surrounding the city had been going on, while means of long distance communication had brought part of the recreational functions, which formerly took place in communal centres, into people's houses (Figs. 814 and 815). This was the ideal theorized about by Wright in Broadacre City. The problem of reconciling concentration with the individual needs of every dwelling, quantity with quality, was therefore greatly lessened; the problem of the house could be posed in mainly qualitative and more complex terms, which could not be reduced to a minimum standard.

Gropius embarked upon this path eagerly, because he felt that this could be the start of a new urban environment, one with a greater degree of continuity, where functions were not rigidly classified and separated, but interlinked and jointly present to some degree, in the various places. But he also saw the danger of settling permanently for a formula like Broadacre, of emphasizing quality and individuality, and of ceasing to consider the requirements of standardization and quantitative control.

It may have been to solve this dilemma that in 1941 Gropius began to work with Konrad Wachsmann (b. 1901). With him he continued the studies on prefabrication which he had begun in Germany in 1931 for the Hirsch Kupfer und Messingwerke A. G., and between 1942 and 1945 he worked on the 'packaged-house system' for the General Panel Corporation.

Of the two lines of thought that Gropius put forward to solve the problem of residential building – the work on the distribution of well-scattered multi-storey units for intensive building, and on constructional matters with prefabrication in mind for less concentrated building – the second seemed the best suited for America. The aim was always economy, but the problems of town-planning were also now always borne in mind. In fact prefabrication – provided it stopped short at the single elements and left the architect free to combine them in many different ways – was possibly the best means of maintaining some sort of order and unity in the multiform extensive building of American suburbs. For this reason Gropius insisted on the need to reconcile standardization of the various elements with freedom of the whole, to escape the two opposite dangers of mechanical repetition and individualistic sprawl:

'The true aim of prefabrication is certainly not the dull multiplication of a housing type *ad infinitum*; men will always rebel against attempts at over-mechanization which is contrary to life. But industrialization will not stop at the threshold of building. We have no other choice but to accept the challenge of the machine in all fields of production until men finally adapt it fully to serve their biological needs . . . . Very gradually the process of building is splitting up into shop production of building parts on the one hand, and site assembly of such parts. More and more the tendency develops to prefabricate component parts of buildings rather than whole houses. Here is where the emphasis belongs . . . .

The coming generation will certainly blame us if we fail to overcome those understandable though sentimental reactions against prefabrication. If we are determined to let the human element become the dominant factor for the pattern and scale of our communities, prefabrication will be beneficial'.[22]

Wachsmann on the other hand was particularly interested in the technical mechanism and its potentially infinite possibilities. He regarded the various types of building as combinations of unvarying standardized elements, and concentrated on obtaining the greatest variety of combinations with the least variety of pieces. In this context he was interested primarily in the study of relationships, and therefore not so much in the form of the single pieces as in the way they were put together:

'The development of a joint, using the most advanced methods of technology, becomes a basic task which will largely determine the final characteristics of a structure. The study of such joints, not merely limited to the connecting of two, three, four or more parts, and not merely in a simple fashion, but in such a way as to make any type of combination possible, three-dimensional as well and in such a way as to transmit the stresses from one part to the other is to-day the very essence of the secret of the art of building. (This may give rise to) a continuous order, starting from the basic elements which produce the joints, which produce surfaces, and structures, rooms, buildings, roads, squares or parts, urban complexes, the future panorama of the civilized world'. [23]

These devices could be developed only in a workshop, after a long series of theoretical experiments, far from the bustle of professional practice: 'for this reason [Wachsmann concluded] we must for the moment accept a separation of thought and action.'

But it is quite possible that Gropius would not have agreed with this statement. In fact, his research with Wachsmann was only a stage in his development, after which he devoted himself once more to active planning, gathering some former pupils around him [24] in a studio called The Architects' Collaborative (T.A.C.).

5   Mies van der Rohe

In 1938 Mies was appointed to run the architectural department of the Armour Institute, which later became the Illinois Institute of Technology. As early as his opening lecture the themes of his American activities were stated:

'All education must begin with the practical side of life. Real education, however, must transcend this to mould the personality. The first aim should be to equip the student with the knowledge and skill for practical life. The second should be to develop his personality and to enable him to make the right use of his knowledge and skill. Thus true education is concerned not only with practical goals but also with values. By our practical aims we are bound to the specific structure of our epoch. Our values, on the other hand, are rooted in the spiritual nature of men. Our practical aims measure only our material progress. The values we profess reveal the level of our culture. Different as practical aims and values are, they are nonetheless closely connected.

For to what else should our values be related if not to our aims in life? Human existence is predicated on the two spheres together. Our aims assure us of our material life, our values make possible our spiritual life. If this is true of all human activities, where even the slightest question of value is involved, how especially is it true in the sphere of architecture. In its simplest form Architecture is rooted in entirely functional considerations, but it can reach up through all degrees of value to the highest sphere of spiritual existence, into the realm of pure art. In organizing our architectural education system we must recognize this situation if we are to succeed in our efforts. We must fit the system to this reality. Any teaching of Architecture must explain these relations and inter-relations. We must make clear, step by step, what things are possible, necessary and significant. If teaching has any purpose, it is to implant true insight and responsibility. Education must lead

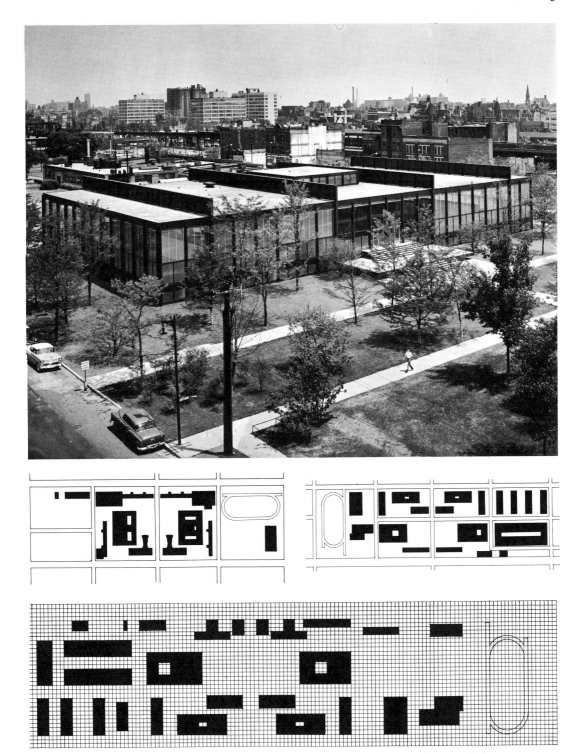

825, 826   *Chicago, The campus of the I.I.T. (Mies, 1939): a view and three successive ground plans*

us from irresponsible opinion to true responsible judgment. It must lead us from chance and arbitrariness to rational clarity and intellectual order. Therefore let us guide our students over the road of discipline from materials, through function, to creative work'.[25]

The distinction between the practical aims and values was similar to that made in 1930 between the 'how' and the 'what'; but now Mies seemed to want to start all over again, exploring the most simple facts – constructional materials – and seeing how the most simple values arise from them:

'Where can we find greater structural clarification and intelligent order than in the wooden buildings of old? Where else can we find such unity of material, construction and form? Here the wisdom of whole generations is stored . . . and buildings of stone as well: what natural feeling they express! What a clear understanding of the material! How surely it is joined! What sense they had of where stone could and could not be used! . . . We can also learn from brick. How sensible is this small handy shape, so useful for every purpose! What logic in its bonding, pattern and texture! What richness is the simplest wall surface! But what discipline this material imposes!

Thus each material has its specific characteristics which we must understand if we want to use it.

This is no less true of steel and concrete. We must remember that everything depends on how we use a material, not on the material itself'.[26]

Mies was certainly annoyed by the superficial nature of the spread of the modern movement everywhere. He did not doubt the validity of the method, but he did have reservations about the way in which it had been exercised hitherto and above all about the excessive speed with which the field of

its uses had broadened, logically diminishing the severity of control. He believed that it was necessary to increase methodical rigour even at the cost of restricting the field of activity.

'The long path from material through function to creative work has only a single goal: to create order out of the desperate confusion of our time. We must have order allocating to each thing its due according to its nature. We should do this so perfectly that the world of our creations will blossom from within. We want no more; we can do no more. Nothing can express the aim and meaning of our work better than the profound words of St Augustine: "Beauty is the splendour of Truth".'[27]

The American cultural scene, confused and incoherent but vast and multiform, welcomed Mies' experience eagerly, but put up great resistance to its development; similarly the townscape of Chicago, because of the precarious and fragmentary nature of its elements, absorbed Mies' buildings without difficulty, but only as finite and circumscribed episodes.

Mies' plan for the new campus for the University of Chicago was highly significant. In the first draft of 1939 the various departments were grouped within a few blocks, arranged symmetrically around a large enclosed space crossed by an aerial road, but while the symmetry was very strict in the centre of the complex, certain limited deviations from it appeared round the edge which lessened the rigidity of the whole and prepared for its introduction into the surrounding areas. In the following plan of 1940, since a second road crossing the first in the centre of the complex had to be retained, the enclosed central square was lost and the composition became more fluent. Finally Mies gave up trying to subordinate the whole to a single visual outline, based the composition on a modular framework

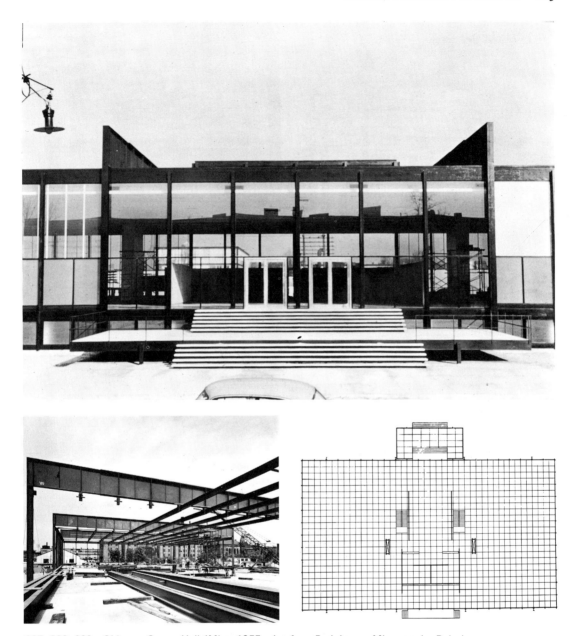

827, 828, 829 *Chicago, Crown Hall (Mies, 1955; plan from P. Johnson,* Mies van der Rohe*)*

and placed the various departments in so many buildings, freely distributed over the empty space (Figs. 825–9).

The buildings were built gradually, from 1942 onwards.[28] The town-planning module established the intervals between the constructional elements, but not always in the same way and without demanding repetition of the same details, as in Perret's plan for Le Havre. Mies showed that by following the

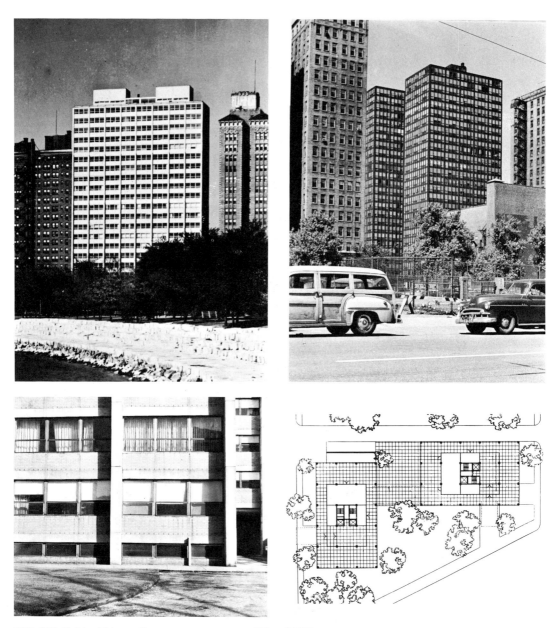

830, 831 *(left)   Chicago, Promontory apartments (Mies, 1946)*
832, 833 *(right)   Chicago, Lake Shore Drive apartments (Mies, 1951)*

guideline of a uniform rhythm and using the same materials – metal supporting structures, filled in with brick and tiles – an immense variety and wealth of solutions could be obtained, provided that the proportions, the textures, joins and details were not mechanically repeated, but re-established on each occasion with equal and unflagging spontaneity: in this way every element acquired an extraordinary expressive intensity and added

834 *Chicago, Detail of the Lake Shore Drive apartments*

to the harmony of the whole with its own individual tone. Isolated in the tumultuous and precarious fabric of the city, the campus enclosure was like a fragment of an ideal city, where every aspect – forms, colours, proportions – had been subjected to a process of rigid control.

Mies' fame increased after the exhibition of his works organized in 1947 by the Museum of Modern Art. He received more commissions every year, but approached each new subject with infinite caution and subjected it to a long selective process, eliminating secondary aspects and laying bare certain essential aspects which formed the nucleus of the problem; this led to an impoverishment of formal appearance, but made it possible for the designer to concentrate his energies on a few decisions and to have absolute control, through these

835   *Chicago, Lake Shore Drive apartments*

decisions, of the whole building.

The first plans for the Promontory apartments, on the banks of Lake Michigan, were made in 1946.[29] Having settled upon a rigid distribution plan and a suitable reticular structure, Mies worked on two constructional solutions, in reinforced concrete with filling in brick or steel and glass. He was taking up a possibility already worked on by the masters of the Chicago school, abandoned by Sullivan and more or less ignored ever since the concept of the multi-storey building not as a finite and compositionally complete organism – an effect which would be aimed at by differentiating various portions of façade and emphasizing vertical links – but as a rhythmically open organism, made up of the repetition of many identical elements. This made it possible suddenly to resolve the compositional conflict between the scale of the whole and that of the details, since proportional considerations stopped at the single element, while the overall composition depended on quite other criteria and was not complete in itself, but was resolved by its relationship with infinite landscape (and did in fact require a great deal of surrounding

free space, as happened here). This was the meeting point of this American concept of the unité d'habitation, and the European one; in both cases the overall composition based on rhythmic repetition made it possible to retain a human scale whatever the size of the building, and to build a multi-storey house without its losing the character of a house or becoming transformed into a monument.

The solution in reinforced concrete, selected for the execution of the block, allowed a very slight hint of aesthetic unity, in the offset of the pilasters which protrude, almost imperceptibly, differentiating the four ascending zones of the building (Figs. 830 and 831). This expedient was necessary to give visible support, below, to the fairly heavy structural network, and it was discreet enough not to disturb the rhythmic continuity of the wall, but became superfluous in the successive apartment houses – 860 Lake Shore Drive apartments, 1951[30] (Figs. 832–5), Commonwealth Promenade apartments, 1957 – with steel skeletons and covered with uniform glass walls; all the architecture depended, as in an ancient Greek temple, on the carefully considered proportions of a single element, the rhythmically repeated panel.

In the house for E. Farnsworth, of 1950, Mies gave his own personal interpretation of the detached American house standing in green surroundings; a glass prism detached from the ground and supported by well-spaced metal supports, with an intermediate platform making it possible to sit in the open air without going down to the ground. In the plan of the '50 × 50' house (1951) the solution is even more uncompromising: the supports are reduced to four, placed in the middle of the four sides, and the panes of glass meet at the corners without the encumbrance of any structure.

These disciplined and perfect pieces of architecture stand outside in the American countryside as isolated objects, set down in an empty square of city or in the untouched countryside, and they exclude any relationship with their surroundings, apart from with certain natural backdrops: the stretch of Lake Michigan, the wood surrounding the Farnsworth house. They are works which have a point to prove; they do not resolve present day conflicts but point to the image of an ideal city where these conflicts might finally have been settled.

This image, if it had no direct hold on reality, was nonetheless very effective indirectly: it aroused the imagination of other designers, inspired clients and administrations, even to some extent modified the habits of industry.

Through his collaboration with various local designers, Mies gradually assumed the figure of a superdesigner, a creator of exemplary forms which he transmitted to others so that they could be repeated and adapted to actual circumstances. He had no need of a large studio, because many fashionable firms (Holabird and Roche, Pace Associates etc.) were in a certain sense his clients.

American industry realized that Mies'

prestige could be exploited for publicity value, and this was the start of a series of great prestige commissions: the Seagram buildings in the heart of New York, the Bacardi headquarters in Cuba.

The Seagram building[31] (Figs. 836 and 837), completed in 1959, was realized with exceptional means: the visible metal parts were of bronze, the panelling in polished marble or pink glass; the installations were of the most perfect possible; even the actual volumetric solution was intrinsically very expensive, since by leaving open the small square in front of the building the owners were giving up a good portion of the cubic space that could have been utilized on that site. Although all this – the prodigality of the use of the site – constituted so much publicity for the firm, Mies did not object to working on this project and did it in the only correct way, by transposing quantitative exception into qualititative exception, the availability of large amounts of money into absolute perfection.

The economic sacrifices were not in vain, since the square isolates the building from the traffic of Park Avenue, allows the visitor to contemplate it more peacefully, to establish a calmer relationship with the architecture; the materials chosen guaranteed the durability of the outer surface and the absolute control of the chromatic features; the impeccable design of the installations ensured that the perfection of the building would not be marred, because of some unexpected defect, in the course of the execution and upkeep. Rather than a contemporary building, this is in a sense a prototype, to be utilized in many later works; this justified the enormous amount of money spent, as happened with industrial models, and only in this way could the publicity-seeking intention be made morally acceptable, since the public's attention was solicited on behalf of a particular interest, but received an objective contribution in exchange, an enrichment of its experience and a probable

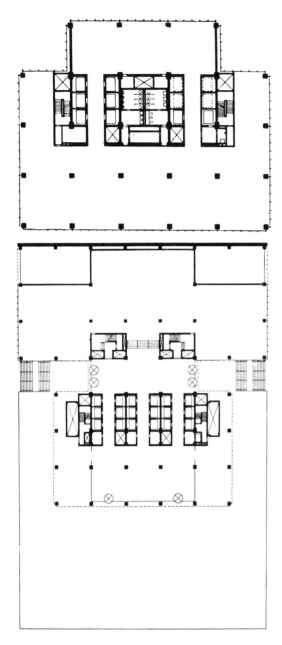

836, 837   *New York, Seagram building (Mies, 1956)*

stimulus to the improvement of future building activity.

In a recent conversation Mies used this phrase: 'I don't want to be interesting, I want to be good'.[32] American patrons regarded him as interesting and so they offered him opportunities of designing; he

accepted that they should be drawn by curiosity, by desire for publicity, or by any external motive whatever, but for his part he committed them to a severely moral course of action, offered them continual lessons in moderation, coherence and clarity.

It is not yet possible to say whether this

attempt has any chance of success. It is a walk along a razor's edge and the danger of formalism is continually present, just as it was thirty years ago in the works of the Germans. But present day reality, particularly American reality, probably does not leave the architect any other possible choice. It is in fact impossible to embark on any discussion on the level of ideas alone and it is vital to talk with facts; Neutra said: 'The architect, like any other artist, can never prove things. They must prove themselves to others';[33] Mies' buildings are precisely such silent demonstrations set in the heart of American cities and available to everyone, all the time.

In order that they might be implemented, an initial compromise had to be made with patrons, executors and with the public itself. The whole difficulty lay in not yielding any further ground, by aiming at the perfect coherence and integrity of the architectural result and by simplifying the means of expression greatly, if necessary. This attempt could be sustained only by total, unremitting commitment, and only by as persistent a character as Mies van der Rohe.

6 Recent developments in American architecture

In the first ten years after the war there was constant discussion of the differences between European and American architecture, and a current distinction, in America, between a group of 'Europeanizing' architects, and other purely American ones.

This problem was dealt with in the book *The Modern House in America* (1940) which contained a series of statements by American architects, and in the *Storia dell'Architettura Moderna* by Bruno Zevi, who named the members of the two groups: the first included M. Abramowitz, G. Ain, B. Fuller, P. Goodwin, W. K. Harrison, F. Kiesler, Kocher and Frey, E. Stone, as well as the immigrants P. Belluschi, L. Kahn, R.

Soriano, O. Stonorov; the second, W. Wurster, G. A. Dailey, J. E. Dinwiddie, A. H. Hill, F. Langhorst, F. J. McCarthy, G. F. Keck, R. Royston, F. Violich, E. Williams, H. H. Harris, H. P. Clark, A. B. Dow, R. V. Hall, V. de Mars. For the latter, the inevitable point of reference was Frank Lloyd Wright, who had in fact theorized about the 'American' tendency in architecture.

In the first edition of this book we gave an account of this controversy, pointing out how irrational it was. We considered the works of some European architects who had emigrated between 1920 and 1940 not so as to contrast them with the work of American architects, but to show their liberating effect on local culture, just at the moment when the 'New Deal' was mobilizing both in an unprecedented effort of co-ordination.

According precisely to the theses of the European movement, a direct transplantation of European results would have been inadmissible and instead it became possible to tackle American problems in a really open-minded way; one need mention only the town-planning activity which, within the framework of the New Deal, brought about the following innovations, in order of time:

a The 'green belts' realized by the Federal Resettlement Administration from 1936 onwards: Greenbelt in Maryland, Greendale in Wisconsin, Greenhills in Ohio: they derived from Howard's model of the garden city (already transferred to America by C. Stein, who founded Radburn, on the outskirts of New York, in 1928) but were interesting because of the new solutions they produced, linked to the American way of life: the motor traffic meant a broader network of roads and an increase in the size of the blocks – which contained facilities for recreation – to keep pedestrian routes separate from those for motor vehicles (Figs. 840–2).

b The agricultural villages financed at the same time by the Farm Security Admini-

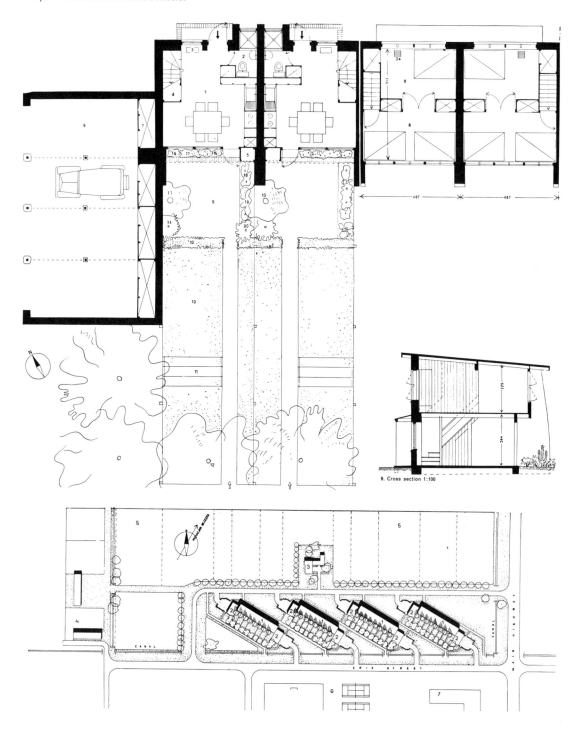

6. Cross section 1:100

838, 839   *Chandler, Arizona, Village of the Farm Security Administration (B.S. Cairns and V. de Mars, 1937; from A. Roth,* La Nouvelle Architecture, *1940)*

stration: Woodville and Yuba City in California, and Chandler in Arizona. The planners had to make use of prefabricated or mobile houses, or else local building systems; in Chandler, adobe (a mixture of straw and mud) was used, though imitation of traditional buildings was avoided, because the adobe was not used for external walling, but for transversal partitions, joined by wooden structures. Thus the architectural result retained just the degree of traditional reference that derived logically for the constructional system (for instance the spur shape of the wall ends) introduced into a modern and rationalist composition.

c The workers' villages built during the war, designed by many of the best American architects of the time, as well as Gropius, Breuer, Neutra, Saarinen, Howe, Wurster and Stonorov. In tackling such a restricting subject, and forced to base their work on rigorous functional analysis, even the most formalist of them, such as Wurster, gave the best of themselves, abandoning individual and national ambitions.

Looked at some years later, the absurdity of the controversy about European and American tendencies emerges clearly without any need of explanation. Today, what conditions the activity of American designers is not reference to their respective origins, but the variety, the urgency and rapid changes in the concrete requirements which architects must fulfil, due to the peculiar character of current American reality.

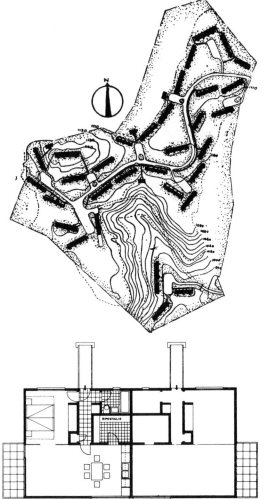

840 *(above)* *Plan of Greendale, Wisconsin*
841, 842 *(below)* *Workers' village at New Kensington, Pennsylvania (Gropius and Breuer, 1940)*

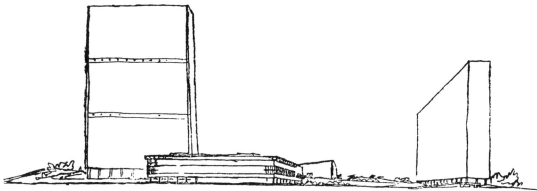

843, 844 *New York, U.N. headquarters (Harrison and Abramowitz, 1948–50) and the sketch for it by Le Corbusier of 27 March 1947 (from* Oeuvre Complète*)*

One primary need, which was already clearly felt just after the war, was that of the revival of the business centres in the cities, where a new type of building had to be found for the great office blocks, in the place of the Romantic tower-like skyscrapers.

The first practical opportunity was the building of the United Nations building in

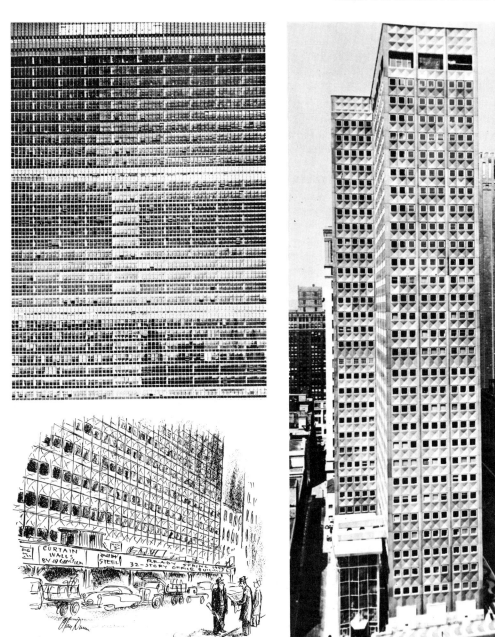

'Very good—14 hours flat—but they're all upside down!'

845 *(above, left)* *New York, One of the façades of the U.N. building*
846 *(below, left)* *Cartoon from the* Architectural Record, *April 1955*
847 *(right)* *Pittsburgh, A.L.C.O.A. building (Harrison and Abramowitz, 1952)*

848　*Pittsburgh, A.L.C.O.A. building*

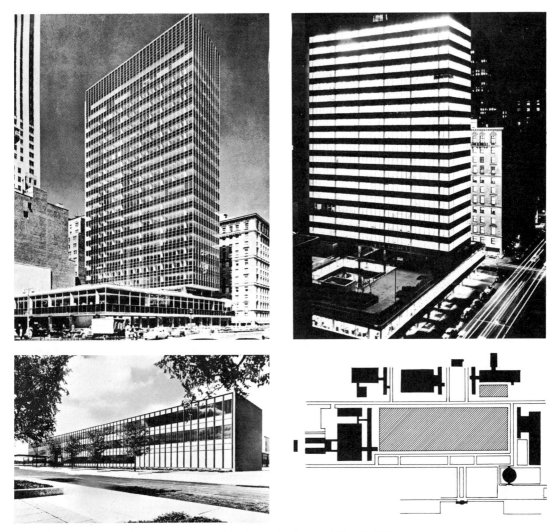

849, 850 *(above)* *New York, Lever House (Skidmore, Owings and Merrill 1952)*
851, 852 *(below)* *Detroit, General Motors buildings (E. & E. Saarinen, 1951)*

New York. In 1947 the United Nations authorities appointed a commission of advisers from the various countries,[34] including Le Corbusier. He arrived in New York two months before the others and drew up a volumetric plan, between January and March, which was subsequently accepted by the Commission, proposing to house the secretariat, the Meeting Halls and the General Assembly in three separate blocks, the first two being 'Cartesian skyscrapers' set at right-angles to one another (Fig. 844). As usual, Le Corbusier's suggestion was a prelude to a more complete plan which he wanted to develop in his own way; but his efforts were unsuccessful and the executive plan was drawn up by Wallace K. Harrison (b. 1895) and Max Abramowitz (b. 1908) between 1948 and 1950 (Fig. 843).

It is probable that Le Corbusier would

have tempered the contrast between the scale of the skyscrapers and that of the element of the single office with appropriate modifications in the uniform fabric of the façades, as in the theoretical plan for Algiers of 1938 and in the European 'Unités d'habitation'; Harrison and Abramowitz on the other hand accepted this contrast in an almost brutal manner. The lesser façades have no openings and are absolutely smooth, covered in white marble, while the long façades are two immense glassed surfaces, made up of the repetition of a very small module – the window, which appears over 2,730 times on each one. Thus no proportional relationship is established between the module and the whole, between the human scale and the scale of the building, and the glass façades appear almost as two joined slabs like the solid terminal walls, partly because the green colour and brightness of the glass blurred the minute design of the metal supports (Fig. 845).

The architectural solution is certainly schematic but in a certain sense is bolder and more courageous than any previous one, since it brusquely poses the problem of the modern skyscraper, formed of an indefinite repetition of a module on a human scale, without subjecting it to the optical and proportional precepts imposed by tradition. As in Paxton's Crystal Palace – built just a century earlier – the relative lack of cultural preoccupation may possibly have thrown a shaft of light into the future and revealed the need for a re-examination of certain habits possibly ill-suited to the new scale of problems.

In 1952 the same designers built a second important building, in which they developed a similar concept: the A.L.C.O.A. building in Pittsburgh[35] (Figs. 847 and 848). The skyscraper, built by the Aluminium Company of America, was entirely covered with pre-fabricated panels in aluminium, faceted like diamonds for greater rigidity and with gaps for the windows where necessary. The marked chiaroscuro of each panel made the compositional process of the simple juxtaposition of the pieces even more obvious and it is here so frank and direct as to suggest comparison with children's construction games. Furthermore the whole followed certain laws of its own, which had nothing to do with the elements themselves: with respect to the dimensions of the whole, the dimensions of the panels disappear, and the façades appear as airy and uniform fields of colour, barely ruffled by the alternate light and shade of the diamond points, as happened in old buildings in rusticated ashlar; but here there was no intermediate element between the boss and the building and the general shape, disengaged from the implications of texture, can be read with absolute spontaneity like an abstract diagram.

This way of building had a rapid success, since it offered appropriate solutions to certain problems connected with the rate of building, the cost and maintenance of commercial buildings; it introduced a mechanical, almost a casual character into architecture, which Americans themselves noted with irony (Fig. 846) and lent itself to certain decorative experiments, as in the Socony Building, also by Harrison and Abramowitz. Here the standard panel in stainless steel had a sort of ornamental rosette stamped on it, but because of its indefinite repetition the motif was not really decoration as it was traditionally understood, i.e., a plastic or pictorial comment on the composition as a whole.

Mies, too, made a contribution to this kind of building; what in the A.L.C.O.A. had been a raw problem, was more thoroughly explored and meditated upon in the Chicago apartments and Seagram building, and the juxtaposition of the various elements became a calculated process of modular composition, making rigorous control possible even in large complexes.

This research of Mies' was complementary to the general direction taken by much of the

American building industry; for this reason his experience was widely influential and raised the standard of public and industrial building considerably during the last decade.

Between 1950 and 1951 Eliel and Eero Saarinen (1910–61) built the technical centre of the General Motors in Detroit, and applied Mies' modular composition on a really vast scale, with a rigour that is still unsurpassed.

The production of the well known firm of Skidmore, Owings and Merrill improved from 1951 onwards, when Gordon Bunshaft (b. 1909) designed Lever House in New York for them: a square block of eighteen floors, suspended on a series of low blocks, where the irregular rooms were housed. This was followed by the US Consulate at Düsseldorf (1954–5), the offices of the Inland Steel Company in Chicago (1956–8), of the Crown Zellerbach Corporation in San Francisco (1957–9), the Harris Trust and Saving Bank in Chicago (1957–60), the Union Carbide Corporation in New York (1957–61) and the Chase Manhattan Bank in New York (1957–61), whose sixty floors merged with those of the other great skyscrapers of the past on the Manhattan skyline. But in other buildings by the same firm, for instance the buildings for the John Hancock Mutual Life Insurance Company in San Francisco (1958–9), the modular composition was burdened with ambiguous stylistic allusions.

In fact, modular composition was used frequently, around 1960, as a support for the most gratuitous decorative inventions, which inevitably turned into references to period styles: by Harrison and Abramowitz in the concert hall and opera house for the Lincoln Centre in New York, by Skidmore, Owings and Merrill in the design (also by Bunshaft) for the Lambert Bank in Brussels, while Philip Johnson (b. 1905), the former collaborator with Mies, theorized about this tendency while making use of classical forms for the Sheldon art gallery of the University of Nebraska and the theatre in the Lincoln centre.

At the same time the technique of the 'curtain wall', i.e. of the façade made entirely of light panels, spread and was commercialized, sometimes being reduced to a decoration applied to already existing buildings, even stone ones, to modernize their outward appearance.

Thus throughout building production, the method of modular composition threatened to become only a variation on the treatment of the façades, without affecting the organization of space.

The effect on town-planning was no different from that of the traditional tower skyscraper: the new parallelepipeds, glass or metal, were crowded together into a small space, cancelled one another out and did not diminish the chaos of American cities, indeed they possibly even added to it.

To get an idea of the confusion one should remember Le Corbusier's argument in connection with the United Nations Building. Presenting the model of his suggested building in his *Oeuvre Complète*, he made this comment: 'the appearance of an element of the "ville radieuse" in the checker-board system of New York's streets' (Fig. 843). The Cartesian skyscraper was therefore the architectural sample of a new concept of town-planning, incompatible with the traditional chess-board system and destined to replace it.

The vitality of the American gridiron system, and the difficulty of replacing it with a new layout, was due to the fact that the gridiron had hitherto functioned by initially disengaging from one another the buildings that could be put up on the individual lots. As long as this basic unit continued to correspond to the size of the various enterprises, the basic chess-board would be continually confirmed, even if the buildings changed their shape and size; but the chess-board was threatened by undertakings whose very nature was contrary to the shape of the sites: urban railways and motorways, port and industrial installations, some public

853, 854   *Armchair designed by C. Eames and desk by G. Nelson for the Miller collection*

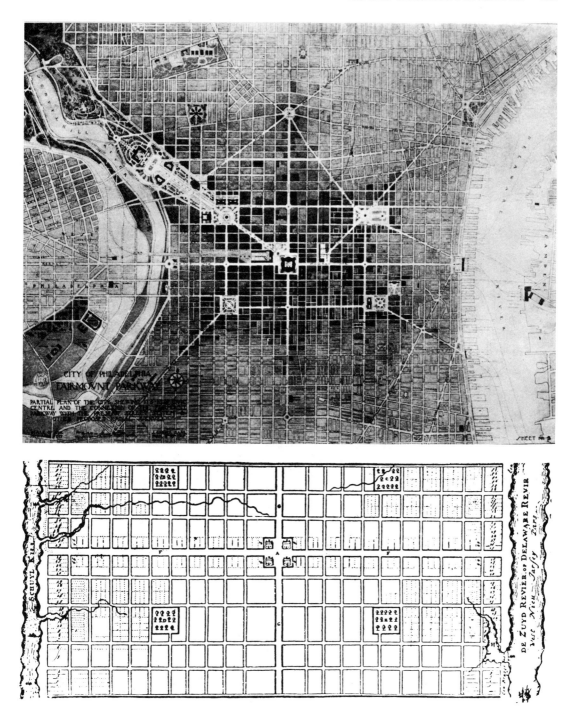

855, 856 *Philadelphia, Gréber plan (1917) compared with Penn's plan*

857   *Boston, Construction of an urban motorway*

services of the same dimensions. Each of the undertakings had been regarded as an exception and was able to be implemented only by destroying a corresponding part of the old fabric of the city; but now the exceptions had become so numerous that, as a whole, they formed a new town-planning framework, its meshes wider and less regular than the old one.

The central problem of modern American architecture is that of effecting a timely transference from the old to the new urban structure, and of drawing from it all the consequences in the field of the designing of buildings. The technique of the curtain wall, by disengaging the dimensions of the building elements from those of the whole, is one of the indispensable instruments for tackling the new scale of planning.

The scope of this method of planning is

being realized both deductively, i.e. by elaborating development schemes for the re-structuring of city centres – for instance Philadelphia, Dallas and Boston – and inductively, when a single building enterprise reaches the dimensions of the World Trade Centre recently designed by Yamasaki in New York.

Another field in which recent developments pose new tasks for architects, and where general clarification *vis-à-vis* town-planning is urgently needed, is that of residential building.

The development of extensive building on the outskirts of cities, and therefore the increase of metropolitan areas continued at an ever greater rate; the idea of controlling the architectural quality of houses by partial prefabrication, as Gropius suggested after the war, has become less and less relevant, because the interest of the consumer has moved from the actual outward building to the installations – ever more numerous – and to the degree of comfort that they can ensure. This comfort is made available to ever larger sectors of the population by means of standardization applying preferably to the whole house, rather than to its parts, as in the case of the motor-car.

Meanwhile the spread of suburban districts has made vital a new distribution of these services which cannot be realized in the home, and primarily of commercial ones; hence the shopping centres with large car-parks, where an increasing variety of activities, including entertainment, take place.

The most disconcerting aspect of these developments is the speed with which things change, making impossible the repetition of earlier attempts and making series of convergent experiments necessary, in the present state of cultural organization, to attain acceptable results.

This is probably at the root of the unease prevalent in American culture, the unevenness of the activities of some of the most gifted American architects, for instance Paul Rudolph (b. 1918), Minoru Yamasaki (b. 1912) and the occasional search for absolutely new forms – as in certain plans by Louis Kahn (b. 1901) which do not aim to demonstrate any Utopian viewpoint but which are the result of an impatient desire to anticipate the development of facts, which on the contrary always precede artists' interpretations.

To this acceleration of everyday experience pop art painters and sculptors reacted by registering images and fragments of the surrounding world and these, immobilized and abstracted from the rhythm of existence, revealed their disturbing significance.

But we believe that architects can do more, if they set themselves to seek a new distribution of the human energies at present being applied to the problem. Ideally they should give up hope of solving the problem on their own from the start, and should take their place in a communal and co-ordinated effort, the only effort that can have any hope of success.

nineteen

Europe after the Second World War

The Second World War left behind it greater material destruction than the first.

The damage looked so serious, at the end of the war, that it seemed likely to hamper the recovery of the countries affected for a long period of time; but for various reasons – because of American aid, the favourable course taken by the world situation in general, the progress of modern technology – the war was followed by a period of economic expansion which made great social changes necessary, changes that were deeper and more sudden, in some countries, than at any other time in their history. Since this process was a very rapid one, there was conflict almost everywhere between the emergency measures necessitated by the war damage and long-term measures necessitated by economic development; in short, between reconstruction and planning. In the technical field, this was the dominant problem in post-war Europe.

In the cultural field the situation was quite different from that which followed the First World War. The countries which had fought in the First World War belonged, until a few years ago, to the same system of balance, they had largely common institutions and traditions, and some of these still remained. But the parties of the Second World War represented antithetical institutions and traditions, as in the old wars of religion; in the conquered countries, political and social régimes crumbled, leaving emptiness behind them, while in the victorious countries political and social conflicts became acute, and tended to amount to basic alternatives.

The boundaries between technology, politics and morals, which seemed clear at first, were now no longer recognizable. The enormity of certain crimes, such as the death of many millions of Jews, transcended political assessment, and the possibility of destruction inherent in the most modern means of warfare laid responsibilities on technicians which went beyond the technological field. The obvious connection between remote and immediate causes, intentional and non-intentional ones, made every decision difficult and uncertain.

When the war was over the main reaction was one of simple elementary relief. Then came a feeling of weariness, a desire to avoid basic problems, to be content with immediate, tangible results: unpropitious conditions for the careful consideration demanded by the gravity of contemporary problems.

It is not possible, within the limits of this chapter, to give a definitive judgment, or even a complete review of the works of reconstruction in European countries. We shall restrict ourselves to describing certain of the more significant facts, which may clarify the current situation and point towards possible future developments.

1 Rebuilding in England

As happened a hundred years ago at the time of the first sanitary laws, English town-planning experience acted as an example and as a stimulus to the other countries of Europe.

The town-planning law of 1932 empowered local administrations to control the transformations in the use of land when these were actually taking place, but not actively to intervene to bring them about; since these transformations were controlled by very considerable interests, the administrations soon proved incapable of restraining them and of bearing the political weight of the decisions which should limit private activities. Plans were drawn up slowly, and amid many difficulties; in 1942 only three per cent of Britain's land was accounted for by any plan actually in force.

The problems created by this situation soon became evident, both because of the economic crisis, which revealed the functional shortcomings of English industry and agriculture – due in part to the actual territorial distribution of these activities throughout the country – and because of the insistent criticism put forward by the town-planners. Howard died in 1928 but his ideas were taken up by his disciples, particularly by C. B. Purdom and F. J. Osborn; the old Garden Cities and Town-Planning Association, which took the name of Town and Country Planning Association, published a journal of the same name, edited by Osborn, and it kept alive the awareness of the need for a reform of current legislation. Furthermore an enquiry on garden cities in 1935 bore witness to their vitality and recommended the extension of this experiment,[1] though

without success.

The crisis forced the Government to intervene in economic life much more firmly than before, abandoning among other things the principle of free enterprise after more than a century; in this way the premises were laid down for greater coercive action in the field of town-planning as well.

In 1937 a Royal Commission was set up to study the distribution of the industrial population, headed by Sir M. Barlow. Its aims were expressed as follows:

'To inquire into the causes which have influenced the present geographical distribution of the industrial population of Great Britain, and the probable direction of any change in that direction in the future; to consider what social, economic or strategical disadvantages arise from the concentration of industries and·the industrial population in large towns or in particular areas of the country, and to report what remedial measures, if any, should be taken in the national interest'.[2]

The report was published in 1940, together with twenty volumes of documentation, and used very harsh words to describe the disadvantages of demographic and economic concentration around large cities; it recognized that the administrations and laws currently in force were incapable of remedying them, because they could improve the internal pattern of the cities, but not regulate their growth; it suggested the setting up of a central authority which should be in control of building land and which – as one of the technical solutions suited to correcting the distribution of centres of settlement – advised the formation of new towns or the development of existing ones where this was appropriate.

This report might have remained simply a theoretical recommendation if the war had not intervened; the enormous bombardments of London and Coventry played the same part, in the formation of the new

English town-planning laws, that the epidemics had played a century before in the formation of the first sanitary laws.

During the discussion on how to rebuild London, two committees were appointed in 1941 to complete the work done by the Royal Commission: the first, headed by Scott, to study the use of land in rural areas and the second, headed by J. Uthwatt, to work on a solution to the urgent problem of compensation, on which town-planning control of the use of building land depended.

The two reports were published in 1942, one shortly after the other.[3] The Scott committee had noted that agriculture was seriously threatened by the thoughtless developments on the edges of the industrial cities, and re-stated the need for the distribution of industrial activities on agricultural land to be regulated by a plan. The Uthwatt report on the other hand started from an overall concept of public intervention, which led to the fresh formulation of the problem:

'The notion of town-planning which we are taking as the basis for our deductions has a breadth which neither public opinion nor the law have yet recognized. Its application must constitute a concrete and permanent element in the internal policy of this country, must aim to obtain the best possible utilization of the land in the interests of the community and of individual well-being, and implies the subordination to the public good of personal interests and the desires of landowners. The unreserved acceptance of this concept of town-planning is of vital importance for the policy of reconstruction, because all aspects of the country's activities depend, in the last analysis, on the use that is made of its land. The denser the population, the better controlled this use must be, so that the limited land can supply the vital services; the more complex the social organization, the more severe must be the control of the use of land, in the common interest'.[4]

With regard to the instruments of public control over the use of building land, the Uthwatt report, like the preceding one, started from the concept that the increase in value produced by these transformations should go to the community, not to the single land-owners, and it suggested that the value of compensation should be determined by reference to the value of the land in 1939; neither report made any explicit statement of the need for the complete nationalization of building land, but they posed it implicitly as an objective of future legislation.

Meanwhile work was going on on the development plan for London. In 1942 the M.A.R.S. group produced a theoretical plan,[5] which broke the continuity of the fabric of the town into a series of districts separated by green belts and joined by the crossing of a main axis going through the historic centre and industrial parts, running along the Thames. In 1943 the Royal Academy published a plan for the centre in accordance with the traditional concepts of formal layout. But in 1944 the L.C.C. preliminarily adopted the plan by Abercrombie and Forshaw;[6] this kept a reasonable distance from any concept of geometrical regularity and any too basic intervention in districts already built, but aimed at inverting the process of concentration followed hitherto, with a series of measures on a regional scale, going beyond the limits of the city as it then was.

Based on a detailed examination of the existing built up area, the plan distinguished several concentric zones:

a   The *inner ring*, which included the whole area of the county of London and which was characterized by excessive density; this zone was to be progressively thinned out with the removal of over 400,000 inhabitants.

b   The *suburban ring*, whose density was not excessive but which needed to be reorganized and provided with suitable amenities.

c The *green belt*, an extensive area of green surrounding the existing city and which was to remain as it was, unbuilt up. This concept derived from Howard and indicated the intention, from now on, of limiting the growth of London as a compact organism.

d The *outer ring*, where the new centres were to develop, in the form not of dormitory suburbs but of new towns, large enough to have lives of their own (Fig. 861).

The street network was based on a new system of fast radii, converging on an internal ring made in the inner ring, and on an outer ring, between the green belt and the outer ring. Since the success of the new plan was believed to be dependent on public approval, no means were spared to make the concepts underlying it known, and popular exhibitions, debates and informative publications proliferated.[7]

Meanwhile a new central planning authority was being set up. In 1941 in the House of Lords, the Churchill government declared their intention of creating a central organ to co-ordinate town-planning activities; in 1942 the functions of the Ministry of Health were assumed by the Ministry of Public Works, which became known as the Ministry of Works and Planning (an act which had an almost symbolic significance, since it was from sanitary legislation that modern English town-planning had sprung); finally in 1943 the Ministry of Town and Country Planning was set up.

In the same year a temporary law subjected all building activity to the approval of the new Ministry, during the preparation of the new plans; in 1944 another law authorized compulsory purchase by the Ministry of the land needed to carry out the works of reconstruction in areas which had suffered war damage, or developments in the areas where the utilization of the land was no longer compatible with modern needs.

When the Labour Government came to power in 1945, town-planning was given a further, decisive stimulus. In the autumn, the new Minister of Town-Planning, L. Silkin, appointed a committee for the new towns, with the following duties:

'To consider the general questions of the establishment, development, organization and administration that will arise in the promotion of New Towns in furtherance of a policy of planned decentralization from congested urban areas; and in accordance therewith, to suggest guiding principles on which towns should be established and developed as self-contained and balanced communities for living'.[8]

The prompt and effective work of this committee made it possible for the New Towns Act to be passed less than a year later, on 1 August 1946; for each new town[9] (Figs. 863–8) a relevant body was set up, independent of local administrations and closely linked with the central authority: the Development Corporation, which had the power to acquire land, establish the way in which it was to be used, build basic installations and obtain the subsidies provided for by the 1936 Housing Act to realize the districts of subsidized housing. These organizations completely took the place of local authorities in the task of giving life to the new towns, but they were thought of as temporary, and for this reason could not control the permanent public services.

So far it was a question of particular measures, which concerned certain sectors and were basically emergency steps. In 1947 a new English town-planning law was passed, concluding this cycle; this unified planning methods over the whole country and prepared for the re-absorption of all emergency measures into the orbit of normal administration.

Following the English tradition, the law left the task of town-planning to local authorities, but so as not to split this task among too many bodies it stated that the plans should be drawn up by the County

858   *Allegory of building speculation (from C. B. Purdom,* How should we rebuild London?, *1945)*

859, 860 *Two cartoons from Purdom (*op. cit.*)*
861, 862 *The London plan of 1943 by Abercrombie and Forshaw. From the inside: the county of London (in black), the inner ring, the suburban ring, green belt and outer ring, where the new towns are*

Councils, i.e. by the local bodies with the most extensive territorial powers. These might come together among themselves and form Joint Planning Boards, to draw up more extensive plans, and when the plans were actually being implemented they could delegate their powers to the lesser bodies, to the District and Town Councils. The Minis-

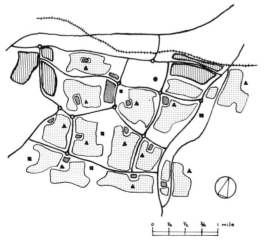

residential districts
shops and offices
industry
▲ primary school
■ secondary school
● college

863–865 *Part of the new town of Harlow (plan from L. Rodwin,* The British New Towns Policy, *1956)*

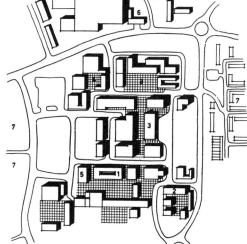

1 civic centre   5 church
2 offices   6 fire station
3 shops   7 houses
4 playground

866, 867, 868 *Views of the new towns round London: a residential district in Harlow, the centre of Hemel Hempstead and an industrial district in Crawley*

try of Town-Planning initiated and sanctioned all planning activity, it had the power to take the place of the local authorities if these evaded their duties, and kept control of all financial operations with regard to land, through the Central Land Board. Parliament had not warmed to the concept of total nationalization of land, already contained in the Labour electoral programme, and arranged to compensate landowners for the loss of the potential increase in value within five years, fixing the compensation according to the current value of the land and setting aside for this end, for the whole of England, an overall sum of £400m.; this increase in value was offset with a tax, to be paid by the landowners on the execution of all future works.

This law marked an enormous advance over the previous ones, but it had various shortcomings, too: it did not define the criteria for determining compensation nor the development tax questions which were referred to future decisions by the ministries, and it did not resolve relations between the Ministry of Town-Planning and other ministries, which also took important decisions in matters of planning: the Ministry of Transport which was concerned with the roads, the Ministry of Trade which were responsible for locating new industries, the Ministry of Defence which was in charge of military installations.

The realization of the plans and the building of the new towns went ahead rapidly, particularly at first; at the end of 1954 about half the population anticipated for the seven new towns around London had settled into them. When the Conservatives returned to power in 1951 none of the enterprises begun by the Labour Government was abandoned, but their meaning was partially altered. The mechanism for the recovery of the increase in land value was revised in 1953, so that the exceptional character of the new towns under the aegis of the Development Corporation was accentuated. Furthermore,

as the town-planning programme gradually became reality, it gave rise to a series of building problems whose solutions had to be found gradually, by trial and error; for this reason the image of the new town was slow to emerge with any precision, and gave an impression of uncertainty, as was the case with Paris during the first decades after Haussmann's transformations.

To these difficulties, after 1952, was added the debate on urban landscape, which characterizes recent town-planning thought in England and of which we shall say more later on.

Along with the general town-planning programme, as soon as the war finished, there were certain other sectorial programmes, one of the most important of which concerned schools and had its roots in the Education Act of 1944, which raised the school leaving age to fifteen.

Between 1945 and 1955 about 2,500 schools were built in England, for a total of 1,800,000 pupils. This scheme, too, was managed by the counties, which generally took planning measures through special technical offices. Of these, that of the Hertfordshire County Council achieved particular distinction, run by Charles H. Askin (1893–1959) who worked out a very successful system of prefabrication (metal supporting structure, ceilings and wall panels in reinforced concrete) and built a large number of exceptionally fine primary and secondary schools.

The work of the architects was based on that of the educationalists, who attributed a variety of functions, both educational and recreational, to the English primary school; in this sector too, therefore, English experience served as a model for that of many other countries.

The greatest merit of English technicians and authorities is that they considered the rebuilding after the war not as a self-contained problem, but as an inseparable part of an overall process of planning; for

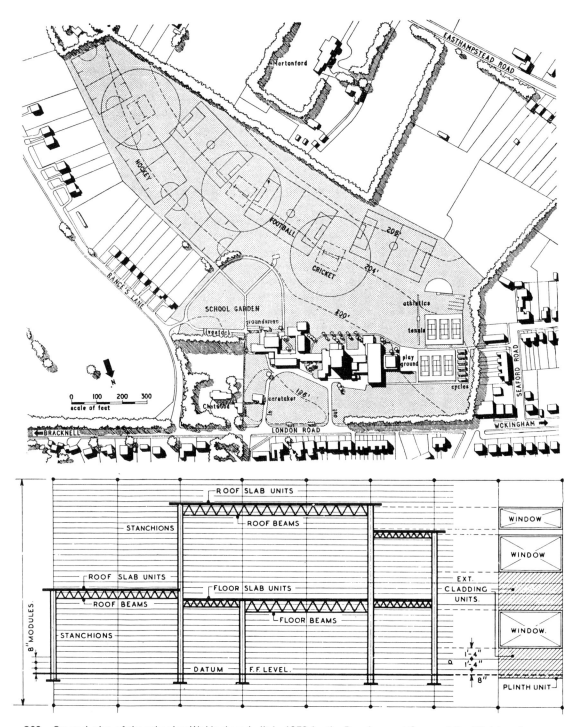

869   *Ground-plan of the school at Wokingham built in 1952 by the Development Group of the Ministry of Education to try out the new measures on a secondary school*
870   *Hills scheme of prefabrication, also adopted by the Hertfordshire County Council*

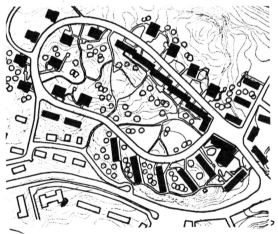
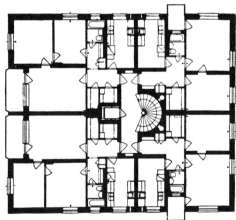

871, 872, 873 *Stockholm, Torsviks district at Lidingo (Ancker, Gate and Lindegren 1943–6; plans from Urbanistica)*

this reason, apart from certain partial failings, English experience has an enormous methodological importance and has been followed with exceptional interest throughout the world. Discussion of the reasons why the initial objectives were not always com-

874   *Hall in the school at Solna (N. Tesc and L.M. Giertz, 1945)*

pletely attained is also of general interest.

The politicians certainly underestimated the implications of decisions in town-planning, which implied a basic upheaval of the structures serving communal life and a shifting of the fundamental principles on

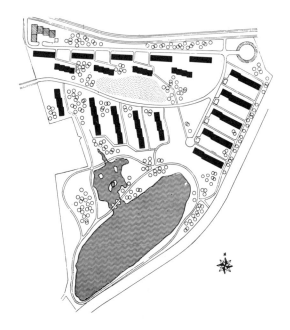

875, 876, 877 *An intensive district near Copenhagen (the Bellahöy, 1951) and an extensive district (Sollerod Park, designed by N. & E. Koppel, 1954)*

which the balance of English society had rested for over a century and a half.

The viability of the experiment derived precisely from the fact that town-planning measures, for the first time since the beginning of the industrial revolution, were not taking place after technical and economic upheavals but in various ways were actually preceding them. This led to a series of difficulties that were in a sense the reverse of the traditional ones; these difficulties, furthermore, stimulated English architec-

tural thought into making an exceptional theoretical and experimental effort, which is still bearing fruit today.

2 Continuity and progress in Scandinavian building

If the English experience was the inevitable model for town-planning in other countries, after the war Swedish experiment acquired a similar exemplary value as far as building design was concerned.

878, 879, 880   *Helsinki, Pension Bank (A. Aalto)*

Sweden, which remained neutral during the war, experienced no war damage, nor did her building production slow down enough to produce a housing crisis. Thus the country almost entirely escaped the difficulty that arose elsewhere, i.e. the antagonism between reconstruction and planning; on the contrary the wartime lull gave Sweden the time to formulate, in the post-war period, an extensive and well-ordered programme of town-planning reorganization in the main cities.

The town-planning law of 1948, like the

881, 882 *(left)* *A. Aalto, furniture for Artek; part of the plan for Rovaniemi, 1945 (from* Werk*)*
883, 884 *(right)* *Säynätsalo, Town Hall (A. Aalto, 1951)*

English one of the year before, gave local administrations the power to determine the time and place of all building enterprises, in accordance with a general town-planning scheme which was to be renewed every five years, and with minutely detailed plans. The law allowed compulsory purchase only for sites destined for public use, while those destined for building had to be acquired on the free market and leased to private individuals or building concerns for sixty years. But the big cities had for some time been

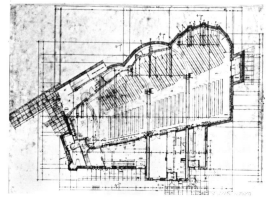

885, 886, 887   *Imatra, Church (A. Aalto, 1958; plan from* Casabella)

buying outlying sites as farming land; Stockholm, which had begun the process in 1904, owned nineteen thousand hectares by 1952, i.e. most of the building land outside the nineteenth-century nucleus.

The new buildings were financed partly by municipal building societies, partly by co-operatives and private concerns; the state, which at first had restricted itself to financing lodgings for the poorest classes, now embarked on a large-scale programme of encouragement and part subsidy for most

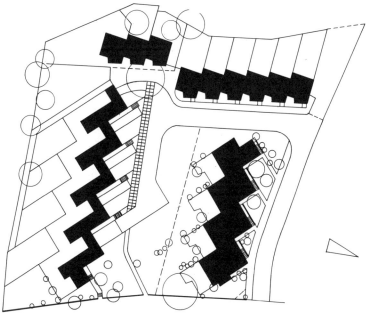

888, 889   *Terrace-houses by Jacobsen at Soholm, near Copenhagen (1950–5; photo shows the houses of 1950)*

Swedish building, both to increase building production and to control rising rents, for building costs were more than double those of the pre-war period.

Since the town-planning schemes were very detailed, the relations between the municipal offices, the architects and the building bodies were rather complex, and the plans were often the result of a repeated exchange of suggestions. This organization was not without its difficulties, but it made it possible to put aside certain basic problems of attitude, which were implicitly determined by the balance between the interests at stake, and to utilize the forces of architectural culture in the most fruitful way, by concentrating discussion on the details rather than on the basic attitude.

In this way Swedish planning, thanks to the happy and possibly momentary balance of social, political and economic needs, developed essentially in the sphere of architectural compositions and the decisions which were expected of the town-planners were concerned far more with form than content; many varied and even contradictory formal experiments could also be carried out, because they had a stable organizational basis.

It was in this atmosphere, in the immediate post-war period, that the neo-empiricist tendency developed. The definition was that of the English critic E. De Maré, who commented on Swedish production as follows in 1948:

'In general it is a reaction against a too rigid formalism. The first excitement of structural experiment has gone and there is a return to workaday common sense. There is a feeling that buildings are made for the sake of human beings rather than for the cold logic of theory. The word *spontanietet*, so often on the lips of young Swedish architects, perhaps gives the key to the approach .... Why, they ask, make windows larger than necessary just to show that we can create a wall entirely of glass? Why flat roofs when they always start to leak in the spring? Why avoid traditional materials when they do their job well and provide pleasant texture and colour at the same time? Why eschew fantasy and decoration for which, in our hearts, we long?

Planning has become much freer and far less concerned with the pattern on paper than with the formal reality. Fenestration, too, is freer and windows occur at the places and of the sizes which needs dictate and as the pattern pleases. Indigenous traditional materials are used both inside and out, especially brick and timber. In domestic work cosiness is coming back and there is a tendency among the more sophisticated at any rate to mix furniture of different types .... Buildings are married carefully to the sites and to the landscape, and flowers and plants are made an integral part of the whole design'.[10]

Obviously, this description did not characterize all Swedish production; there existed a whole range of different tendencies, from the rigorous probings of Sven Markelius (b. 1889) to the decorative experiments of Ralph Erskine (b. 1914). Foreign observers have created an image of Swedish architecture which seems conventional in Sweden but which was a working reality in many other countries where it had a notable influence on the initial phase of reconstruction.

In considering this fact one must bear in mind that what was at stake was not simply a formal choice. Swedish architects worked in conditions that were on the whole favourable: they knew precisely what society wanted from them, they worked with adequate technical and financial means, they built their districts within the framework of good town-planning schemes and therefore at the appropriate time and place. These were not ideals to be fought for but circumstances that had been created, at least temporarily; the remaining margin was mainly of a compositional order and the architect could return to his job, almost as in the olden days.

But in the countries that had been through the war this balance was hampered by many preliminary obstacles: uncertainty of political and social aims, shortage of funds and technical means, lack of town-planning discipline; hence the fascination of Swedish architecture, where these obstacles appeared to have been easily resolved.

The interest, therefore, was at first less concentrated on forms than on methods; the variety of formal experiment attracted attention because it demonstrated the stability of the content. But the close relationship between form and content was transferred from reality to outward symbol, and the implicit conviction arose that by repeating those forms the corresponding content would also be reproduced.

Imitation was therefore distorted by an initial contradiction: the diversity of cultural conditions was what made the forms of Scandinavian architecture seem desirable, but it was also the obstacle that prevented them from becoming acclimatized and taking on a life of their own elsewhere.

Denmark and Finland – unlike Sweden – suffered war damage, which they had to remedy with emergency programmes. But the economico-social similarity, the high level of technical education and the influence of Swedish models blurred initial differences after a few years.

Here too there existed a basic homogeneity, in building-production during the first decade after the war; the contributions of the youngest designers, like Nels and Eva Koppel, J. Utzon, H. and K. Sirén, fitted smoothly into place beside that of the older ones such as K. Fisker.

So, during the first years, did the work of the best-known masters, for instance Aalto and Jacobsen.

When the war was over Aalto was already a world-famous figure. After the success of his pavilion at the 1939 Exposition in New York he was invited to America, taught at the Massachusetts Institute of Technology and in 1949 built the famous student dormitory with its undulating plan. Nonetheless, unlike the German masters, he did not adapt himself to the American atmosphere and the Boston building, however brilliant the plan, was not on the level of the masterpieces of Paimio and Viipuri, partly because the general conception did not take on convincing reality in the final details, which were weak and even careless.

Meanwhile Aalto was working on various town-planning schemes in Finland (the regional plan for the valley of Kokemaki in 1942; the plan for the rebuilding of Rovaniemi in 1945; the plan for the island of Säynätsalo from 1942 until 1949) and after 1950 a new series of splendid architectural works: the Säynätsalo Town Hall (1949 to 1952) (Figs. 883 and 884), the Rautatalo block of shops and offices at Helsinki (1953–5), the building for the Pension Bank (1954–6) and, also in the capital, the House of Culture (1954–6).

This is possibly Aalto's most successful work. The deep identification with his native environment sustains and makes up for his limitations as an individualist; if before 1950, when he was considered as the leader of the organic school in Europe, he himself delighted in repeating certain of his schemes – for instance the undulating line applied on various different scales, from the Boston dormitories to glass vases – in the following decade he gave up all stylized simplification and stuck closely to the needs of the subjects he was tackling, without losing his sensational capacity for inventing new forms (as much cannot be said for his more recent works – the church of Imatra of 1958, the Enso Gutzeit offices in Helsinki of 1961 and the buildings he designed abroad, the apartment block in Bremen, the Wolfsburg recreation centre, the Carré

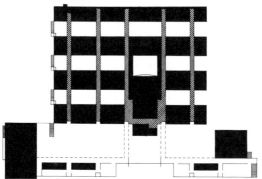

890, 891, 892   *Copenhagen, School at Gentofte (Jacobsen, 1952–6)*

house near Paris – where his passion for a preconceived programme and diminished concentration on detail once again weakened the architectural result).

Jacobsen – who lived in Sweden during the war and concentrated on applied art – designed mainly residential centres after he returned to his own country (Ibstrupparken II, 1946; Jaegersborg, Gentofte, 1947;

Soholm, 1950, next to the Bellavista of 1934; Islevvaenge, Rodovre, 1951; Alléhusene, Gentofte, 1952) where the empiricist repertoire was simplified, with an evident taste for geometrical abstraction. But the course taken by Jacobsen was almost the opposite to that taken by Aalto; his initial confidence in his native environment gradually faded and a feeling of unease came to the surface, which after 1952 led him towards other experiments, in definite conflict with Danish tradition. This phase began with the school at Gentofte, of 1952, where Jacobsen gave up the usual articulated organism (which he had used a few years earlier in the school at Harby) and adopted a solid plan, which enabled him to organize the internal and external spaces with inflexible rigour (Fig. 891).

We shall return to the later developments of his work in the final chapter.

3 Rebuilding in the USSR

During the last phase of the war the principles that had emerged from previous experience had been elaborated in a sort of code,[11] which served as a guide for the reconstruction of the cities that had been destroyed.

According to Parkins these principles were:

a The size and population of the city must be laid down in advance, in accordance with a programme of general development; the growth of the big cities must be appropriately limited.

b The distribution of the buildings must be planned together with that of all basic services and public amenities.

c The difference between towns and villages must be eliminated, making communications easier between large and small centres, and between city centres and suburbs; the solution of satellite towns was rejected.

d The basic unit, for residential zones, was to be the super-block (kvartal) of about 6,000 inhabitants, provided with a school, day-nursery, shops, playing-fields, post-offices and restaurants.

e The concept of public services was to include all equipment to satisfy political, economic, recreational and aesthetic needs of the population.

f Every city was to be planned with its own criteria and with due respect for its own individual characteristics.

g The traditional styles of Russian architecture were to be respected, though duly adapted to modern techniques and materials.

h Residential building and its requirements were to take precedence over all the rest.

i Town-planning and architecture must follow the principles of Socialist realism, and the value of the principles of criticism and self-criticism was to be recognized, within appropriate organizations.

The bulk of building reconstruction in Russia was realized within the course of the fourth Five Year Plan (1946–50), and then entirely under the Stalinist régime. From the start the operation was rigidly controlled by central authorities and in 1943 a committee for building affairs was set up, within the Council of the people's commissars with the task of 'ensuring state control of building and town-planning works in the process of reconstruction of towns and villages destroyed by the German aggressors'.[12]

At first building was done rather at random, with emergency means and plans so as to re-house homeless citizens as soon as possible. The poor quality of these buildings was repeatedly noted by official inspectors, and particularly by a general enquiry organized in 1948 by the Committee for Architectural Affairs,[13] and on each occasion it was decided that this should be remedied by the broader application of models. In this way, while official statistics declared that in 1947 only a quarter of building production was standardized, in 1948 it had risen to 60 per cent, and in the same year the authorities ruled that all production should be modelled, from now on, on a scale of plans laid down by the authorities. The USSR Academy of Architecture was asked to draw up the plans (Figs. 898–900) and the Committee on Architectural Affairs approved a series of fifty prototype plans for dwellings, plus two hundred

893, 894 (above)   *Moscow, Skyscraper near Krasnye Vorota and Hotel in Kalanchevskya Street*
895, 896 (below)   *Reconstruction in the U.S.S.R.; paintings in the Soviet pavilion at the universal exhibition in Brussels in 1958*

for public buildings, taking into account the differences in climate, habit and technical resources of five main regions: northern Russia, the Baltic states, southern Russia, the Urals and Siberia, central Asia and Transcaucasia.[14]

But the fault which weakened Russian reconstruction was not the poor quality of

897 *(left)   Building in Moscow, near the Lenin hills (from* Urbanistica*)*
898, 899, 900 *(right)   Moscow, Building of the Stalinist period: Novo-Peschanaya Street, Komsomolskaya
Street and one of the prefabricated houses designed by the Soviet Academy of Architecture*

the plans nor poor technical work, but the ambiguity lurking in the illusion that one could treat 'style' as a fixed, material ingredient of planning, to be adapted subsequently to material needs. The adoption of prototype plans, far from remedying the shortcomings that had been complained of, eliminated the possibility that any methodical illumination might emerge from so vast and varied an experiment, confirming the initial ambiguity and disseminating its consequences throughout thousands of copies.

A glance at one of the official apologias on Russian reconstruction, gives one an idea of the results obtained:

'The central motif employed in these, as in all Stalingrad's buildings, is Russian classical architecture with a slight flavour of the East, which must be given a place in its architecture as the city stands on the old route that joined the east to the west. In the very centre of the group will stand a monument to the Stalingrad victory, a tower nearly 60 metres high surmounted by a bronze statue of a trumpeter proclaiming victory[15] . . . the frontal façade of the new building for the City Executive Committee will also be on this square . . . [it will have] a ten-storey tower, surmounted by an oriental gilded dome at the corner . . . .[16]

[At Rostov] Academician Semenov proposes to introduce some of the classic forms used in the architecture of the ancient towns of the Black Sea Basin in addition to the Russian Empire and Russian classical styles . . . .[17]

[In Voronezh the Academician Rudnev] does not intend to rebuild the city so that it will be unrecognizable; he wants to retain and improve the old Voronezh with all its beauty and charm. This, of course, leads to a number of problems of style and character in building, the selection of architectural forms and materials and in

determining the scale and composition of the groups of buildings. Voronezh took form during three centuries and each added its contribution to the art of the city. Rudnev has selected early nineteenth century as his style, the period of Russian classicism, the spirit of which is felt with great strength in the architecture of old Voronezh. The colour of the buildings is closely connected with this decision: Leon Rudnev has categorically rejected cement and ferro concrete – their grey-green barrack like tone would completely ruin the lively clarity of the style.[18]

[In Istra, which was based on an eighteenth century gridiron plan] the new plan follows the old, with the streets widened to form boulevards and some diagonal streets added; Administration Square will contain the buildings of the District Executive Committee with a high square tower arcaded at the top, a large hall for meetings and a façade look-out on public gardens and the square where demonstrations will be held . . . . The Executive Committee building will be carried out in red brick with a white stone arcade and an abundance of majolica decoration, concording in style with the motifs and forms of the seventeenth century. This building determines the character of the architecture of the town as a whole'.[19]

It is easy to discern the political concern behind these architectural considerations. Diverting the attention of the planners to imaginary problems left more space and greater possibilities for restrictive action. The supposed adherence to ancient traditions and popular customs was a conventional ploy which was used to avoid the emergence of a realistic discussion capable of interfering with the authorities' directives, and guaranteed that every enterprise would be set within known cultural forms.

A similar architecture was imposed on the

socialist countries of eastern Europe, even where there had been a consistent modern tradition as in east Germany, Czechoslovakia and Hungary. Almost everywhere monumental roads sprang up, flanked by highly ornate palaces and set along the axes of imposing skyscrapers, on which the odd remaining supporter of period styles or some ambitious young man lavished the most absurd ornaments.

After the death of Stalin and the new course taken by internal Soviet politics, things changed to some degree. The decision of the central committee of the CPSU and of the Soviet Council of Ministers on the elimination of the superfluous in planning and building (November 1955) clearly denounced the stylistic excesses of Stalin's reconstruction:

'The work of many architects and architectural organizations has been greatly influenced by that kind of exterior which delights in massive superfluity . . . . Absorbed by the thought of the impressive appearance the building could have, many architects have concerned themselves solely with beautifying the façades, ignoring the improvement of internal installations and the layout of houses and apartments, and the indispensable need to create a commodity for the population, a commodity required by both the economy and the normal purposes of buildings. There is no possible way of justifying the towered summits, the innumerable decorative columns, the porticos and other architectural superfluities, which have been dug out of the past and which constitute a quantitatively enormous phenomenon in the design of residential and public buildings; as a result, much State money has recently been wasted on the building of dwelling houses'.[20]

There followed a list of buildings where such wastage had occurred; in a block of houses in Leningrad 'a series of superfluous columns two storeys high had been planned'; in an administrative building in Tbilissi 'a tower fifty-five metres high was built, with no practical use and at a cost of three million roubles'; the public buildings of Baku 'are riddled with complicated arcades, loggias and towered superstructures'; in the nursing homes in the south unnecessary arcades were built, colonnades and towers, expensive finishing materials, artificial marble, top quality wood, bronzes and plaster statues; the entrances to the sub-station at Nogiski 'were of polished granite, with two enormous marble globes near the entrance'.[21]

There is no reason to believe that these reproofs were not sincere and did not express a real economic concern. The idea that style and functionality are separate requirements made it possible, in many cases, for a conflict to arise between the two needs, and for convenience to be sacrificed to beauty or for costs to be increased by a gratuitous show of ornament.

But the proposed remedies – to modify the criteria of planning, giving greater importance to functional needs and ensuring that these directives were closely applied by standardizing all production, more strictly than in the past, with new prototypes – were ineffectual, since they attacked effects, leaving the causes unaltered and indeed confirmed.

The above-mentioned decision made it obligatory for central and local organizations, planners and executors radically 'to modify their own works of planning or construction as soon as possible; to examine within three months the advance documentation on plans for buildings with the aim of eliminating from these plans excesses in architectural finish, and in distributive and constructional solutions; to ensure an unconditional execution of the prescribed prototype plans and to take the indispensable measures for the elimination of the delay that there has been in connection with this matter'. Furthermore 'it was considered vital, by 1 September 1956, to have worked out new prototype

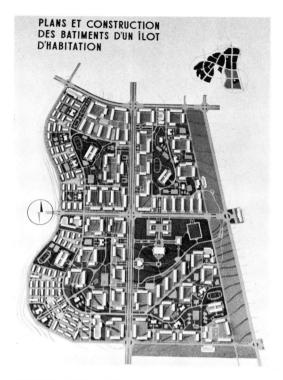

901–904   *New Soviet buildings, in the models shown at the Brussels universal exhibition of 1958*

plans of residential buildings of 2, 3, 4, and 5 storeys, of schools for 280, 400 and 800 pupils, of hospitals for 100, 200, 300 and 400 patients, of crèches, shops and collective food suppliers, cinemas, theatres, nursing homes, hotels and rest homes, making use of the best Russian and foreign experience in planning and building'.[22]

As long as the Russians continued to talk in these terms, the problem was insoluble. The functional problems of architecture are solved only if a method is found of making the various requirements compatible, by considering them together as part of a single conception. Otherwise the task awaiting the architect – that of modifying the physical scene according to the needs of his contemporaries – becomes fragmented into so many separate and abstract tasks: stability, distribution, convenience, economy, style, outward decorum, and so on, so that he tries in vain to satisfy them all at once, because each one, conceived in this form, can be satisfied only at the expense of the others.

The material exhibited at the universal exhibition in Brussels in 1958 gives an idea of the results produced by the new turn taken in Russian architecture and town-planning: a huge alabaster model proudly reproduced the Moscow University skyscraper, with its Stalinian pinnacles and colonnades, but in the residential building (Figs. 901–4) the architectural orders, the decorations and carving, have disappeared. The plans for the dwellings and districts are no longer disturbed by concern for symmetry, therefore they may be presumed to be more workable, yet the buildings are very similar to the earlier ones in the same style, without the ornament.

4 Reconstruction in Italy, France and Germany

While in England and Russia – with very different means – an exceptional effort was made to adjust town-planning schemes to the needs of rebuilding, and while in the Scandinavian countries (where the need for reconstruction was less urgent) the balance between town-planning and building concern had been already attained, in the other countries involved in the war – and particularly in Italy, France and Germany – rebuilding did not stimulate equivalent reorganization in town-planning, indeed in the first two cases it came into conflict with the existing town-planning measures and hastened their moment of crisis.

In this way the demands of production and those of co-ordination hindered one another, or at least they made themselves felt at two different stages, making the

achievement of any degree of balance extremely problematical.

In Italy this conflict was at its most serious, because of the extent of the housing shortage which it was vital to remedy – due not only to the war but also to earlier, longstanding backlogs – and because of the fragility of town-planning institutions. In France it was lessened because the need to build was less urgent, in Germany because of the greater strength of the instruments of town-planning control.

Italy emerged from the Second World War without really serious material damage – about 5 per cent of her houses were demolished – but at that moment she received perhaps the most violent political and social shock of her recent history.

A long authoritatian régime had collapsed ignominiously, suddenly revealing the precariousness of its foundations; in every field of thought new men were coming to the fore, replacing the old, not so much because of a relaxation in the political atmosphere, as because the old ruling class, which had lived in the restrictive and artificial climate of Fascist protectionism, was at a loss when faced with the dimensions and complexity of the new problems.

The new ruling class, composed of young men or people who had formerly been out of favour, was full of enthusiasm but could not be said to be really equipped to deal with the serious tasks awaiting it. The fight against Fascism had acted as a limiting factor, directing the most worthy efforts towards a very useful but purely negative goal. In the field of architecture, some of those who had waged the first battle for modern architecture, and perhaps the greatest, were dead: G. L. Banfi, R. Giolli, G. Pagano, E. Persico, G. Terragni.

But at first these uncertainties were swept aside by a new, intense sensation: that of having once again made contact with reality, of seeing the things around one with new eyes, as if for the first time, and particularly those closest to one, hitherto masked by patriotic rhetoric or veiled with platitudes. It was this sensation that gave rise to so-called 'neo-realism' which found its best means of expression in the cinema, but influenced Italian culture in general in a variety of ways. The films of Rossellini and De Sica, the theatre of Eduardo, the paintings of Guttuso, the architecture of Ridolfi at Terni and the Tiburtino district in Rome have in common the desire to keep close to everyday reality, concrete and solid, with a preference for popular and dialectal forms, interest restricted to one's immediate environment, the rejection of the abstract and the exotic.

But there were also important differences. Examining the dates, one sees that architectural neo-realism arrived some years later, when cinematic neo-realism, for instance, was already on the decline. The chronological delay is noticeable in the tone, too: while the cinema, with the immediacy available to it, promptly registered the fleeting but genuine atmosphere of that short period, architecture received it indirectly, in a reflected and almost conventional form, and slipped easily from the popular to the folksy, from spontaneity to artifice.

During a first period, up to 1947, the enthusiasm and activity of the architects were directed mainly towards building technique; since almost nothing was being built, architects concentrated largely on studies and theoretical suggestions, often clumsy and amateurish, which did not have much effect but which were indicative of the conviction that this was the way to begin, by mastering technical processes and particularly the usual, common processes which constituted Italian building practice and which suddenly appeared immensely interesting (this, in fact, was really the connection with neo-realism).

This tendency was illustrated by the preparatory work for the VIII Milan Triennale (1947) and the district QT8, and

in Rome by the *Manuale dell'architetto* (Fig. 905) assiduously compiled by C. Calcaprina, A. Cardelli, M. Fiorentino and M. Ridolfi for the National Council of Research and the U.S.A. Unlike the old books, based on a study of theoretical cases and centring mainly on distributive problems, like that by Neufert,[23] the authors of this book had attempted to gather together in an organic corpus details of current constructional usage in Italy, to abstract theory from practice, avoiding all generalization. It was in this atmosphere that Milanese architects worked on the preparatory studies for their city – a number of committees were set up to investigate the various districts – and those for the Piedmont regional plan, already begun during the war and published in 1947[24] by G. Astrengo, M. Biano, N. Renacco and A Rizotti: this was a work of technical analysis and elaboration, but it was also an intriguing voyage of discovery of Italy and its unknown territory.

Meanwhile attempts were being made to give these aspirations exact theoretic formulation. In 1945 Bruno Zevi (b. 1913) published his essay 'Towards an Organic Architecture' and suggested using this term (with reference to the American controversy and the work of Frank Lloyd Wright) for a programme of revision of the pre-war cultural heritage, which was becoming known by the contrasting term of 'rationalist'. In Rome, Turin and Palermo, and other cities, Associations for Organic Architecture were formed, while Milanese architects, insisting on continuity with pre-war experiments, formed an independent association, the Movimento Studi d'Architettura. The quarrel between supporters of organic architecture and those of rationalist architecture began, but without either the passion or the asperity with which similar disagreements of outlook had been conducted in the period after the First World War. The architects willingly accepted cultural labels as they did political ones, because they were

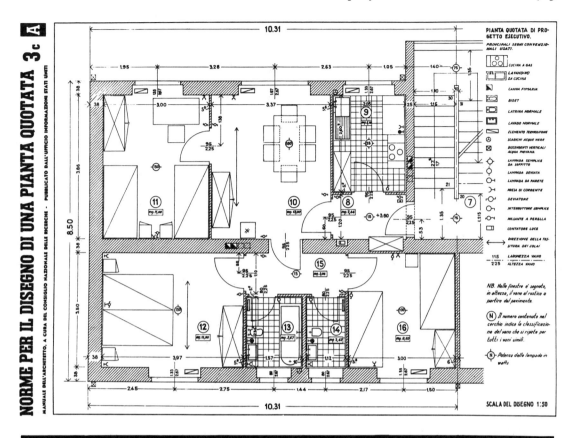

905 *A page from the* Manuale dell'architetto *(1946)*
906 *Plan entered for the competition for the* Stazione Termini *at Rome (Cardelli, Carè, Ceradini, Fiorentino, Quaroni, Ridolfi, 1947)*

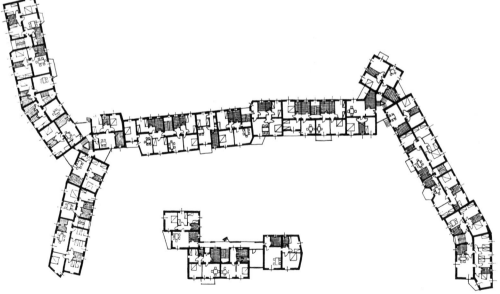

907, 908   *Roma, INA-Casa Tiburtino district: square amid houses by Ridolfi, Quaroni and Fiorentino; plan of houses by Quaroni and Fiorentino (from* Casabella*)*

909, 910 *Rome, Part of the Tiburtino district; Matera, the church in the village of La Martella (Quaroni, 1950–4)*

911   *Rome, Gallery in the* Stazione Termini *(Calini, Montuori, Castellazzi and Vitellozzi, 1948–50)*
912, 913   *Pistoia, Commodity market by Michelucci (1950)*

914, 915 *(left)   Parma, I.N.A. building (Albini, 1955)*
916, 917 *(right)   Genoa, Interior of the Cathedral
Treasury and of the Palazzo Bianco (Albini, 1950–7)*

eager to take sides; as Bo said, 'the need for
choice was a method like any other of finding
a family, of escaping from one's solitude.'[25]

But when the first choices were presented
to them, the problems left unsolved in the
'taking sides' necessarily emerged.

The idea of having (or having not) to
produce an organic architecture proved
particularly harmful to the clarity of the
discussion. What was organic architecture?[26]

The terms which in Wright had a meaning closely connected with his individual experience and which already had an inaccurate and second-hand meaning in American discussion, became vaguer still when transferred to Italy.

Zevi gives a broad theoretical definition of the term (organic architecture equals human architecture) and a limited historical illustration, referring to the remote and incommunicable examples of Wright, Aalto and the young Americans. In fact this became a label applied *a posteriori* to a great variety of works – two small buildings by B. Zevi and S. Radiconcini, the traumatological hospital designed in 1948 by G. Samonà, the Falchera district of 1951 by G. Astengo and others, and later the works of Carlo Scarpa (b. 1906).[27]

On the other hand the controversy associated with 'organic architecture' had a very important indirect consequence, since it accustomed people to conceiving the modern tradition in unduly restricted terms, definitively classifying the European movement between the two wars with the correlative terms of 'rationalist architecture' and strengthening the prejudices connected with it, described in Chapter 14.

This must be recognized as one of the causes of the confusion into which it subsequently fell. In fact discussion had moved, unobserved, back into the old cultural terms and the history of modern architecture appears in line with that of ancient architecture as an uninterrupted series of formal tendencies, succeeding one another ad infinitum. As early as 1948 Zevi took this step,[28] deducing from the organic tendency a 'spatial interpretation of architecture' and describing 'the various space ages', i.e. giving precise and conclusive definitions, using the terms of art criticism, of all the stages of modern architectural history.

On this ground architects and art critics could be reconciled once and for all and the conviction gained ground that the naïve

initial propositions of the modern movement had been left well behind, and that a mature position had at last been reached.[29]

The sound and fury of this discussion and the slight hold gained by the modern movement in Italy prevented reflection on the relations between the first experiments made after the war and the theses of the modern movement, and the development from these experiments of a broader method, capable of making its mark on the increasingly important subjects that faced Italian architects. In this way the interest in current constructional processes was gradually replaced by an interest in the forms in which these processes were traditionally embodied. What counted was not the passing from the rationalist and international repertoire to the popular, local one – which altered only the point of application of the architect's energies – but the passing from an active and innovating attitude to one that was mainly receptive and retrospective.

This took place about 1950; this was the period of the architectural works that are known as neo-realist – the houses by M. Ridolfi in Rome and Terni, F. Albini's at Cervinia, a villa by I. Gardella in the country near Pavia – and which might more accurately be called post-neo-realist, because the reference to that cultural moment was already projected into the past. The excellence of these works, where the inadequacies and naïveté of the first post-war attempts were successfully corrected, constituted a very persuasive argument in its favour; the perfection of the results could be set against the goodness of the intentions. The commodity market built at the same time by Michelucci in the centre of Pistoia showed that an intelligent integration of the current and traditional repertoires made it possible to fit a modern building harmoniously into a historic setting.

Because of the characteristic mobility of Italian architectural culture, the experiments in literal re-utilization of the traditional

918 *(left)*   *Brussels Window of the* salon d'honneur *in the Italian pavilion at the 1958 exhibition (I. Gardella)*
919 *(right)*   *Milan,* Torre Velasca *by the studio B.B.P.R. (1957)*

forms had a short life, and architectural thought moved on towards other sources of inspiration. But meanwhile many of the best architects had begun to adopt the attitude typical of tradition, i.e. the tendency to treat each subject more as an isolated instance than as an opportunity for the renewal of the town.

The path opened up by such an attitude was that of the search for qualitative perfection; the situation that had emerged was particularly well-suited to drawing out the compositional skill of certain architects and to producing brilliant exceptions, which made up for the general low level.

Outstanding among these works were the church of the Madonna dei Poveri in Milan by Figini and Pollini (1952), the I.N.A. building in Parma by F. Albini (1954), the Savings Bank in Florence by Michelucci (1957), the Olivetti shop by C. Scarpa in Venice (1959) and some interiors by Albini –

the museum of the Palazzo Bianco and the Museo del Tesoro of the Cathedral of S. Lorenzo in Genoa – which were of a very high standard (it is interesting to note that the best results were reached in buildings whose purpose was basically something rather exceptional).

In the Torre Velasca in Milan (completed in 1958) the studio B.B.P.R. carried off the singular attempt at treating the façade of a skyscraper as a formally finite episode, while this type of building was almost always interpreted as a rhythmic structure, open and potentially extensible. The elevation of the tower is divided into two perfectly inter-balanced parts, while the vertical supporting elements, protruding from the base to the summit, serve to mediate between the general bulk of the building and the uniform openings of the single floors – as in Sullivan – by replacing the uniform rhythm with a continuous gradation and by a particularly careful modulation of the detachment of the projection (Fig. 919).

In this way there is a mainly contemplative relationship between the building and its urban setting. According to Rogers, the tower aims, without actually following the style of any of its buildings, 'culturally to summarize the atmosphere of the city of Milan, its elusive yet pervasive mood';[30] its singularity and uniqueness derive precisely from the fact that it appears as an isolated contrast, a summary of the pre-existing landscape; it would be impossible to see in it even the faintest allusion to any building type which could be multiplied to change that same landscape.

These works are no longer, like those mentioned before 1950, isolated facts in the midst of a uniform production, but they have a precise relationship to current building, which was influenced by them in varying degrees. The need to make single works intensively individual, the habit of exaggerating formal stimuli, of concentrating concern for planning within a certain scale, constituted a large area for understanding between major and minor architects, working in large towns and small, between designers and executors, specialists and laymen. This understanding was based largely on the acceptance of the working methods and scale of values proper to tradition; the ease with which it became established proved that traditional habits were still very much alive, i.e. that modern Italian society was still very similar – in this way – to old Italian society. The momentary reconciliation of tradition and modernity also aroused the interest and almost always the approval of foreign observers.[31]

Now, some years later, only a small part of this activity constitutes a valid contribution to the solution of certain marginal problems of the modern city – museography, the art of setting new buildings amid old monuments – while certain implicit limitations weighed negatively on successive experiments, with far more serious results:

a The habit of transferring the need for historical continuity on to formal grounds which led, between 1957 and 1960, to an interest in the imitation of forms of the past. The experiments which have become known as 'neo-liberty'[32] were based on considerations of content (the recovery of the values of intimacy and urbanity contained in the architecture of the first decades of this century) which were promptly reflected on the formal plane, giving rise to a short-lived revival;

b A limited idea of architectural composition, similar to that theorized about by Perret, which became a common delight in symmetry and centrality. Telling examples of this are the superstructure of a house in via Mercadante in Rome by M. Ridolfi (1957), the *salon d'honneur* of the Italian pavilion at Brussels by I. Gardella (1958) and a long series of churches, including the one by G. Michelucci at Larderello (1959). This prejudice hindered the activity of P. L.

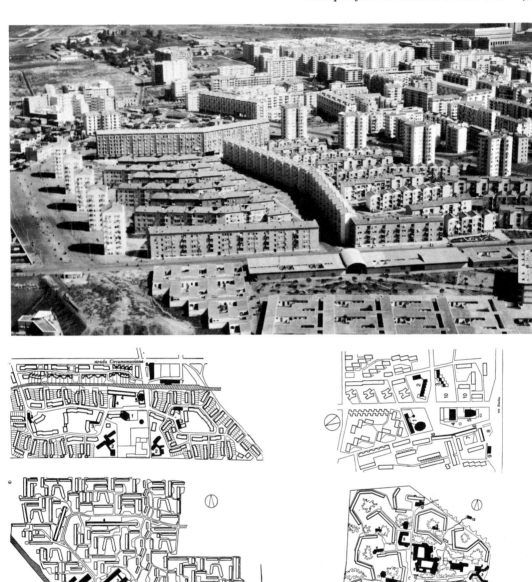

920-924 *I.N.A.-Casa building: (top) Tuscolano district in Rome (in the foreground is the 'unité d'habitation' by A. Libera) and ground-plans of (left) the Ponticelli district in Naples (office plan), the Cesate district in Milan (Albini, Albricci, Castiglioni, Gardella, B.B.P.R.), (right) Borgo Panigale in Bologna (G. Vaccaro) and Falchera in Turin (G. Astengo; from* Architettura-cantiere*)*

Nervi, keeping him this side of the barrier already crossed by Maillart; his exceptional constructional talent was forced to exercise itself within geometrically conventional schemes – in the hall of Torino-Esposizione, in the Palazzo dello Sport in Rome – applying itself to final details rather than to the invention of the static organism;

c The difficulty of tackling, above a certain scale, the problems which were ever more rapidly conditioning the life of the modern city, and therefore the failure in continuity between architectural and town-planning involvement. This is the crucial point in present day Italian architectural thought, and it is only by considering all other facts within this framework – including the excellent production of the best architects – that one can assess their significance.

During the war, in 1942, the first general town-planning law was passed in Italy, which provided for a scale of plans of various kinds – general, intercommunal, communal and detailed – to be extended to the whole country. After the war was over, town-planners had at their disposal a new and progressive technical instrument; but no simultaneous steps were taken to strengthen the control of the planning authorities over individual interests, public and private, while the economic situation soon invested these interests with a strength and aggressiveness certainly unforeseen by the legislators, who had been working at their desks at a moment of almost complete economic standstill.

In this way the need for production typical of reconstruction soon had the upper hand over the need for co-ordination; indeed, in the confusion caused by the passage from the old to the new town-planning discipline, effective public intervention in each of the sectors could be ensured only by maintaining firm vertical organizations, and therefore by further weakening the remaining horizontal links.

In the sector of popular building, after various experiments conducted with mainly quantitative criteria, a new body was set up in 1949 (I.N.A.-Casa, financed by a tax deducted from the wages of all workers) which exerted a central control over the technical and economic management of relevant works, committing their execution to the peripheral bodies already in existence. In this way, still with the aim of making the organization of this sector autonomous as had been done from 1903 onwards, the advantages of this approach could be exploited to the full, creating a single driving force at the centre but exempting it from the greater part of bureaucratic work; apart from concentrating on quantity (hitherto I.N.A.-Casa had built 400,000 dwellings) it could also concentrate on quality, by selecting designers from the centre and soon bringing the level of sub-sidized building – traditionally lower than average – almost to the absolute maximum that Italian architecture today is capable of achieving.[33]

The first districts designed around 1950 very plainly reflected the conflicting tendencies of these years; the particular circumstances of I.N.A.-Casa planning – the large amount of freedom granted to the architects and the lack of practical relations with other forces active in the same field, due to the failure in horizontal co-ordination with other forms of planning – led automatically to more intense concentration on form.

The Tiburtino district in Rome, designed by C. Aymonino, C. Chiarini, M. Fiorentino, F. Gorio, M. Lanza, S. Lenci, P. Lugli, C. Melograni, G. Menichetti, L. Quaroni, M. Ridolfi and M. Valori, was the most notable example of so-called 'neo-realism'; (Figs. 907, 909) but above all the variety of the architectural results that emerged in the various districts – which went much further than natural differences in climate, customs and building methods from place to place – bore witness to the conditions of isolation and uncertainty in which the planners found themselves (Figs. 920–4).

925, 926 *(left)*   *Two electric power stations in Sicily (G. Samona)*
927, 928 *(right)*   *Florence, Savings Bank (G. Michelucci, 1958)*

While the Italian cities, through the work of I.N.A.-Casa and private industry were once more growing at a tremendous pace, there was much more delay in applying the town-planning control laid down by the law of 1942. It was not until 1953 that the first general development scheme was passed for Milan,[34] and not until 1954 that a first list of a hundred communes obliged to draw up a new planning scheme was published.

929 *(left)   Larderello, Tall houses by Michelucci (1960)*
930 *(right)   Milan,* Torre Galfa *(M. Bega, 1959)*

But in all cities the plans met with difficulties; at the end of 1958 only thirteen of the hundred relevant communes had an approved plan, and in all Italy only forty-three out of about 8,000.

The lack of town-planning control jeopardized the fabric of old historic centres, which were now exposed to the attacks of the speculators. The laws and authorities supposedly the guardians of historical and artistic values constituted another administration, different from that making the town-planning schemes, so that the demands of preservation could never be rationally considered in relation to those of renovation, and the latter easily gained the upper hand, giving rise to an increasing number of acts of artistic vandalism and arousing protests that often came too late.[35]

But even more worrying was the degeneration of the urban organisms as a whole. All cities, including the most famous, were surrounded by extensive suburbs characterized – independently of the quality and architectural exterior of the single buildings – by the disorder and squalor typical of the early industrial areas, and this was the result of the same disparity between the scale of the process and the scale of the measures taken to deal with it.

This description of the development of town-planning is strictly complementary to

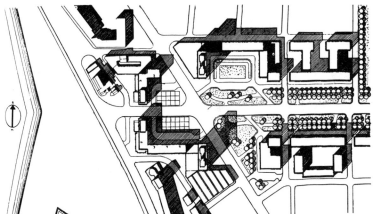

931, 932   *Le Havre, Perret's scheme for the port: avenue Foch and the port Océane (plan from* Casabella*)*

the preceding one of architectural tendencies. The same combination of causes propitious to the solving of certain isolated problems hindered the progress of town-planning, and put Italian architects face to face with a basic choice. In the years from 1957 onwards a series of events – the discussion of the new plan for Rome,[36] the crisis in the Faculties of Architecture,[37] the preparation of a new town-planning law, finally included in the government's programme in 1962[38] – make the extent of the crisis of Italian architecture today abundantly clear.

As was only natural, the present day debate is dominated by certain basic problems – firstly, that of a new town-planning discipline, and that of a new legal ruling on building land – which go beyond the field of architecture itself and are of general importance.

In fact the architects, after having pinpointed and discussed them theoretically, handed them over to the politicians, who were responsible for their solutions. But architecture could contribute to their solution if it became recognized as an integral part of political action; at the same time, from 1957 onwards, an increasingly important part was played by architects who agreed as a result to modify their professional activity and to maintain an equal degree of involvement in both building and town-planning.

In France the problem of rebuilding after war damage (about 450,000 dwellings had been destroyed, i.e. about five per cent of those existing in 1939) was now added on to the housing shortage which had been serious even before the war, because of prolonged stagnation in the building industry.

The crisis was connected with deep-rooted economic and social changes which were tending to re-distribute the population throughout the countryside; but the remedies devised to solve the problems of this re-distribution – rent freezes, state subsidies to provide workers with accommodation at regulated prices – did nothing but increase the stickiness of the process and ended up by crystallizing settlements, sometimes in overt contradiction with economic requirements.

After the war an alternative was presented: either the authorities could adhere resolutely to town-planning, and re-examine the distribution of dwellings in relation to the sources of employment, bearing in mind foreseeable economic problems, or they could accept distribution as it was and make good existing deficiencies in a technically correct manner.

In 1944 the Ministry of Reconstruction and Town-planning was set up, which included both urban and rural planning, and subsidized building. But the laws on repairs of war damage, based on the concept of reconstructing the ruined buildings in their original positions, only contributed further to hardening the situation and made it more difficult for the problem of housing to be fitted into the general framework of town-planning.

E. C. Petit, the Minister of Reconstruction and Town-planning between 1948 and 1953, attempted to implement a sweeping programme of planning, by creating a new study group for the plan of Paris, whose task was to update the Prost plan in the light of a regional programme[39] and by instituting a study group for the national plan in 1950, flanked by regional groups 'with the participation of geographers, specialists in agriculture and industry, economists, doctors, in short persons of very different callings, chosen because of their capacities, their authority and the interest they feel in the problems of territorial planning, excluding the 'notables' whose action is too widely dispersed to be really effective'.[40]

The functional crisis of the political system in France, during the years of the Fourth Republic, made it impossible to continue firmly along the path of general town- and country-planning. Aware of these difficulties, from the start Petit moved in another direction as well, instigating several isolated and very important acts of public intervention, to shatter public inertia with a practical demonstration and thoroughly to exploit the advantages offered by the current legislative attitude, aiming at a high technical level and making use of the most lively forces

933, 934 *Amiens, Two views of Perret's building*

in French architectural culture. Petit described the aims of this activity as follows:
'Working on a large scale is clearly the only
way to reduce costs and improve quality
and we are opposed to the attempt to lower
prices by competition and outdated
techniques. It becomes possible to plan, to
reduce equipment, to prefabricate on the
site, to employ mechanical maintenance and
organize the building yard.

Building technique is undergoing a
change of which the outcome is still
uncertain. Professional traditions and the
attitudes they breed are quite inadequate
to modern needs. This is no small obstacle,
and demonstration alone of the effectiveness
of newer methods can eliminate it . . . . A
further satisfactory result of such large
scale operations is their encouragement of
architectural creativeness, which links up

with the great traditions in providing monumental solutions, the use of masses, and research into functional adaptations'.[41]

In this way the great complexes of Strasbourg, Saint Étienne, Angers and Lyon were realized; but the most significant experiments, in relation to preceding cultural history, were Perret's works in Le Havre and Amiens, and Le Corbusier's 'unité d'habitation' in Marseilles.

Perret was appointed to work on the plan of reconstruction for Le Havre – whose centre had been almost completely destroyed – as early as 1944, but work did not begin until 1947, and continued until the death of the master, in 1954. In reality, Perret's plan was an architectural programme, which demanded to be developed coherently, down to the smallest executive details; in fact Perret took on the burden of designing the main buildings, the hôtel de ville, the church and various groups of houses (Figs. 931 and 932), and organized a special *atelier* for this purpose.[42]

The whole layout was based on a constant module of 6·21 metres which made possible the standardization and prefabrication of many constructional elements; in some buildings of the whole structure – girders, uprights, ceilings – in others only of the panel walls, door and window frames and stairs. Care was taken that the uniformity of the elements should not produce monotony in the whole, and the arrangement of volumes and rhythmical combinations was varied accordingly, various exceptional elements being introduced after careful consideration.

This great experiment demonstrated the advantages, but also the limits, of Perret's thought, and his remoteness from the problems of modern town-planning. He had no town-planning methodology which would enable him to stagger decisions over various times and places; however broad the field, he still saw his subject as an architectural plan, where the whole was regulated by the same criteria of symmetry, order and proportion valid for the single parts.

For this reason Perret tried, in a single act of designing, to create completely a new urban organism, but he met with insurmountable barriers of time and space; of space, because a single designer or group of designers manages to control a certain quantity of work, beyond which the problem of internal organization becomes impossibly complicated; of time, because the whole operation was bound up with the economic social and administrative situation as it appears at the moment of the initial formulation, and must be completed before the situation has changed too much.

The increasing complication of technical matters and the speed of social and economic change progressively narrowed these limits, making Perret's basic premise even more natural. The architect registered this situation faithfully; Perret and his team could keep up with the pressure of external changes only by accentuating the mechanical aspect of their compositional repertoire, and he concentrated his attentions on the most important buildings, falling into a weary exaggeration of his own former style.

This unproductive confusion was accentuated in the scheme for Amiens (Figs. 933 and 934). This was a huge square interrupting the circle of the *boulevards* in front of the railway station, with uniform buildings with porticos and a tower, over a hundred metres high, which stood out on the skyline not far away from the famous cathedral. Here the forms were openly neo-classical, particularly in the station façade; this was the last of the large-scale schemes in the old French tradition, now decisively out of keeping with the spirit of the times.

Le Corbusier was equally sure of the resolutive power of architecture, but unlike Perret he had at his disposal a method of town-planning which had already been amply developed theoretically, and his initial problem was the finding of a suitable scale for overall architectural intervention, which would bring together, within a single organism, a certain number of residential cells and their communal services.

This was the germ of the concept of the 'unité d'habitation' which had been maturing slowly in Le Corbusier's thought throughout his life, since the basic inspiration dated back, according to the author, to 1907,[43] and its first architectural appearance from 1922, with the 'immeuble-villas'.

The old city had been composed of houses and big buildings, and its dynamics was assured by the mutual separation of these elements, each controllable by a separate process of planned intervention.

The attempt at extending to whole districts of the city, or indeed to a whole city, the criteria of overall planning valid for a single building answered the need to control more complex systems, but froze the dynamism of the whole, as in the case of Le Havre. The real problem lay in finding the dimensions of a new component element, larger and with more complex functions; the separateness of these new elements was to guarantee the dynamism of the modern city, because their mutual co-ordination would be distributed over different times and different spheres of competence.

This very possibility of separateness made it possible to begin with a single experiment, which could however hint at the image of the whole of the future city.

For about a decade, as we have said, Le Corbusier's activity was almost exclusively theoretical; immediately after the war he took part in the first attempt at reconstruction by putting forward suggestion after suggestion – dry assembly,[44] 'murondin' constructions,[45] flying schools for evacuees,[46] the 'logis provisoires transitoires'[47] – he defined his concepts of architecture and town-planning – the 'brise soleil',[48] the four routes,[49] the four functions of town-planning,[50] the three human settlements,[51] the 'modulor'[52] (Fig. 935), the seven roads[53] –

and he was writing new books to represent his schemes of the past or to comment on experiments that had been made.[54]

In 1944, working on a new system of mass-produced emergency accommodation, Le Corbusier suggested the building of very deep blocks crossed by an internal road which would separate dwellings on two levels, separated by transversal masonry partitions. These buildings would be called 'unités d'habitations transitoires' and would have only two storeys, so that they could be easily built and demolished. But by applying this idea to tall blocks it was possible to concentrate a large number of dwellings in a single compact block, leaving each independent of the others and open on both sides. This was the germ of the idea of the 'unité d'habitation de grandeur conforme', which comprised about four hundred dwellings and contained within it and in its extensions all the services necessary to complete family life; parking space, shops, a day nursery, a laundry, space for recreation and physical exercise. This was the basic cell for the tissue of the modern city, since it made it possible to keep most of the ground as green space, while retaining high density, and to simplify the street system keeping the various types of traffic separate (Fig. 936).

In the reconstruction plans drawn up for Saint Dié, Saint Gaudens[55] and La Rochelle, Le Corbusier was insistent on this idea; at last in 1946 he was asked by the Ministry of Reconstruction and Town-Planning to try out the first actual experiment in Marseilles (Figs. 938–41). Amid many conflicts and differences the building was completed in 1952; the architectural result was so impressive that it fired even the general public in a way that had been unknown for a long time, but there were certain persistent differences with regard to its actual functioning: part of the accommodation remained empty and the communal services on the seventh and eighth floors – food shops, bars, cafeteria, cigarette shop, hairdresser, newsagent, florist and

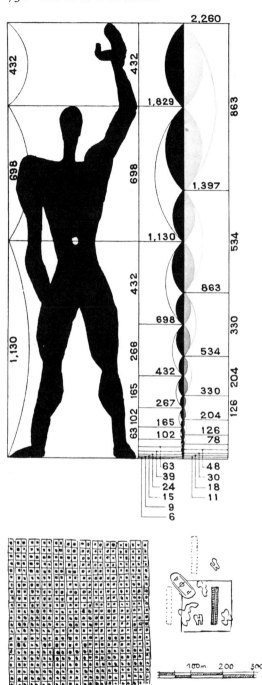

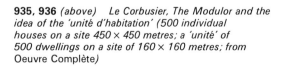

935, 936 *(above)   Le Corbusier, The Modulor and the idea of the 'unité d'habitation' (500 individual houses on a site 450 × 450 metres; a 'unité' of 500 dwellings on a site of 160 × 160 metres; from Oeuvre Complète)*

937, 938 *(above)   The 'unité' under construction in Berlin and the completed Marseilles 'unité'*

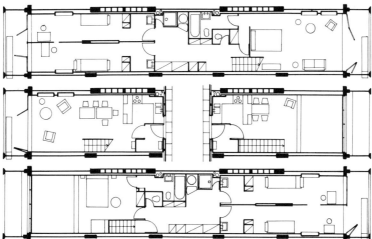

939–941 *Marseilles, Two aspects of the 'unité d'habitation' and plans of two typical dwellings*

post-office – were not realized. Thus for several years the building functioned like a sort of monument, visited each day by three hundred paying visitors; art exhibitions and meetings were organized, and tourist advertisements described it unequivocally as the 'ville radieuse'. In other words, the first 'unité' actually built was still, in many ways, a persuasive proposal, like so many others already conceived of by Le Corbusier.

After this a second 'unité' was built at Nantes, for a private co-operative (1953–5),

a third at Berlin, commissioned by the Citizens Administration for the occasion of the 1957 Interbau, while a fourth has been finished at Briey-en-Forêt. Those at Nantes and Berlin had no communal services, while the last one (which contains three hundred and sixty average-sized apartments) is part of a complex which is also to include forty-nine larger terrace dwellings and two hundred smaller ones, by M. Pingusson, as well as communal services housed in a separate building. In 1960 Le Corbusier had a contract with the Renault factory for the mass production of 'unités', using a metallic structure.[56]

The enthusiasm and perplexity aroused by these experiments are connected with the town-planning programme which is implicit in the very idea of the 'unité'; with respect to this programme, each of the 'unités' actually realized acts as an isolated model, and cannot therefore be judged as an autonomous architectural object.

The idea of the 'unité d'habitation', is perhaps the most important hypothesis in present day town-planning thought. It can be formulated in purely functional terms: it was a question of filling the gap, by now too large, between the dimensions of the modern city and those of the single building, and therefore of not conceiving of the city in terms of houses or public services, but of introducing a sub-multiple – or a series of sub-multiples – within which there should be a pre-established balance between residences and services. It remained to be seen whether this sub-multiple should be a single block or an articulated system of buildings; in fact, if there are going to be a series of sub-multiples varying in size according to the various types of services, it becomes plain that each one, generally speaking, must be articulated in an architecturally complex fashion.

At the moment town-planning thought is centred around this formulation, with different results, varying from the districts by Bakema and Van den Broek to the Brazilian *supercuadros* and the Soviet *kvartal*.

Le Corbusier concentrated his attention on the smallest sub-multiple of the scale – which comprised 400 dwellings, i.e. 1,200–1,500 inhabitants (as in Fourier's *Phalanstère,* or Owen's Parallelogram), enough to require a basic provision of communal services, i.e. nursery, kindergarten, spaces for children to play – and invariably translated it into a single plastic image. In fact his main concern – after battling for thirty years almost always

unsuccessfully – was to protect his field of action as an architect, within a calculated and repeatable dimension, i.e. one that was correct from a town-planning point of view. And the 'unité' fits into the fabric of the existing city with complete plastic autonomy, hinting, at the same time, at an overall town-planning alternative.

But this autonomy, which was fully attained by even a single sample unit, did not bring with it a corresponding functional autonomy. The correct functioning of every 'unité' could be obtained only in relation to the presence of others around it, because the relations between residences and services – even at the most basic level – could not be conceived in a rigid and one-sided manner, in the sense that these inhabitants had perforce to take advantage of these services, but they had to admit of two-way choices, which are the very essence of social life.

In this way the fact of living in a certain 'unité' was too weak an argument to make a person decide to have their hair cut by a certain barber, to take the children walking in a certain place. This explains the impossibility of installing communal services halfway up the building as had been intended in Marseilles; if in theory four hundred families were sufficient customers for a foodshop, there was no saying that these families had to use this shop.

The installation of communal services on the ground floor, as in Briey-en-Forêt, seemed to offer the answer to the integration of the 'unité' within a more complex residential fabric. Le Corbusier, concentrating on the finishing touches of the plastic image of the 'unité', did not seem to be aware of this aspect of the argument; having had to do away with communal services within the building itself, in Nantes, he wrote: 'Communal services half-way up the building were regretfully abandoned, because here the economic demands of a budget and of a legislation had actually mutilated an idea: the "unité d'habitation" is valid because of its communal services.'[57]

On the other hand the experimental phase of the 'unité' as an isolated episode had been prolonged more than necessary. After Marseilles, Le Corbusier had to be content with a few other opportunities offered him by private individuals or abroad, and he had no means of directly influencing schemes in French public building. In France too there was the same contrast between exceptions of a high level and current production, which remained at a low level for a long time, until the spread of the new processes of heavy prefabrication, which we shall discuss later.

The French exceptions – at least in the case of Perret and Le Corbusier – were based on far longer cultural preparation and were in a position to influence successive developments more broadly than was the case in Italy. The recent systems of prefabrication in fact applied certain technical experiments begun by the two masters during the previous fifty years, on an industrial scale; but it was precisely the indirect character of this development that impoverished French architectural culture, endangering the permanence of the results attained.

Reconstruction in Germany took place under very special circumstances, because of the extent of the war damage, which was greater than that in any other country: of the ten and a half million dwellings in Western Germany, almost five million were damaged, 2,350,000 being completely destroyed.

Naturally, the cities suffered worse than the countryside: almost all the centres of any size had at least half their buildings demolished, with as much as 70 per cent in Cologne, 75 per cent in Würzberg and even more in Berlin, where one might almost say that the original city no longer exists and that two others have risen painfully from its ashes, East and West.[58]

There has been a large-scale exodus of the population from the large cities: Cologne, which had half a million inhabitants, had less than 50,000 in 1945. Also, it has been calculated that ten million people have moved from East Germany into West Germany; so that the population distribution has been greatly altered.

Until 1948, when the currency was reformed, no effective measure could be made for rebuilding; between 1949 and 1950 100,000 dwellings were built and in 1950 the new housing law was passed, aiming to build 1,800,000 new homes in six years. From then on, rebuilding went ahead at a steady rate and today the housing problem may be regarded as almost solved.

In the planning field, difficulties were greater. Town-planning legislation left the whole responsibility for planning to local authorities, so that individual interests weighed more than was necessary on the planning schemes for German cities and nowhere was a large scale programme of compulsory purchase and re-organization carried out, as the Dutch had done for Rotterdam.

In the German cities that have been rebuilt, the remaining traces of their old and traditional faces were often assiduously preserved. Many ruined or even completely destroyed monuments were carefully rebuilt exactly as they had been, and sometimes whole complexes, like the riverside houses in Cologne near St Martin's, were reconstructed exactly. Important experiments were made in this field and the Germans demonstrated, with their meticulous technical processes, that it was possible to produce a plausible imitation not only of masonry frameworks but also – within certain limits – of details and original decorations, recreating a by no means arbitrary image of works which had seemed to be lost for ever; one need mention only the Bishops' Palace at Bruchsal and, in eastern Germany, the Zwinger in Dresden: these are, so to speak, life-size models of real works, which naturally do not really replace them but which make their critical recon-

942   *One of the new streets in Frankfurt-am-Main*
943, 944   *The new theatre at Münster (Deilmann, Hausen, Rave, Ruhnau, 1955) and the old centre at Lübeck*

struction easier, and re-establish their presence in the townscape.

This way of understanding reconstruction was due as much to attachment to the image of the traditional city as to the pressure of private interests, which encouraged an identical use of the sites as far as possible. Nonetheless the vast areas of building-land owned by almost all the administrations restricted building speculation, so that an

945, 946, 947 *Düsseldorf, Mannesmann A.G. offices (P. Schneider-Esleben, 1960)*

excessive density of building in the city centres was successfully avoided (Fig. 944).

The lack of an adequate town-planning framework and the high cost of materials as compared with that of labour gave German architecture, particularly in the years just after the war, a somewhat homespun quality; but as industry developed, as supplies improved and wealth spread making the cost of labour rise, the opposite tendency began to appear, that of a highly industrialized architecture. The contrast was echoed and even strengthened on formal grounds, since one part of German production made a great show of producing brick walls, over-hanging roofs and traditional carving, while another made use of an extremely up-to-date repertoire, often with a polemical delight no longer common in European architecture. Examples of this were certain theatres, with lively and intentionally surprising ground plans (the State Theatre in Kassel, by H. Scharoun and T. Mattern; the Liederhall in Stuttgart by A. Abel and R. Gutbrod, the municipal theatre in Münster, (Fig. 943) and certain office buildings of impeccable and rigorous modular composition, for instance the recent Mannesmann building in Düssel-dorf (P. Schneider-Esleben and H. Knothe, 1960).

This latter tendency was determined both by Germany's relationship with the United States – particularly by the presence of various American firms active in Germany, like Skidmore, Owings and Merrill who built the U.S. Embassy in Bonn – and by the influence of nearby Switzerland where, after 1933, many of the experiments cut short in Germany by Nazism, were carried on.

The Americans rightly observed that this imitation was more apparent than real,[59] since the modular structures of the German buildings did not depend on standardization of the elements but on a formal choice, and the buildings were then executed with methods that they judged more or less primitive. But this situation allowed German architects greater freedom in designing and enabled workmen to give more time to the control and perfection of each element, generally achieving a standard of finish attained in the United States only on exceptional occasions and at much greater cost.

The use of craftsmanship in the building industry was made possible by the application on a large scale of the UNI norms for the unification of measurements; in this way it was possible to build the single elements in small series, with the certainty that they would always be made to fit together in the actual assembling.

The ideological meaning of this trend is worth considering; the gap between crafts-manship and industry – which was Gropius' basic problem in 1919 – was not bridged but conventionally settled, and while functional relationships were guaranteed, cultural ones were frozen because of the rigorous separation of the two fields of action. This way of building, furthermore, was workable only while the cost of labour was low, but now this cost was rising, and the problem necessarily arose of how to transfer the traditional skills of the workers to mass-production; this then was a larger-scale version of the problem Gropius had faced forty years before in the Bauhaus, with the same general implications.

There were not the same resources of human energies as there had been after the First World War; the best men of the older generation had had to leave Germany, the next generation had been scattered and disorientated by the disastrous experience of Hitler's régime, and the youngest, which was now beginning to work, no longer found sufficient support and guidance from its elders.

The only remaining architects who had lived through the beginnings of the modern movement in the Weimar republic, were those who had not been driven out by Nazism: Bartning, Scharoun, the Luckhardt brothers, but they were the most concerned with following their own personal paths and

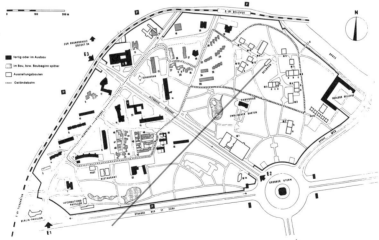

948, 949 *Berlin, New Hansa district, site of the Interbau 1957 (ground-plan from official catalogue)*

therefore all the less suited to exercising a formative influence and giving German reconstruction a unified outlook.

The similarity between these circumstances and those after the First World War made people think that it might be possible to repeat Gropius' experiment and found a new Bauhaus. This time the enterprise sprang from a private foundation, the Geschwister-Scholl-Stiftung, set up in 1950 by I. Aicher-Scholl in memory of two brothers killed by the Nazis. Max Bill (b. 1908) a former student of the Bauhaus, built the school's new headquarters at Ulm and ran it for the first two years, after which his position was held by T. Maldonado until the school was closed in 1968.

Gropius opened the building in 1955 with a hopeful yet prudent speech, stressing the importance and difficulties of the enterprise:

'I would like to express my hopes that Max Bill, Inge Scholl, the Faculty and students . . . keep to the high ideals they have set themselves in the inevitable struggles that will ensue: I mean, not to pursue a style, but to continue in constant experimental research of new expressions and new truths. I know how difficult it is to maintain such an attitude, when the end product of habit and conservative tenacity is constantly put forward as the will of the people. Every experiment demands absolute freedom as well as the support of far-sighted authorities and private individuals, who will be present with their goodwill at the pangs, often misunderstood, that accompany the birth of everything new. Give this "University of Form" time to develop in peace'.[60]

Interbau 1957 was in a certain sense the conclusion and summary of this phase of German architecture.

In 1953 the Berlin Senate stated that the rebuilding of the Hansaviertel – a central nineteenth-century district between the Spree and the Tiergarten almost completely destroyed by the war – should be combined with an international exhibition of modern architecture and should offer architects, scientific institutes and industries the opportunity to try out the most modern solutions to the problems of urban settlement.

A competition was organized for the town-planning scheme and was won by G. Jobst and W. Kreuer. From the beginning it was decided that the new district should be made up of blocks isolated in green spaces and that the density agreed upon should be obtained by tall buildings, leaving most of the land not built up; meanwhile a company was set up to acquire the sites from their original owners and to redistribute them rationally according to the new plan. The town-planning scheme was modified by Jobst in 1954 to introduce a greater variety of types, was submitted to the group of designers invited to design the buildings and finally was drawn up in an executive form by a limited committee chaired by O. Bartning. The initial compositional unity was naturally lost and the district was composed of many disparate buildings, well-spaced and set freely within the uniform green space.

As in the Weissenhof of 1927, the variety of the types – tall, medium or small blocks, some detached and some terraced – served to exemplify the alternatives at the disposal of a modern city; but on the earlier occasion the freedom granted to the various architects served to underline the harmony of the styles and gave a persuasive picture of the future, while now the Interbau reflected a far more confused cultural situation. Each was speaking for himself – in a sense there was a certain amount of agreement between them in the form of constructional technique, where the various solutions could usefully be compared – but it seemed that the gulf which, thirty years before, had seemed to be almost bridged, had re-opened between technical and formal decisions: general planning and executive details were often superimposed as two independent factors, and in many cases they were the product of two different people, the foreign planner and the local collaborator.[61] From this there emerged a much more ambiguous lesson for the contemporary city: clearly defined attitudes on individual matters and confused general attitudes, 'precision in means and confusion in ends'.

950 *(above)   Berlin, T.A.C. building at Interbau 1957*
951, 952 *(below)   Berlin, manifesto and poster for Interbau 1957*

The discord evident at the Interbau was in a sense the image of what was happening in the cities of Europe. It was very much to the organizers' credit to have reflected this situation clearly, by juxtaposing the products of the various tendencies within the restricted area of the Hansaviertel. Rather than propose hurried syntheses, they preferred patiently to consider all contemporary experiments and continue to give the debate all the scope it needed.

5   Rebuilding and planning in Holland

Once again, the Dutch experience was the happy exception in the European picture.

At the basis of this experience, as in Scandinavia, lay the balance between architecture and town-planning that had already been achieved in the pre-war period; but war damage, and particularly the economic and social changes that followed the war, set Dutch technicians wider and more pressing tasks, which they tackled and resolved without breaking the continuity of tradition.

The Dutch achievements can therefore more rightly be considered exemplary than the Scandinavian ones, because they were not conditioned by a demographic and social balance that could not be found elsewhere, but were achieved in a country where the population was growing at a greater rate than anywhere in Europe, where there were zones of great industrial concentration and where the geographical form of the territory was changing.

Of the cities which suffered from war damage the case of Rotterdam was exemplary: it had first to remedy serious war damage and then to cope with the consequences of rapid development, which made it the biggest port on the continent.

The centre of Rotterdam had been destroyed in a single day, 14 June 1940, by a German raid followed by a tremendous fire. 260 hectares were razed to the ground, with 25,000 dwellings, 2,400 shops, 70 schools,

2,000 offices and storehouses, while over 78,000 people were left homeless. For over ten years the city appeared to visitors with a great hole in the place of the old centre; this was how it appeared to the sculptor Zadkine, and the image of the mutilated city inspired him with the famous sculpture of the man with his heart torn out, now placed near the Leuvenhaven not far from the remaining statue of Erasmus.

The day of the bombardment the Army Commander-in-Chief surrendered to the Germans, after five days of *blitzkrieg*. But already the municipal administration was thinking of reconstruction; on 17 June they began clearing away the debris, on 18 June they appointed the Chief engineer W. G. Witteveen to work on a new plan, and in the same month – while Belgium was surrendering and the English expeditionary corps was gathering on the dunes at Dunkirk – they gained permission from the commander of the army, who had been delegated power by the government in exile, for the compulsory acquisition of the whole of the centre of the city, i.e. of the sites and bombed buildings.

The compensation fixed upon for the owners was not paid immediately, but the sums were inscribed in the so-called Great Book of Reconstruction and retained at an interest rate of 4 per cent: in exchange every landlord was to receive a new site of equivalent value to the old, but not necessarily in the same place and only when it was possible to build on it; furthermore he was to start the reconstruction within a certain period of time and he would receive the compensation for the bombed building only after having spent an equivalent sum on the new one.

The first scheme in the new plan was presented on 8 June – while the battle for France was being fought – and it was concerned with the most urgent works: the disposal of 5 million cubic metres of débris, temporary accommodation for the homeless, the completion of certain works already under way, for instance the tunnel under the Meuse.

At first the idea was to rebuild the destroyed property once again in the centre, but then the authorities realized that part of the population would have to be transferred to the suburbs to made way for the development of offices and public amenities; for this reason they compulsorily acquired a further 640 hectares in the suburbs, and in 1941 a certain number of small outlying communes were annexed to the city, so that a broader development scheme could be envisaged. In June 1942 all works under way were suspended:

'From that moment – says a municipal publication – an almost uncanny peace reigned over the building sites, but the offices were humming with activity, with secret discussions for the rebuilding of the city. Gradually we felt ourselves freed from the grievous image of the city as it had been and the conviction that the new city should be organized in a different way gained ground'.[62]

The definitive plan, directed by C. Van Traa, was passed in 1946 (Fig. 954). The street network in the centre was independent of the old one and was traced in an intentionally elementary way, to regularize the building lots as far as possible within the uninspiring triangular perimeter and make the intensive exploitation of the precious ground possible. Possibly this concern weighed more heavily than it need have done and prevented the planners from completely exploiting the opportunities offered by the lack of restrictions in the way the land could have been divided up; but the plan could be executed without compromise, in fact it gained in coherence and variety through the architectural details, whereas usually the reverse was the case.

The most important work so far built in the centre of Rotterdam was the Lijnbaan complex of shops and dwellings, by Jacob Van den Broek and B. Bakema (b. 1914). Here the plan provided for two parallel roads at the Coolsingel, with shops on the ground floor and private accommodation on the two upper floors, but landlords and architects were in agreement in choosing a new solution: the shops were concentrated around a broad pedestrian street, so as to form a real business centre, complemented by two large stores at the entrance to the Binnenweg; a great deal of attention had been lavished on the details (shelters, kiosks, benches and parking places); the apartments on the other hand had been concentrated in seven large ten-storey blocks set on nearby sites amid generous green spaces. The most profitable solution economically had also proved the best artistically, and the architecture had a confidence and fluency which call to mind the best works of the Rotterdam school between the wars.

The southwards expansion of Rotterdam beyond the Meuse had 200,000 inhabitants, and it was to be the centre of a number of new districts; for this reason the plan, while it had decided that all the business functions were to remain on the north bank, provided for a secondary centre here, cultural and recreational, set round a tall building erected in 1949 by Van Tijen and Maaskant (the authors of the Bergpolder and the Plaslaan). The designers described their third tall building as follows:

'In the residential building at Zuidplein we have tried to provide something for those who look for the impressive and the important in life. We have tried to build apartments where people could live in the heart of the city in spacious surroundings and where, at just 40 metres above street level, they could find a sense of security and intimacy. We built a hall which is indeed very high, but where the inhabitants can feel that they are at home and can delight in their status as citizens of

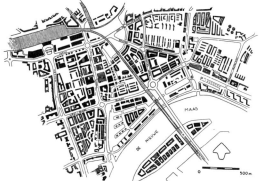

953, 954, 955   *Rotterdam, The new centre: aerial view (in the centre is the new Bijenkork by M. Breuer with the sculpture by Gabo, behind, the Lijnbaan by Bakema and Van den Broek), general ground-plan (from Casabella) and view of the De Klerk & Zn. stores (Bakema and Van den Broek, 1955)*

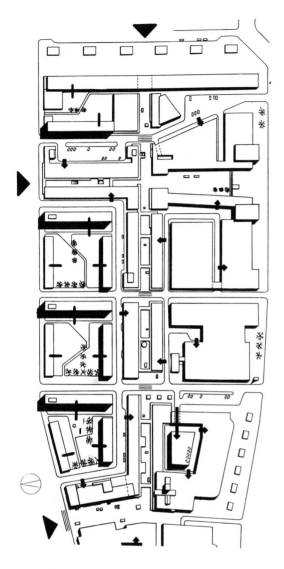

956, 957 *Rotterdam, Plan of the Lijnbaan (large arrows indicate entrances for pedestrians, small ones those for traffic) and a view from above*

Rotterdam. We have built a roof terrace where people can sit out in bad weather as in an ocean liner and from which they can see the harbour in all its splendour. By day the ugly Rotterdam-Zuid becomes a lovely patchwork of green, red-brick and deep blue, by night it is an expanse dotted with lights'. [63]

But the dominant factor, in the recent development of the city, was the growth of the ports towards the estuary of the Nieuwe

Maas, which by now had transformed the city's structure from a centralized into a linear one.

It is important to note that the new shape of the city was determined not by the accumulation of residential districts and business districts, but by the trappings of industry; for instance, the canals and locks which had defined the pattern of the medieval Flemish cities. In comparison with the size of the harbour installation, the residential districts and services rightly remained in a

958, 959, 960   *Rotterdam, Alexanderpolder (in collaboration with Van Tijen) and two views of the Montessori school (Bakema and Van den Broek, 1957)*

subordinate position, but it become important, within them, to retain the limited
dimensions typical of family life and of the
serried relationships between residences and
basic services.

Some of the most striking of the recent
districts of Rotterdam are those that have
been built around the small town of Vlaardingen – Ambacht, Westwijk and Vlaardingen Noord – whose authors were Van

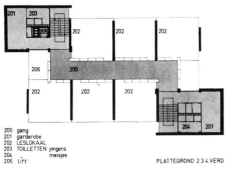

200 gang
201 garderobe
202 LESLOKAAL
203 TOILLETTEN jongens
204 ̈   meisjes
205 lift ·

PLATTEGROND 2.3.4.VERD

961, 962, 963 *Plan and details of the Montessori school at Rotterdam*

Tijen, Bakema and Van den Broek; because of their size (about 800,000 inhabitants) and their relatively remote position *vis-à-vis* the present-day main centre of Rotterdam, they form a particularly rich and complex urban whole, where the planners have had to tackle problems different to those typical of normal suburban districts.

A second aspect of Dutch reconstruction was connected with the draining and recla-

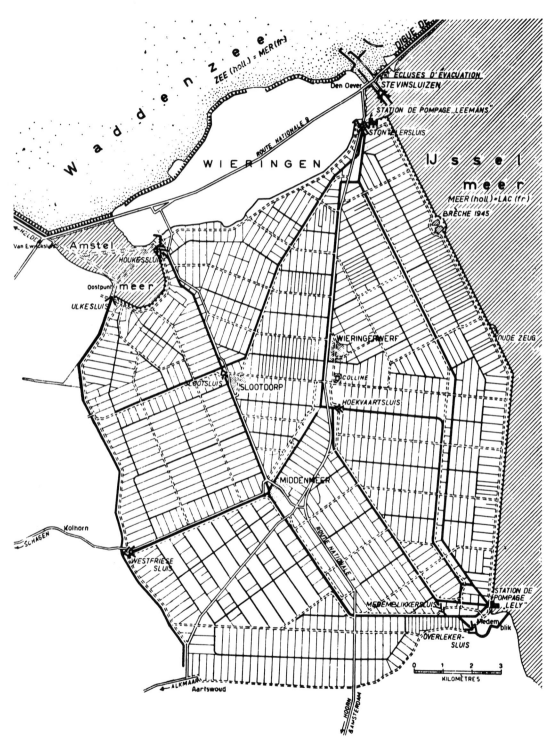

964   *Plan of the cultivation of the polder of Wieringermeer (canals shown in black; from* Urbanistica)

mation of the Zuiderzee, begun in 1918 and made possible by the building of the great dyke which separated the Zuiderzee from the open sea; this, one of the greatest feats of engineering of our time, was closed on 28 May 1932, where the monument designed by Dudok now stands.

The scheme provided for five big *polders*, in the earth that had been used to fill in the sea; the first, Wieringermeerpolder, was completed between 1927 and 1930, but flooded by the Germans in 1945 and rebuilt after the war; the second, Nordoostpolder, was reclaimed between 1937 and 1942 and built in the following decade; work is still going on on the last three, eastern Flevoland – now complete – southern Flevoland and Markenwaard. While in the first *polder* the new settlements were scattered, never amounting to more than a village, in the second a new town was built, Emmeloord, which was to hold 10,000 inhabitants, and the southern *polders* were to have an even bigger centre, Lelystaat.

Even in this case the productive problem which was at the basis of the undertaking – the transformation of the sea into agricultural land – conditioned every stage of the operation, from the reclaiming of the land to the layout of the farms and urban settlements, so that the formal result was apparently rigid, because of the constancy of the dimensions of the elements, but in reality elastic and variable, because of the open-minded way in which the instruments available had been adapted to the various local conditions.[64]

Finally, the disastrous flood of 1953 forced the Dutch government to work out a general hydraulic system for the mouths of the Rhine and Meuse, linked with a large-scale town-planning scheme; in fact, the problem presented was that of the cities concentrated in the western zone – Amsterdam, Haarlem, the Hague, Rotterdam, Delft and Utrecht – which were on the verge of merging into one single built up area with five to six million inhabitants and the same overcrowding problem as the other great metropolitan areas.

This congested area might find an outlet to the south, in the river zone, where a new city of 500,000 inhabitants had been planned along the Haringvlietriver, linked with the development of the harbour installations all along the mouths of the rivers.[65]

Faced with these grandiose plans, it was to the credit of Dutch architecture that it was able – almost always successfully – to bridge the gap between the geographical dimension of infra-structural action and the much smaller dimensions of urban life, collective and individual.

Among the best results were some parts of Amsterdam – including the new public park of 900 hectares, planted artificially on sandy ground between 1935 and 1955 – the town of Nagele – one of the smaller centres of the Noordoostpolder, planned by the Dutch group of the C.I.A.M. – and many of the districts jointly planned by Bakema and Van den Broek. The instrument which made possible the successful link up between town-planning schemes and architecture was the use of a scale of sub-multiples, derived from detailed study of the concept of 'unités d'habitation'; on the unwavering principle that the elements of the new urban fabric were not to be single dwelling houses, but systems formed of the association of houses with services, a scale of these systems was picked out, including a number of dwellings proportionate to the services of varying sizes. Bakema and Van den Broek also applied this method on a territorial scale; in the plan for the district of Noord-Kennemerland; but we shall say more about these experiments in the final chapter, to emphasize their importance in international town-planning thought.

twenty

The new international field

At the beginning of the Second World War the modern movement had affected countries throughout the world, but what happened outside Europe and America was only a consequence of the European and American experiments already described; the international repertoire was adapted to local customs but did not draw from them the impetus for new and original developments.

On the other hand after the Second World War there began a widespread movement of reconsideration of the contributions made hitherto and in at least two cases – in Brazil and in Japan – the results were of international importance, no longer linked to Europe or to American models, but actually able to stimulate the experiments under way in the old as well as the new world.

In this way the foundations were laid for a new movement of cultural interests, which we are only now beginning to discern.

It is impossible to give a systematic account of a picture which is altering so rapidly and disconcertingly; we shall simply allude to the two episodes which have already been recognized as being of international interest – the Brazilian and the Japanese – and to Le Corbusier's experiment in Chandigarh, India, which is the most serious attempt by a European architect at interpreting the pre-existing styles of a remote country, without slackening his own commitment to international culture.

Le Corbusier's name recurs frequently in the exposition of Brazilian and Japanese events too. Today his architecture acts as a guideline for the most lively and advanced experiments in many widely scattered countries.

1 Brazil

After the First World War Brazil felt the echo of the battle of the *avant-garde* that was being waged in Europe; its most clamorous manifestation was the 'week of modern art' organized in 1922 at Sao Paulo, with exhibitions of painting and sculpture, concerts, recitals and lectures.

In 1925 G. Warchavchik published a 'manifesto of functional architecture',[1] inspired by the ideology of Le Corbusier, and in 1928 he built the first 'modern' house; in 1927 in the competition for Government House of the State of Sao Paulo, F. de Carvalho scandalized the public and judges with a strictly rationalist design. As well as turning toward Europe, this period also tended to re-appraise local tradition and the 'anthrophagist' movement (1928) actually

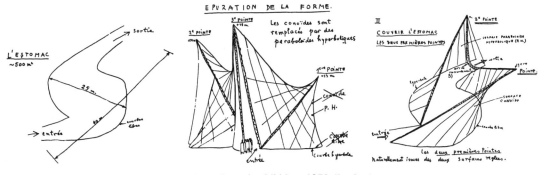

965, 966 *Brussels, Philips pavilion at the universal exhibition, 1958 (Le Corbusier)*

suggested a return to the pre-Columbian heritage. In 1929 Le Corbusier, on his way back from the Argentine, stopped at Sao Paulo and Rio, gave various lectures and was received officially by the authorities, with whom he began to discuss certain town-planning projects.

The turning point for the Brazilian movement coincided with the revolution of Getulio Vargas, in 1930. The political class now in power came from the milieu which supported the *avant-garde* artists, who from now on were no longer confined to the opposition but became part of the ruling élite.

Immediately after the Revolution, Lucio Costa (b. 1902) was made director of the School of Fine Arts at Rio de Janeiro; he appointed G. Warchavchik and A. Budeus as professors of composition and planned a complete renewal of traditional teaching, but this caused such an upheaval that after less than a year he was forced to resign. The students took his part, organized a strike and even attempted to found a new school: the most important of them were J. M. Moreira, E. Vasconcellos and C. Leao, who were to play an important part in the development of the Brazilian movement.

The conflicts caused by the 1930 revolution prevented normal building activity for several years. In 1935 a competition was organized for the Ministry of Health and Education, in which several of the best modern architects took part unsuccessfully. But the minister G. Capanema gave the task of drawing up the executive plan to L. Costa, O. Niemeyer, A. E. Reidy and E. Vasconcellos. In 1936 Costa suggested that Le Corbusier should be called in as an adviser; Le Corbusier spent a month in Rio, worked with the local group and reconsidered the whole basis of the plan, also requesting, in vain, that the proposed site should be replaced by another, more spacious and better situated.

In 1937 the definitive plan was ready, based on Le Corbusier's suggestions; its execution took several years and in 1939 Costa gave up his position as leader of the group and was replaced by Niemeyer, but continued to follow and support the works of the younger architects. In 1946 he wrote to Le Corbusier, inviting him to visit the finished building:

'I am certain that you will be immensely moved and reassured when you actually see the Ministry building for the first time, and lay your hand on the magnificent *pilotis*, ten metres high. You will also be gratified to note that of the seeds so generously scattered to the four corners of the world – from Buenos Aires to Stockholm, from New York to Moscow – those sown in our beloved Brazilian soil have produced – thanks to the exceptional though hitherto unsuspected talent of Oscar and his team – a flowering of architecture whose Ionic charm owes much to you'.[2]

This was in fact the first realization of a building type of which Le Corbusier had been thinking for some time – the Cartesian skyscraper for administrative purposes, designed in vain for Paris, Algiers, Nemours, Buenos Aires – and here all the points of his architectural programme were rigorously applied: 'pilotis', roof garden, 'pan de verre', 'brise soleil'. As always, its practical demonstration was extremely effective, because the unprejudiced attitude of the designers had made it possible to make good use of the restricted site, fitting this inspiring pointer to a possible new urban scene into one of the most crowded corners of Rio; (Figs. 967 and 968) the building also has various works of sculpture – including a statue by Lipchitz – and a covering of Portinari majolica, henceforward to be widely used in Brazilian architecture.

From 1936 onwards there were an increasing number of opportunities for modern architects: Marcelo and Mauricio Roberto won the competitions for the headquarters of the Printing Association and the Santos Dumont Airport, A. Correa Lima that for the seaplane station in Rio; Costa and Niemeyer built the Brazilian Pavilion at the New York Exposition of 1939.

In 1942 the American critic P. L. Goodwin and the photographer E. Kidder-Smith went to Brazil to gather material for an exhibition which was organized the following year at the Museum of Modern Art in New York.

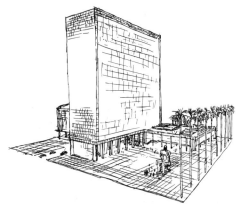

967, 968 *(left)   Rio de Janeiro, Ministry of Education and Health (Costa, Leão, Moreira, Niemeyer, Reidy, Vasconcellos, 1937–43)*
969, 970 *(right)   Rio de Janeiro, The 'brise-soleil' of the Banco Boavista by Niemeyer and the original sketch by Le Corbusier for the Ministry of Education and Health (from* Oeuvre Complète*)*

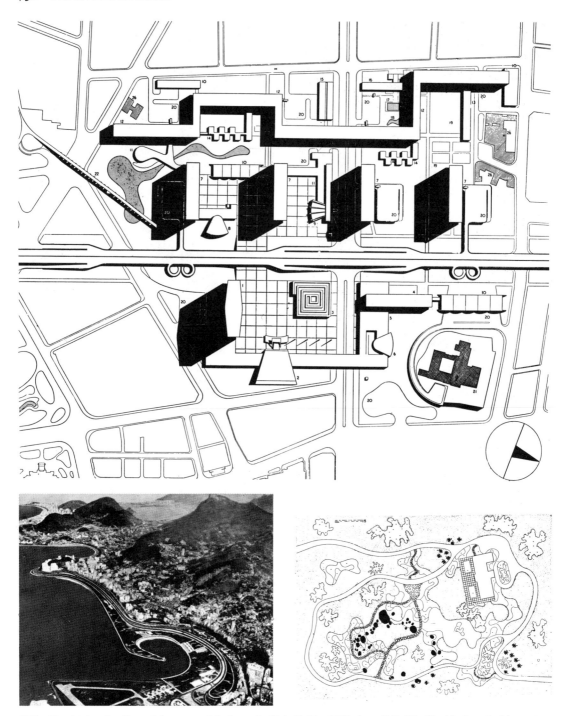

971   *Rio de Janeiro, New civic centre of S. Antonio (E.A. Reidy, 1948; from H.E. Mindlin,* Modern Architecture in Brazil, *1956)*
972, 973 *(below)   Rio de Janeiro, Building up of the coastline in accordance with the planning scheme, and a garden designed by R. Burle-Marx (from Mindlin, op. cit.)*

1 reservoir
2, 3, 4, 5   apartment blocks
6 primary school
7 gymnasium
8 changing rooms
9 swimming bath
10, 11, 12 playing fields
13, 14   laundries
15 market
16, 17, 18 asylums
19 pedestrian underpass
20 existing factory

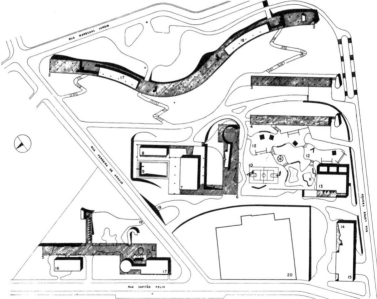

974, 975   *Rio de Janeiro, Pedregulho residential complex (Reidy, 1950–2)*

The two authors published the book *Brazil Builds*,[3] which marked the beginning of the international acclaim of the Brazilian movement.[4]

Oscar Niemeyer (b. 1907), already well known for his buildings in Pampulha between 1942 and 1943 (the church, casino, yacht club) built the Banco Boavista in Rio in 1946, the Aeronautics Technical Centre at Sao José dos Campos in 1947, from 1951 onwards the buildings in the Ibirapuera park in Sao Paulo and several residential complexes in Belo Horizonte, Sao Paulo and Rio.

In these works he moved towards an intentional simplification of the rationalist repertoire, slackening the dense structural counterpoint typical of Le Corbusier and replacing it with a few elementary motifs, decisive and strongly spaced. The architectural image is sometimes impoverished almost to the point of nudity – in the Banco Boavista – yet the whole organism acquires a decorative value by becoming transformed almost into a gigantic piece of moulding (particularly in his own house at Rio, in 1953) with an immediacy hitherto unknown, and which nonetheless appeared indispensable to stand up to the sensational surrounding landscape.

But Niemeyer's tendency must be considered as a limit, from which Brazilian production as a whole remained firmly distant. Similar in intent, but with greater variety of tone, were the works of Lucio Costa – he built the exemplary residential blocks Nuova Cintra (1948), Bristol (1950) and Caledonia (1954) in Rio, M. and M. Roberto, H. E. Mindlin, R. Levi and, of the immigrants from Europe, G. C. Palanti and S. Papadaki.

The most obvious shortcoming of contemporary Brazilian production is the lack of an adequate town-planning framework; the formal agitation was undoubtedly determined partly by a defensive attitude towards the dense and chaotic urban surroundings.

The main exceptions – apart from the large-scale planning schemes of which we shall say more later – are certain building complexes by Alfonso Eduardo Reidy (1909–1964): the new civic centre of S. Antonio (designed in 1948 and now being built); (Fig. 971) and particularly the residential complex Pedregulho in Rio (1950–1), where buildings, services and outside spaces are interbalanced with great skill (Figs. 974–5). Yet one of the most gifted landscape architects of our time, R. Burle-Marx, is working in Brazil at present; so far he has been employed only on marginal and decorative tasks such as the gardens of several private houses and public buildings (the Santos Dumont airport, the Canadian embassy in Rio).

While Brazilian architecture is becoming ever better known, partly through the direct experience of visitors who come from all over the world, judgments are becoming increasingly discordant and the first reasoned dissent is being expressed.

After the Biennale at Sao Paulo in 1953, when many critics of all nationalities came to Brazil, the *Architectural Review* printed statements by P. Craymer, Ise and W. Gropius, H. Oyre, M. Bill and E. Rogers.[5]

Gropius, with his usual sympathy, was delighted at the originality of the Brazilian movement, by the adaptation of international contributions to the climate and customs of the country, and he was particularly enthusiastic about the works in which architectural planning had a balanced relationship with town-planning, for instance Reidy's Pedregulho.

In a lecture at Sao Paulo M. Bill was firmly critical of Brazilian architecture as a whole:

'Architecture in your country stands in danger of falling into a parlous state of anti-social academicism. I intend to speak of architecture as a social art; an art which cannot simply be set aside, one of these days when it no longer seems to meet the case, because "style" has changed – because wiping out values which run into millions or billions is not as easy as putting away a few canvases or pieces of sculpture deemed bad or mediocre'.[6]

He believed that in Brazil the elements of the international repertoire – organic forms *à la* Arp, the curtain wall, the 'brise soleil', the 'pilotis' – had become conventional formulae, like the columns and pediments in neo-classical times, i.e. that they had been accepted in obedience to a pre-ordained poetics, not to resolve the real demands of the country; in this connection Bill criticized the Ministry of Education, too, which had been built before the war under Le Corbusier's supervision (but he made an exception for Il Pedregulho, which he found absolutely acceptable).

The accusation of formalism was certainly not groundless, and particularly when levelled at the more original architects like Niemeyer, but it should lead to a closer examination of the causes and possible developments of the Brazilian experiment.

It may be noted that formalism arose, as in Scandinavia, in the presence of a very particular social pattern – in Scandinavia, of a socially very equal society and an economy based on co-operation, in Brazil, of a hierarchical society and recently born but flourishing capitalism – which for this reason demanded appropriate symbolic representation. The international repertoire was not applied at all literally, in fact it was powerfully transformed, particularly in the relations between geometrical form and scale, since every single formal motif was charged with an emotive significance which enabled it to stand on its own; in this way composition became elementary, allusive, and the texture of the buildings singularly rarified while the shape of the whole could be taken in at first glance, with the immediacy of a diagram.

This method of composition contained in essence a new concept of the urban scene, absolutely foreign to the fabric of the traditional cities – and for this reason the new architecture did not take root in the old centres, where it simply created a feeling of disorder – but realizable through town-planning action on an appropriate scale.

In 1955 the governor of the state of Minas Gerais, J. Kubitschek – who together with Capanema, Valadares and Vital had hitherto been one of the protectors of the modern movement in Brazil – was elected President and gave new impetus to town-planning, enabling Brazilian architects to draw upon, on this new scale, the consequences of the experiments so far achieved. This period saw the beginning of various large-scale works provided for by the plan for Rio (worked on from 1938 to 1948 by a commission headed by J. de Olivera Reis); to place certain installations on open land, in the shelter of the existing city, the authorities decided to build great artificial embankments along the sea-shore, superimposing a planned landscape upon the natural one and using the same firm, sweeping curves that had been used for buildings (Fig. 972).

But Kubitschek's great enterprise, for which the nation's finest talent was mustered, was the founding of Brasilia, the new capital which was rising out of the desert in the hinterland. This decision was linked to a vast programme to move part of the population and economic enterprises from the coast into the interior. The transfer of the seat of politics was regarded as indispensable to set the process in motion, and from the start it was the task of the new city visibly to represent this aim.

First Kubitschek appointed a commission to choose the site; the American firm D. J. Belcher and Assistants, with local officials and experts from Cornell University, was appointed to carry out research and suggested five possible localities, of which the one finally chosen was on a slightly undulating plateau in the state of Goias.

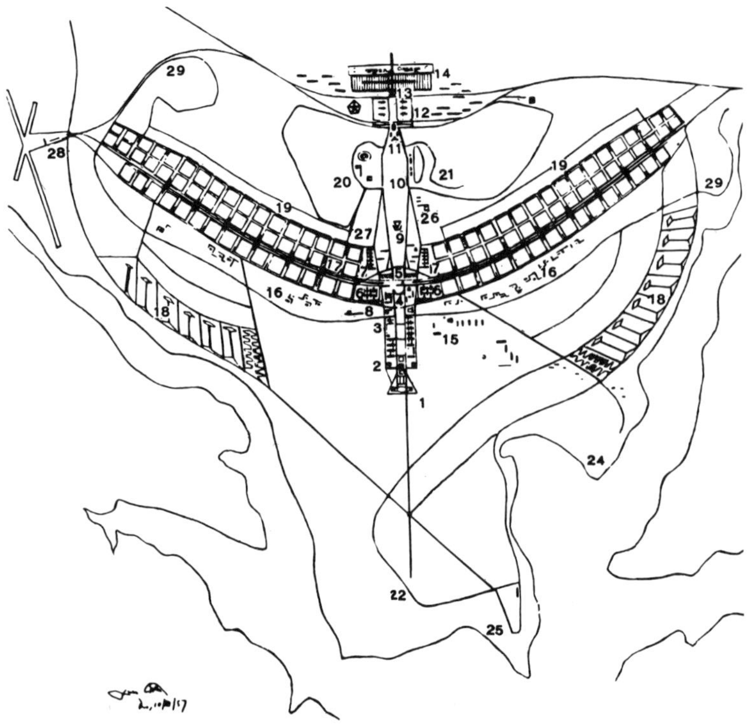

1   plaza of the Three Powers
2   ministries
3   Cathedral
4   cultural sector
5   entertainment centre
6   banks and offices
7   commercial sector
8   hotels
9   television tower
10   playing fields
11   square of the Town Hall
12   barracks
13   railway station
14   storehouses and small
    industries
15   university
16   embassies and legations
17   residential zone
18   single houses
19   horticulture
20   botanical garden
21   zoological garden
22   golf club
23   bus station
24   yacht club
25   Presidential residence
26   riding club
27   amusement park
28   airport
29   cemetery

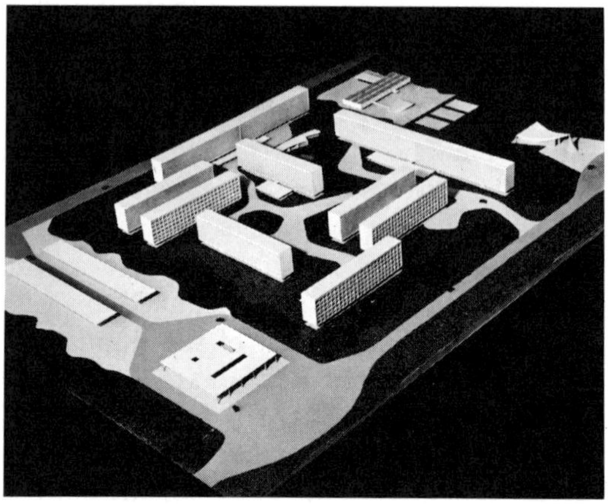

976, 977, 978   *Brasilia, Ground-plan by Lucio Costa (1957) and models of a residential super-block and complex of banks (Niemeyer, 1958)*

An executive body was then set up ('Novacap') similar to the English development corporations, to acquire the site, to do the groundwork and erect the public buildings. Niemeyer was appointed the head of the department of architecture and town-planning, and was immediately commissioned to build the first two buildings (the

979, 980 *Brasilia, Central traffic crossing and some 'supercuadras'*

Governor's Residence and a hotel for official visitors).

For the general plan Niemeyer suggested a competition of ideas, which was organized in September 1956, to be closed six months later. The competitors were given a mass of research material, but were asked for only two pieces of work: a basic layout on the scale 1:25,000 and a report.

The competition was judged by the representatives of the professional organization of Brazilian architects and engineers (P. A. Ribeiro and H. Barbosa), of the Departments of Architecture and Town-planning (Niemeyer and Papadaki) and two foreign experts (A. Sive from Paris and W. Holford from London); as Holford describes in an article in the *Architectural Review*,[7] the judgment was disputed, because some of the projects claimed to deal exhaustively with all technical problems, with numerous analytical plans, while others simply outlined the form of the city, justifying it with reasons of a general order. Of the first, the most ponderous was the plan by Marcelo and Mauricio Roberto, who saw the future city articulated in seven 'unités d'habitation', hexagonal in shape, which could be increased to up to fourteen, and which fixed the economic balance which the future city would have to maintain, from the start.

Of the second the most notable was that by L. Costa, contained in five plates including the text of the report and the illustrative sketches, all drawn freehand. Costa described the basic conception of the new organism as follows:

'It was born of that initial gesture which anyone would make when pointing to a given place, or taking possession of it: the drawing of two axes crossing at right angles, in the sign of the cross. This sign was then adapted to the topography, the natural drainage of the land, and the best possible orientation: the extremities of one axial line were curved so as to make the sign fit into the equilateral triangle which outlines the area to be urbanized'.[8]

The north-south axis was equipped as a modern motorway and carried the outside traffic – i.e. the flow of communications with the surrounding territory, for which Brasilia was being created – into the heart of the city; along this axis all the residential districts were set, while the entertainment districts were positioned at the crossings with the minor roads, equipped with platforms at various levels.

The east-west axis on the other hand linked the business areas and formed the monumental radial artery of the new political centre; the main buildings – the Presidential Palace, the Supreme Court and Congress – were grouped around a triangular piazza, the 'Plaza of the Three Powers' while the Cathedral was set apart, to offset its monumental qualities.

The residential zones were articulated in large super-blocks, which were to be designed in a uniform style. Costa wrote:

'I feel that the super-blocks should not be subdivided and suggest that not the land, but shares in the land should be sold.
The price of these shares would depend on the vicinity and the height regulations.
This would overcome any obstacles in the way of present planning and any possible future replanning of the internal arrangement in the super-blocks. Such a plan should be preferably worked out before the shares are sold; but there is nothing to prevent purchasers of a substantial number of shares from submitting their own planning scheme for a specified super-block to the approval of the development company'.[9]

Space in the huge city, Costa concludes, would be controlled and unified by two main instruments: 'on the one hand, the use of highway technique; on the other, the technique of the landscaper, planting parks and gardens.'[10]

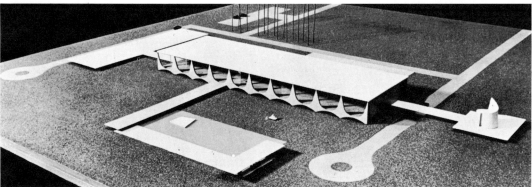

981, 982 *Brasilia, Presidential palace (Niemeyer, 1958) and model*

As is well known, Costa's plan was chosen by the jury,[11] despite Ribeiro's disagreement; whatever may be the judgment as to its absolute value, it was certainly the one which best fitted into the direction taken hitherto by the Brazilian movement, transferring its merits and defects on to a town-planning scale, and therefore the best suited to act as a framework to the architecture which was to spring up in the new city.

As in the later works of Niemeyer, the organism was based on an intentionally simple and elementary image, a positive gesture as Costa says, i.e. the Sign of the Cross formed by the two axes. However, since the minor axis has a markedly celebratory character, the planner tended to keep the two arms of the major axes symmetrical, giving the whole organism a bilateral symmetry which gives it a vaguely zoomorphic flavour, probably intentional for symbolic reasons (Fig. 976).

This was the main weakness of Costa's plan since it introduced an extrinsic factor into the very structure of the city, a metaphor which disturbed its practical reality.

This defect is still more obvious in the present state of the work; while the city designed by Costa has taken shape on the site, many building enterprises were settled elsewhere, and have almost entirely occupied the bank of the artificial lake. So that the symmetrical figure conceived of by the designer no longer corresponds to the whole urban organism, but is only an inner core around which formless outskirts are growing up, as happened with the old centres with their enclosed and finite form.

But the way in which the initial image took architectural form in the various parts, without losing in freshness and simplicity, was masterly. The super-block was the means that made it possible to keep the mesh of the city's fabric broad and well-spaced, just as the summary divisions of the 'brise soleil' or the walls of glass by Niemeyer kept the texture of his buildings rarified. In this way the organism of Brasilia, despite its half million inhabitants, retained a basic aspect that was immediately legible, which meant that the energy and character of the general plan could be grasped from all points of the enormous area. What is striking is the new relationship between formal invention and the space in which it is applied. Holford points this out in financial terms as well:

'One of the press comments after the Award was to the effect that Lucio Costa had spent 25 cruzeiros to win a million. But with this expenditure – still only a tenth of what is needed in these days of inflation to buy a good French Impressionist painting – the Brazilian government had made, in my opinion, one of the best investments in urban development that the twentieth century has produced'.[12]

In designing the buildings of Brasilia, Niemeyer was following the same criteria. Each of these was born of a very simple, in fact elementary, basic formal idea – the motif of the sickle-shaped marble screens for the Presidential Palace, of the scrolled wall for the nearby chapel, of the convex dome for the Senate and the concave one for the House of Representatives, of the ring of moulded pillars for the Cathedral – developed with extreme parsimony of constructional detail (Figs. 981–6).

Often these motifs have no relationship to the supporting structure: for instance, the screens which surround the Presidential Palace were made with a covering of specially-moulded marble slabs, and they look like an enormous decoration superimposed upon the organism, certainly deplorable. Yet because of its scale this decoration no longer belongs exclusively to the building but involves the surrounding space, forcing the presence of the building itself upon one's attention from a distance much greater than that necessary optically to discern its true texture, necessarily linked to the human scale.

In following this aim Niemeyer was led to force the effects that could be obtained from the usual constructional elements, or to distort their meaning by presenting them in isolation from their usual context, like enormous *objets trouvés*; in this way his architecture took on a surrealistic tone which has been noted several times,[13] and some details – for instance the marble elements, shaped and polished like animal bone – are undoubtedly reminiscent of

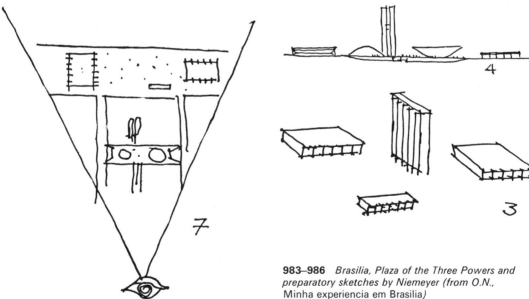

983–986 *Brasilia, Plaza of the Three Powers and preparatory sketches by Niemeyer (from O.N., Minha experiencia em Brasilia)*

certain images by some surrealist painters from Dali to the contemporary Brazilian O. de Andreade Filho and A. Bulecao.

Like Haussmann in his time, Costa and Niemeyer aimed at creating a new urban landscape by experiment on a new scale with

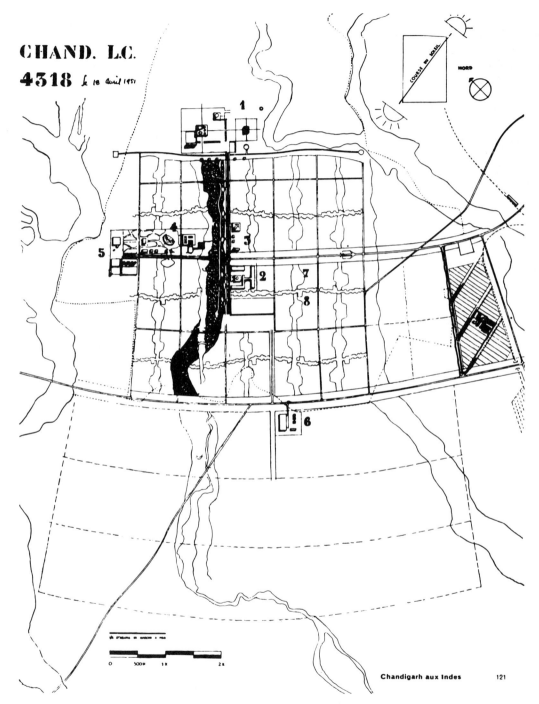

987   *Chandigarh, General ground-plan of 1951 (from Oeuvre Complète of Le Corbusier): 1 the Capitol; 2 commercial centre; 3 reception centre; 4 museum and stadium; 5 university; 6 market; 7 green spaces with recreational facilities; 8 the four ways (commercial)*

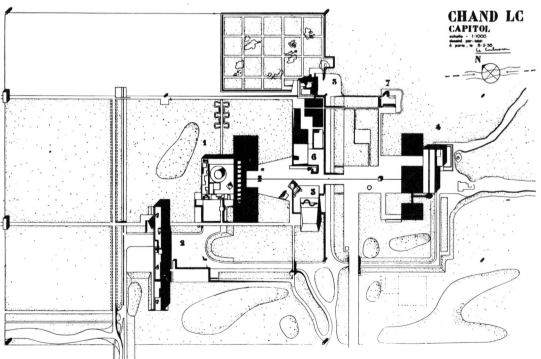

988, 989 *Chandigarh, view and general ground-plan of the Capitol (1956; from* Oeuvre Complète*): 1 Assembly; 2 Secretariat; 3 Governor's palace; 4 Law Courts; 5 the 'Fosse de la considération'; 6 pools in front of the governor's palace; 7 the open hand*

certain already established compositional formulae. Even the criticism levelled today at Brasilia make one think of those levelled a century ago at Haussmann's Paris: critics emphasize the artifical and abstract character of the instruments adopted, without taking into account the methodological importance of their use in such new circumstances and the lessons, however problematical, that derived from them for the planning of the future city.

One may judge the buildings of Brasilia severely, but one should at least judge them for what they are, i.e. the component parts of a new urban space to which they are giving shape. For this reason the experiment of Brasilia involves present day town-planning thought and in various ways anticipates its possible developments.

2 Le Corbusier in India

In 1950 Le Corbusier was in contact with the Indian government and was appointed to supervise the building of Chandigarh, the new capital of the Punjab, to replace Lahore which was now in Pakistan.

Appointed with him were the English architects Maxwell-Fry and Jane Drew (b. 1911) and Pierre Jeanneret, his cousin and former colleague. The four of them met together on the site in February 1951 and within six weeks they had drawn up the town-planning scheme, so that the work on the roads could begin the following summer.

The city was to hold 150,000 inhabitants (to be increased to 500,000) of whom about a third were to be employed in administrative positions; the state was to build the public buildings and houses for these employees and therefore a good part of the city, and the planners had to control *a priori*, according to a precise programme, the whole course of the affair from the basic town-planning formulation to the final architectural details.

By applying the theory of the seven ways,[14] Le Corbusier conceived of a street system of fast roads of varying degrees of importance (Roads 1, 2 and 3) which would intersect at right-angles, creating a chess-board system of great rectangular 'sectors', each of about 100 hectares. Each sector was divided among the thirteen social classes which made up the city's population, housed in thirteen different categories of accommodation and grouped in different portions of the sector, although making use of the same public services; in this way Le Corbusier was able to put rigorously to the test his theory of mixed sectors, where the various residential zones were differentiated according to density. The sectors were crossed in one direction by Road 4 (Commercial), off which Roads 5 and 6 branched, leading to the actual doors of the houses, and at right-angles to Road 7, which wound through green spaces and linked scholastic and recreational facilities.

The administrative buildings – the Government Headquarters, the Parliament, the Secretariat (where all the ministries were) and the Law Courts – were grouped together outside the city, on a stretch of flat ground artificially enlivened with variations in level, pools, plantations and symbolic figures (Fig. 989).

As always, Le Corbusier tended to make architectural planning and town-planning coincide – he immediately designed an admirable building type for the houses of the pariahs (Fig. 999) – but since plainly uniform conditions were not possible for the whole of his work, his responsibility was restricted to the buildings of the Capitol. Here Le Corbusier committed himself completely, convinced that in India he might be able to realize the definitive public work that could never be born in the cramped spaces of Europe. He set out to forget all preconceived models, to deduce a new architecture from the very reality before him; nonetheless, his methodology demanded an immediate formal qualification of the environmental data, and he preferred to start from the unchanging facts of the climate rather than from the changeable ones of social relationships:

'Sun and rain are the two components of an architecture which must be sunshade and umbrella at the same time. The roofs must be treated as problems of hydraulics and the problem of shade is the most important. The concept of the *brise soleil* here acquires its full value as as a breaker of acquired habits, and should be extended from the window to the whole façade, indeed to the very structure of the building'.[15]

The rooms in the Law Courts (Figs. 990–1) were protected by a broad undulating covering, beneath which air and light passed freely, penetrating into every part of the structure; within its cavities ran horizontal and vertical routes, linked by gently sloping ramps, while the glass walls of the halls and offices were protected by an elaborate 'brise soleil', which brought the impressive dimensions of the main framework down to human proportions. This architectural framework was boldly enclosed by blank walls at the two ends, so that the building rises out of the great clearing as a compact block.

The civic importance of the subject inspired Le Corbusier with one of his most suggestive architectural images, but one which also respects the humble people who walk there, to whose stature the dimensions of all the spaces are subordinated.

The Secretariat (Fig. 994) was a simpler and more conventional organism where variations of structure and internal distribution did not interrupt the compact volume, but were reproduced in two dimensions by the highly elaborate design of the 'brise soleil'. The Parliament (Fig. 993) and the Government Palace, not yet completed, have a more pronounced plastic outline, particularly the second which crowned the landscape of the Capitol. There was some difficulty in going from the monumental scale to the domestic – since this was a residence, however grandiose – and indeed

the plan did have to be changed repeatedly.

While he was working in Chandigarh, Le Corbusier designed a building for the Association of Spinners at Ahmedabad, a museum and two splendid private residences, utilizing the same planning criteria in a more limited setting, criteria based on a cosmic and super-historical interpretation of the local environment (one of the villas, designed for a client, was successfully adapted for another owner and another site almost without alterations).

At this point in time, the experiment of Chandigarh is not yet concluded. Le Corbusier encountered increasing difficulties in carrying out his work and awaited the complete realization of the monumental complex, 'now regulated down to the last centimetre as a whole and in every detail',[16] to reply to his critics.

While this was probably the most impressive measure of his talent, Le Corbusier undoubtedly wanted to leave a very personal mark on the Capitol, using his personal symbols as focal points of the layout.

One may legitimately wonder which was the more fruitful, such an experiment, where the designer gave all he could without any limit, or the more reticent one of the foreign specialist trying to immerse himself in the previous habits of the people, without presuming to contrast them with new forms and new models of behaviour.

Only the future will allow us to make any certain judgment. Hitherto Indians have taken little from this work for the modernization of their architectural tradition. The value of Le Corbusier's teaching ends where he was unable to intervene in person, and some buildings built at Chandigarh by other European designers or by Indians (Figs. 996–8) demonstrate, in the most persuasive way possible, with their poverty and the mechanical repetition of certain conventional motifs, the unique character of this, Le Corbusier's last experiment.

What had not yet happened could, how-

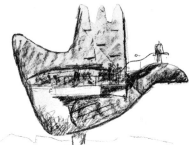

990, 991, 992   *Chandigarh, Law Courts and the open hand*

ever, happen some time in the future.

As usual, Le Corbusier gave himself thoroughly to the task; he provided his humble users with forms that were perhaps incomprehensible, but which were the result of a generous and unconditional communicative effort, whose effects cannot yet be measured.

3   Japan

Japan is perhaps the only country where a tradition different from that of the west, and not naturalistic or primitive – as in Latin America – but cultured and highly sophisticated, has been affected by western contribution and has developed in an original way, attaining results of international importance,

993, 994   *Chandigarh, Parliament and Secretariat*

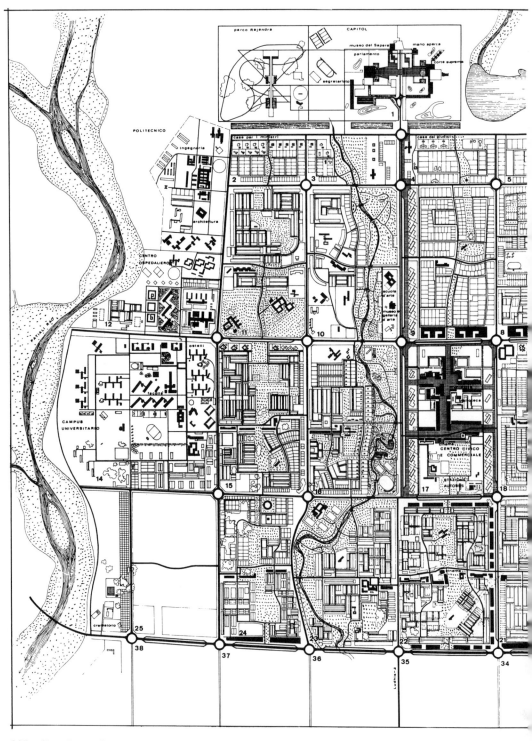

995   *Chandigarh, Ground-plan brought up to date, 1965; public buildings are shown in black, and*

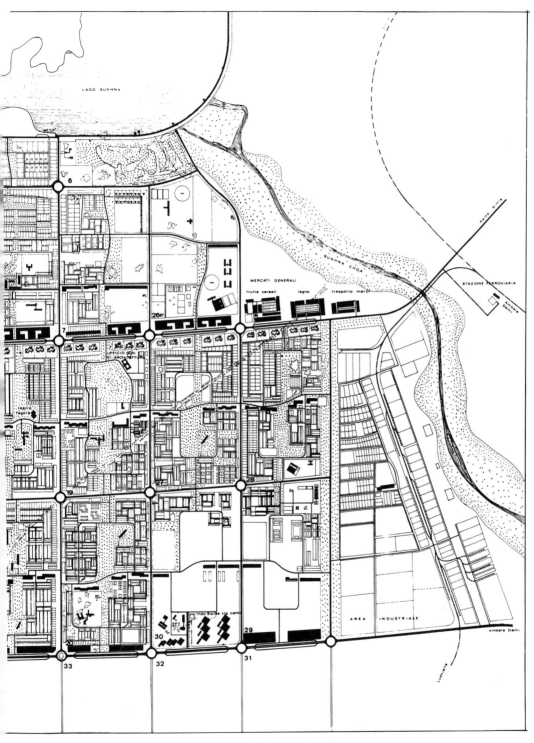

green spaces by dots (drawing by Preti, Caldini and Natali)

though amid many difficulties. It is therefore important to consider how it was that this happened, and what were the exact relationships between modern Japanese architecture and the heritage of tradition.

In the first place one must consider the influence of the Japanese tradition on the formation of the modern movement in the west. From 1854, when the Americans had the Japanese ports opened for their trading, the products of Japanese art began to circulate in the west, and were an important stimulus in the imminent movement for the reform of the applied arts.

H. Cole and O. Jones used Japanese and Chinese examples in their publications; W. Crane was strongly influenced by the Japanese models with which he came into contact between 1859 and 1862, when he worked as an engraver for W. J. Linton, and communicated his enthusiasm to the Arts and Crafts Society; Japanese prints began to circulate in Paris in 1856, through the activities of the etcher Braquemond, influencing the painting of the period and, particularly from 1866 onwards, that of Whistler; in the 1860s the vogue for Japan spread rapidly: Mme de Soye's shop for Japanese *objets* opened in Paris and was frequented by the Goncourts, Baudelaire, Dégas and Zola, and M. Marks' opened in London; furnishings in the Japanese style became increasingly popular.

In 1886 the first book on Japanese architecture appeared, *Japanese Houses and their Surroundings*, by the American E. S. Morse, and in 1889 the great work *Kunst und Handwerk in Japan* by the German J. Brinkmann. These works certainly influenced the dawning *art nouveau* movement, but they considered Japanese architecture mainly from an external and picturesque point of view.

References to the art of the far east were still present, in a less literal and more subtle way, in the *avant-garde* experiments of the period after the First World War; it has been suggested that the basic germ of the attitude Mondrian adopted in his painting was influenced by Japanese art[17] and it is well known that Itten, in his course at the Bauhaus, made use of Sung painting, the texts of Lao Tse and Chuang Tse.[18] Finally Wright – who lived in Tokyo from 1918 to 1922 – described as follows his contacts with Japanese art, which was to have such a startling influence on his subsequent production:

'During the last years I spent in the workshop at Oak Park, Japanese prints had attracted me and had taught me a great deal. The elimination of the insignificant, the process of simplification on which I had already embarked, found confirmation in these prints. From the moment I discovered the beauty of its prints, Japan had an immense fascination for me. Later I ascertained that Japanese art and architecture had a really organic character. The art of the Japanese was a more autonomous product of more autochthonous conditions of life and work, therefore in my view much closer to the modern spirit than the art of any European civilization, living or dead'.[19]

While in the west, Japanese and Chinese art acted mainly as an indirect stimulus – as we pointed out in Chapter 6 – in Japan the repertoire of western architecture was utilized *à la lettre*, from 1869 onwards, during the enforced Europeanization of the country promoted by the emperor Mutsuhito.

In considering this literal use of European style one must consider the extraordinary speed with which the process of transformation was carried out: in 1869 the Constitution was proclaimed – on the model of the French one – in 1872 compulsory education was introduced, and in 1873 so was compulsory military service, eliminating at its source the power of the warrior caste of the Samurai which was definitively defeated in 1877 by the regular army; in 1880 freedom of worship

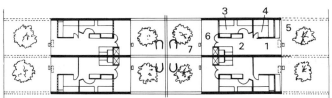

1 *veranda*
2 *kitchen*
3 *parents' bedroom*
4 *children's bedroom*
5 *brise-soleil*
6 *shower*
7 *W.C.*

996, 997, 998 *(above)   Chandigarh, Buildings designed in collaboration*
with Le Corbusier
999 *(below)   Chandigarh, Houses designed by Le Corbusier*
(from Oeuvre Complète*)*

was introduced, as were the Gregorian calendar, a weekly day of rest and a modern penal code; in 1889 a new Constitution was promulgated on the Prussian model, in 1898 a new penal code was introduced and lastly in 1899 consular jurisdiction for foreigners was abolished. At this point Japan – which had won the war against China in 1895 – became a fully-fledged participant in the theatre of world politics.

During the first two decades of the new era the government employed mainly foreign experts. In 1870 a building department was set up at the Ministry of Engineering and various European architects were invited to Japan to design the necessary new public buildings; among these were the Italian C. V. Capelletti – who built the historical

1000 *Katsura, Detail of the imperial villa*

1001   *Mondrian,* Composition in red, yellow and blue, *1928*

Museum and offices of the General Staff in 1880 – the American R. P. Bridgens, the Englishman J. Condor, the Frenchman C. de Boinville and the German H. Ende.

Since there was now absolutely no local point of reference, these designers applied the precepts of eclecticism most rigorously and built every building in the style adapted to its function: public offices in the Renaissance style, the churches in medieval style and so on.

Meanwhile in 1875 a course of architecture was inaugurated at the Faculty of Engineering and visits by Japanese students to Europe were encouraged in every possible way, so that they should become personally acquainted with western methods of design and execution. In this way there grew up a generation of native architects who in the third decade of the new era gradually replaced the Europeans, though continuing to use the same styles; some of the more distinguished of them were K. Tatsuno, the designer of the School of Engineering, the Bank of Japan and the Tokyo Central station, and T. Yokogawa, author of the Imperial Theatre. Meanwhile new methods of building arrived there promptly: the first building in steel (a store) was built in 1895, the first in reinforced concrete (the headquarters of an insurance company) in 1912.

Western concepts of building were absolutely foreign to the Japanese mentality; there was not even a word equivalent to 'architecture', i.e. one that referred to all buildings in so far as they had any artistic value. In traditional language there was the term *Zoka* (which referred to the building of houses) and the term *Fushin* (concerned with the collection of funds for the construction or reconstruction of temples) but they could not be generalized, since they were inseparable from their respective ritual modes of procedure.

So a new term was coined, *Kenchiku*, equivalent to the western word 'architecture'; scholars intended it to indicate mainly the artistic value of a building, but in popular speech – as a contemporary student of architecture, Shinji Koike,[20] has pointed out – this term is used rather to indicate the totality of technical operations in the building field. This shows that the Japanese concept differs from the western one not so much in extent as in mental framework; Europeans, following the Renaissance conception, had in mind an abstract and general value, concerned with a single aspect of building activity, while the Japanese – like the men of the Middle Ages – had in mind a concrete and particular activity, whose various aspects were perceived as a single unified whole.

But this traditional conception was regarded as an obstacle for the cultural modernization of Japanese architecture, and the most advanced intellectuals were concerned to abstract and emphasize the artistic value (for instance the phrase 'aesthetic architecture' came into use) by submitting

the architectural heritage of their country, too, to the scrutiny of western critical methods. In 1887 Professor K. Kigo gave the first course in the history of Japanese architecture and after this C. Ito and T. Sekino, with their comparative studies on eastern and western architecture, drew from ancient building production the complex of general characteristics which could be called the 'Japanese style'.

At this point it became possible to draw a two-way comparison between the Japanese style and the European; in 1910 the Japanese Institute of Architecture organized a discussion of the subject, during which indiscriminate imitation of foreign forms was criticized and a mingling of eastern and western ones was put forward as an ideal, mainly to take into account differences in climate and habits.

In these terms any fruitful relationship between European architectural thought and the Japanese tradition became impossible; imitation of European models had not only supplanted local tradition, but had caused it to disintegrate and had rendered it virtually unutilizable, by splitting it up into a number of abstract components. The inadequacy of this approach to the problem became evident soon after the First World War, when various *avant-garde* literary men, for instance S. Yoshino, promoted the building of the first private houses in European style (*Bunka Jutaku*). A. Drexler wrote:

'While the exteriors of such houses suggested English or Dutch villas, the number of western style rooms they actually contained depended on financial resources and on the amount of discomfort the family was prepared to endure. At the back of the house there was likely to be a Japanese garden and clean, airy rooms of traditional Japanese design, ostensibly for less adaptable parents or grandparents, but often as a refuge for the whole family'.[21]

At the same time, however, echoes of the

new architectural thought maturing in Europe also reached Japan. Soon after the First World War a group of *avant-garde* architects was formed – K. Ishimoto, S. Horiguchi, M. Tazikawa – known as 'Bunriha' (Secession), inspired by the similar Viennese movement and proclaiming its dislike of all historical styles; in 1918 Frank Lloyd Wright began work on the Imperial Hotel, placing an inspiring example of his own extremely personal style in the heart of the capital; in 1921 a European architect of considerable talent, A. Raymond, settled in Japan and exercised a lasting influence on young Japanese architects, many of whom worked in his studio.

The 1923 earthquake, which almost completely destroyed Tokyo and Yokohama, made a vast programme of rebuilding necessary and forced designers to consider carefully the advantages and disadvantages of the various building systems. These urgent technical tasks encouraged the spread of the rational theses; the Association of Young Architects (Shinko Kenchikuka Remmei) was formed and, soon afterwards, the far more important one, the Nihon Kosaku Bunka Remmei (Japanese Association for Industrial Design) whose members included H. Kishida, S. Horiguchi, K. Ichiura, K. Maekawa, Y. Taniguchi and S. Koike; their programme was inspired by the Deutscher Werkbund and their aim was to bring all artistic energies together, putting them into contact with the world of industry; the group also published a journal, the *Gendai Kenchiku* (Architecture of Today).

Meanwhile there was direct contact with the masters of the modern movement of Europe. During his travels Prof. K. Imai met Gropius, Le Corbusier, Mies and B. Taut; Kunio Maekawa (b. 1905) from 1928 to 1930 and Junzo Sakakura (b. 1904) from 1931 to 1936 worked in Le Corbusier's studio, and finally from 1933 onwards B. Taut spent some time in Japan and made a decisive contribution to the study of local

tradition,[22] distinguishing the short-lived elements from the permanent ones, still capable of development.

He was the first to draw attention to the examples where wooden construction was developed with rigour and sobriety (the shrine of Ise, Katsura's Imperial Villa) contrasting them with better known ones like the Buddhist temples, where the same processes degenerate into excessive decoration. From the first one could learn a general method that was always valid, from the second only a repertoire of images that were suggestive but by now culturally lifeless.

Taut stressed this distinction which is still basic for the development of Japanese architectural thought; real continuity with the past could not establish itself through images linked with incidental situations, but through methods, which could be generalized by means of critical reflection.

'Naturally I do not wish to contest that locally-conditioned peculiarities do not have a great influence on architecture, but these are things which can never be understood by a non-Japanese, and which therefore remain sterile even for the further development of Japanese architecture.

For what are they essentially? They are – this may be sacrilege to many Japanese – the tea houses with their rooms for the tea ceremony. Their beauty – often great – is beyond question, and yet in spite of all its fineness it is in itself sterile for modern Japan. This is not architecture, but improvised lyricism, so to speak. But lyricism does not, as in poetry, readily convey itself in wood, bamboo, *shoji*,[23] mats, stucco and so forth. The old masters of the tea ceremony stressed the unique subjectivity of the pure beauty of this atmosphere. They declared that it would be lost in repetition and they would certainly pronounce all the elements of the tea house to be "cheap": entrances made of trees left in their natural state,

1002 *(above)   'Jo-an' tea house (early eighteenth century)*
1003, 1004   *Tokyo, School of dentistry (B. Yamaguchi, 1934) and Wasaka house (S. Horiguchi, 1939)*

stucco applied on round bamboo, and even the rustic fence, the irregular stones in the garden, and the garden itself with its thousands of imitations in hotels, restaurants and private homes . . . . What was meant to be a unique expression of spiritual personality of a restful character turned out to be petrified rules and dry

1005, 1006 *(left)* *Hiroshima, Peace Centre (K. Tange, T. Asada, Y. Otani, K. Matsushita, 1949–55)*
1007, 1008 *(right)* *Kagawa, Prefecture (Tange, Asada, Kamija, T. Oki, Y. Tsuboi, 1954; from* Bauen + Wohnen*)*

academicism – not only in the architectural details but in the tea ceremony itself'.[24]

In the short period between 1930 and 1937 the Japanese modern movement produced its first important works: some houses by S. Horiguchi, where for the first time real, structural integration was achieved between eastern and western contributions, the Japa-

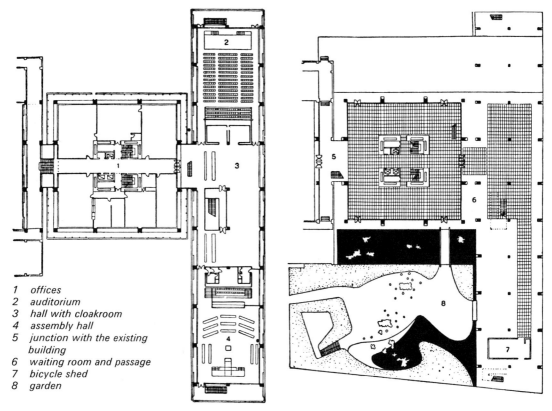

1   offices
2   auditorium
3   hall with cloakroom
4   assembly hall
5   junction with the existing
      building
6   waiting room and passage
7   bicycle shed
8   garden

1009   *Kagawa; plans of the prefecture (from* Bauen+Wohnen)

nese pavilion by Sakakura at the Paris Exhibition in 1937, reproduced in Roth's book
among the twenty works which best represent the decade, and the Teishin Tokyo
hospital built in the same year by M. Yamada.

From 1937 onwards, when the Japanese
régime hardened into a totalitarian and
nationalist position, these activities were cut
short, and here too there was an artificial
exhumation of traditional forms.

Japan was heavily bombed during the
war; rebuilding, slow at first and furthered
mainly by the American forces of occupation,
became more intense after 1950 when the
first law on subsidized building was passed,
setting aside 5 milliard yen for the building
of 80,000 dwellings. In the same year the
legal status of architects was defined,
distinguishing between a grade-one qualifi-

cation given by the central government and a
grade-two qualification given by local
authorities.

The execution of this programme posed
the problem of reconciling European and
Japanese habits on a large scale. For economic
reasons the dwellings were grouped in collective buildings, thus breaking the relation
between dwelling place and nature on which
the organism of the traditional house had
been based; inside there was usually a
compromise: first of all there was a living
and working room furnished in the European
style, and where shoes were worn, then one
or more rooms floored with *tatami*,[25] for
sleep or rest.

The same ambiguity was also to be found
in the organism of the town. C. Perriand,
who is at present working in Japan, describes

1010   *Kagawa, Detail of the prefecture* (*from* Bauen + Wohnen)

the capital as follows:

'Tokyo 1956: modern buildings, forts in glass and concrete, housing the most unexpected things piled one on top of another: a railway station, an underground station, large shops, restaurants, theatres. At their feet a city of eight million inhabitants built of wood and paper . . . . It's like going back to a Paris straight out of the middle ages, which has kept all its old customs and which has modern buildings into the bargain. Do you realize what might come out of it?'[26]

The juxtaposition of these motley elements was made even more precarious every day by economic and social development: it is against this background that the 'Renaissance' of Japanese architecture, which is arousing interest throughout the world, should be set.

The architects of the generation which grew up between the two wars continued to produce works of a very high standard: among the most noteworthy were the Museum of Modern Art at Kamakura by J. Sakakura (1951), the Nippon Songo Bank in Tokyo (1952), the offices of the *Readers' Digest* by A. Raymond (1952) and the Pensioners' Hospital by M. Yamada (1953), also in the capital. But the Japanese scene was shaken by another group of works, less perfect but more fruitful and influential and which embodied a clearer alternative to the chaos of contemporary urban organisms.

Kenzo Tange (b. 1913), a former assistant of Maekawa's, began his career after the war with several tough, contrived buildings – an exhibition hall at Kobe in 1950, the Hiroshima memorial began in 1951 – where the structural mechanism was insistently displayed, giving the architecture a summary, elementary solidity (Figs. 1005 and 1006).

In the Prefecture of Kagawa (Figs. 1007–10), begun in 1954, he tackled the distributive aspects of the subject with the same determination and created a work completely new to Japan: not a closed, hostile office block,

but a civic centre, open and welcoming, with a ground floor open to pedestrians; on this stood the low block of the rooms for public use and the quadrangular tower of the offices; the structure in reinforced concrete is still strongly marked, with contrived points of juncture, particularly in the rows of balconies which surround the office tower, in vague imitation of the rows of roofs of the old pagodas. By Tange's building, Maekawa built a library with a music room, where the forms were more discreet but still largely surrounded by open or covered spaces for pedestrians, and the whole formed a real civic centre in the European sense.

At the same time and for the same University Hiroshi Oe, a contemporary of Tange's, planned a group of buildings designed to facilitate communal student life; here too the site was left open by means of the 'pilotis', and the layout of the external spaces was particularly carefully planned, in close relation to the assembly halls on the ground floor.

In the nineteen-fifties Tange also built a most controversial work, the Tokyo City Hall; in front of the block of offices is a paved pedestrian plaza, which extends on under the 'pilotis' and is beautified by the most exquisite resources of traditional gardening. In this way the usual concept of such an organism was reversed: visitors and not employees were the chief elements in its functioning. *Architectural Forum* noted a statement by one of Tange's colleagues: 'it appears that the elevators are too small; the reason being that we assumed peak traffic would occur during the hours when employees were coming to work or leaving, whereas in fact the peak comes in the middle of the day when sightseers arrive *en masse*.' And the editor commented: 'A public building should have that kind of trouble'.[27]

Tange had to overcome very strong resistance in order to realize this building, and his architecture has aroused equally

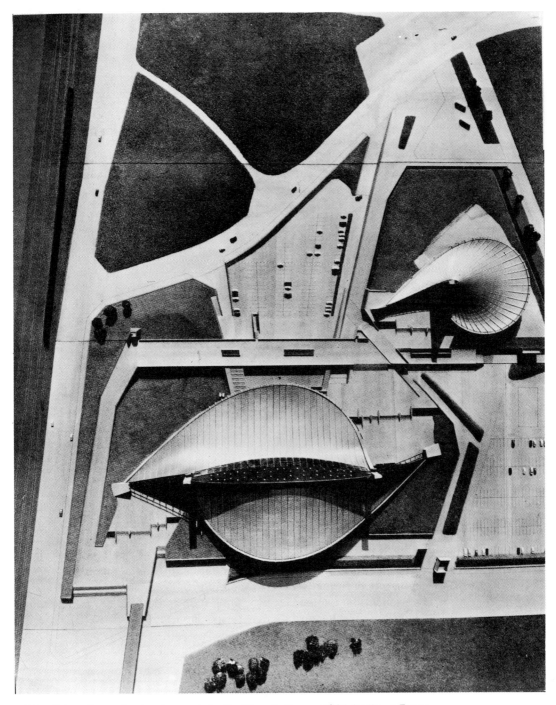

1011   *Tokyo, Covered swimming pools for the Olympic Games, 1964, by Kenzo Tange*

strong feelings of approval and disapproval in Japan. But he suddenly became famous on the Continent, received the 'Grand Prix d'architecture et d'art' from the review *L'Architecture d'Aujourd'hui* and in 1960 gave a lecture course at the Massachusetts Institute of Technology. International acclaim finally consolidated his position in Japan as well and has recently earned him several important official commissions, including the designing of the splendid covered buildings for the Olympiad in 1964 (Fig. 1011). It would be no exaggeration to say that his influence has been responsible for all that is most vital in Japanese production of the last few years; even the more established designers are building the most violently controversial buildings – for instance Maekawa's 'unité d'habitation' in Tokyo, which upset traditional domestic organization by applying the principle of Le Corbusier, and T. Murano's town hall in Yonago, where the architecture seemed to be repeating the expressionist tones of the famous Sogo store at Osaka of 1935 – giving more fuel to the arguments for and against tradition. Maekawa and Sakakura supervised the building of the Museum of Western Art in a Tokyo park, designed by Le Corbusier with his usual polemical incisiveness (Fig. 1012).

After Japan had accustomed us to sophisticated, carefully considered combinations of old and new, these works, brusque and cursory but full of energy and immediacy, bore witness to a promising cultural revival. For the first time the ambiguity of formalism was broken, and this was something that had been hanging over Japanese architecture since the juxtaposition of the two notions of *Zoka* and *Kenchiku*.

The movement that is under way is only one aspect of the great effort that is made to develop Japanese society in a democratic direction, and its fate depends on the overall success of this effort; however, it is certain that Tange and the others have behind them a very powerful stimulus, which seems capable of overcoming very many difficulties.

Their experiment also contains a methodological lesson valid for everyone. Chiefly it puts us on our guard against facile and idyllic schemes of total integration between old and new; in the presence of an illustrious tradition, one still rooted in the habits of the majority – and precisely while architectural thought was in a position to distinguish its external and picturesque aspects from the basic ones, by recognizing for instance the modernity of the traditional house with its unified elements, the continuity between interior and exterior and its organic capacity for extension – the young Japanese architects have realized that it is impossible to aim for the preservation of the old harmony, indissolubly connected with a series of social limitations that would be unthinkable today.

So they accepted the risks of a partial break, firmly shifting the emphasis from form to content and bringing to the fore the concern for social innovation inherent in the modern movement with an enthusiasm that seems to have become dulled in the west.

Continuity with tradition was no longer a basic prejudice but a possible point of arrival in so far as old values could be retained in the new forms of society.

Conclusion

The association of American architects (AIA) at its 1949 convention in Houston added to its mandatory rules a new paragraph 7: 'An architect may not engage directly or indirectly in building contracting'. At the AIA meeting in Chicago in March 1952 Gropius delivered a long and convincing speech against this rule:

'In the great periods of the past the architect was the "master of the crafts" or "master builder" who played a very prominent role within the whole production process of his time. But with the shift from crafts to industry he is no longer in this governing position.

Today the architect is not the "master of the building industry". Deserted by the best craftsmen (who have gone into industry, toolmaking, testing and researching), he has remained sitting all alone on his anachronistic brick pile, pathetically unaware of the colossal impact of industrialization. The architect is in a very real danger of losing his grip in competition with the engineer, the scientist and the builder unless he adjusts his attitude and aims to meet the new situation.

Complete separation of design and execution of buildings, as it is in force today, seems to be altogether artificial if we compare it to the process of building in the great periods of the past. We have withdrawn much too far from that original and natural approach, when conception and realization of a building were one indivisible process and when architect and builder were one and the same person. The architect of the future—if he wants to rise to the top again—will be forced by the trend of events to draw closer once more to the building *production*. If he will build up a closely co-operating *team* together with the engineer, the scientist and the builder, then design, construction and economy may again become an entity—a fusion of art, science and business.'

About the new paragraph added to the AIA rules, he expressed his dissent very energetically:

'I have very great doubts about the wisdom of this rule which would perpetuate the separation of design and construction. Instead we should try to find an organic reunification which would return to us the mastery of the know-how in building. Of course, the intention of this mandatory paragraph has been a good one, namely to block unfair competition. But I am afraid that it casts away the baby with the wash, that it represents merely a negative veto and does not try to solve our dilemma constructively.

Let us not deceive ourselves as to the strength of our present position in the eyes of our clients. For instance, at the beginning of the last war high officers of the Army and Navy were not complimentary to us and showed a shocking ignorance of the character of our activities. The average private client seems to consider us members of a luxury profession whom he can call in if there is some extra money available for "beautification". He does not seem to consider us as essential for the building effort as the builder and the engineer. . . .

When a client is in the building mood, he wants to buy the complete package for a fixed price and at a definite time of delivery. He is not at all interested in the question of the division of labor between architect, engineer and contractor. Since he senses subconsciously that it is rather artificial to keep design and building so wide apart, he usually concludes that the architect may be the unknown "X" in his calculations, in terms of money as well as time.

And what else can we expect? Are we not in an almost impossible position, having to meet a preset price, though we have to start almost every commission with a kind of research and laboratory approach? Compare that with the long process in industry from paper design to test model to final product. In our field of design we have to absorb all the cost of research ourselves, for with us the model and the end-product are one and the same. Has this not become an almost unsolvable task, particularly because it is subject to changes caused either by the client or by public agencies?

We often question the soundness of the business angle of our activities when we realize that the greater the ingenuity and the harder the work we devote to reducing costs, the more we are penalized by lesser payment. The client on the other hand assumes that it must be in the material interest of the architect to increase the building cost deliberately, since this would also increase the architect's percentage fee. So he often tries to settle for a lump sum fee. Of course we have to oppose that tendency of the client, as it is quite unfair to us, but that does not solve the ticklish problem in either direction. Here indeed is our greatest ethical dilemma. It often causes distrust on the part of the client, because of its inherent injustice to both parties; it even keeps many clients from seeking our service altogether.

This does not happen to the designer of industrial products, who is usually paid for his initial service to develop the model, plus royalties from multiplication of the product. He benefits from the success of his work not only financially, but also in stature as a legitimate member of the team to which he belongs, along with the scientist, the engineer, and the businessman. This process, developing more and more in industry, is carrying the previously isolated artist-designer back into the fold of society.

I am convinced that a similarly co-ordinated teamwork will also become the trend within the building industry. This should give the future architect, who is by vocation co-ordinator of the many activities concerned with building, once more the opportunity to become the Master Builder – if we are only willing to make the necessary changes in attitude and training. We then must climb down from our brickpile and train the rising generation in conformity with the new means of industrial production instead of a training at the platonic drafting board, isolated from making and building.

The machine certainly has not stopped at the threshold of building. The industrialization process of building seems only to take longer to complete than it took in other fields of production, since building is so much more complex. One component part of building after another is being taken out of the hands of the craftsman and given to the machine. We have only to look at manufacturers' catalogues to become convinced that already an infinite variety of industrialized component building parts exists at our disposal. In a gradual evolutionary procedure, the handbuilding process of old is being transformed into an assembly process of ready-made industrial parts sent from the factory to the site. Furthermore, the proportionate percentage of mechanical equipment in our buildings is steadily increasing. Prefabrication has penetrated much further into the building of skyscrapers than into residential building. Some 80% to 90% of the new Lever House in New York City and the new apartment buildings by Mies van der Rohe in Chicago consists of industry-made parts assembled, not made, at the site. Many other buildings show the same trend.

But, to be honest with ourselves, we must admit that only relatively few of us architects have directly taken part in influencing and performing this great change, or in designing those component parts which we all use in building. It is the engineer and the scientist who have been instrumental in this development. That is why we have to speed up to regain lost ground by training our young generation of architects for their twofold task: 1) to join the building *industry* and to take active part in developing and forming all those component parts for building, and 2) to learn how to compose beautiful buildings from these industrialized parts. This presupposes, in my opinion, much more direct participation and experience in the workshop and the field in contact with industry and builders than our usual training provides.'

The conclusion of the speech becomes unusually forthright:

'I have merely tried to put the light on the crossroad to which our profession has come. One of the two roads appears rough but wide and full of venture and hope. The other narrow one may lead into a dead end.

I have made my personal choice where to go, but being along in years, all I can do is to urge my students, who will represent the next generation, to search for a constructive solution how to correlate again design and execution in their future practice by direct participation in industrial and building production. But, of course, I have to tell them that, as things stand now, they then could not join the AIA. I confidently hope that the AIA will reconsider and remove that fatal paragraph No. 7, which bars the road to a most promising creative development. If not, I want to be kicked out of membership as a rebel against this unfortunate and timid rule. For I cannot convince myself that if a young architect and a young builder should decide to join hands and to build up a complete modern service – both design and building execution – this would show a lack of integrity on their side. Instead the AIA should actively encourage such a natural combination.

I have been asked whether this would not leave the client high and dry when he is deprived of the trustee control of his architect. My reply is that we do not need trustees for buying our everyday goods: we select them on account of the good reputation of the make or of the manufacturer. I do not see any difference as to buildings and their component parts. Of course, I know that the task of reconciling design and execution – which should be inseparable – will still meet a great many difficulties which can only be slowly solved in practice. But it is always a change of attitude first which precedes any implementation of a new course of direction.

This country in its new if unwanted position of world leadership has been called upon to create the magic which would equip it beyond its might and wealth with the creative means for peaceful world guidance. We are all aware that consolidation of the American genius on the cultural level, in addition to our material strength, would bring salvation to us and to others. It is not enough then that we defend our democracy only; we must wage and win the battle of ideas to make democracy a positive force, and we architects must find the dynamic means to make these ideas visible in our environment.

Our disintegrating society needs participation in the arts as an essential counterpart to science in order to stop its atomistic effect on us. Made into an educational discipline, it would give our environment the unity that is the very basis of culture, embracing everything from a simple chair to the house of worship.'

This speech was published in *Architectural Forum* in May 1952 and gave rise to a wide debate which was reported in the June issue. The AIA spokesman found the profession 'in excellent health, suffering only from normal growing pains'. The architects seemed worried about the possibility of keeping an important job as professional men in the future building organization rather than about the whole arrangement proposed by Gropius. The replies of the other professional men are more interesting – some of them putting forward their claims to the authority the architects felt they would lose. J. W. Dunham, an official of the federal administration, thought that 'the counterpart of the old master builder might be considered to be the leader of the team that has taken his place. This person must be a leader and an administrator'; J. Feld, an engineer, wrote:

'As an engineer who for 30 years has worked for, with and against architects, I record full agreement and sympathy with Dr. Gropius' attempt to awaken architects to the facts of life. It is fortunate for them that they have such prophets unless, of course, the profession is satisfied to continue on its present path to extinction, becoming as outmoded as the dinosaur. (Extinction will come for the same reason – the unbalanced design of important organs.)

The architect in placing himself outside and above the level of the industry which he serves (most of them would not even agree to the word "serves") has lost the confidence of the client for whom the industry exists. Whereas the engineer is considered an economically desirable expense, the architect, because of legal requirements and the customs of the financial interests, is considered a necessary nuisance.

The architect will not convince the client that his services are economically desirable until he can clearly explain the purpose of his services, and that he cannot do before he understands the problem himself.

Since any structure is merely a tool to serve a purpose, the architects' part in the team to produce that tool is to understand its purpose, to crystallize the owners' requirements, and to modify the owners' ideas where they are not consistent with a plan which is consistent within itself, balanced in its various departments and progressive enough to provide for the future trend in the owners' needs.

If he does not see the problem, the architect will eliminate himself from the industry; and, frankly speaking, the engineer is ready to take over.'

Some teachers considered impartially the situation of the art of building. B. L. Pickens wrote:

'If we are to improve the status of the architect and the quality of our architecture, we need certain other changes in addition to the repeal of AIA rule No. 7.

Suppose, as things are now, every AIA firm were encouraged to team up with a builder or an industrialist. How many would produce better buildings and better communities? How many would, for one reason or another, get beaten down to the level of the "builder-architects" who now operate in every large city, usually outside AIA restrictions?

Dr. Gropius weakens his argument by pointing to the industrial designer as a successful member of a team. Is he not in most instances rather a creature of the sales and advertising executives? Look at his most conspicuous product – the automobile. Where is the overall design correlation in the sense that Dr. Gropius conceives it – a fusion of art, science and business?

The root of the problem lies in the crass inversion of this tripartite entity. It was well stated by Dr. Gropius, himself, in the first half of his original appraisal.'

And E. Pickering:

'Architecture is struggling to remain a profession, but it is so very much concerned with the production of a form of capital goods—buildings. Law and medicine are each a profession; they sell a service, not a product to be built or manufactured.

The building public is less interested in a service than in the finished product. Clients want buildings, complete with walls, openings, roofs, equipment and landscaping. They care little about traditional ethics, professional standards or the separation or amalgamation of designer and builder. The architect has difficulty explaining his business philosophy to those accustomed to buying a ready-made suit of clothes or a ready-made house.

The architect designs – he lays his brain child on the doorstep of the builder and, from a distance, watches it grow and develop. Except for improving his

techniques or strengthening his position, he has gone as far as he can in the matter of planning, awarding contracts and supervising construction. He, then, has three alternatives: (1) Continue as at present as a professional man, with an aggressive effort to "sell" his services. (2) Become a business man by associating himself with a builder or builders. (3) Become an industrialist for the actual production of buildings – with the aid of assembled materials.

With the last two schemes of operation, creative design as we have known it would probably become a second-rate art, subordinate to big business. Except for headaches not of our choosing – architecture is now so much fun! Anything much different is unpleasant to contemplate.

What should the architect do? What can he do? He is part of a confused mood of changing political, economic and social patterns. The future of the profession will probably be decided by forces over which the individual architect has little control. In the meantime – if an architect wants to get into the business of building and if he can retain his creative ability and his professional integrity, let him try his hand at the new approach'.[1]

Like the discussions on the law of Le Chapelier, this could be regarded as a controversy regarding merely the function of an architect, but it had a much broader significance.

What was at stake was not the fate of a function but the fate of certain spiritual values, which had long been regarded as the responsibility of architects.

The Industrial Revolution had changed things, not only by increasing the possibilities of production to an extraordinary degree, but also by modifying the demand for available goods, including the spatial modifications with which architecture is concerned; it afforded glimpses of the possibility that everyone might be able to take part in them, in accordance with Morris's formula, and offered hope for the fulfilment of a desire deeply rooted in the spiritual heritage of our society; for this reason it has aroused tremendous expectations, which are the hidden source of the energies, courage and patience drawn upon to give life to modern architecture.

Its task is inseparable from the other transformations under way in the various aspects of communal life. The reader will have noticed the connection between Morris's formula 'an art of the people for the people' and Lincoln's definition of democracy as 'government of the people, by the people and for the people'. In both cases the problem posed is that of adapting the legacy of values handed down from the past – by freeing it from the formulations connected with the hierarchical structure of the old society – to alter it to the new joint conception of cultural and political rights. The system of these values (which is always evolving) is what Lippmann calls a 'public philosophy' and the theses of the modern movement are a part of this philosophy whose historical continuity and perfectibility must both be stressed simultaneously.

But the trends of architecture are a real component of the general or political balance, not a consequence to be deduced from an already given political tendency. The responsibility of the architects or the operators who will replace them, is only limited, not taken over by the responsibility of the other sectors involved. For this reason architecture may succeed or fail, it may make a positive contribution to democratic life or may hinder it with the limitations which derive from an unfair or mistaken organization of space.

Therefore the organizing of spatial changes is always a specific problem, even if it can be divided up technically in many possible ways.

Which, among the ways hitherto experimented with, has managed simultaneously to safeguard the technical efficiency and cultural responsibility of which Gropius speaks? In the interim what convincing answers have been given to the challenge he launched in 1952?

No single organizational proposal can be regarded as completely satisfactory: the figure of the 'master-builder' of whom Gropius talks is perhaps only a historical comparison, and finds its full realization today neither in an individual nor a team. Both individual research and collective research still seem indispensable for the progress of architecture; but one can point, among current experiments, to at least three characteristic groups which follow different tendencies and which have been able to give convincing if partial replies to the 1952 challenge.

The first group utilizes exclusively individual research and concentrates on the creation of types, of organisms from the scale of interior décor to that of full-scale building and town-planning.

The second group aims at controlling and rationalizing current industrial production, i.e., the single organisms of widest consumption, including between the scale of interior décor and building as a whole, making use of close collaboration between individual research and collective research.

The third group aims at controlling the transformation of urban organisms and, in certain cases, at creating new cities and patterns in land use, with the means typical of public authority, hence with collective research and the occasional collaboration of independent individual researchers.

These three groups of experiments are equally important and tend – in the best cases – to be super-imposed one upon the other; Le Corbusier's work belongs to the first group, but tends to extend into the second and third; the work of Mies van der Rohe belongs simultaneously to both the first and second group; the work of the professional studios which make up 'team X' – particularly of Bakema and Van den Broek, Candilis, Josic and Woods – is moving from the first to the third group. The activity of some of the best organized public bodies is directed mainly towards experiments of the third type, but is in a position to produce important results in the first and second as well.

1 Creation of types

Individual research, as a means for the creation of types, is still necessary, indeed irreplaceable because of the legal, economic and cultural limitations which largely compromise building production and the activities of the public bodies.

For this reason, a limited number of small private studios, which design a very small part of general production, make the most important contributions to the progress of the common repertoire of solutions, from the small to the large scale.

But this research, even as an exception, has not yet found a satisfactory place in productive organization, particularly in Europe; it remains a nonconformist adventure, dependent on few and precarious opportunities for work. For this reason too large a part of these studies or proposals remains on paper and is finally wasted, i.e., it is not experimented with in time before being overtaken by technical progress or changes in social requirements.

This isolation may easily become a state of irresponsible freedom; so that another portion of this work is lost because it is spoiled by the designer's whims and excesses.

The architect who has hitherto best resisted this temptation, but who has borne this isolation to the full and with incredible tenacity, and who has experienced the falling through of almost all opportunities for work and therefore the squandering of most of his ideas, is Le Corbusier.

Le Corbusier died in 1965, at the age of seventy-eight, and when a great artist reaches this age, in our era of rapid change, he is almost always the surviving witness of a moment of the past, when he made his decisive contribution. Modern criticism is quicker to recognize these contributions; great artists need no longer expect purely posthumous glory; in their last years they may personally witness their own entry into history and be honoured as monuments to themselves.

The aged Le Corbusier too has received this treatment and has had to accept many medals, diplomas and honorary degrees for which he did not conceal his distaste. In fact, while authorities and academics lavished conventional honours upon him, his work still remained the centre of a fierce debate, perhaps a little more decorous and circumspect than in the past but no less crucial; rejected or accepted, it remains a biting alternative to what is being done all over the world, and cannot in any way be regarded as an affair of the past.

The aim of this work has always been quite clear: it is not the modification of the form of buildings within the framework of the traditional city, but the creation of a new city, independent of the limitations regarded as possible under the old hierarchical society and able to supply an adequate answer to modern society's demands for freedom and equality. The search for new standards to organize the functions of the modern city, and for the variation of these standards when necessary so that they can be adapted promptly to transformations under way, is the dominant aim of all the master's activity, from after the First World War until today; all the rest – the eloquence of his plastic forms, the interplay of historical and symbolic references, the richness of his creations, the marvellous facility and felicity of the visual presentation – is only the manifestation of the impassioned, confident, brazen tone in which he conducted his rational work of demonstration.

1012   *Tokyo, Sketch by Le Corbusier for the museum of western art (from* Oeuvre Complète*)*

Like Brunelleschi, Le Corbusier is therefore involved in a fundamental process of cultural transformation, which challenges a division of labour and a typology of urban functions on which an immense number of established institutions, habits and interests depends. Hence the violence of the protests aroused by Le Corbusier (as in his time by Brunelleschi, who during discussion about the dome 'was carried by ushers bodily out of the hearing, believed to be completely mad').

Malraux, in his speech at Le Corbusier's funeral, recalled this relationship between the importance of his contribution and the intensity of the reactions to it: 'Le Corbusier has known several great rivals, some present here, some dead. But none has made so strong a mark on the revolution in architecture, because none has been so long and so patiently insulted.'[2]

A list of the attacks received by Le Corbusier in the sixty years of his working life would be the best praise for his achievements and would indeed give an impressive if paradoxical measure of the changes wrought by him in the previous system of values.

Together with the attacks of his enemies – innumerable and heterogeneous – one must also recall the attacks of friends and admirers, who cannot or will not recognize the methodological consequences of his work.

Contemporary criticism – I am referring to the most up-to-date and favourable to modern art – has made an impressive effort to reduce his stature to that of traditional artist: it has almost always tried to separate the works from the writings and theoretical programmes, has given lavish praise to the plans or buildings realized (endowing them with an imaginary permanence and over-looking their problematic and perfectable character, in so far as they are part of a continuous process of research) only to deny the very continuity of this research and the value of the standards gradually elaborated; it has noted every nuance of tone and every broadening of the formal repertoire with exaggerated attention, anxious to find the stylistic contradiction which would reveal the lack of objectivity of the rules and models.

Writings of this kind have become insistent – if accompanied by growing signs of respect – in connection with Le Corbusier's latest works, where a natural withdrawal and a desire for recapitulation (the only signs of an old age which has never slackened the coherence of the 'recherche patiente') have been mistaken for escapes into the totally independent realms of pure poetry.

Even in 1956 a well-known Italian architect was composing this (completely mistaken) prophecy:

'The experience of the Great Master will continue to nourish us but I am certain that, with time, we shall become increasingly detached from it and shall perhaps begin to regard Le Corbusier as we do Gaudi: as a great creator of works of the highest poetic value but remote from our immediate interest and so far from our problems as to appear positively exotic'.[3]

It would not be worth devoting any time to these writings had they not had reper-cussions on the work of Le Corbusier, by conditioning his possibilities of immediate success.

Accepted up to 1930 only by a restricted clientèle of connoisseurs, excluded from programmes of public building until after the Second World War and deprived of specific opportunities for town-planning work until Chandigarh – he was free to realize his plans only when his fame as an artist was established, and by virtue of the unquestionable authority traditionally al-lowed to artists. Hence the tragic difficulty of his professional relations: he aimed at demonstrating the excellence of his plans, not at imposing them with an arbitrary act, but he could succeed only in the measure in which his personal prestige put him above argument.

Therefore all he could rely on was the irrefutable strength which sprang from numerous interlinked experiments, but he alone could guarantee the consistence of his work; in fact solitude increased in proportion to his success, and weighed heavily upon his behaviour as an individual, especially during the last years of his life. It will be interesting now to summarize the main lost opportuni-ties of his career.

The first was the competition for the League of Nations building in Geneva in 1927. As is well known, four of the judges were in favour of modern architecture and four against; thus the vote of the ninth member – Victor Horta, President of the Jury – finally decided Le Corbusier's defeat. Le Corbusier's plan was initially awarded a prize *ex aequo* with eight other heterogeneous projects; implicitly Le Corbusier was accep-ted as representing the 'modern style', to be put on a par with other backward-looking styles. But in the second stage of the compe-tition he was excluded and the commission was given to four academic architects, who adopted Le Corbusier's distributive plan almost in its entirety in their definitive version, disguised under conventional forms; Le Corbusier spread the scandal, attempted legal proceedings and wrote a book to give vent to his bitterness (this was Brunelleschi's situation when he took part in the compe-tition for the lantern of the dome and said of the model of a competitor: 'Ask him to

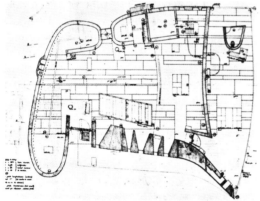

1013, 1014, 1015 *Details of the church at Ronchamp*

make another and he will make mine'; however, Brunelleschi did win the competition). In other words Le Corbusier analysed the subject and found the right solution, which was accepted even by his rivals for its intrinsic logical value; however judgment was never based on the objective features of the solution but on the style, i.e., on the subjective

variable, and in 1927 Le Corbusier's prestige as a champion of the modern style was not yet great enough to influence the jury.

Twenty years later, Le Corbusier was asked to represent France on the committee of ten experts called to New York to supervise the planning of the United Nations building. He arrived in New York in

1016 *Inside view of the hall in the Chandigarh Parliament*

January 1947, two months before the others, made contact with Harrison, chief of the office of executive planning, and prepared a distributive scheme which was accepted as it stood by the committee; the only point left undecided was the grouping of the three blocks. However, the definition of the distributive scheme was not regarded as the beginning of a continuous work of planning, but as an antecedent and Le Corbusier was dismissed from the executive planning which remained in the hands of Harrison's office.

After another five years Le Corbusier was

1017   *Inside view of the hall in the Chandigarh Parliament*

asked, with four other celebrities (Gropius, Costa, Markelius and Rogers) to sit on the panel of judges for the plans of the Unesco building in Paris. The initial commission had been given to Beaudouin, who had prepared a plan and numerous variants, none of the quality demanded by the importance of the undertaking. The committee of five now questioned both the choice of designer and of site and when invited to propose a new architect, Le Corbusier's four colleagues took upon themselves the responsibility of naming Le Corbusier himself as the only possible designer, waiving the conventional

1018 *The architecture of the Capitol, Chandigarh*

practice which forbids a judging panel to choose one of its own members. But it was the cult of conventional practice which invalidated this designation, and the commission was given to three other architects, who created the disappointing building on Place Fontenoy. This time Le Corbusier did not agree to provide suggestions without being able to control their development and,

after it was all over, he made this bitter declaration:

'When the first plan was submitted to us and put up on the wall, I reflected as follows: there are two methods of working: the first when the plans are on the wall and your hands in your pockets, the second when the plans are on the drawing boar and your hands on the pencil; I demand that one should keep to this second method'.[4]

When, at the age of sixty-three, for the first time he received a commission on a scale proportionate with his theoretical commitment – the creation of a new city of a hundred thousand inhabitants in India – Le Corbusier drew up a general plan, exercised a feeble control over the collaborators commissioned to develop it, but kept for himself the plan of the area with the four governmental buildings, and could write in 1957: 'The composition of the Capitol, is today worked out down to the last centimetre in every one of its overall and detailed measurements.'[5] It is significant to think that this is the only large building complex that Le Corbusier managed to take as far as the executive plan; indeed the control of the whole range of the planning, from the town-planning layout to the individual architecture, remains the only way the completed work can speak for itself, rising above the bickerings during the planning stage. But Le Corbusier died without being able to finish its execution and we do not know if his project can be totally translated into reality. (Brunelleschi, who had experienced the same difficult circumstances, had put into his Will the request that the lantern of the dome 'should be built exactly as the model was, and as he had put down in writing'.)

The list of Le Corbusier's lost opportunities, of the buildings he never realized and the rejected plans might well prove a source of other none too hopeful reflections.

One need only recall the idea of the 'unité d'habitation', born in 1909 after a visit to the Certosa in Florence and worked out fully for the first time in 1923, in the plan for the 'immeuble villas'. But in 1923, and during the twenty years that followed, Le Corbusier regarded this building type as secondary and insisted on continuous residential blocks 'à redents', giving rise to a new urban fabric, presented as an alternative to the traditional one. Even within the area of the 'îlot insalubre', worked on in 1936, he has two sections of 'redents' which theoretically could extend into the rest of the city, so as to stress the contrast between new and old fabric.

In 1937, on the occasion of the universal exhibition, Le Corbusier suggested building a model-district at Vincennes, also 'à redents'; when this possibility vanished and he was promised a smaller area at the bastion Kellermann, he designed a 'unité d'habitation' for 4,000 inhabitants, as a sample, but this too was made impossible by bureaucratic quibbling.

During the war Le Corbusier did further work on the concept of the 'unité d'habitation' in as far as one field of previous research, on the standardization of housing, coincided with another, on the rational grouping of dwellings in relation to the scale of communal services; the unit of 1,200–1,500 inhabitants seemed the smallest organism in which the integration of dwellings with certain basic services was feasible – the 'prolongements du logis' – and it was the basic cell of the new residential fabric within which integration with secondary and tertiary services became possible.

The post-war development plans for Saint Dié, Saint Gaudens and La Rochelle were based on this model; finally Le Corbusier obtained permission from the minister Petit to create a trial 'unité' in Marseilles, which was built amid all manner of difficulties between 1947 and 1952. But the 'unité' was accepted as an exceptional building, not as a prototype of a new urban fabric, and remains an isolated architectural fact; indeed, the difficulties and failures it met with are largely dependent upon this isolation. Today the building is mentioned in city guides, written up on sign posts and referred to as the 'cité radieuse': but the city is just what it always was, ordinary houses are crowded around the park of the 'unité' and just recently there has been talk of selling the park land itself as building lots, since it has been reduced to a zone of respect for the new concrete monument.

Later at Nantes, Berlin, Briey-en-Forêt and Firminy the same mistake was made; the 'unité' was always taken as an exception, it must be deprived of communal services or fit into an ordinary type of suburban district, as was arranged for at Briey. The 'unité' as a repeatable organism, integrated into a broader associative system and therefore linked to the whole scale of urban services, remains an abstract model, which has not yet been put to any serious concrete test.

It was then that the so-called turning point in Le Corbusier's career took place. In 1954 the church at Ronchamp was opened (Figs. 1013–15) and most critics talk of a crisis of his usual rationalism; but after the initial surprise, today, it is easy to recognize the continuity of the master's experiments, confirmed by his masterly last works: the monastery at La Tourette, completed in 1961, the buildings of Chandigarh, the figurative arts centre in Harvard and the hospital designed for Venice (Fig. 1019).

What has changed, to some degree, is the artist's psychological attitude, linked no doubt to the obstacles that still hindered experimentation with his town-planning proposals.

As he reached the end of his career his tone became more intimate, autobiographical, without losing its usual penetration and adaptability in the face of concrete opportunities, as was shown by his frank concern for religious themes, through his friendship with father Couturier. This tremendous capacity for participation, which remained intact in the passage from the general to the particular, enabled Le Corbusier to avoid the pitfall of excessive individualism.

In the preface to the sixth volume of *Oeuvre Complète* he wrote:

'Recently, on an air trip, I noted in my sketchbook the titles for three works asked for by different publishers, the ideas for which occurred to me at different times.

These titles are:

1 End of a World: Deliverance
2 The Base of the Matter
3 Indefinable Space

These describe an atmosphere in which a living human being, compelled by others in all sorts of endeavours and inventions, performs an acrobatic feat, unsurpassed and unrelenting in proportion, function, final aim and efficiency: at the crisis one is breathless while waiting to see if the man will reach the end of a hanging rope by means of a perilous jump. One does not know if he trains for this every day, if, for it, he renounces a thousand frivolities of the soft life. Only one thing matters: has he arrived at his goal – the end of the rope at the waiting trapeze? A somewhat similar peril exists in the course of successive twenty-four-hour days which are the daily course of a life, having to accomplish the necessary feats which lead to the end of the course: the forming of exact aims, regulating and consistency of effort, exactitude and minuteness of manner, choice of time, steadfast morale etc. . . . Ladies and Gentlemen, the heart of the matter is this, that having done everything, compensated or not, won or lost, the proposed objective provokes an emotion so intense, so powerful, that one strives (from time to time – exceptional days) to qualify the "indefinable", a word which describes one of the paths to happiness and which, extraordinarily, is not translatable into certain languages (why, I ask?)'.[6]

These are the thoughts of a man who, throughout his life, tried with great lucidity to communicate, to make his own achievements available to others. The effects of his work will be felt beyond his direct experience, but meanwhile circumstances are still hostile to him and he remains definitively tied to the attitude of revolt he chose at the beginning of his career.

1019   *Venice, The new hospital by Le Corbusier*

By now it is too late for particular polemics, which can be pursued by others who have more time before them; Le Corbusier must settle his accounts, and the final balance is 'indefinable', i.e., communicable only at the deepest level of consciousness, beyond any particular circumstance. The proof of the efficacy of these last experiments is their international acclaim, for they seem able to overcome all diversity of historical and geographical environment, and influence activities from Brazil to India, from Japan to England and Switzerland (as witness the activities of Atelier 5).

In 1964, when his book *La Ville Radieuse* was reprinted, Le Corbusier added this comment:

'I have corrected the proofs of the reprint of this book written between 1931 and 1933 and published in 1935. Well, M. Le Corbu, congratulations! You posed the problems of forty years ahead, twenty years ago! And what they earned you was a generous and unfailing ration of kicks in the behind.

This book contains an impressive collection of complete and detailed development plans, ranging from the detail to the whole, the whole to the detail. They said to you: No! They treated you as though you were mad! Thank you! Have you "no" men ever considered that in these plans lay the total and disinterested passion of a man who spent his life thinking of "his brother men" in a brotherly way? But of course, the righter he was, the more he upset the agreements made or to be made. He upset . . . etc. etc.'[7]

One should indeed consider these bitter words written a year before his death, now that Le Corbusier is universally recognized as the main protagonist of the modern movement.

It is not a question of knowing whether Le Corbusier is regarded as a great artist, particularly now that he is dead and it is easy to relegate him to that shrine of art he wanted to escape from; but whether his work has indeed upset the shape of things today enough to demand their reconsideration, at least in part, or whether these things have stood their ground, to such an extent that those chiefly concerned may recognize his genius without danger, after having removed its sting.

The work of Le Corbusier, as we have observed, continues to have a widespread influence in the most varied places and on all forms of architectural research today. Le Corbusier's characteristic research – individual research, directed towards the typological creation of the modern city, from small to large scale – is being carried on almost everywhere, with particular concentration on inventive town-planning (which is the aspect still inaccessible, or almost, to other forms of research).

The results of this research, intentionally independent of contemporary means of realization and current economic, legal and administrative circumstances, are often presented as 'utopias'; the most important are those worked on by the Japanese around 1960 and a recent one which appeared in the English review *Archigram*.

The new Japanese architecture, which we discussed in Chapter 20, found its logical complement in certain town-planning proposals, put forward by Tange and others after 1959. The polemical energy that distinguished previous experiments appeared in the uncompromising and sometimes Utopian character of these proposals, which have aroused great interest throughout the world.

In 1959, during the course held at the M.I.T., Tange and his students worked on the plan for a community of 250,000 inhabitants in Boston Bay, where streets, houses and services were laid out at various levels within a great trestle structure.

'This space organization is expressing the hierarchy which consists of several levels of scale: the scale of nature itself, the superhuman scale of linkages of all kinds, the mass human scale which is created by human activities in mass and,

ultimately, the human scale involved in the everyday life of individuals . . . At this microscopic level, the details and placing of the house can be left open to individual taste; the significance of these houses is that they permit the individual to identify himself within the system and make this identification comprehensible'.[8]

In 1960 Tange, together with K. Kamiya, A. Isozaki, S. Watanabe, N. Kurokawa and H. Koh, published a plan for Tokyo, where this idea became the means to create a new linear structure within the metropolis, capable of breaking out of the centripetal scheme that was no longer appropriate (Figs. 1020–21).

The planners recognized that the metropolis with over ten million inhabitants was a necessary fact, in so far as it corresponded to the increasing importance of tertiary activities, which required a traffic system of a new type, i.e., suited to carrying more intense traffic and having closer and more continuous points of exit and entry. Hence the idea of a great axial road going from the modern business centre to right out into the waters of the bay, forming the framework of the new commercial, residential and recreational districts, organically interlinked.

'Organizing a metropolis so as to impress order on to the various levels of urban space, both public and private, it is necessary to arrange these spaces according to some clear plan, within the ambit of the urban structure.

When tackling the problem of residential housing, one comes up against the need to build a dynamic, unitary whole, with a progressive order going from the house to the playground for children, quiet meeting places, large open spaces, big recreation and sports centres; from the crèche to the elementary school, secondary school, other recreational and social institutions; from parking places to squares for transport vehicles, to motorways. The measure of these different components must be set

1020, 1021   *Tokyo, Two aspects of Tange's plan: model of the commercial zone and general layout* (from Bauen+Wohnen*)*

1022, 1023 *(opposite page) Drawings from* Archigram *for 'Plug-in-city'* (from Architectural Design): *section across the area of highest density; plan and elevation of a living unit; elevation of a tower occupied by many dwellings.*
In the plan of the single unit: 1. *canalizations*
2. *kitchen and bath*
3. *pneumatic elevator*
4. *furnished wall*
5. *movable wall*
6. *service doors*
7. *plugs for facilities*
8. *storage unit*

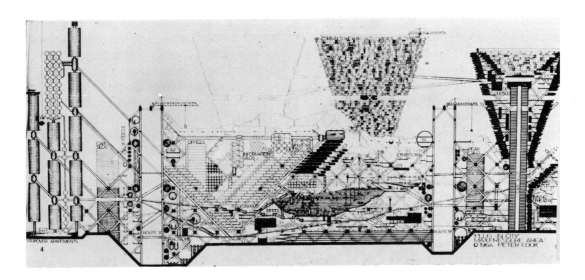

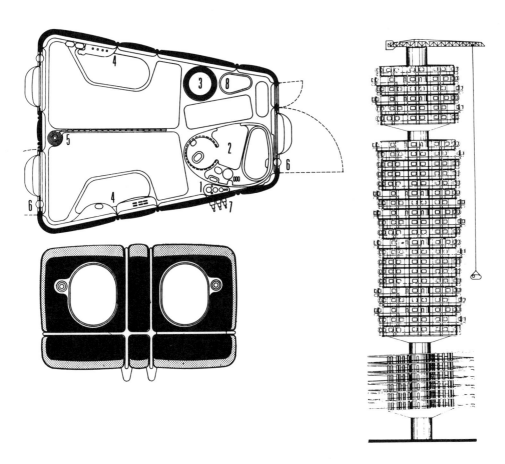

within an organic whole well connected with private houses, and which at the same time is adapted to variability, continuity, expansion, contraction.'⁹

The great framework, formed of the circulation system and canalizations for the various installations, gave the plan its gigantic and costly character, which however, according to the planners, was not purely Utopian, since it was the equivalent of traditional building activity which, by extending the metropolis, mobilized sums that even today are incredibly high.¹⁰

The great size of the main framework was the most striking but perhaps the most superficial feature of the plan and gave rise, in Japan and elsewhere, to many idle discussions of the 'new dimension' which was proudly cherished as a victory in itself. But what should rather be assessed is the value of an attempt at making the various dimensions coexist within a single system, where the needs of life find a calculated balance; the doubt is about the hierarchy of functions needed to realize this balance; it is still the old hierarchy, which gives tertiary functions precedence over all the others, as in the traditional radiocentric city.

The proposal in *Archigram* is presented in quite a different architectural guise. The authors are not concerned with defining the form of the new city as a fixed entity of the traditional type. 'Plug-in-city' can have no definitive and stable appearance, but is based on a series of communal installations, on to which the single dwellings, capsules of light material, can fairly easily be plugged or unplugged; the installations would develop along with technology generally and the capsules would be continually replaced by new models produced by industry, just like the other machines we use (Figs. 1022–23).

Therefore the landscape of the new city can be designed only in an ironical and challenging form, like a science-fiction vision. But the method of its formation is not arbitrary or capricious: it is based on the definition of the minimum element, to be mass-produced, and on its infinite repetition, so as to pose the least number of obstacles to the freedom of combinations.

An excess of formal characterization – as is found in Tange's building production and in that of some English architects – was perhaps inseparable from the polemical aim of this study; it should be regarded as an allusion to the great unsolved problem, to which the shortcomings and shakiness of our architectural thought can be reduced: the problem of the modern city, not as the result of a more or less prudent adjustment of the traditional city, but as an original invention which may be regarded as a qualitative jump from the previous cities, as the medieval city was from the ancient one.

2 Control of industrial production

The progress of the building industry, though slowed down by deficiencies in town-planning, has complicated the interplay of the parts which contribute to the realization of a building, and has produced, side by side with the traditional figures of the client and the designer, at least three other figures: that of the builder, the final user (who may be identified, either separately or together, with the client, but may also be distinct from him) and that of the supplier, i.e., the maker of the separate pieces of the building.

Gropius observes that already in 1952 '80 per cent or 90 per cent of Lever House in New York and Mies' new apartment building in Chicago consists of assembled industrial elements;' the maker of these elements may be compared to Gropius' 'master-builder' because he designs and creates his product within a single industrial organization. But the montage of these elements to form the building cannot as yet be described, even in America, as an industrial operation, and it is hardly ever dealt with by a producer-seller, but by a producer on behalf of a seller, for the largely unknown requirements of a future user.

To help the seller – or sometimes the user – in negotiating with the builder, a category of professional studios has grown up which are in a position to control all the operations necessary to realize the building, i.e., which are capable of carrying out the 'overall design' through the collective work of a large number of specialists. Some of these studios, particularly in America, are simply enormous, with a thousand or more dependents, but they tend not to produce the synthesis Gropius hoped for: they help to make planning, i.e., one of the terms of the synthesis, a more efficient if belligerent affair and to ensure authoritative intervention between commission and production; furthermore, because of their size, they become important economic enterprises, where a seller of the planning service appears in his turn, as well as a producer of this service, two distinct entities who fight for control of the enterprise.

Experience teaches that a satisfactory result can be obtained when an external co-ordinator intervenes, not linked with any of the parties and capable of rationalizing the whole production process. This co-ordinator must be a designer, contributing his own individual research but remote from the many-sided figure Gropius describes: free of permanent ties with the client, with the builder and also with the organization doing most of the executive planning, but in a position to make the decisive choices, both of a distributive and a constructional kind.

This too is a difficult position, which can degenerate into stylistic caprice, passive subjection to pre-established choices of the big organizations, and often into a combination of the two. Exceptional rigour is needed to safeguard the real independence of this role, and the most successful at it was Mies van der Rohe in America (he died in 1969).

Mies' last works – from the Seagram building onwards – are still largely neglected by critics. They have no interest for those in search of novelty, and they appear so similar to previous ones that they might almost be considered repetitions of them. Yet Mies' rigour, and his ability to return to problems gradually to improve their solutions, have just now produced their most important results.

The features of the volume and construction of the Seagram, at first mistaken for gratuitous exhibitions of extravagance, have served to clarify two general problems connected with tall office buildings:

1   The setback of the building with regard to Park Avenue, and the square surrounding it are not just expedients to set off an isolated volume, but contain a basic criticism of the traditional skyscraper (from Hood to Lescaze, from Harrison and Abramowitz to Bunschaft in his Lever House which stands opposite) in so far as it rises from a base occupying the whole surface of the site, reconstituting, below, the continuity of the corridor-road, and it serves to disengage the tower from the fabric of the town, like the old bell-tower (the most obvious example is the Empire State building, absurdly out of scale with regard to its site, because of a desire to dominate the Manhattan skyline vertically).

Mies, since he had the head of a block at his disposal, grouped together the few supplementary rooms necessary to the lower floors in the blocks at the back, which backed on to the adjacent buildings, and put the prism of the skyscraper right on the ground, in contact with the open space of the lot; in this way the distinction between site and street also disappeared, and the nineteenth-century street network was no longer projected upwards, thus becoming a mere plan for dividing up a single free plane into zones for traffic and pedestrians.

This reasoning has been repeated in many recent enterprises. Skidmore, Owings and Merrill, commissioned to build the Chase Manhattan Bank on two adjacent sites in the city, put three possible solutions to their clients: that of filling the first block with a

1024   *Seagram building among the buildings of Manhattan*

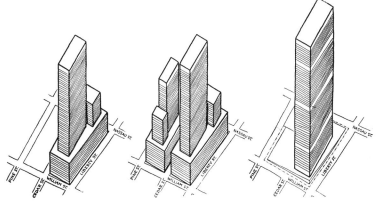

1025, 1026 *(above)   Seagram building, New York, compared with the glass skyscraper designed by Mies in 1921*
1027, 1028 *(below)   Chase Manhattan building, New York, with three volumetric solutions submitted by Skidmore, Owings and Merrill to clients*

traditionally tiered mass, of filling both blocks with such volumes, interrelated to one another, or of joining the two areas to form a single pedestrian plaza, concentrating the volume of the building into an isolated tower on 'pilotis' (Figs. 1027–8). The third solution was chosen and now, near the Chase that is already built, the same firm is putting up another building with the same criteria; in this way, a new civic space is being opened

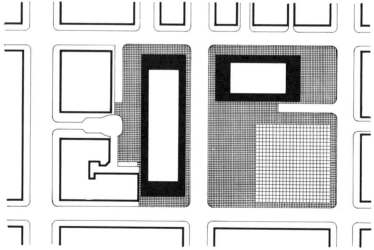

1029, 1030   *Chicago, Federal Center with the building of the federal court of justice (Mies, 1964)*

up off the deep-sunk streets of the city, consisting of terraced pedestrian squares that can be crossed in all directions and overlooked by the aerial prisms of their buildings.

The other parts of the city where several enterprises of this kind have been carried out – a stretch of Sixth Avenue, and the district around the Seagram where Skidmore, Owings and Merrill have put up the Union Carbide building – although they still bear the mark of the original cadastral chaos, do still allow glimpses of the possibility of a future use of urban space very different from the present one, and reveal an as yet unexplored margin of transformation, based on the chess-board system of 1811.

2 The curtain wall of the Seagram, of bronze and brown athermic glass, gives the great uniform prism an exceptional prominence, precisely because no attempt has been made at any chromatic distinction between the design of the metal cagework and the expanses of glass, which tend to blend together into great opaque and tonally uniform panes (while the surrounding buildings flaunt absurd flourishes of graphic detail and shining surfaces that diminish their dimensions).

In this way Mies demonstrated how appropriate it was to give tall buildings a monochrome, opaque finish, which enhanced their size, eliminating contrasts between the various metallic frames, also used in his Chicago buildings before 1955. But the same result could be obtained with the more usual black iron and grey athermic glass, used in fact by Mies in his latest apartment houses in Chicago and the Federal Center, still under construction.

These latest works – together with the One Charles Center and Highfield House in Baltimore – are perhaps Mies' masterpieces. The first of the three buildings intended for the Chicago Federal Center[11] destined for the Federal Court, was finished in 1964 and occupies an irregular area, a narrow space

between the buildings of the Loop, but the aerial volume of the building rises, detached from the ground, which has been laid out as a continuation of the adjacent pavement; the body of the building, thirty-five metres deep, made it possible to place two rows of offices along the façades, with the courtroom – two storeys high – in the middle section, thus including all the rooms necessary to a modern court within a single compact block.

The Highfield apartment building,[12] completed in 1965, was built in reinforced concrete, and the supporting pillars appear on the façade, determining the width of the glassed openings; this structure too is treated with Mies' usual rigour, without hiding or emphasizing its particular features.

Is the rigour of Mies' method inseparable from the presence of his personality? Statistically, the answer would be yes; Mies' models influence much of American production, but only in a few cases have other designers shown that, as well as his formal appearances, they also accept the master's logical approach.

In at least one case, however, the continuity between Mies' work and that of his successors is so evident as to suggest a complete depersonalization of his method. This is the case in the new buildings for the I.I.T. designed by Skidmore, Owings and Merrill: the library and the Hermann Hall. Here one cannot talk of imitation, because the distribution and structure of the two buildings is basically different from earlier ones, but of continuity of architectural reasoning, which confirms the validity and perfectability of the standards elaborated by Mies in the preceding years; the organism of Hermann Hall is derived from that of Crown Hall and from the plan for the Mannheim theatre, except that the supporting pillars are inside, bearing the sheet-metal girders visible above the roof. The interior is enlivened by an unusual variety of detail – the wooden framing of the secondary rooms, glass windows treated in a variety of ways – and it houses the various recreational and cultural amenities for which it is destined, in an orderly and effortless way.

In Europe, the most consistent attempt at gaining control of industrial production with a method similar to that of Mies at the end of his life – but taking into account the differences between American and European building technique – was made by Jacobsen during the last ten years.

The new direction taken by Jacobsen's activity, which can be seen in the school of Gentofte of 1952, produced its most important results from 1955 onwards.

That same year he built the Rodovre Town Hall (Figs. 1031–3) and offices for Jespersen and Son in Copenhagen, in 1957 a group of terrace houses at Ornegardsvej for the same firm, in 1960 the S.A.S. air terminal in Copenhagen, and from 1956 onwards a series of exemplary industrial buildings.

Now Jacobsen was using the curtain wall, sometimes contained between masonry walls on the short sides, sometimes extending to all the outer walls, as in the S.A.S. skyscraper which was overtly inspired by the latest American skyscrapers.

The loss of all reference to traditional architecture in stone demanded, here as in America, a special intensification of chromatic control: in this way Jacobsen's architecture (like that of Mies and Bunschaft) was very different from the rationalist examples of the thirties: no longer white, pure colours and deliberate tonal clashes, but a tonally unified harmony of glazed, sophisticated colours; even among natural materials those preferred were the ones with a less obvious grain and which would blend more easily with artificial ones – examples of this are the bronze of the Seagram building and the black stone of the terminal walls of the Rodovre Town Hall. But the work of the Americans was closely related to the advanced degree of mechanization of the building industry, because of which there was continual contact between the most advanced experiments and current production; Jacobsen on the other hand was working in an environment where manual labour was preponderant over mechanized labour and he utilizes architectural design as an instrument to provoke and stimulate the development of the environment itself.

His curtain wall, panelled internal walls, accessories in stainless steel – for instance the beautiful stairway in the Rodovre Town Hall – were built and mounted with the methods that belonged to the sphere of craftsmanship. It was as though Jacobsen were utilizing the separate parts of the usual Danish repertoire and aiming to broaden their possibilities of application with a different system of assemblage, less sophisticated and more casual, using the American modular buildings as models.

This tendency naturally strained and upset all customs of planning and execution. Inevitably Jacobsen encountered various technical difficulties and a notable increase in costs. He also tended to dismiss from architectural consideration the supporting structure, which could not be manipulated like the final details. Both in Rodovre, in the Jespersen offices and in the S.A.S. the skeleton in reinforced concrete is inside the building, completely hidden and covered by the curtain wall; the pillars can be seen only from the inside, and even there they are usually disguised by cylindrical coverings in plastic or some other material very different from concrete.

Jacobsen occupies a position similar to that of the *avant-garde* artists of a generation before; he works on a different plane to that of his Danish colleagues, he cannot compromise himself beyond a certain limit in executive matters (for the S.A.S. he worked with a specialist firm, Kamsak, with a relationship similar to that of Mies and the American firms) and he has a very individual method of working, preferring to draw his own plans personally with great care. His repertoire even contains explicit references to the *avant-garde* of thirty years ago, for instance his love

1031, 1032 *Rodovre Town Hall, Copenhagen (A. Jacobsen, 1955)*

1033   *Staircase in Rodovre Town Hall*

1034 *A. Jacobsen, a chair designed for F. Hansen*
1035 *Copenhagen, the SAS headquarters*
1036 *Lettering for the SAS*

of lettering.

Even with these difficulties, Jacobsen's attempt is one of the liveliest in Europe, and it aims to retain, simultaneously, both local and international references and to find a new meeting point between craftsmanship and industry; his method appears to bear consistent fruit in the field of industrial design (particularly the chairs designed for the F. Hansen Cop.) while it may perhaps find its limit on a town-planning level, where his proposals are incomplete and hesitant (see the comparative plans for the University of Bochum, in comparison with the splendid one by Bakema and Van den Broek).

3　Control of urban changes

It is clear that the planning and control of large building complexes – new districts, new towns and new settlements of all kinds – can be assured only by collective research, promoted or controlled by public bodies.

Only collective research, in fact, can develop the ideas produced by individual research with continuity, and can absorb the contributions of other branches of activity at the right moment; furthermore only public bodies, in present-day economic conditions, are in a position to direct industry towards the production of economic housing and primary services – schools, hospitals etc. – completely or partially bearing the cost of these works, which form the main fabric of the modern city.

But public intervention depends on a series of political conditions: town-planning laws, control of the market of areas of building land, the technical equipment of the central and other administrations. These conditions vary from country to country; we shall consider several countries which have carried out the most satisfactory or significant experiments in our field, i.e. – in decreasing order of merit – England, Holland, France and the United States.

a England

After the rush of activity during the immediate post-war period, English experiments went ahead without a break, endlessly extending and criticizing the results achieved, and must today be considered, as a whole, the most advanced in the world.

The speed with which the programme of the new towns was conceived and realized was soon to reveal the casual unfinished character of the new urban landscape, and in many cases too the feeling of emptiness produced by a density that was too low. This realization (popularized by the *Architectural Review*, which coined the word 'subtopia' to describe the new atmosphere created by the planners) was the point of departure for a line of activity for the formal control of the countryside on the new town-planning scale, making use of the traditional line of studies on landscape, though eliminating the contrast between town and country that was so vital in Ruskin, Howard and Geddes.

This renewed interest in the urban scene and its trimmings was not long in bearing fruit, and during the fifties some of the most perfect residential districts of average and high density were built – particularly by the L.C.C.: Loughborough Estate, 1955, Roehampton Estate (Figs. 1037–9) – and some carefully considered and articulated civic centres in the new towns, with a particularly fine one at Stevenage.

At the same time town-planners studied the structural causes of the defects noted in the new towns and became aware of the need to correct them with still broader and more radical plans of action. The lack of vitality of the new centres might have come from their being too small (about 50,000 inhabitants); starting from this hypothesis, the L.C.C. worked on a plan for another new town in Hampshire, Hook, with 100,000 inhabitants; the project was shelved by the County Council, but the work done on it, collected together in volume form[13], is still one of the most important contributions to contemporary town-planning (Figs. 1040–3).

Traffic difficulties – which have given rise to many plans for the re-structuring of cities, one of the most important of which was William Holford's (b. 1907) for Piccadilly Circus – were tackled in a general way in the report by C. D. Buchanan, commissioned in 1960 by the Ministry of Transport and issued in 1963.[14] This study strengthened the suspicion that solutions hitherto realized to canalize motor traffic were only partial remedies, and that motorization should lead to a new definition of the conceptual terms connected with road systems and hence become a point of departure for theoretical and practical developments as yet largely unexplored (Fig. 1044).

The New Towns by Sir Frederick Osborn and Arnold Whittick – the first large and exhaustive survey of English town-planning in the twenty years since the war – appeared in the same year 1963. The plans for the final sizes of the existing new towns, settled in December 1962, were reported in this book; almost all the figures were much higher than 50,000: 80,000 for Stevenage, Hemel Hempstead and Harlow, and 106,000 for Basildon. This new size required new architectural patterns for residential areas and especially for town centres. At Cumbernauld, Hugh Wilson planned a compact commercial and administrative centre on the top of a hill, shaped as one big building – the climax of the whole town's skyline – and based on different levels of circulation for cars and pedestrians (Figs. 1045–6). Now this centre is almost completed and can be appreciated as an exciting architectural experience; but it is so important in the town organization that a hierarchy rises again among the residential areas, according to their distance from the town centre, and the industrial areas become suburbs outside the town as in a traditional urban organization. So new experiences are bringing new unsolved problems too. In some of the most recently planned new towns an attempt is being made to find a closer connection between residential and industrial areas; perhaps the most interesting is the plan for Runcorn near Liverpool (for 90,000 people) prepared by Arthur Ling. The industrial areas form a continuous belt all round the town so that the relationship between living and working facilities can be planned in one standardized way.

But some new social and economic pro-grammes are already proposing a bigger size for new towns and that is another challenge for town-planners and architects. The programme for the area south-west of London, prepared in 1964, includes a new town for 250,000 near Southampton and two for 150,000 near Newbury and Bletchley. For overseas countries, English and American consulting agencies have planned even larger new towns: new capitals like Chandigarh and Islamabad in India, or extensions of existing towns like El Tablazo near Maracaibo in Venezuela for 330,000 and Tuy Medio near Caracas for over 400,000. Will town-planners be able to get a new persuasive architectural environment out of this new dimension?

The habit of maintaining close relations between building planning and town-planning during the last few years has given English architecture a dry, summary and sometimes aggressive character, which was denoted (from an aesthetic point of view) a few years ago by the term *brutalism*; but now after much experiment, it has become reconciled to the landscape and general setting.

b Holland

Holland is the country where modern tendencies were most readily absorbed into the practice of public bodies – one need mention only Berlage, Oud, Dudok and Van Eesteren – and where these tendencies have been developed with the greatest continuity, with all their technical consequences.

The development plan for Amsterdam, begun in 1928 by the Van Eesteren group, has been developed consistently up to the present day; the new districts of expansion to the west, outlined in the plan of 1935, are today a splendid reality and offer a persuasive demonstration of the advantages to be gained from a forward-looking attitude in urban development, even with all the limitations inherent in the state of research forty years ago. No single district is designed in an exceptional way, but the general tone

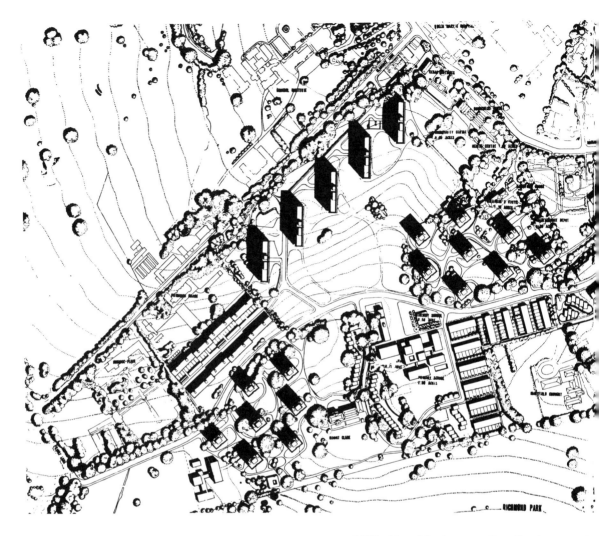

1037   *Plan of Roehampton (from Bruckmann and*

of the building is higher than that prevalent in Europe today, and some open spaces – the Sloterplas lake, with its circle of recreational facilities, and the wood of almost 1,000 hectares created from scratch during the last twenty years – are the most inspiring examples of the new landscape which can be realized with the scientific organization of public intervention, and with the collaboration of many specialists, from engineers to botanists and child care experts.

But precisely because it was modernized so long ago, Dutch planning is no longer in a position easily to absorb the latest developments in architectural research. Dutch public bodies have always made eager use of the work of *avant-garde* architects; but while in England such architects find that public bodies tend to welcome their most advanced experiments, in Holland for at least fifteen years the most progressive proposals have been made in private studios and have only

Lewis, New Housing in Great Britain)

partially influenced the practice of the public administrations.

Outstanding among these was the studio of Aldus Van Eyck – author of a splendid school in Amsterdam (1958) and of specimen plans for the schools and playing fields of Nagele – and particularly that of Bakema and Van den Broek, which carries on the liveliest experiments of the pre-war period.

Van den Broek went into partnership with Brinkmann in 1937 on the death of Van der

Vlugt, and joined with Bakema who was younger, in 1948. In this way the new studio was linked directly to the experience of Brinkmann and Van der Vlugt, whose importance we noted in the thirties.

The idea of the 'unité d'habitation', which with Le Corbusier became translated into a unitary architectural image, was linked on the other hand to the amenities around which the dwellings gravitated, on which their number and the size of the unit depended.

1038, 1039   *Views of Roehampton (London County Council, 1956)*

1040, 1041, 1042, 1043   *Hook new town: network of roads and of pedestrian ways; plan of civic centre, with separation of pedestrian and motor traffic; cross section through a residential area (from the London County Council book, 1961)*

The two Dutchmen broke down the overall volume into various blocks – terrace houses, collective houses with three to four storeys, tall houses – and worked on the association of the simplest units (already articulated within more complex groups, each integrated by the services adapted to its size).

The articulation introduced within the simplest unit was justified by the need for formal variety – Bakema and Van den Broek used the term 'visual groups' – and by the need, on this most basic level of association, to offer a scale of different choices, corresponding to different ways of living: with and without contact with a garden, with and without the encumbrance of internal com-

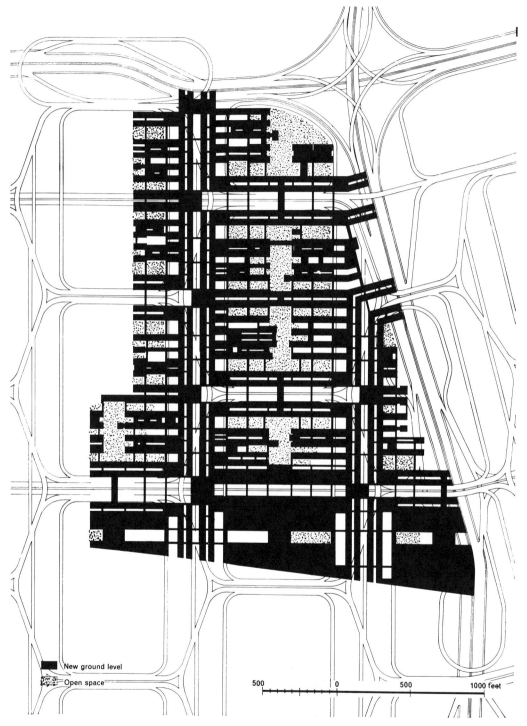

1044   *Diagram from the Buchanan report: the black shows the elevated 'new land' which serves as a base for the buildings and beneath which traffic flows freely*

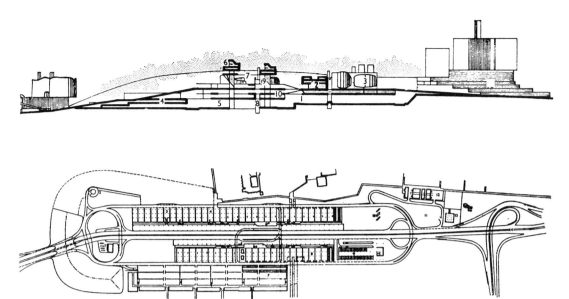

1045, 1046 *Cumbernauld new town; cross section and plan of civic centre*

munications. The association of the simpler units gave rise to a further and fruitful complication of the volumetric systems and social choices, so that the study of the district gradually led to the study of the town and of the surrounding countryside.

The two planners began to develop this method in 1949, when the Opbouw began their study of the district of Pendrecht, near Rotterdam, and they discussed it at the C.I.A.M. at Aix-en-Provence in 1953; subsequently they used these criteria to draw up the plan for the Alexanderpolder (1953–6), the development of Leeuwarden (1956–62) (Fig. 1051), the regional plan for Noord Kennemerland (1957–9), the competition plan for Wulfen in Germany (1961) and the plan for the linear extension of Amsterdam (1966). But the only plan realized was that for the small district Klein Driene in Hengelo (1956–8) (Figs. 1049–50).

Up till now, the plan for Amsterdam has been the most important result of this long research. During the sixties the new developments on the west forecast by the plan of 1935 (described in Chapter 17) were almost completed (Fig. 1048). So the merits of the plan – the independence of the buildings from road fronts, the careful balance between volumes, open spaces, woods and water – and even the deficiencies – the casual arrangement of buildings in the estates, the complicated network of roads and canals, the waste of many little green areas to space out the buildings – were by then concrete evidence. But public administration seemed unable to discuss the planning method as a whole and to point out the possible alternatives. Bakema and Van den Broek carried on in their studio a proposition for an extension of Amsterdam eastwards, on a series of islands to be created in the Ij lake.

This new urban district includes thirty-five units, each one for 10,000 people, linked by a high-speed line of traffic, a highway and a mono-rail to the very heart of the town and to the eastern polders. Each unit includes high density, middle density and low density buildings; but every house or flat looks directly on to both the built-up space within the unit, with schools and shops, and the open space between the next two units, with water, woods and sports fields (Figs. 1052–5). So the differences between one type of

1047   *Cambridge, Churchill College, accommodation for fellows (Sheppard and Robson, 1960)*

residence and another are only technical differences, and they can be chosen freely according to the convenience of families instead of social and economic differences, imposed by the inequalities of income and social standing.

The authors make an impressive comparison between the new residential system, based on repeated units, and the old one carried on in Amsterdam (Fig. 1056); the

actual problem is how is it possible to pass from the old system, accepted by public bodies, to the new one proposed by individual research?

While this problem remains unsolved, the architects can try to show the possibility of a new townscape only by little specimens, that is by single buildings, as in the early stages of the modern movement. Later Bakema and Van den Broek realized many exemplary buildings, where the neo-plastic contribution and that of the most lively experiments of the Dutch *avant-garde* were used to create a mature and balanced planning; apart from the Lijnbahn and the Montessori school already mentioned, some isolated houses, the tall blocks on the Hansaviertel in Berlin (1957–60), a school in Brielle (1955–7), the radio building in Hilversum (1956–61) and the Marl Town Hall in Westphalia, still being built.

The two Dutch architects also played an important part in the break up of the last C.I.A.M. at Otterlo in 1959. Soon afterwards they promoted the setting up of 'team X', a group of European planners whose common interest was precisely to direct the activity of the public administrations in the field of economic building and urban development; as well as Bakema and Van den Broek, the team includes Candilis, Josic and Woods, Alison and Peter Smithson, Ralph Erskine, Stefan Warweka.

c France

French enterprises, which have aroused such interest in recent years, were made possible by the new legislative situation: in 1954 the passed, bringing all previous rulings together into a single law; in 1957 a law was passed authorizing the formation of regional plans, and in two stages, in 1958 and 1962, lists of 'zones à urbaniser en priorité' (Z.U.P.) were published, where funds for subsidized building were to be concentrated.

The interest of these new settlements lay in their unprecedented size – usually thirty thousand to forty thousand inhabitants, but the Z.U.P. of Toulouse-le-Mirail (Fig. 1058) reached one hundred thousand, and that of Aulnay-sous-bois, near Paris, seventy thousand, while the centre had to serve the twenty-five thousand inhabitants of the four surrounding communes – and in the processes of heavy prefabrication adopted on a large scale, this being another reason why a simple, summary compositional layout was preferable. It is easy to recognize the older French tradition behind these characteristics but, also, the teachings of Le Corbusier on the new urban scale and the use of concrete.

Together with the assessment of these positive features one must however put forward serious reservations about the lack of integration between the 'grands ensembles' and the already existing towns, and in general on the lack of any town-planning framework proportionate to the importance of this new strain put upon the surrounding territory – and on the repetition on a large scale of conventional building types, already superceded in English and Dutch experiment.

The shortcomings in the town-planning framework can be made good by the development of institutions and planning practice, today jeopardized by the contradictions of French politics; however, the lack of typological research seems to be connected with a thoroughly established tendency of the building trade which, assured of increasing demand because of state financing, is encouraged to perfect building methods but, since it does not receive adequate directions as to the qualitative characters of the dwellings from public bodies, keeps to the most ordinary distributive patterns, applicable to the largest possible number of occasions.

This failing can be corrected, today, only by the individual abilities of certain planners, i.e., by a research which finds its continuity in the private sphere rather than in the public. The studio which has done most work in this direction is the one already mentioned of Candilis, Josic and Woods; among their main works are the districts in Africa (Casablanca, Carrières centrales; Oran, Burre Mirauchaux, 1954; competition for the semi-rural building in Algeria, 1960; Fort Lamy, Tchad, 1962) and in France (Bagnols-sur-Cèze, 1956–60; Toulouse-le-Mirail, 1961–6), the plans for the universities

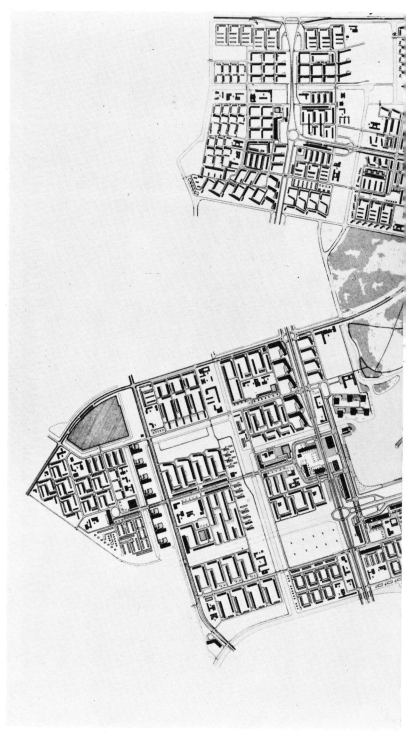

1048   *Amsterdam, the Western development around the*

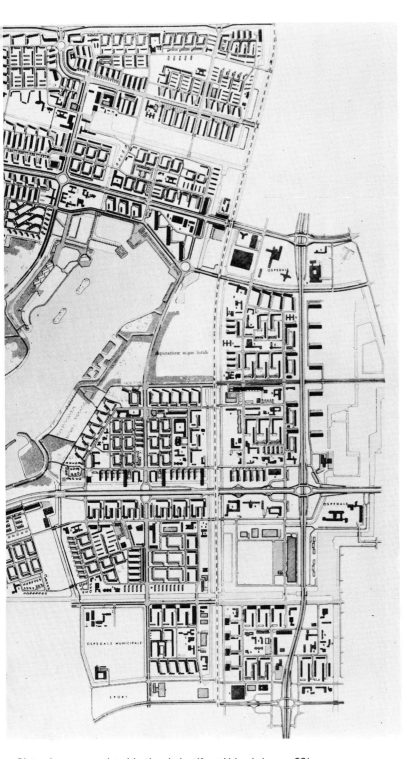

Sloterplas, as completed in the sixties (from Urbanistica, *n. 38)*

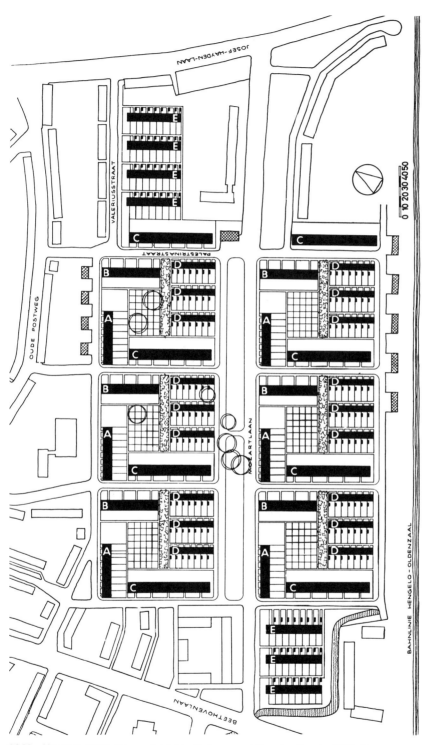

1049   *Hengelo, Klein Driene district by Bakema and Van den Broek, 1956–8*

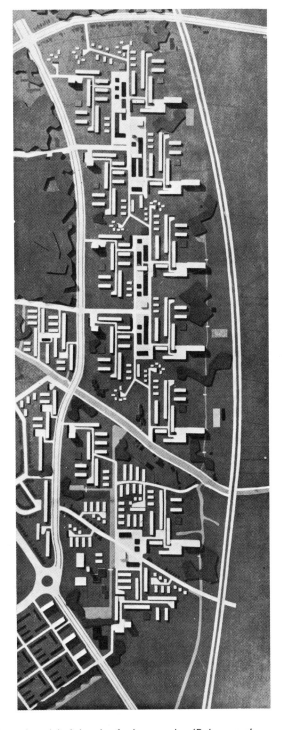

In the plans
1   entrance
2–7   day rooms
8   staircase
9   bedrooms

On the opposite page in Fig. **1049**
A big terrace buildings
B four-storey terrace buildings
C three-storey terrace buildings
D small terrace buildings
E big terrace buildings

1050, 1051   *Plans of building types D and E at Hengelo and model of the plan for Leeuwarden (Bakema and Van den Broek, 1959–62)*

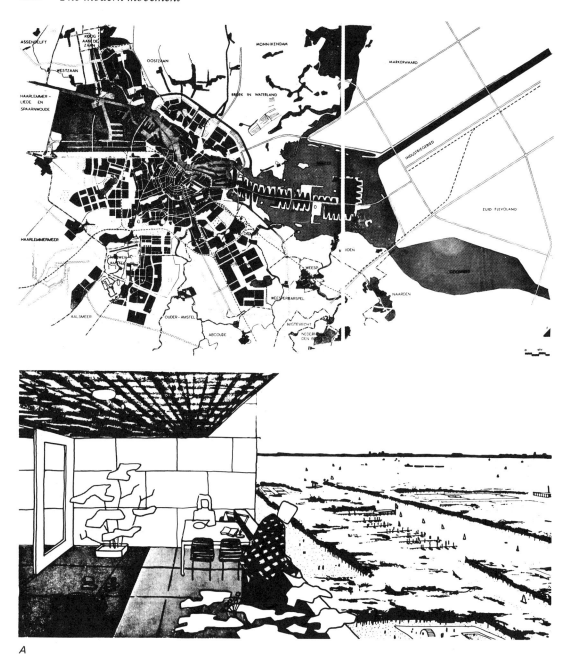

A

1052, 1053, 1054, 1055   *Plan for Amsterdam-Pampus (Bakema and Van den Broek, 1965); general layout; views of recreational area (A), local area (B) and central area (C)*

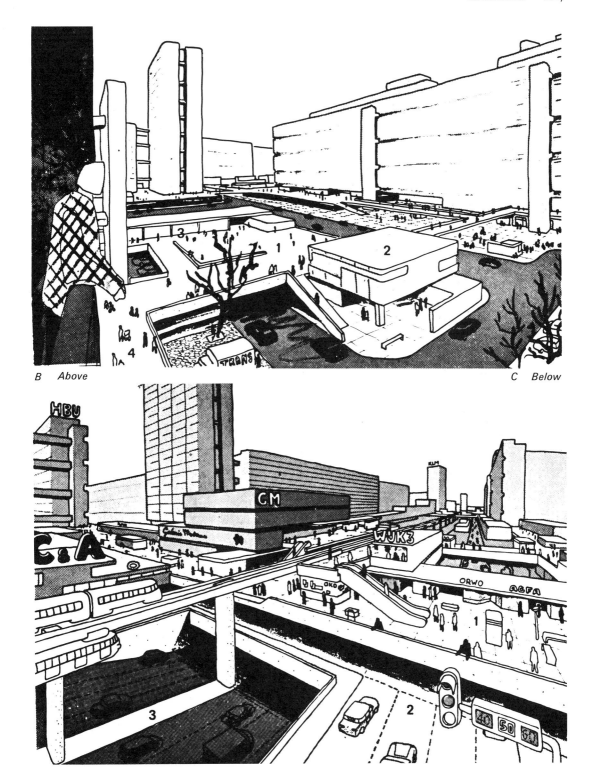

B   Above

C   Below

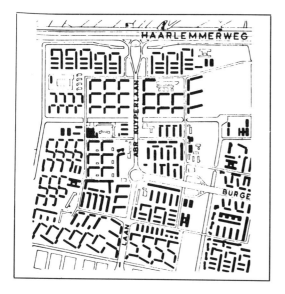

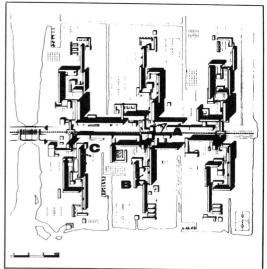

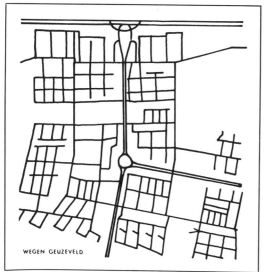

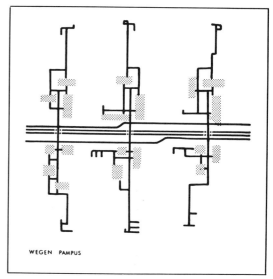

1056, 1057   *Plan for Amsterdam-Pampus. A comparison between a traditional estate (Geuzeveld) and a section of Pampus, of the same size; a view of a unit for 10,000*

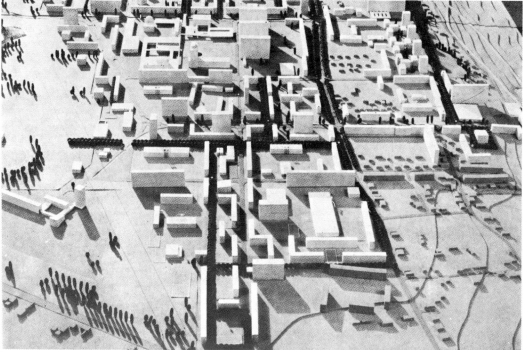

1058, 1059 *Models of the grands ensembles of Toulouse-le-Mirail (équipe Candilis) and of Massy-Antony (P. Sourel and J. Duthilleul)*

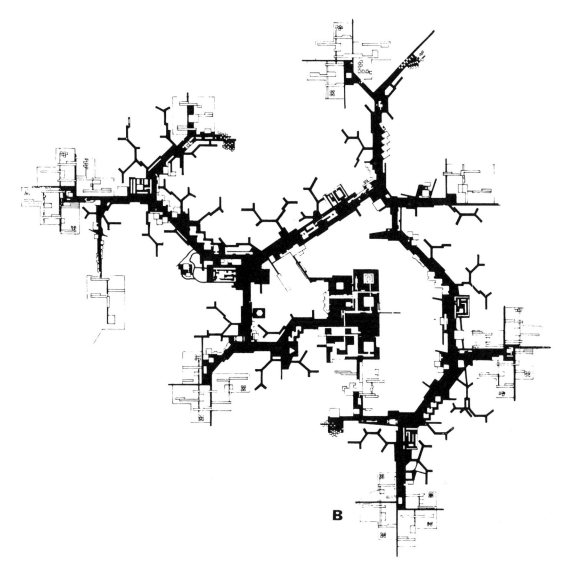

B

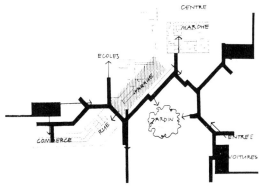

1060, 1061 *Toulouse-le-Mirail, network of pedestrian ways and diagram of connections between houses and facilities*

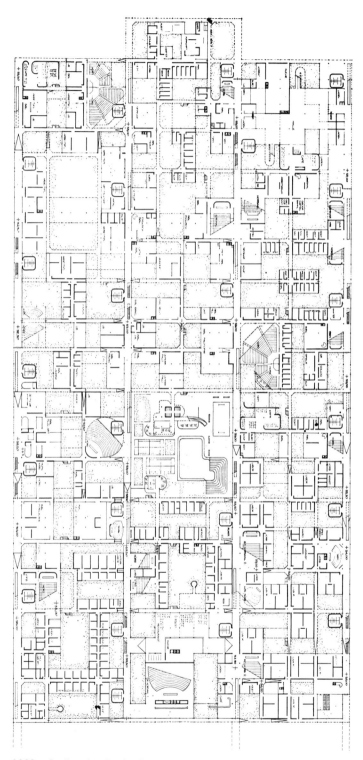

1062   *Berlin, plan for the Free University (équipe Candilis)*

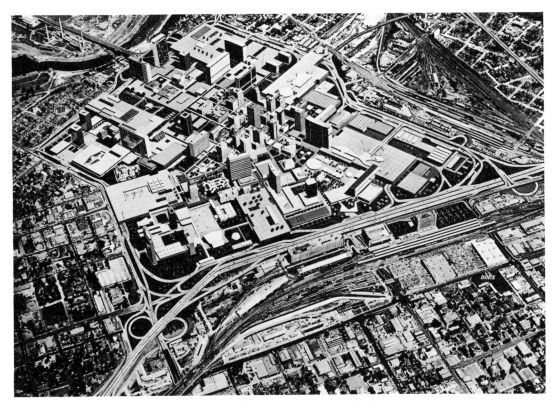

1063   *Fort Worth, Plan for the new civic centre (V. Gruen Associates, 1954)*

of Bochum (1962) and Berlin (1963) (Fig. 1062).

The theoretical and practical studies on horizontally grouped dwellings have proved applicable to temporary residential districts and centres: hence the plan for the winter tourist centre at Belleville of 1962 (in collaboration with Charlotte Perriand, Jean Prouvé and Ren Suzuki) and the recent sweeping plans for the urbanization of the coast of Languedoc.

In the districts designed by Candilis, Josic and Woods research into distribution and construction find an acceptable balance; collaboration with Prouvé has proved valuable in many cases (Blanc Mesnil district, 1956). One still unsolved problem is the introduction of this twofold research into the technical and administrative mechanism of public intervention. The experiment of

Candilis, Josic and Woods, unlike that of Le Corbusier, is already biassed in such a way as to be easily absorbed into the workings of public bodies. But the obstacles which cut the old master out of French mass production applied, to a large extent, to his ex-pupils too; the district of Le Mirail, which was to have been the great demonstration of the advantages of the new criteria of planning, was only partially realized, at random and defectively. But the planners' 'patient research' is still under way, and may meet with better opportunities in the future.

d   The United States

As has been noted, the chief difficulty of American experiments was connected with the crisis of the traditional urban structure, whose former elasticity, based on Jefferson's gridiron system, had become singularly rigid as a result of changes which involved the basic device.

The elasticity and automatism of the grid-iron system have so far made co-ordinating public intervention relatively unnecessary, and have allowed individual sectorial action to remain independent; but the crisis of this device poses the problem of town-planning anew, with the qualitative and quantitative requirements we talked of in connection with European countries.

As often happens in the United States, the new proposals containing an alternative to the traditional mechanism of urban development were first formulated by private individuals – by design studios, industries, cultural associations – and taken up by public bodies only at a later date. Among these the most important are:

I

The studies for the restructuring of the 'downtowns', of which the first example was the plan by Victor Gruen (b. 1903) for the centre of Fort Worth, Texas (1954) (Fig. 1063). Gruen suggested gradually freeing certain stretches of the network from motor traffic, concentrating parking lots in certain areas and recovering the pedestrian spaces necessary to social life, around the new commercial and business buildings.

The logic of this plan was similar to that which tended to develop the shopping centres serving residential suburbs, to transform them into complex centres of commercial and recreational activity; noteworthy among the more recent plans are that for San Mateo, California (W. Belton and Ass.) for Milwaukee, Wisc. (J. Graham and Ass.) for Nassau County, New York (I. M. Pei and Ass.) and the Lloyd Center being built at Portland, Oregon (J. Graham and Ass.) which also includes a hotel and office block.[15]

II

The residential quarters built in the big cities, in great green spaces, in the form of multi-storey collective buildings; the most striking among these are Lafayette Park in Detroit, designed by Mies, and Lake Meadows in Chicago, by Skidmore, Owings and Merrill (Fig. 1064).

In comparison with similar European districts, these have a much lower density, with huge open spaces, and at the moment form a more satisfactory alternative to the extensive suburbs of one-family houses, though they are still very expensive;

III

Plans for the alteration of the centres of the great cities; the first in order of time was that for Philadelphia, begun in 1942 by the City Planning Commission, run by E. N. Bacon.

This plan had publicity, including a special exhibition in 1947, but only in 1960 did it take the concrete form of a development plan. These town-planning schemes did tend to remain on paper for a long time, in the United States, but during the last five years there has been a noticeable and rapid increase of awareness on the part of the authorities and public opinion on these matters, which may be linked with the coming to power of the Democrats, in 1960, and to the notable development of theoretical studies on the city, encouraged mainly by the Joint Center for Urban Studies, set up in 1959 by M.I.T. and Harvard.

It was in this atmosphere that the Government Center Project was born, worked on by Adams, Howard and Creeley for the City Planning Board of Boston, from 1958 onwards. This undertaking was important not so much for the quality of the plan, as because it was based on the needs of public administration, which was the guiding element of urban layout. In 1962 a competition was organized for the new City Hall, won by G. M. Kallmann, N. M. Mackinnell and E. F. Knowles with a plan that was very individual but strongly integrated with the surrounding spaces (Fig. 1066).[16]

In Philadelphia and Boston the considerations connected with the separation of traffic and the three-dimensional organization of urban spaces have been extended to the scale of a big city. It is probable that in the near future there will be other similar experiments in America.

IV

The new towns – Foster City, Redwood Shores, Reston, Valencia, Columbia – planned as business enterprises by private corporations. Master plans and executive plans were also prepared by private firms (Victor Gruen and Ass. for Valencia, the Architects Collaborative for Redwood Shores, Whittlesey and Conklin for Reston) and approved by public authorities. These are small and limited experiences, compared with the huge spread of traditional towns, and do not change the balance of general urbanization as in England and other European countries. New towns are different from normal residential districts because they attempt to escape the traditional patterns of north American suburbs: a double network of motor and pedestrian ways instead of the usual undifferentiated grid; new patterns of housing – for instance terrace houses assembled in neighbourhood groups instead of the endless succession of individual houses; commercial and recreational facilities planned together with residential areas.

The current problem is learning to consider town and country planning as one general process that is not controlled by private and independent enterprises; in this trend the United States are far behind Europe but are now moving. In 1967 a new department of Housing and Urban Development was established; the strong reaction of public opinion against the perils of pollution will force the government to set up, perhaps in the near future, a new, efficient system of public controls on urbanization and the general environment.

The experiments enumerated here seem today to be the most full of inspiration for the future; some are really encouraging, but all, to some degree, share the contradictions of our time, and none is a perfect model.

The ideals of the modern movement, like those of the good society mentioned by Lippmann, 'fall far short of perfection, and in speaking of them we must not use superlatives. They are worldy ideals, which raise no expectations about the highest good. Quite the contrary. They are concerned with the best that is possible among mortal and finite, diverse and conflicting men'.[17] Modern architecture does not promise a perfect world, it does not set itself up as the fulfilment of any historical prophecy; it is a hopeful attempt, but it is no guarantee of unconditional success.

In the near future the city will certainly undergo greater and more rapid transformations than those that have taken place in the past. Possibly the methods hitherto experimented with will make it possible to keep up with events and to invert the process of the disintegration of our environment, as has been the case so far. On the other hand it could be that the results obtained might depend on the limited extent of the changes achieved so far, and that the attempt is destined to fail on the new scale. In such a case it is not the fate of any particular tendency that is at stake, but the continuation of the European artistic tradition, which has been re-elaborated by the modern movement to the point of losing every incidental link with the old social, economic and productive organization. By doing this the masters of the First World War period were in a sense burning their own boats and made any return to previous positions not only inapposite but also downright impossible. If this cultural heritage cannot adapt itself to the dimensions of the modern world, this would really mean the breaking off of relations with the past and the abandoning, in the new society, of any attempt at pre-

1064 *(above)   Chicago, Lake Meadows plan (above on the left is the school, below on the right commercial services; Skidmore, Owings and Merrill, 1950–60)*

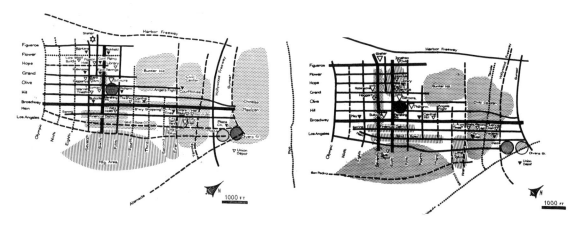

1065   *Two schemes for Los Angeles drawn from verbal and graphic interviews (from K. Lynch,* The Image of the City, *1960)*

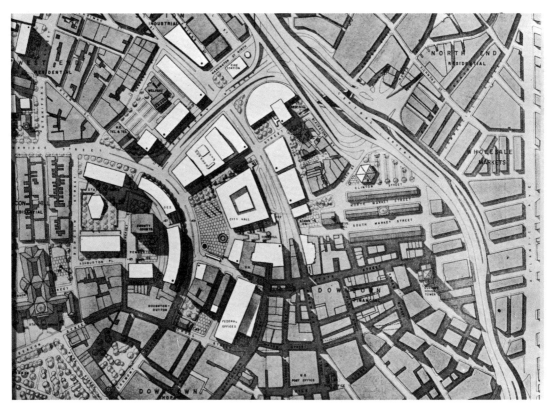

1066 *(above)   Plan of the new Boston centre (from* Casabella*)*

serving the hierarchy between permanent and contingent values.

Therefore, if the modern movement was to be outgrown, this must be an 'outgrowing' far more radical than any that had hitherto taken place: things would have to begin again from the beginning, with completely different aims. The realization of the gravity of this dilemma certainly does not help modern architects to find peace of mind, but it does project duty and hope on to a specific target.

1067   *Chicago, the I.I.T. Campus, with the Crown Hall and the new buildings by Skidmore, Owings and Merrill; in the background the Loop*

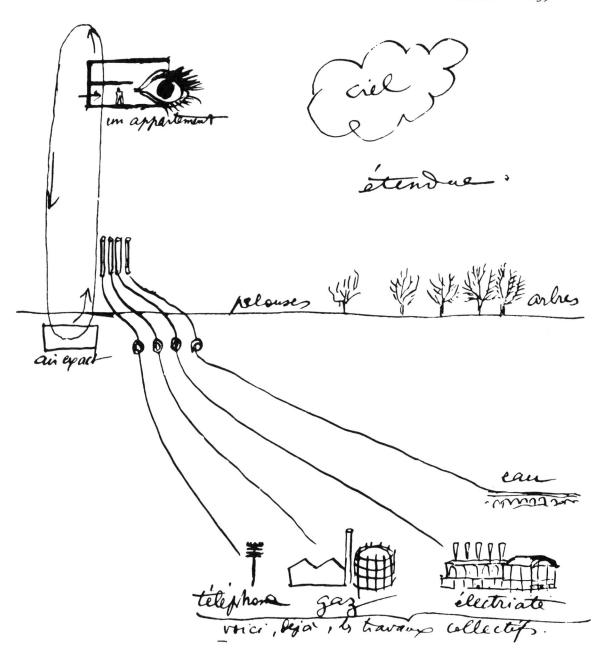

1068   *The task of modern architecture: to bring the improvements of modern techniques to the service of man's home (drawing by Le Corbusier)*

Notes

Chapter 12

1 B. Russell, *Freedom and Organisation,* 1814–1914, London, Allen & Unwin, 1934, p. 357.
2 Quoted in N. Pevsner, *Pioneers of the Modern Movement,* London, Penguin Books, 1960, p. 35.
3 G. C. Argan, review of 'Eliante o dell'architettura' by C. Brandi in *Casabella,* n. 16 (1957), p. 44.
4. W. Gropius, *Sind beim Bau von Industriegebauden künstlerische Gesichtspunkte mit praktischen und wirtschaftlichen vereinbar?* Leipzig, 1911.
5 W. Gropius, 'Die Entwicklung moderner Industriebaukunst' in *Jahrbuch des deutschen Werkbundes,* Jena, 1913, p. 22.
6 *Die Grundzüge der linear-perspecktivischen Darstellung in der Kunst der Gebrüder Van Eyck und ihrer Schule,* Leipzig, 1904. 'Die Anfänge der zentralperspecktivischen Konstruktion in der italienischen Malerei des XIV Jahrhunderts' in *Mitteilungen des Kunsthists. Institutes in Florenz* 1912, p. 39.
7 'Masaccio et la théorie de la perspective' in *Revue de l'art ancienne et moderne* 1914, p. 145.
8 'Das perspektivischen Verfahren L. B. Alberti' in *Kunstcronik,* 1915, p. 505.
9 'Die Perspektive als symbolische Form' in *Vorträge der Bibliothek Warburg,* 1924–5, Berlin, 1927, p. 258.
10 Conversation with Zervos, *Cahiers d'art,* 1935, quoted in W. Hess, *I Problemi della pittura moderna,* Italian translation, Milan, 1958, p. 74.
11 G. Braque, *Cahiers,* Paris, 1948. Hess, *op. cit.,* p. 76.
12 Quoted in D. H. Kahnweiler, *J. Gris, sa vie, ses oeuvres, ses écrits*; W. Hess, *op. cit.,* p. 85.
13 W. Hess, *op. cit.,* p. 75.
14 G. Apollinaire, *The Cubist Painters, Aesthetic meditations,* Paris, 1913, New York: Wittenborn, Schultz Inc. 1949. 'The utilitarian end aimed at by most contemporary architects is responsible for the great backwardness of architecture as compared with the other arts. The architect, the engineer should have sublime aims: to build the highest tower, to prepare for time and ivy the most beautiful of ruins, to throw across a harbour, or river, an arch more audacious than the rainbow, and finally to compose to a lasting harmony, the most powerful ever imagined by man.'
15 W. Hess, *op. cit.,* p. 84.
16 Quoted in M. Calvesi, 'Il futurista Sant'Elia' in *La Casa,* n. 6 (1959), p. 123.
17 R. Banham, 'Futurist manifesto', in *Architectural Review,* Vol. 126, n. 751 (1959), p. 78.
18 Printed 20 May 1914 on the occasion of the first exhibition of the group Nuove Tendenze, at the Famiglia Artistica in Milan.
19 Published 11 July 1914; see Fillia, *La nuova architettura,* Turin, 1931.
20 From 'Futurism and modern architecture', by R. Banham in the *Journal of the R.I.B.A.,* Third Series, Vol. LXIV, Feb. 1957.
21 W. Gropius, 'The Formal and Technical Problems of Modern Architecture and Planning' in the *Journal of the R.I.B.A.,* May 1955, p. 65.
22 Particularly because of the formula 'the futurist house like a gigantic machine', reminiscent of Le Corbusier's 'machine à habiter'.
23 See A. Sartoris, *Gli elementi dell'architettura funzionale,* Milan, 1941.
24 F. Marc, *Briefe, Handzeichnungen und Aphorismen,* Berlin, 1920. W. Hess, *op. cit.,* p. 111.
25 W. Kandinsky, *Essays,* Stuttgart, 1955; W. Hess, *op. cit.,* p. 122.
26 W. Hess, *op. cit.,* p. 108.
27 W. Gropius, *The New Architecture and the Bauhaus,* London, 1935, p. 48.
28 Quoted in B. Zevi, *Poetica dell'architettura neoplastica,* Milan, 1953, p. 35.
29 P. Mondrian, *Plastic Art and Pure Art,* New York, 1947. W. Hess, *op. cit.,* p. 145.
30 B. Zevi, *op. cit.*
31 Letter from J. J. P. Oud to B. Zevi, in *op. cit.,* p. 161.

Chapter 13

1 *Programm des staatlichen Bauhauses in Weimar* **1919**, quoted in H. Bayer, W. Gropius, I. Gropius, *Bauhaus 1919–1928*, London, Allen and Unwin, 1939, p. 18.
2 W. Gropius, 'My Conception of the Bauhaus Idea', (1935) in *Scope of Total Architecture*, London, Allen and Unwin, 1956, p. 29.
3 W. Gropius, *op. cit.*, p. 31.
4 W. Gropius, *op. cit.*, p. 33.
5 W. Gropius, *op. cit.*, p. 26.
6 A. Hauser, *Social History of Art*, London, Routledge and Kegan Paul, 1952, Vol. II, p. 823.
7 This is the text quoted in the preface, note 2.
8 W. Gropius, *op. cit.*, p. 13.
9 The reasons for this disagreement have been discussed objectively several times by Gropius (*Bauhaus 1919–1928*, p. 38); B. Zevi (*Poetica dell'architettura neoplastica*, Milan, 1953) interprets it as a figurative polemic between Expressionism and neo-plasticism, while its cultural premises have been clarified by G. G. Argan, *M. Breuer*, Milan, 1957, p. 10, and in the second edition of *W. Gropius e il Bauhaus*, Turin, 1957, p. 79.
10 *Satzungen, Staatliches Bauhaus in Weimar*, Munich, 1922.
11 *Staatliches Bauhaus in Weimar 1919–1923*, Munich, 1923.
12 Published in A. Meyer, 'Ein Versuchshaus des Bauhauses in Weimar', in *Bauhausbücher*, n. 3, Munich, 1925.
13 W. Gropius, *Idee und Aufbau des staatlichen Bauhauses in Weimar*, Munich, 1923.
14 Quoted in H. Bayer, W. Gropius, I. Gropius, *Bauhaus 1919–1928*, pp. 22–31.
15 The list is the following: (1) W. Gropius, *Internationale Architektur*, Munich, 1925. (2) P. Klee, *Pädagogisches Skizzenbuch*, 1925. (3) A. Meyer, *Ein Versuchshaus des Bauhauses in Weimar*, 1925. (4) *Die Bühne im Bauhaus*, 1925. (5) P. Mondrian, *Neue Gestaltung*, 1925. (6) T. Van Doesburg, *Grundbegriffe der neuen gestaltenden Kunst*, 1925. (7) *Neue Arbeiten der Bauhauswerkstätten*, 1926. (8) L. Moholy-Nagy, *Malerei, Photographie, Film*, 1926. (9) W. Kandinsky, *Punkt und Linie zu Fläche*, 1926. (10) J. J. P. Oud, *Holländische Architektur*, 1926 and 1929. (11) K. Malewitsch, *Die gegenstandlose Welt*, 1930. (12) W. Gropius, *Bauhausbauten in Dessau*, 1931. (13) L. Moholy-Nagy, *Von Material zur Architektur*, 1932.
16 For instance F. H. Ehmke and A. Müller quoted in *Bauhaus 1919–1928*, *cit.*, pp. 92 and 95.
17 T. Van Doesburg and K. Teige in *Stavba* 1924: *op. cit.*, p. 93.
18 In *Das Werk*, September 1923.
19 In *Deutsche Allgemeine Zeitung*, 2 October 1923.
20 Quoted in *Bauhaus, cit.*, p. 95.
21 A society, called 'Friends of the Bauhaus' gave Gropius moral and material support in the difficult years: the managing board included H. P. Berlage, P. Behrens, A. Busch, M. Chagall, H. Driesch, A. Einstein, H. Euleberg, E. Fischer, G. Hauptmann, J. Hoffmann, O. Kokoschka, H. Poelzig, A. Schönberg, A. Sommerfeld, J. Strzygowsky and F. Werfel.
22 In *Die Tat*, 1932.
23 Quoted in *Bauhaus, cit.*, p. 95.
24 *Op. cit.*, p. 97.
25 Quoted in *Bauhaus, cit.*, p. 206.
26 P. Portoghesi in a lecture given in 1958 at the Galleria d'Arte Moderna, Rome.
27 Gropius wrote in 1953: 'One of the U.S. Supreme Court Justices once discussed the substance of democratic procedure and I was highly interested to hear him define it as "essentially a matter of degree". He did not base his decision on abstract principles of right and wrong, but wanted to consider every case in its particular circumstances and relative proportion, because he felt that it was the soundness of the whole social structure that mattered and that what might contribute to its detriment today might be inconsequential tomorrow under changing conditions, and *vice versa*.' *Scope of Total Architecture*, p. 15.
28 W. Gropius, 'Architect, Servant or Leader?' 1954, in *Scope, cit.*, p. 99: 'Should the architect be a servant or a leader? The answer, already implicit in what I said before, is simple: put an "and" in place of the "or". Serving and leading can be inter-dependent.'
29 W. Gropius, 'Is there a Science of Design?' in *Scope, cit.*, p. 49.
30 P. Klee, lecture on modern art given in 1924, quoted in Hess, *op. cit.*, pp. 117–18.
31 S. Giedion, *Walter Gropius, Work and Teamwork*, London, Architectural Press, 1954, p. 42.
32 It sometimes seems as though Gropius thinks that certain laws of composition can be deduced from the characteristics of the human eye, and as though he conceives of rationality in a restricted, naturalistic way; see his interest in optical illusions 'Design Topics', 1947, in *Scope, cit.*, p. 29. In 1939 he wrote: 'For a long period, however, no common denominator has guided our expression in the visual arts. But today, after a long and chaotic period of "l'art pour l'art", a new language of vision is slowly replacing individualistic terms like "taste" or "feeling" with terms of objective validity. Based on biological facts – both physical and psychological – it seeks to represent the impersonal cumulative experience of successive generations.' (*Scope, cit.*, p. 58). Later, to defend himself from the more superficial meanings of the designation 'rationalist' and the accusation of materialism it carried with it, Gropius seemed to give rationality only the value of a means, and came near to re-establishing the old antagonism between technique – means, and art – end. For instance in 1952: 'Good planning I conceived to be both a science and an art. As a science, it analyses human relationships; as an art, it co-ordinates human activities into a cultural synthesis.' (*Scope, cit.*, p. 158).
33 Le Corbusier-Saugnier, *Vers une architecture*, Paris, 1923, p. 3.
34 *Ibid.*, p. 11.
35 A. Rossi in *Casabella*, n. 246 (1960) n. 4.
36 Le Corbusier and P. Jeanneret, *Oeuvre Complète 1910–1929*, Zurich, 1956, pp. 41–3.
37 In *Urbanisme* Le Corbusier confirms his historical preferences: 'We are enthusiastic about the lucid order of Babylon and turn eagerly to the terse spirit of Louis XIV; we underline this date and regard the great King as the first western town-planner since the Romans'.
38 *Oeuvre Complète 1910–1929, cit.*, p. 128.

39 Quoted in B. Zevi, *Poetica dell'architettura neo-plastica, cit.*, p. 123.
40 M. Bill, *Mies van der Rohe*, 2nd edition, New York, 1953, p. 195.
41 Quoted in M. F. Roggero, *Il contributo di Mendelsohn alla evoluzione dell'architettura moderna*, Milan, 1952, pp. 63–4.
42 See P. H. Riepert, *Die Architektur in Eisenbetonbau*, Charlottenburg, 1914; L. Hilbersheimer and J. Vischer, *Beton als Gestalter*, Stuttgart, 1928.
43 For instance in the essays by R. Furneaux-Jordan, 'Dudok and the Repercussion of his European Influence', in *Architectural Review*, (Vol. 115, 1949, p. 237, and by G. Canella, *Il caso Dudok riferito anche ad alcune esperienze italiane*, in *Casabella*, n. 216, (1957), p. 79.

Chapter 14

1 W. Gropius, *The New Architecture and the Bauhaus*, London, 1935.
2 Le Corbusier, letter to Martienssen of 23 September 1936, quoted in *Oeuvre Complète 1910–1929*, Zurich, 1956, p. 5.
3 Le Corbusier, *op. cit.*, p. 162.
4 For instance the Gemeente Museum in the Hague, 1935.
5 P. Nenot, J. Vago, C. Lefebvre, M. Broggi.
6 See *Une maison, un palais*, Paris 1928 and *Oeuvre Complète 1910–1929*, pp. 160–73.
7 The Weissenhof is illustrated in H. and B. Rasch, *Wie bauen?* Stuttgart, 1927, and C. Behrendt, *Der Sieg des neuen Baustils*, Stuttgart, 1927.
8 Vaillat, in *Le Temps*, 21 May 1930, quoted in Giedion, *op. cit.*, p. 51.
9 A. Alexandre, in *Le Figaro*, 16 May 1930, quoted in Giedion, *op. cit.*, p. 51.
10 Quoted in S. Giedion, *Walter Gropius*, p. 49.
11 The words of Kandinsky seem the most appropriate comment, although metaphorical, on the work of Mies: '[The empty canvas] apparently really empty, silent, indifferent, almost stupid. But actually full of tensions, with a thousand subdued voices, big with expectation. A little frightened, because it may be violated, but docile. It does what you ask of it, only it asks for mercy. It can receive everything, but it can't bear everything. The empty canvas is a marvellous thing, more beautiful than many paintings. Such simple elements. A straight line, a straight surface, slight, rigid, undaunted, affirming itself without scruples, apparently obvious, like a destiny already lived out. This way and no other. A free curve: vibrant, retiring, yielding, elastic, apparently indeterminate, like the destiny awaiting it. It could become something else but it doesn't. Hard and soft. A combination of both, infinite possibilities. Each line says: here I am! It proclaims itself, shows its expressive face: listen, listen to my mystery! A line is a marvel. A little dot, lots of little dots, here smaller, there slightly bigger. They've all dug themselves a hole but they remain soft, so many tensions constantly repeating, in chorus: listen, listen! Little messages gradually swelling into the great yes. A black circle, distant thunder, a world on its own apparently taking no notice of anything, wrapped up in itself, an instant conclusion. A: here I am, spoken slowly, coldly.

A red circle, well-placed, proclaiming its position, leaning in on itself. But at the same time it is moving, because it would like to be everywhere at once, it spreads beyond all obstacles to the farthest corner. Thunder and lightning both. A: here I am, spoken passionately. The circle is a marvel. But the most marvellous thing of all is that all these voices together and so many more can still come together in a single voice, the whole painting has become a single: here I am!' (Quoted in Hess, *op. cit.*, pp. 131–2.)
12 L. Hilbersheimer, *Internationale neue Baukunst*, Stuttgart, 1926.
13 G. A. Platz, *Die Baukunst der neuesten Zeit*, Berlin, 1927.
14 P. Meyer, *Moderne Architektur und Tradition*, Zurich, 1928.
15 H. R. Hitchcock Jr., *Modern Architecture, Romanticism and Reintegration*, New York, 1929.
16 B. Taut, *Die neue Baukunst in Europa und Amerika*, Stuttgart, 1929.
17 M. Malkiel-Jirmounsky, *Les tendances de l'architecture contemporaine*, Paris, 1930.
18 S. Cheney, *The New World Architecture*, London, 1930.
19 Fillia, *La nuova architettura*, Turin, 1931.
20 A. Sartoris, *Gli elementi dell'architettura razionale*, Milan, 1932.
21 *Moderne Bauformen*, 1927, p. 325.
22 B. Taut, *op. cit.*, p. 6.
23 Quoted in P. Chiarini, *Bertolt Brecht*, Bari, 1959, p. 164.
24 E. Piscator, *Das politische Theater*, Berlin, 1929, pp. 40–1.
25 B. Brecht, *The Measures Taken*.
26 B. Brecht, Preface to *Three-penny Opera*.
27 W. Gropius, *Internationale Architektur*, Munich, 1925, p. 7.
28 E. Persico, 'Un ristorante automatico a Praga', in *Casabella*, January 1954, quoted in *Scritti politici e polemici*, Milan, 1947, p. 262.
29 See for example G. Giovannoni, 'Il momento attuale dell'architettura', in *Architetture di pensiero e pensieri sull'architettura*, Rome, 1945, p. 271.
30 Le Corbusier, *op. cit.*, p. 175.
31 Gropius was not present at this first meeting, since he was busy moving from Dessau to Berlin.
32 Text in *La Charte d'Athènes*, Paris, 1957.
33 Le Corbusier-Saugnier, *Towards a New Architecture*, London, 1927, p. 102.
34 G. C. Argan, *Walter Gropius e la Bauhaus*, Turin, 1951, pp. 16–19.
35 W. Gropius, 'C.I.A.M. 1928–1953', in *Scope, cit.*, p. 103.
36 Le Corbusier and P. Jeanneret, *Oeuvre Complète 1929–1934*, Zurich, 1952, p. 24.
37 Le Corbusier, *op. cit.*, p. 24.
38 Published respectively in the First Vol. of *Oeuvre Complète*, pp. 186–7, and in the second, pp. 24–5.
39 E. Persico, in *Casabella*, November 1931; see *Scritti critici e polemici, cit.*, pp. 238–40.
40 J. Posener, assisting on this work, noted that the building was more beautiful before the horizontal panels were fixed to the slender, close-set pillars which formed the outer structure; Mendelsohn, too, said: 'Every

building is better before completion. This is the stage, when the architect learns what to do next time.' Quoted in A. Whittick, *Eric Mendelsohn*, London, 1964, p. 93–4.

Chapter 15

1 Quoted in A. Verneuil, *La législation sur l'urbanisme en Grande-Bretagne*, 1948, p. 4.
2 A. Klein, 'Neues Verfahren zur Untersuchung von Kleinwohnungsgrundrissen', in *Städtebau* 1928, p. 16.
3 A. Fischer, C. M. Grod, O. Haesler, W. Lochstampfer, W. Merz, W. Piphahn, F. Roeckle, F. Roessler, H. D. Roesiger.
4 In collaboration with O. Bartning, F. Forbat, H. Häring, Henning, H. Scharoun.
5 In collaboration with H. Häring, R. Salvisberg, M. Wagner.
6 W. Gropius, 'Die Soziologischen Grundlagen der Minimalwohnung', in *Die Justiz*, Vol. 5, n. 8, 1929; see *Scope, cit.*, p. 112.
7 W. Gropius, 'Flach, Mittel- oder Hochbau?' in *Rationelle Bebauungsweisen*, Stuttgart, 1931, p. 26.
8 W. Gropius, preface to A. Meyer, *Ein Versuchhaus des Bauhauses*, Munich, 1925, ('Bauhausbücher' n. 3); see *Scope, cit.*, p. 146.
9 E. Persico, 'Profezia dell'architettura' (1935) in *Scritti critici e polemici, cit.*, p. 205.
10 H. Kampfemeyer, *Wohnstätte und Arbeitstätte*, quoted by F. Fariello in *Architettura*, 1937, p. 605.
11 Le Corbusier, introduction to *Oeuvre Complète 1929–1934*, Zurich, 1952, p. 11.
12 Le Corbusier, 'Le parcellement du sol des villes', in *Rationelle Bebauungsweisen*, p. 49.
13 Le Corbusier, *op. cit.*, pp. 51–2.
14 Le Corbusier, *op. cit.*, p. 57.
15 *Rationelle Bebauungsweisen*, edited by V. Bourgeois, S. Giedion, C. Van Eesteren, R. Steiger, Stuttgart, 1931.
16 'Stellungnahme des Brüsseler Kongresses zu Flach, Mittel- oder Hochbau', in *op. cit.*, p. 74.
17 These were Amsterdam, Athens, Brussels, Baltimore, Bandung, Budapest, Berlin, Barcelona, Charleroi, Cologne, Como, Dalat, Detroit, Dessau, Frankfurt-am-Main, Geneva, Genoa, the Hague, Los Angeles, Littoria, London, Madrid, Oslo, Paris, Prague, Rome, Rotterdam, Stockholm, Utrecht, Verona, Warsaw, Zagreb, Zurich.
18 The C.I.A.M. met in 1937 in Paris, and after the war, in 1947 in Bridgewater; in 1949 in Bergamo, in 1951 in Hoddesdon, in 1953 in Aix-en-Provence, in 1956 in Dubrovnik and for the last time at Otterlo in 1959. In its original form the association proved unsuited to solving the problems of the new cultural situation, and its protagonists were in agreement as to its dissolution.

Chapter 16

1 For instance in the originally unpublished work by G. Pagano, 'Aspetti e tendenze dell'architettura contemporanea', of 1928, later printed by C. Melograni in his *G.P.*, Milan, 1955, p. 55; or in the International Exhibition of Modern Architecture at the V Triennale, see E. Persico in *L'Italia letteraria*, 2 July 1933.
2 *Moderne Bauformen*, 1929, p. 304.
3 *L'Architecture d'Aujourd'hui*, 1933, I, p. 68.
4 For the school of Hoffmann *Moderne Bauformen*, 1927,

p. 373; for the school of Strnad, 1928, p. 49.
5 E. Kaufmann, 'C. N. Ledoux', in *Thieme Becker Kunstler-Lexicon*, Vol. 22, 1928; 'Von Ledoux bis Le Corbusier', Ursprung und Entwicklung der autonomer Architektur, Vienna, 1933; 'Die Stadt des Architekten Ledoux', in *Kunstwissenschaftliche Forschungen*, 1933, p. 131.
6 R. Bauer, K. A. Bieber, A. Brenner, O. Breuer, J. F. Dex, M. Fellerer, J. Frank, H. Gorge, J. Groagh, O. Haerdtl, C. Holzmeister, J. Jirasek, E. Lichtblau, O. Niedermoser, E. Plischke, G. Schütte-Lihotzky, W. Sobotka, H. Vetter, E. Wachberger, H. Wagner, J. Wenzel, O. Wlach; see *Moderne Bauformen*, 1932, p. 435.
7 Biographies of the Bauhaus teachers in *Bauhaus 1919–1928, cit.*, p. 220.
8 Bonatz also designed an excellent series of bridges for the *Reichsautobahnen*, built from 1935 onwards. See F. Tamms, *P. B., Arbeiten aus Jahren 1907 bis 1937*, Stuttgart, 1937.
9 'Les tendances de l'architecture dans le Troisième Reich' in *L'Architecture d'Aujourd'hui*, 1936, n. 4, p. 9.
10 *Ibid.*, p. 21.
11 This was the title of an exhibition organized in 1935 at the Oesterreichisches Museum in Vienna.
12 J. Posener, *op. cit.*, p. 23.
13 *Ibid.*, p. 40.
14 N. Brunov 1931, quoted in A. Voyce, *Russian Architecture*, New York, 1948, p. 104.
15 Lenin, 1920, quoted in A. Voyce, *op. cit.*, p. 125.
16 Kamenev 1919, quoted in A. Voyce, *op. cit.*, p. 124.
17 Quoted by B. Lubetkin in *Architectural Review*, May 1932.
18 This period of Soviet architecture has recently been dealt with in the excellent study by V. De Feo, *U.R.S.S., architettura 1917–1936*, Rome, 1963.
19 11 January 1921; *Archivi del futurismo*, I, Rome, 1958, p. 56.
20 *Scena illustrata*, 1939.
21 A. Soffici, *Spirito ed estetica del fascismo*, quoted in E. Garin, *Cultura e vita morale* ('La Casa' fasc. 6, 1959, p. 137).
22 E. Garin, *op. cit.*, p. 137.
23 G. Muzio, 'Alcuni architetti d'oggi in Lombardia', in *Dedalo*, 1931, p. 1086.
24 *Ibid.*, pp. 1087–90.
25 *Ibid.*, pp. 1097–107.
26 M. Piacentini, *Architettura d'oggi*, Rome, 1930, p. 34.
27 *Architettura e arti decorative*, 1931, p. 215.
28 *Ibid.*, p. 246.
29 Gruppo 7, 'Architettura', in: *Rassegna italiana*, December 1926 (quoted in B. Zevi, *Storia dell'architettura moderna*, Turin, 1955, p. 231–2).
30 *Ibid.*, p. 232.
31 Published 31 March 1931, see Zevi, *op. cit.*, p. 650.
32 Published 5 May 1931, see Zevi, *op. cit.*, p. 651.
33 For instance M. Piacentini, 'Problemi reali più che razionalismo preconcetto', in *Architettura e arti decorative*, 1928, p. 103; Dove è irragionevole l'architettura razionale, in *Dedalo*, 1931, p. 527.
34 G. Pagano in *Casabella*, April and June 1931.
35 See G. Veronesi, *op. cit.*, p. 34; this is what Persico calls 'the grotesque manifesto: the chocolate box mani-

festo of Italian art' (*ibid.*, p. 35).

36 *Casabella*, February 1937.

37 'Brinkmann e Van der Vlugt', in *Casabella*, March 1935, *Scritti, cit.*, p. 185.

38 'Decadenza di J. Hoffmann', in *L'Eco del mondo*, 23 March 1935; *Scritti, cit.*, p. 287.

39 'Errori stranieri', in *L'Italia letteraria*, 28 May 1935; *Scritti, cit.*, p. 169.

40 *Domus*, November 1934; *Scritti, cit.*, p. 236.

41 *Casabella*, June 1937, p. 52.

42 *Architettura*, June 1937.

43 *Casabella*, June 1937.

44 *Casabella*, February 1941.

45 G. Pagano, in *Casabella*, March 1940.

46 See Chapter 6.

47 Statement published in *Casabella*, June 1934.

48 Le Corbusier, preface to *Oeuvre Complète, 1929–1934, cit.*

49 G. Giovannoni, *Architetture di pensiero e pensieri sull'architettura*, Rome, s.d., p. 286.

50 A. Lunacharsky, 1938, quoted in Voyce, *cit.*, p. 149.

51 A. Speer, *Neue deutsche Baukunst*, Berlin, 1940, pp. 7–8.

52 'We think that art should be in a state of permanent revolution. Forget about the dead, about *faits accomplis*' (*L'Architecture d'Aujourd'hui*, 1937, n. 7, p. 7).

53 'We love balance, logic, purity. In houses we prefer light to shade, gay tones to gloomy ones. We offer the eyes and the mind a rest, after the worries, the haste and the chaos of our days' (*ibid.*, p. 10).

54 'It is the almost indisputed criterion of a standard form that, to be easily made and naturally utilizable, it must necessarily be beautiful' (*ibid.*, p. 8).

55 See *L'Architecture d'Aujourd'hui*, 1933, n. 4, p. 101: Austria, Spain, Hungary, Poland, Czechoslovakia and Yugoslavia were represented.

56 *L'Architecture d'Aujourd'hui*, 1933, n. 5, p. 120.

57 F. Léger, lecture given on 9 August 1933 during the Fourth C.I.A.M. in Athens; Italian translation in *Casabella*, n. 207 (1955) p. 69.

58 *L'Architecture d'Aujourd'hui*, n. 1, p. 6.

59 *L'Architecture d'Aujourd'hui*, n. 1, p. 5.

60 The four successive plans are illustrated in the third Volume of *Oeuvre Complète, cit.*, pp. 140, 148, 152 and 158.

Chapter 17

1 *Casabella*, October 1932; see E. Persico, *Scritti, cit.*, p. 354.

2 E. Mendelsohn, *Buildings and Sketches*, Berlin and London, 1923.

3 H. G. Scheffauer, 'The Work of Walter Gropius', in *Architectural Review*, August 1924, p. 50.

4 *America, Architect's Picture-Book*, London, 1926.

5 *Towards a New Architecture*, London and New York, 1927.

6 *The City of Tomorrow and its Planning*, London 1929.

7 E. Maxwell-Fry, 'Walter Gropius', in *Architectural Review*, Vol. 117, (1955), p. 155.

8 W. C. Behrendt, *Modern Building, its Nature, Problems and Forms*, New York, 1937.

9 S. Giedion, *Space, Time and Architecture*.

10 *Oeuvre Complète*, Vol. II, p. 48.

11 *Oeuvre Complète*, Vol. III, p. 125.

12 See E. Persico, 'L'ultima opera di Berlage', in *Casabella*, September 1935; *Scritti, cit.*, p. 277.

13 This building and the Plaslaan are fully illustrated in A. Roth, *La Nouvelle Architecture*, Zurich, 1940.

14 The general plan of Amsterdam, the detailed plans and the enquiries connected with them are published in the series *Grondslagen voor de Stedebouwkundige ontwikkeling van Amsterdam*.

15 E. Persico, 'La cooperativa Foerbundet', in *Casabella*, August 1935; *Scritti, cit.*, p. 271.

16 E. Persico, *Scritti, cit.*, pp. 272–273.

17 See for instance 'The Humanizing of Architecture', in *Technology Review*, November 1940 and in *The Architectural Forum*, December 1940.

18 *Schweizerische Bauzeitung*, 1 January 1938, quoted in M. Bill, *Robert Maillart*, Zurich, 1955, p. 17.

19 U.S.A.: A. Lawrence-Kocher and A. Frey, holiday house; R. Neutra, experimental school in Los Angeles; V. de Mars and B. Cairns, co-operative farm in Arizona. France: Le Corbusier, house at Mathes; Beaudouin and Lods, school at Suresnes.
Sweden: E. Friberger, pre-fabricated house.
Switzerland: M. E. Haefeli, two Goldbach houses; A. and E. Roth and M. Breuer, two Doldertal houses; the Neubühl; M. E. Haefeli and W. Moser, bathing establishment at Zurich; M. Bill, Swiss section at the 1936 Triennale.
Holland: the Bergpolder; the Plaslaan; J. B. van Loghem, indoor swimming pool in Rotterdam; A. Boeken, indoor tennis courts in Rotterdam; Merkelbach and Karsten, radio building in Hilversum.
Italy: sun therapy colony at Legnano, by studio B.B.P.R.
Japan: J. Sakakura, Japanese pavilion at Paris exhibition, 1937.
Finland: A. Aalto, library at Viipuri.
Czechoslovakia: J. Havlicek and K. Honzik, office block in Prague.
England: E. Owen-Williams, Beeston factory.

20 *Introduction*, p. 7.

21 *Ibid.*, p. 8.

22 *Ibid.*, p. 8.

Chapter 18

1 J. Gréber, *L'Architecture aux États Unis*, Paris, 1920, Vol. I, p. 14.

2 J. Gréber, *op. cit.*, Vol. II, p. 12.

3 J. Gréber, *op. cit.*, Vol. II, p. 160.

4 Le Corbusier, 'La catastrophe féerique', in *L'Architecture d'Aujourd'hui*, 1939, n. 1, p. 15.

5 J. Gréber, *op. cit.*, Vol. II, p. 16.

6 In collaboration with Fouilloux, Reinhard and Hofmeister, Corbett, Harrison and MacMurray.

7 *Survival through Design*, O.U.P., 1954, p. 56.

8 R. Neutra, *op. cit.*, p. VII.

9 J. Ruskin, 'The Lamp of Truth', XVI, in *The Seven Lamps of Architecture*, London, 1849.

10 R. Neutra, *op. cit.*, p. 72.

11 R. Neutra, *op. cit.*, p. 303.

12 H. R. Hitchcock, *In the Nature of Materials, the Buildings of Frank Lloyd Wright, 1887–1941*, New York, 1942.

13 See Chapter 10 ('L'influenza internazionale di Wright') in the *Storia dell'architettura moderna* by B. Zevi, who quotes the following judgments: L. Mies van der Rohe, *Frank Lloyd Wright*, written in 1940 for the catalogue of an exhibition of Wright's work at the Museum of Modern Art in New York, reproduced in P. Johnson, *Mies van der Rohe*, New York, 1947, p. 195; E. Mendelsohn, in H. Vijdeveld, *The Life-Work of the American Architect Frank Lloyd Wright*, Sandpoor, 1925; J. J. P. Oud, 'Ollandische Architektur', *Bauhausbücher*, Munich, 1926; see also: 'Architettura e lavoro in collaborazione', in *Metron*, 1952, n. 1, p. 7.

14 Wright, *Architettura e democrazia*, (1930).

15 Wright, *The Future of Architecture*, Horizon Press, N.Y., 1953, p. 247.

16 *Bauhaus 1919–1929, cit.*, New York, 1938.

17 *Ibid.*, pp. 7–9.

18 *Ibid.*, p. 8.

19 *Architectural Record*, May 1937, in *Scope, cit.*, p. 21.

20 W. Gropius, 'Apollo in the Democracy', speech given at Hamburg on 5 June 1957 on the occasion of the awarding of the first Goethe prize, in *Zodiac*, n. 1, 1958, p. 5.

21 W. Gropius, 'Blueprint of an Architect's Education', in *Scope, cit.*, p. 50.

22 Quoted in S. Giedion, *Walter Gropius*, p. 76, from an article published in the *New York Times*, 2 March 1947.

23 'Concetti di architettura', lecture given 11 April 1956 at the Circolo Artistico in Rome.

24 J. Bodman-Fletcher, N. C. Fletcher, J. C. Harkness, S. Harkness, R. S. McMillan, L. A. McMillen, B. Thompson.

25 See P. Johnson, *Mies van der Rohe*, New York, pp. 191–2.

26 *Ibid.*, pp. 193–4.

27 *Ibid.*, pp. 194–5.

28 In 1943 the Mineral and Metal Research Building, in 1944 the Engineering Research Building, the Library and Administrative Offices, in 1946 the Alumni Memorial Hall and the Metallurgy and Chemical Research Building (in collaboration with Holabird and Root); in the same year the Chemistry Building was built, in 1950 the Institute of Gas Technology and the Central Research Laboratory for the American Railways Association, in 1952 the Chapel, the Mechanics Research Building and the Architecture and Design Building, in 1953 the Mechanical Laboratory for the Railways Association and the Student Common Building (in collaboration with Friedmann, Alschuler and Sincere); also in 1950 the Boiler Plant (with Sargent & Lundy and F. J. Kornaker), in 1953 the Faculty and Student Apartment Building (with Pace Associates), after 1955 Bailey Hall, Cunningham Hall and Crown Hall.

29 In collaboration with Pace Associates and Holsmann, Holsmann, Klekamp & Taylor.

30 In collaboration with Pace Associates and Holsmann, Holsmann, Klekamp & Taylor.

31 In collaboration with P. Johnson, Kahn & Jacobs.

32 *Conversations Regarding the Future Architecture*, collected by J. Peter on a record made for the Reynolds Metals Company (1956).

33 R. Neutra, *op. cit.*, p. 384.

34 Australia: G. A. Soilleux; Belgium: G. Brunfaut; Brazil: O. Niemeyer; Canada: E. Cormier; China: Ssu-Ch'eng Liang; France: Le Corbusier; Sweden: S. Markelius; U.S.S.R.: N. D. Bassov; England: H. Robertson; Uruguay: J. Vilamajo.

35 In collaboration with Mitchell & Richey and Altenhof and Brown.

Chapter 19

1 *Garden Cities, Satellite Towns*, (Report of the Department Committee), London, H.M.S.O., 1935.

2 *Report of the Royal Commission on the Distribution of the Industrial Population*, London, H.M.S.O., 1940, p. 1, quoted in Rodwin, *The British New Towns Policy*, Cambridge, Mass., 1956, p. 17.

3 *Report of the Expert Committee on Land Utilization in Rural Areas*, London, H.M.S.O., 1942; *Report of the Expert Committee on Compensation and Betterment*, London, H.M.S.O., 1942.

4 Quoted in A. Verneuil, *La législation sur l'urbanisme en Grande-Bretagne*, Paris, 1948, p. 6.

5 *Architectural Review*, June 1942.

6 P. Abercrombie and J. H. Forshaw, *County of London Plan*, London, 1944.

7 P. Abercrombie, *Greater London Plan 1944*, a Report Prepared on Behalf of the Standing Conference on London Regional Planning at the Request of the Minister of Town and Country Planning, London, H.M.S.O., 1945.

8 *New Towns committee, Interim Report*, London, H.M.S.O., p. 3; quoted in L. Rodwin, *op. cit.*, p. 21.

9 Seven were around London: Basildon, Bracknell, Crawley, Harlow, Hemel Hempstead, Stevenage, Welwyn-Hatfield (which included the old Garden City) and four elsewhere: Aycliffe, Corby, Cwmbran, Peterlee, and three in Scotland: East Kilbride, Glenrothes, Cumbernauld.

10 E. De Maré in *Architectural Review* January 1948.

11 V. Semenov, in M. F. Parkins, *City Planning in Soviet Russia*, Chicago, 1953, p. 51.

12 N. Voronin, *Rebuilding the Liberated Areas of the Soviet Union*, p. 14.

13 Quoted in M. F. Parkins, *op. cit.*, p. 80.

14 Quoted in M. F. Parkins, *op. cit.*, p. 60.

15 N. Voronin, *op. cit.*, p. 29.

16 *Ibid.*, p. 33.

17 *Ibid.*, p. 34.

18 *Ibid.*, p. 40.

19 *Ibid.*, p. 59.

20 *Casabella*, n. 208, (1955, p. 1).

21 *Ibid.*, II.

22 *Ibid.*, III–IV.

23 E. Neufert, *Bauentwurfslehre*, Berlin, 1936.

24 In *Metron*, n. 14, (1947).

25 C. Bo, 'Una cultura senza nome', in *Communità*, n. 60, (1958), p. 2.

26 See B. Zevi, *Towards an Organic Architecture*, Faber, 1950, p. 66, with quotations from Wright, Lescaze, Giedion, Hitchcock, Behrendt.

27 S. Molli-Boffa, M. Passanti, N. Renacco, A. Rizzotti, G. Becker, G. Fasana, M. Grossi, M. Oreglia, P. Perone, A. Romana, E. Sottsass Jr.

28 B. Zevi, *Saper veder l'architettura*, Turin, 1948.

29 B. Zevi, *Architettura e storiografia*, Milan, 1951; *Storia dell'architettura moderna*, Turin, 1951 (especially Chapter 12: 'Il rinnovamento degli studi storici sull² architettura); also: 'Architettura', in the *Enciclopedia dell'arte*, Vol. I, 1958, columns 615–700.

30 E. N. Rogers, *Esperienze dell'architettura*, Turin, 1959, caption facing page 312.

31 See G. E. Kidder-Smith, *Italy Builds*, London, 1955.

32 The term was used for the first time by P. Portoghesi (*Dal neorealismo al neoliberty*, in *Comunità*, n. 65, p. 69); the *Architectural Review* which had already published a hostile note about these experiments (Vol. 24, 1958, p. 281) then criticized them harshly in an article by R. Banham ('Neoliberty, the Italian Retreat from Modern Architecture', n. 747, 1959, p. 231); this article provoked a widespread debate whose participants included E. N. Rogers ('L'Evoluzione dell'architettura, Risposta al custode dei frigidaires', in *Casabella*, n. 228, p. 2) B. Zevi, (*L'Architettura*, nn. 46–47 and *L'Espresso*, 24 May 1959), C. Brandi (*Corriere della Sera*, 10 July 1959), G. Bernasconi (*Rivista tecnica*, n. 8, 1959), P. Portoghesi (*Comunità*, n. 72, p. 78); R. Banham replied to all these in *Architectural Review*, n. 754, p. 341.

33 For the districts of the first seven years (1949–55) see *L'I.N.A.-Casa al IV Congresso di urbanistica*, Venice, 1952, and G. Astengo, 'Nuovi quartieri in Italia' in *Urbanistica*, n. 7, 1951, p. 9; for districts built in the second seven years (1956–62) see R. Bonelli, 'Quartieri e unità d'abitazione I.N.A.-Casa' in *L'Architettura* from n. 31 on.

34 See the special issue of *Urbanistica*, nn. 18–19, (1956).

35 In 1956 the association 'Italia Nostra' was founded to defend Italy's artistic and natural heritage; in the same year a parliamentary commission was formed to alter legislation connected with these matters, but it was dissolved in 1958 without having concluded its tasks; the national town-planning institute devoted its 1957 meeting at Lucca to the defence of the urban and rural landscapes; the number 27 (1957) of the review *Ulisse* was entitled 'Difendiamo il patrimonio artistico'; the XI Triennale organized an international session in 1957 on the 'Attualità urbanistica dei monumenti e dell'ambiente antico'.

36 Three consecutive numbers of *Urbanistica* are devoted to this problem (nn. 27, 28 and 29, of 1959); successive developments are documented in successive numbers of the review, and the definitive plan of 1962 is illustrated in n. 40, of 1964.

A first plan prepared between 1954 and 1958 by a committee of experts (E. Del Bebbio, E. Lenti, R. Marino, V. Monaco, S. Muratori, G. Nicolosi, L. Quaroni, L. Piccinato) was loudly rejected by the Administration in 1958 and replaced the following year by an office plan criticized by all town-planners and cultural institutions. Only in 1962 was it replaced by a more acceptable plan, by M. Fiorentino, P. Lugli, P. Passarelli, L. Piccinato and M. Valori.

37 See the special issue of *Casabella* (287), May 1964. The persistently academic character of the teaching in the Faculties of Architecture met increasing resistance from students from 1960 onwards, and between 1962 and 1963 they occupied the Faculties in Turin, Milan, Florence and Rome, though without obtaining any degree of reform in the methods of teaching.

38 Successive plans are collected together in F. Sullo's book, *Lo Scandalo urbanistico*, Florence, 1964. A first version was prepared by the Istituto Nazionale di Urbanistica and presented at the Rome Congress in November 1960; the Ministry of Public Works was working on an alternative in 1961, limited to altering the law of 1942; when the opening to the left took place, the minister Sullo had a third text prepared, which for the first time envisaged the general compulsory acquisition of building land, and became one of the most controversial points of the 1963 electoral campaign. After this the minister Pieraccini prepared a new text, which was to be modified in conformity with government views in 1964.

39 P. Gibel, 'L'aménagement de la région parisienne', in *La vie urbaine*, 1950, p. 115.

40 Quoted in P. Lavedan, *Histoire de l'Urbanisme, époque contemporaine*, Paris, 1952, pp. 177–8.

41 E. C. Petit, 'Esperienze della ricostruzione francese', in *Casabella*, n. 199 (1953–4) p. 37.

42 Collaborators: P. Branche, P. E. Lambert, A. Le Donné, A. Hermant, J. Poirier, J. E. Tournant; for documentation see 'Urbanisme et habitation' 1953, p. 81; *Casabella*, n. 215, p. 49 (1957).

43 See Le Corbusier, *Oeuvre Complète 1946–1952*, Zurich, 1955, p. 193: 'The idea of the unité d'habitation goes back to a first visit to the Certosa of Ema in Tuscany in 1907'.

44 *Oeuvre Complète 1938–1946, cit.*, p. 38.

45 *Ibid.*, p. 94; see *Les constructions murondins*, Paris, 1941.

46 *Ibid.*, p. 100.

47 *Ibid.*, p. 130.

48 *Ibid.*, p. 103; see 'Le brise-soleil', in *Techniques et architecture*, 1946, p. 25.

49 Earth route, sea route, iron route, air route; see *Sur les Quatre Routes*, Paris, 1941.

50 Living, working, cultivating body and mind, circulating; see *La Charte d'Athènes*, Paris, 1943.

51 Unit of agricultural production, linear industrial town, radio-concentric social city, see *Les trois établissements humains*, Paris, 1944.

52 New system of harmoniously related proportions defined in 1945; see *Le Modulor*, Paris, 1950.

53 Primary, secondary and tertiary streets, commercial streets, branch roads leading to 'unités d'habitation', streets within the 'unités'; see *Oeuvre Complète 1946–1952*, p. 94 and *Le Modulor*, 1950.

54 *La maison des hommes* (with F. de Pierrefeu), Paris, 1942; *Entretiens*, Paris, 1943; *Perspectives humaines*, Paris, 1946; *Propos d'Urbanisme*, Paris, 1946; *Manière de penser l'Urbanisme*, Paris, 1946.

55 In collaboration with M. Lods.

56 J. Petit, 'Le Corbusier propose des unités d'habitation en séries', in *Zodiac*, n. 7, (1960), p. 39.

57 *Oeuvre Complète 1946–1952*, p. 170.

58 Official figures given by the Minister of Housing W. Fey in *Der Aufbau*, August 1953.

59 P. Blake, 'German architecture and American', in *Architectural Forum*, August 1957, p. 132.

60 *Domus*, n. 315, February 1956, p. 4.
61 See O. Bartning, 'Zum Programm der Interbau', *Interbau Berlin 1957*, p. 27; the vicissitudes of the town-planning scheme are well summarized by G. Scimeni, 'La Ricostruzione di Berlino e il quartiere Hansa', in *Casabella*, n. 218, 1958, p. 23. The following is the list of designers (according to the numbering of the buildings): (1) K. Müller-Rehm; (2) Siegmann; (3) A. Klein; (4) H. Müller; (5) G. Gottwald; (6) G. Wilhelm; (7) W. Gropius, T. A. C. and W. Ebert; (8) P. Vago; (9) W. Luckhardt, H. Hoffmann; (10) P. Schneider-Esleben; (11) E. Zinsser, H. R. Plarre; (12) L. Baldessari; (13) E. Eiermann; (14) O. Niemeyer-Filho; (15) F. Jaenecke, S. Samuelsson; (16) A. Aalto; (17) W. Kreuer; (18) G. Hassenpflug; (19) H. Schwippert; (20) R. Lopez, E. Beaudouin; (21) J. H. Van den Broek, J. B. Bakema; (22) L. Lemmer; (23) W. Düttmann; (24) B. Grimmek; (25) P. G. Baumgarten; (26) M. Taut; (27) K. Fisker; (28) O. H. Senn; (29) M. Fuchs; (30) B. Pfau; (32) H. H. Sobotka, G. Müller; (33) F. R. S. Yorke; (34) F. Schuster; (35) G. Nissen; (36) B. Hermkes; (38) H. Scharoun; (39) E. Ludwig; (40) A. Jacobsen; (41) G. Weber; (42) A. Giefer, H. Mäckler; (43) J. Krahn; (44) S. Ruf; (45) W. von Möllendorf, S. Ruegenberg; (46) J. Lehmbrock; (47) W. Fauser; (48) G. Hönov and also Le Corbusier, H. A. Stubbins, W. Düttmann and F. Mocken.
62 *Bureau d'information et de publicité de la ville de Rotterdam, Bulletin d'information n. 3*; see also C. Van Traa, *Rotterdam, die Neubau einer Stadt*, Rotterdam, s.d.
63 Quoted in *Urbanistica*, n. 5, 1950, p. 15.
64 I. Insolera, 'Prosciugamento e pianificazione della Zuiderzee', in *Urbanistica*, n. 22, p. 39.
65 W. Van Tijen, 'Il centro sperimentale di Vlaardingen', in *Casabella*, n. 219 (1958) p. 47.

Chapter 20

1 *Il Piccolo*, 14 June and *Correio de Manha*, 1 November 1925.
2 Letter of 8 June 1946, reproduced in *Oeuvre Complète 1938–1946*, p. 90.
3 P. L. Goodwin, *Brazil Builds*, New York, 1943.
4 Among the books issued after 1943 we may mention S. Papadaki, *The Work of Oscar Niemeyer*, New York, 1950, and *Oscar Niemeyer, Work in Progress*, New York, 1956; L. Costa, *Architetura brazileira*, Rio de Janeiro, 1952; H. R. Hitchcock, *Latin American Architecture*, New York, 1955; H. E. Mindlin, *Modern Architecture in Brazil*, Rio-Amsterdam, 1956. An important exhibition concerned with Brazilian architecture was held at the Building Centre in London in July 1953, and another on Brasilia made a tour of the cities of Europe in 1958.
5 *Report on Brazil*, in *Architectural Review*, Vol. 116 (1954) p. 234.
6 *Ibid.*, p. 238.
7 W. Holford, *Brasilia*, in *Architectural Review*, Vol. 122 (1957) p. 394.
8 Quoted in the article by Holford, *cit.*, p. 399.
9 *Ibid.*, p. 401.
10 *Ibid.*, p. 402.
11 The second prize went to the plan by B. Milman, J. H. Rocha and N. F. Goncalves; the third equally to M. and M. Roberto and R. Levi, R. Cerqueira, L. R. Carvalho-Franco; the fourth equally to H. Mindlin and

G. C. Palanti, to Construtecnica S. A. and to C. Cascardi, J. V. Artigas, M. W. Vieiera, P. de Camargo and Almeida.
12 W. Holford, *op. cit.*, p. 402.
13 A. Rosa Cotta and A. Marcolli, 'Considerazioni su Brasilia', in *Casabella*, n. 218 (1958) p. 33.
14 *Oeuvre Complète 1952–1957*, Zurich, 1957, p. 54.
15 *Ibid.*, p. 117.
16 *Oeuvre Complète 1952–1957, cit.*, p. 54. A recent article in *Architectural Design* (October 1965, p. 504) describes the almost completed city, which 'works very well, better than one would have imagined possible'.
17 D. Gioseffi and C. L. Ragghianti, see *Sele-Arte*, n. 32 (1957) p. 10.
18 H. von Erffa, 'Bauhaus first phase', in *Architectural Review*, Vol. 122 (1957) p. 103.
19 Frank Lloyd Wright (*Io e l'architettura*, Milan, 1932).
20 S. Koike, *Contemporary Architecture in Japan*, Tokyo, 1953, p. 16.
21 A. Drexler, *The Architecture of Japan*, New York, 1955, p. 240.
22 B. Taut, *Nippon mit europäischen Augen gesehen*, Tokyo, 1934; *Japan Kunst*, Tokyo, 1936; *Grundlinien japanischer Architektur*, Tokyo, 1935 (also published in English with the title *Fundamentals of Japanese Architecture*, Tokyo, 1935); *Houses and people of Japan*, Tokyo, 1937.
23 The movable panels which form inner and outer walls.
24 B. Taut, *Fundamentals of Japanese architecture, cit.*, pp. 10–11.
25 The mats, of standard size, which cover the floors.
26 C. Perriand, 'Crisi del gusto in Giappone', in *Casabella*, n. 120, p. 54.
27 R. Bourné, 'Renaissance in Japan', in *Architectural Forum*, September 1959, p. 98.

Conclusion

1 E. Pickering, *ibid.*, p. 117.
2 Quoted in *Architettura*, December 1965, p. 494.
3 *Casabella*, n. 210 (1956) p. 4.
4 Quoted in *Casabella*, n. 226.
5 See Chapter 20, note 16.
6 *Oeuvre Complète 1952–1957*, p. 8 (written 21 September 1956).
7 P. 347.
8 *Casabella*, n. 258 (1961) p. 5.
9 *Ibid.*, p. 16.
10 Partly influenced by Tange's plan, partly for similar reasons, other analogous proposals have been put forward in Japan, for Tokyo and elsewhere by N. Kurokawa, Akui and Nozawa, and by the group Metabolists. But none has the systematic character of Tange's plan, and in fact they should rather be linked with an international vogue, to which Kahn's plan for the centre of Philadelphia and certain Italian, German and French projects belong. See n. 115 of *L'Architecture d'Aujourd'hui* (1964).
11 In collaboration with A. Epstein and Sons, C. F. Murphy Associates, Schmidt, Garden and Erikson.
12 In collaboration with Farkas and Barron.
13 *The Planning of a New Town; Data and Design based on a Study for a New Town of 100,000 at Hook, Hampshire*, London County Council, 1961.

14 *Traffic in Towns; a Study of the Long-Term Problems of Traffic in Urban Areas; Report of the Steering Group and Working Group appointed by the Minister of Transport,* London, H.M.S.O., 1963.

15 See V. Gruen and L. Smith, *Shopping Towns, U.S.A.,* New York, 1960.

16 See *Casabella,* n. 271 (1963).

17 W. Lippmann, *The Public Philosophy,* London, Hamish Hamilton, 1955, p. 128.

Bibliography

In outlining a bibliography of modern architecture one has to take into account the changes that have taken place between the beginning and the end of the period considered, changes which concern not only the value of the architectural experiments but also their conceptual setting.

The word 'architecture' does not designate an unchanging concept, a permanent form of human experience, but a notion which is variable in time in the same way as the human experiences which come within it, though usually more slowly than they, and which can be considered constant within a given period of time only by approximation.

But in the time dealt with this approximation is no longer possible; in fact eclecticism and the modern movement have transformed the accepted meaning and the limits of the term 'architecture' more deeply, perhaps, than any other period. If one wishes to present the main bibliographical sources available on this period in a fair light, one must, therefore, go over the main phases of this transformation and place each single source within the conceptual framework to which it belongs.

Bibliography therefore tends to become fused with real historical narrative, and indeed in the text the reader will find a large number of bibliographical references to the subjects dealt with as he proceeds. Here it seemed useful, however, to provide a summary of the most important sources, which may provide an initial guide in the bibliographical ocean of works on architecture during the last two centuries.

1 Historicist thought

The unity of the traditional concept of architecture – as expressed in the treatises of the Renaissance and Baroque periods, where stylistic and constructional precepts appear side by side – tended to disappear during the second half of the eighteenth century. In the *Encyclopédie* (1751–72) there is a discussion of 'architecture et les parties qui en dépendent' (i.e. interior decoration, exterior decoration and construction) and the technical and stylistic data are still to be found under the same heading, though separately. But towards the end of the century this way of presenting things was no longer common practice and two distinct groups of treatises began to appear, one group concerning the technique of construction and the other, the architectural composition in the strict sense of the word.

The prototype of the first group was the

work of G. B. Rondelet, *Traité théorique et pratique de l'art de bâtir*, Paris 1802–17, translated into various languages and updated until the fourth decade of the nineteenth century. Rondelet's treatise still gathers a multitude of subjects into a single corpus – building technique, hydraulics, road and railway building – which after 1830 became independent, specialized subjects and each gave rise to a literature of their own, which we naturally cannot follow here.

Useful guides to the documentation of technical knowledge as a whole were the dictionaries published during the nineteenth century, for instance S. C. Brees, *The Illustrated Glossary of Practical Architecture*, London 1852.

The prototype of the real architectural treatises was the work of J. L. N. Durand, *Précis des leçons d'architecture*, Paris 1802–5, which remained the basis of French academic teaching throughout the nineteenth century. Starting from the study of *disposition* Durand proceeded to a case history of distributive types – public and private buildings, for the various needs of the modern city – which, however, remained somewhat theoretical, because of lack of experience (the types described in the treatise, baths, museums, markets etc., were based mainly on archaeological considerations).

As experience gradually broadened, this construction of individual cases broadened with it, to constitute the main bulk of successive treatises until the masterly work by J. Guadet, *Eléments et théorie de l'architecture*, Paris 1894, which did not adduce theoretical building types but a large number of concrete examples, and which therefore afford an excellent summary of nineteenth-century production, particularly French. The manuals of 'distributive features' moved along the same lines – whether general or devoted to a particular type of building – and even today they form a large part of current literature.

Nineteenth-century building production was also documented by illustrated collections of examples: we have said that the renewed awareness of the architecture of the past came about mainly through the agency of collections of original reliefs, from the *Recueil et parallèle des édifices de tout genre, anciens et modernes* by J. L. N. Durand, Paris 1800–1, to the *Édifices de Rome moderne* by P. Letarouilly, Paris 1840–55. Similar collections of contemporary buildings were frequently published after 1830, particularly in France; among the most important were:

Gourliet, Biet, Grillon et Tardieu, *Choix d'édifices publics projetés et construits en France depuis le commencement du XIX siècle*, Paris 1825–36.

F. Narjoux, *Monuments élevés par la ville de Paris de 1850 à 1880*, Paris 1877–81.

E. E. Viollet-le-Duc and F. Narjoux, *Habitations modernes*, Paris 1875–9.

C. Lutzow and L. Tischler, *Wiener Neubauten*, Vienna 1876–80 (followed by *Wiener Neubauten in Stil der Sezession*, Vienna 1908–10).

The revivals of styles of the past made it possible for the knowledge of ancient buildings to be linked directly to the planning of contemporary ones; at this time history books were also to some degree manuals of contemporary architecture.

This mixture of historical ideas and operative precepts was particularly noticeable in historical dictionaries, perhaps the most typical product of nineteenth-century historicist thought; the two most important were:

M. Quatremère de Quincy, *Dictionnaire historique d'architecture*, Paris 1832 (neoclassical in inspiration).

E. E. Viollet-le-Duc, *Dictionnaire d'architecture*, Paris 1868–74 (neo-gothic in inspiration).

It was not until the second part of the nineteenth century that historicist production itself began to be considered historically, as a reality independent of its corresponding historical models.

The first general historical works came from England rather than France, perhaps because in France the preponderance of classicism kept up an impression of continuity with the architecture of past centuries, while in England the importance of the neogothic movement made the break with previous eras quite obvious.

Just at the moment when Morris was beginning his career, there appeared the manual by J. Fergusson, *History of Modern Styles of Architecture*, London 1862 (reprinted in 1873 as the fourth volume of the *History of Architecture* which came out in 1865–7).

The expression 'modern architecture' indicated the cycle from the Renaissance onwards, as opposed to the Middle Ages and classical antiquity (even today the distinction is still made between ancient, medieval and modern). This nomenclature was plainly linked to the eclectic vision – the original styles succeeded one another until the Middle Ages, the imitative ones from the Renaissance onwards – and was abandoned only towards the end of the century, partly because of the influence of the *avant-garde* movements which insisted on the antithesis between past and present.

Of the two manuals which gave an authoritative and general view of eclectic culture – B. Fletcher, *A History of Architecture on the Comparative Method*, London 1896, and A. Choisy, *Histoire de l'architecture*, Paris 1899 – the second uses the term 'modern architecture' for the period from the seventeenth century onwards (therefore excluding the Renaissance), the first for the period from 1830 onwards.

Town-planning experiments are not included in the field of interest described hitherto; for this reason information on the growth of the industrial city and the relative systems of control must be sought rather in the economic, legal and political literature, or in city guides.

The only exceptions were the undertakings where the prestige aspect was sufficiently important; Haussmann's organization of Paris was widely documented, for instance in:

M. Ducamp, *Paris, ses organes, ses fonctions et sa vie dans la deuxième moitié du XIX siècle*, Paris 1869–75.

E. Haussmann, *Mémoires*, Paris, 1890.

The technical experience accumulated during the course of the nineteenth century was collected in manuals published in the last quarter of the century; R. Baumeister, *Stadtserweiterung in technischen, baupolizeilicher und wirtschaftlicher Beziehung*, Berlin, 1876; J. Stübben, *Der Städtebau*, Berlin, 1890.

2   Avant-garde experiments up to 1914

Action taken for the renewal of the industrial city up to the last decade of the nineteenth century was mainly theoretical and documented in the writings of the respective promoters:

Robert Owen, *Report to the County of Lanark*, 1820; *The Revolution in the Mind and Practice*, London, 1849.

C. Fourier, *Traité de l'association domestique-agricole*, Paris, 1822; *Nouveau monde industriel et sociétaire*, Paris, 1829.

E. Cabet, *Voyage en Icarie*, Paris, 1840.

J. B. Godin, *Solutions sociales*, Paris, 1870.

Fifty Years of Public Work of Sir Henry Cole, London, 1884.

Owen Jones, *The Grammar of Ornament*, London, 1856.

G. R. Redgrave, *Manual of Design Completed from the Writings and Addresses of R. Redgrave*, London, 1876.

G. Semper, *Der Stil in den technischen und architektonischen Künsten*, Frankfurt, 1860.

Souvenirs d'Henri Labrouste, notes recueillies et classées par ses enfants, Paris, 1928.

E. E. Viollet-le-Duc, *Entretiens sur l'architecture*, Paris, 1863–72.

J. Ruskin, *The Seven Lamps of Architecture*, London, 1849; complete works edited by E. Cook and A. Wedderburn, London, 1903–10.

W. Morris, *Architecture, Industry and Wealth*, London, 1902; *Collected works*, London, 1914–15.

The *avant-garde* movement which arose during the last decade of the nineteenth century brought about an important revolution in architectural literature.

The term 'modern architecture' was now used to indicate the new tendencies as opposed to the eclectic tradition: as in the writings of O. Wagner (*Moderne Architektur*, Vienna, 1895), H. Van de Velde (*Die Renaissance im modernen Kunstgewerbe*, Berlin, 1901), H. P. Berlage (*Gedanken über den Stil in der Baukunst*, Leipzig, 1905) and Frank Lloyd Wright (mainly in the years following these; see for instance F. Gutheim, *Frank Lloyd Wright, Selected Writings*, New York, 1941).

The first attempts at an overall judgment were also made:

W. Rehme, *Die Architektur der neuen freien Schulen*, Leipzig, 1902.

A. D. F. Hamlin, 'L'Art Nouveau, its Origin and Development', in *The Craftsman*, 1902–3, p. 129.

At first, the publications concerning the masters of the *avant-garde* were mainly documentary, and the most noteworthy of these were:

O. Wagner, *Einige Skizzen, Projecte und ausgeführte Bauten*, Berlin, 1891–1910.

Architektur von Prof. Joseph M. Olbrich in Darmstadt, Berlin, 1902–14.

Ausgeführte Bauten und Entwürfe von Frank Lloyd Wright, Berlin, 1910.

The first biographies were those of the names appearing in the first volumes of the *Thieme Becker Künstler-Lexicon* (Behrens and Berlage in 1909).

Monographs on the various masters appeared successively in this order, indicative of the evolution of historiographical tendencies:

F. Hoeber, *Peter Behrens, Vorträge und Aufsätze*, Munich, 1913.

J. A. Lux, *Otto Wagner*, Berlin, 1919 (the documentary volume *Otto Wagner 1914–1918*, by H. Geretsegger and M. Peintner came out in 1964).

J. A. Lux, *Joseph Maria Olbrich*, Berlin, 1919.

K. E. Osthaus, *Van de Velde, Leben und Schaffen des Künstlers*, Hagen i. W. 1920.

J. Gratama, *Dr. H. P. Berlage bouwmeester*, Rotterdam, 1925.

P. Jamot, *A. Perret et l'architecture du béton armé*, Paris, 1927.

L. Kleiner, *Joseph Hoffmann*, Berlin, 1927.

J. F. Rafols and F. Folguera Grassi, *Antonio Gaudí*, Barcelona, 1928 (followed by numerous other studies, up to the recent ones by J. J. Sweeney and J. L. Sert, London, Architectural Press, 1960, and R. Pane, Milan, 1965).

H. Kulka, *Adolf Loos, das Werk des Architekten*, Vienna, 1931.

T. Heuss, *Hans Poelzig*, Berlin, 1939.

G. Veronesi, *Tony Garnier*, Milan, 1943.

N. Pevsner, *Charles Rennie Mackintosh*, Milan, 1950 (followed two years later by the exhaustive biography by T. Howarth, *Charles Rennie Mackintosh and the Modern Move-*

ment, London, Routledge & Kegan Paul, 1952).

There is still no adequate study of Horta, apart from the article by S. T. Madsen in the *Architectural Review* Vol. 118, p. 388. (The periodicals quoted in Chapter 9, section 9, are indispensable for knowledge of *avant-garde* movements).

The historical distance with which the cycle of historicist architecture can now be regarded has made a new assessment of the immediate past possible, whether polemical as in H. von Muthesius, (*Stilarchitektur und Baukunst, Wandlungen der Architektur im XIX Jahrhundert,* Mülheim 1902) or analytical as in D. Joseph (*Geschichte der Baukunst des XIX Jahrhunderts,* Leipzig, 1910).

The movement of revision in the field of town-planning is also documented in the writings of C. Sitte (*Der Städtebau nach seinen künstlerischen Grundsätzen,* Vienna, 1889) E. Howard, (*Tomorrow, a Peaceful Path to Real Reform,* London, 1898) and P. Geddes (*City Development,* Edinburgh, 1904).

In 1962 the memoirs of H. Van de Velde were published (*Geschichte meines Lebens,* edited by H. Curjel, Piper, Munich); these contain a great deal of information on this period.

3   The modern movement

In the first fifteen years after the war the publications of the masters of the modern movement were mainly apologias, as we said in Chapter 14, and offer judgments and documentation that are didactic rather than historical.

Apart from the essays of Le Corbusier, which had an axe to grind (*Vers une architecture,* Paris, 1923; see also Chapter 13, section 2, and Chapter 19, section 4) and of W. Gropius (collected in *Scope of Total Architecture,* London, Allen & Unwin, 1956)

the most important texts are:

W. Gropius, *Internationale Architektur,* Munich, 1925 (the first of the *Bauhausbücher;* the complete list is in Chapter 13, note 15).

L. Hilbersheimer, *Internationale neue Baukunst,* Stuttgart, 1926.

G. A. Platz, *Die Baukunst der neuesten Zeit,* Berlin, 1927.

H. R. Hitchcock, *Modern Architecture, Romanticism and Reintegration,* New York, 1929.

B. Taut, *Die neue Baukunst in Europa und Amerika,* Stuttgart, 1929.

M. Malkiel-Jirmounsky, *Les tendances de l'architecture contemporaine,* Paris, 1930.

A. Sartoris, *Gli elementi dell'architettura razionale,* Milan, 1932.

H. R. Hitchcock and P. Johnson, *The International Style, Architecture Since 1922,* New York, 1932.

Other less important works are cited in Chapter 14, section 3.

At this time too A. Loos' theoretical writings appeared (*Ins Leere gesprochen,* Paris, 1921; *Trotzdem,* Innsbruck, 1931).

The first of the masters of the modern movement to be the subject of monographic documentation were E. Mendelsohn (*Buildings and Sketches,* Berlin, 1923) and Le Corbusier (*Oeuvre complète,* of which eight volumes have appeared: 1910–29, 1929–34, 1934–8, 1938–46, 1946–52, 1952–7, 1957–65, *The last works,* Girsberger, Zurich). The first biographies – apart from the small volumes *Maîtres de l'architecture moderne,* which appeared from 1928 onwards, and *Les artistes nouveaux,* from 1931 – appeared after the Second World War in this order:

A. Whittick, *Eric Mendelsohn,* London, Faber, 1940.

G. Holmdahl, S. Lind and K. Odeen, *Gunnar Asplund arkitekt,* Stockholm, 1943.

P. Johnson, *Mies van der Rohe*, New York, 1947 (followed by the biographies by L. Hilbersheimer, Chicago, 1953, and W. Blaser, Zurich, 1965).

S. Papadaki, *Le Corbusier*, New York, 1948.

M. Bill, *Robert Maillart*, Zurich, 1949.

P. Blake, *Marcel Breuer, Architect and Designer*, New York, 1949.

A. Christ-Janer, *Eliel Saarinen*, Chicago, 1949.

W. Boesiger, *Richard Neutra, Buildings and Projects*, Zurich, 1950 (followed by a second volume in 1959 and by a third in 1966).

S. Papadaki, *The Work of Oscar Niemeyer*, New York, 1950 (followed by *Oscar Niemeyer, Work in Progress*, New York, 1956).

G. C. Argan, *Walter Gropius e la Bauhaus*, Turin, 1951 (three years later Gropius' biography by S. Giedion appeared in English, French, German and Italian; on TAC a documentary volume of Niggli appeared in 1966).

E. C. Nevenschwander, *Atelier A. Aalto 1950–1951*, Zurich, 1954, followed by the second volume of Girsberger in 1963.

W. M. Dudok (Celebration Volume on his seventieth birthday) Amsterdam, 1954.

J. Pedersen, *Arne Jacobsen*, Copenhagen 1957 (followed by the fuller one by T. Faber, *Arne Jacobsen*, Stuttgart, 1964).

U. Kultermann, *Wassili und Hans Luckhardt*, Tubingen, 1958.

T. M. Brown, *Affonso Eduardo Reidy, Bauten und projecte*, Stuttgart, 1960.

H. R. Hitchcock, *Architektur von Skidmore, Owings & Merrill, 1950–1962*, Stuttgart, 1962.

J. Buekschmitt, *Ernst May*, Stuttgart, 1963.

Harry Seidler 1955–1963 (with a Preface by R. Banham) Sydney, Paris and Stuttgart, 1963.

C. Schnaidt, *Hannes Meyer*, Teufen, 1965.

S. Moholy-Nagy, *Paul Rudolph, Bauten und Projekte*, Stuttgart, 1970.

On Italian architects:

J. Joedicke, *The Works of Pier Luigi Nervi*, London, 1957.

G. C. Argan, *Ignazio Gardella*, Milan, 1959.

G. Boaga, B. Boni, *Riccardo Morandi*, Milan, 1962.

C. Blasi, *Figini e Pollini*, Milan, 1963.

Pier Luigi Nervi, nuove strutture, Milan, 1963.

M. Tafuri, *Ludovico Quaroni*, Milan, 1964.

In the period between the two World Wars publications on the modern movement and traditional historiography were usually separated; the chief exception was mainly in Weimar Germany, where a partial integration between the two lines of culture was effected in, for example, the four volumes of the *Wasmuth Lexicon der Baukunst*, Berlin, 1929–32, which retained the form of the nineteenth-century dictionaries.

The grafting of the new experiences on to the trunk of tradition was particularly fruitful in town-planning. Of the numerous general works published at this time we must mention:

A. Rey, G. Pidoux, C. Barde, *La science des plans des villes*, Paris, 1928.

C. Chiodi, *La città moderna*, Milan, 1935.

On the town-planning experiments in the various countries between the wars, the best documentary work is that of B. Schwan, *Städtebau und Wohnungswesen der Welt*, Berlin, 1935.

For the activities of the C.I.A.M. see Chapter 15, section 4. The documentation of the last meeting at Otterlo was published by J. Joedicke, *C.I.A.M. 1959 in Otterlo, ein Wendepunkt der Architektur*, Stuttgart, 1961.

While the crisis of rationalism was emerging, after 1935, a first historical placing of the modern movement as a whole became possible. A basic book in this connection was Pevsner, *Pioneers of the modern movement from William Morris to Walter Gropius*, London, Faber, 1936, which stops just before the First World War but sets up for the first time a relationship of continuity – not just of polemical juxtaposition – between the Modern Movement and previous events.

From this moment onwards there arose a new interest in the age of the pioneers. The year before, the first general study on *art nouveau* appeared: F. Schmalenbach, *Jugendstil*, Würzburg 1935, and, soon afterwards, the book by F. Ahler Anderson, *Stilwende, Aufbruch der Jugend um 1900*, Berlin, 1939; N. Pevsner published his *An Enquiry into Industrial Art in England*, New York, 1937, and an increasing number of studies on the national tradition began to appear in English periodicals; in the U.S.A., after the stimulating studies by L. Mumford – *Sticks and Stones*, New York, 1924, and *The Brown Decades*, New York, 1931 – there began the systematic exploration of the national heritage and the basic monographs on Sullivan – H. Morrison, *L. Sullivan, Prophet of Modern Architecture*, New York, 1935 – on Richardson – H. R. Hitchcock, *The Architecture of H. H. Richardson and his Time*, New York, 1936 – and on Wright – H. R. Hitchcock, *In the Nature of Materials*, New York, 1942; the reassessment of experiments contingent to the orthodox line of the modern movement began (the Museum of Modern Art produced the monograph, by A. Lawrence Kocher and S. Breines, *Aalto, Architecture and Furniture*, New York, 1938, and later the volume by P. L. Goodwin, *Brazil Builds*, New York, 1943, which started the international vogue

for the Brazilian movement).

Meanwhile the first attempts at a general historical appraisal of the Modern Movement were beginning; important among the many works in this connection were:

W. C. Behrendt, *Modern Building*, New York, 1937.

J. M. Richards, *An Introduction to Modern Architecture*, London, Penguin Books, 1940.

S. Giedion, *Space, Time and Architecture*, Oxford University Press, 1941, was the first book in which the limits of the new concept of architecture were explicitly discussed, including within a traditional historical framework architectural experiments as traditionally understood, town-planning and industrial design; however, basically Giedion's work covers the same ground as Pevsner's *Pioneers*, i.e. it analyses the remote formation of the Modern Movement rather than its recent developments.

Immediately after the war B. Zevi's, *Towards an Organic Architecture* (English translation, London, Faber, 1950) appeared, and was later extended to form the *Storia dell'architettura moderna*, Turin, 1950. Starting from the post-war revisionist tendency, Zevi qualified the Modern Movement between the wars with the term 'rationalism', against which he set a new 'organic' tendency, with reference to Wright and the Scandinavians; in this way he was led to bypass the research begun by Giedion on the extent and methodical implications of the new architecture, but by distinguishing the two contrasting moments in the modern movement, he managed for the first time to historicize – even if his intention was to spread a gospel – the events of the last thirty years; for this reason his work of 1950 may be considered the first real history of modern architecture ('history, not pre-history' as Pevsner says).

Zevi's influence has contributed to the resumption of historical studies in Italy (the series of monographs *Architetti del movi-*

mento moderno, came out in Milan from 1947 onwards, with the biographies of the main masters of *art nouveau,* of Wright, Aalto, Asplund and only later of Oud, Mies and Neutra; the choice of subjects is indicative of the cultural trend, but it brought about a rapid absorption of historical studies on modern architecture into the traditional framework of the 'History of Art' (a typical enterprise in this context was the *Enciclopedia dell'arte,* which has been appearing since 1959).

There also appeared various basic contributions to the knowledge of the architecture of the first fifty years of this century:

A. Whittick, *European Architecture in the Twentieth Century,* London, 1950–3.

T. F. Hamlin, *Form and Functions of Twentieth Century Architecture,* New York, 1952.

On nineteenth-century architecture, among the many recent publications:

S. Giedion, *Mechanization Takes Command,* New York, 1948 (an excellent conclusion to the 1941 work).

P. Lavedan, *Histoire de l'urbanisme, époque contemporaine,* Paris, 1952.

H. R. Hitchcock, *Early Victorian Architecture in Britain,* London, Architectural Press, 1954.

L. Hautecoeur, *Histoire de l'architecture classique en France,* Vol. IV–VII, Paris, 1952–7.

S. Tschudi-Madsen, *The Sources of Art Nouveau,* Oslo, 1956, followed by the exhaustive study by R. Schmutzler, *Art nouveau,* Stuttgart, 1962.

All these contributions are summarized in the book by H. R. Hitchcock, *Architecture: Nineteenth and Twentieth Centuries,* London, Penguin Books, 1958, still the most complete general work on this period. Cf. also *The Encyclopedia of Modern Architecture,* London, Thames & Hudson, 1963.

It seems as though the current movement is favourable to objective discussion of the meaning of the modern movement, which by now has a history of fifty years' standing. The book by J. Joedicke, *Geschichte der moderne Architektur,* Stuttgart, 1959, although it undertakes less than those by Zevi, Giedion or Behrendt, has a detached and impartial tone which was hitherto unknown in this type of work.

The editor Karl Krämer is publishing in Stuttgart a series of books directed by Joedicke, *Dokumente der modernen Architektur,* important both for information and for criticism:

1. O. Newman, *C.I.A.M. 1959 in Otterlo* (1961)
2. J. Joedicke, *Schalenbau* (1962)
3. J. Joedicke, *Architektur und Städtebau* (the work of Bakema and Van den Broek, 1963)
4. H. Lauterbach and J. Joedicke, *Hugo Häring* (1965)
5. R. Banham, *Brutalismus in der Architektur* (1966)
6. *Candilis, Josic, Woods* (1968)
7. J. Joedicke, *Moderne Architektur, Strömungen und Tendenzen* (1969).

From about 1955 onwards, there was a notable increase in works on the *avant-garde* movements of the second and third decades of the twentieth century. (See the monographs by W. Grohmann on *Klee,* Stuttgart, 1954, and on *Kandinsky,* Stuttgart, 1959; the essay by H. L. C. Jaffé, *De Stijl,* London, 1956; the publication of Klee's notes, with the title *Des bildnerische Denken,* Basle, 1956, of the *Archivi del Futurismo,* published in Rome from 1958) which have helped to focus attention on that basic point of recent history. Even more significant was Reyner Banham's *Theory and Design in the First Machine Age,* London, Architectural Press, 1960, where this group of experiments was analysed as a whole for the first time.

There is an exhaustive documentary work on the Bauhaus: H. M. Wingler, *Das*

Bauhaus, Bramsche, 1962. See also the discussion aroused by an article by T. Maldonado, *Ist das Bauhaus aktuell?* in the journal of the Hochschule für Gestaltung, Ulm.

The publishers Vincent, Fréal & Cie. have republished the most important texts by Le Corbusier (*Vers une architecture,* in 1958, *L'art décoratif d'aujourd'hui* in 1959, *Précisions* in 1960, *La Ville Radieuse* in 1964 and *Urbanisme* in 1966.

The Berlin publishers Ullstein have published a series of texts from the period between the wars, or of writings on this period, with the title: *Ullstein Bauwelt Fundamente*; of particular note are No. 1 (U. Conrads, *Programme und Manifeste zur Architektur des 20. Jahrhunderts,* 1964) and J. Posener, *Anfänge des Funktionalismus, von Arts and Crafts zum Deutschen Werkbund,* 1965.

From 1960 onwards George Braziller has been publishing a new biographical series, *Masters of Modern Architecture*; the first sixteen volumes are devoted to Mies, Aalto, Nervi, Le Corbusier, Gaudí, Wright, Neutra, Sullivan, Gropius, Niemeyer, Mendelsohn, Khan, Tange, Johnson, Saarinen, Fuller; the architects of the *avant-garde* and those of the modern movement are presented together, profiting from the vogue enjoyed by the 'modern' with the general public.

The essays by H. Seldmayr (*Verlust der Mitte,* Salzburg, 1948, and *Die Revolution der modernen Kunst,* Munich, 1955) and of P. Francastel (*Art et technique,* Paris, 1956) are important for the setting of architecture within present-day cultural thought, and the two works are conceived from two contrary viewpoints but are in agreement in believing that the significance of contemporary experiments can be interpreted by distinguishing 'art' from other functions.

A correct interpretation of the modern movement should rather recognize – in our opinion – the contingent character of the categories inherited from traditional historiography, and agree to bring into the theoretical field the consequences of the operative developments which have had them in a state of crisis for several decades.

Index

Numbers in bold type indicate pages on which illustrations are to be found

A

Aalto, A. 591, 616 ff, 651, 703–4
  works: Imatra church **700**;
  Paimio sanatorium **617–18**;
  Pension Bank **698**; Rovaniemi
  699; Säynätsalo town hall **699**
Aarhus town hall **614–15**
Abel, A. 736
Abercrombie, P. 686, **689**
Abramowitz, M. 671, **674–6**, 677–8
Adam, R. **xxix**, 20, 160
Adler, D. 224, 234, **236**, 239, 240
Ahren, U. 611
Ain, G. 671
Alavoine, J. A. 55, 59
Albers, A. **432**, 548
Albers, J. 414, 424, 651
Albini, F. 595, **600**, **717**, 718–20, **721**
Albricci, G. 721
Alfeld an der Leine, Fagus works 382 ff, **382–4**, **387**, 603
Alfredshof 346
Algiers **533**, 535
Alpago-Novello, A. 562
Alphand, A. 72, 113
Altenhof 346
Amiens **727**, 728
Amsterdam 362–5, 458, 460, **605**, 606–7, 747, 813–14, 819
  Amsterdam-Pampus **826–8**
  Buiksloterham **513**
  Het Blauwe Zand **513**
  nautical club **311**
  offices of *De Nederlanden* **307**
  Stock Exchange 306, **307–8**, 309, **313**
  Sloterplas 814, **822–3**
  Zuid **363–4**, **459**
Ango, M. 23
Apollinaire, G. 393
Aragon, L. 406
Argan, G. C. 565
Arkwright, R. 39
Arnold, K. **271**
Arp, J. 403, **407**
Artaria, P. **622**
Asada, T. **777**
Aschieri, P. 566
Ashbee, C. R. 164, 181, 182, 186, 187
Askin, C. H. 693
Asplund, E. G. **609–10**, 611–12
Asprucci, A. **xxviii**
Atterbury, G. 651
Attleboro (Mass.) **660**
Aubert, A. **584**, 585
Aymonino, C. 722
Azéma, L. 581

B

Baines, E. 127
Bakema, B. 741, 815 ff, 820–1
  works: Amsterdam-Pampus **826–8**; Hengelo **824–5**;
  Leeuwarden **825**; Lijnbaan **742–3**; Montessori school **744–5**
Balat, A. 265
Baldwin, C. W. 224
Ball, U. 403
Balla, G. 390, **394**
Ballio-Morpurgo, V. **572**
Ballu, T. 92

Baltard, L. P. 28
Baltard, V. 68, 90–1, **91–3**
Balzac, H. 133
Bamberg, bridge over Regniz 12
Banfi, G. L. 711
Barbe, P. 576
Barcelona **80**, **491**
  Battló house 318, **319**
  Sagrada Familia church 318, **319**
Barchin, G. 560
Barlow, M. 685
Barnsley 182
Baroni, N. 566, **568**
Barrault, A. 103
Barry, C. **53**, 56
Basildon new town 813
Bauhaus 274, 412 ff, 433 ff, 471, 472, 651–2
  buildings 424, **425–8**, 514
  manifesto **413**
Bavinck 464
Bayer, H. 429
Beardsley, A. **260**, 263
Beaudouin, E. 509, 594 ff, **597**, 794
Beckford, W. 55
Becontree 509
Bega, M. **724**
Behrens, P. 379–85, 424, 479, 486, 546
  works: Linz factory **542**;
  Matildenhöhe **379**; Weissenhof **478**
Belanger, F. J. 20, 91
Belgrand, F. E. 72
Belluschi, P. 671
Belto, W. 834
Bennett, E. H. **230**, 231, **232**
Bentham, J. 149

Berardi, P. N. 566, **568**
Berlage, H. P. 60, 306 ff, 362 ff, 498
  works: *De Nederlanden* **307**;
  Gemeente Museum **310**; Stock
  Exchange **307, 308**; Zuid district
  363
Berlin
  A.E.G. factory **382**
  Alexanderplatz **450**
  Bad Durrenberg **519**
  Britz **513**, 522
  Chancellery **554**
  Columbushaus 499, **504-5**
  exhibitions: (1931) 487-8; (1957)
  738, **739**
  Frederick II monument **29**
  Free University **832**, 833
  Marschallbrücke **16**
  New Hansa **737**
  plan **544**
  Potsdamerplatz **544**
  Siemensstadt **518**, 522
  unité d'habitation **730**, 797
  Universum cinema 454-5, **458**
Bernouilli, J. 5
Bessemer, H. 375
Bethlehem (Penna) 195
Bexhill-on-sea 588
Biano, M. 712
Bill, M. 738, 754-5
Bindesboll, G. 608
Binet, J. R. 316
Birmingham 56, **129**
Blake, W. 263
Bleyl, F. 390
Bloc, A. 576
Boccioni, U. 390, 396, 402
Bochum university 833
Boffrand, G. 23
Bogardus, J. 206
Bogler, F. W. **417**
Boileau, L. A. 581
Boito, C. 256
Boldetti, M. A. xxiv
Bonatz, P. **543**, 546, 595
Bonnat, L. J. 113
Borda, C. 6
Bordeaux, Théâtre français 12
Boscobel (N.Y.) **196**
Boston, town planning **682**, 834-5,
  837
Boullée, E. L. 29, 549
Boulton, M. 9, 19
Bourdais, J. D. 105
Bourgeois, V. **478**, 479
Bournville 351
Boynington, W. W. 220
Bradford 48
Brandt, M. **430, 432**
Braque, G. 390, 393
Brasilia 755 ff, **756-7, 759, 761**
Brazil 748-64

Bregenz 548
Brescia **572**
Breslau, pharmacy **544**
Breton, A. 406
Bridant **58**
Bridgens, R. P. 773
Bridgewater, Duke of 11
Briey-en-Forêt 731, 732, 797
Brighton, Royal Pavilion **16**, 20
Brindley, J. 11
Brinkmann, J. A. 462, **601-2**, 601-6,
  815
Bristol, Clifton bridge 9, **18**, 21
Brno, Tugendhat house 499, 502,
  503
Brown, S. 20
Brunel, I. K. 9, **18**, 20
Brussels 81
  Central station 268
  exhibition **719, 749**
  Floréal 357
  Horta house **269**
  Logis 357
  Maison du Peuple **267**, 268
  Palais des Beaux Arts 268
  Palais Stoclet **295-7**, 301, 365,
  366-7
  Solvay house **269**
  Tassel house 265, **266**, 325
Buchanan, C. D. 444, 812-13, **818**
Buckingham, J. S. 157
Budeus, A. 750
Buenos Aires 535
Buffalo
  Guarantee building **236**
  Larkin building 242
  Martin house **249**
Buildwas, bridge over Severn 19
Burckhardt, J. 255
Burdon, R. **14-15**, 19
Burke, E. xxi
Burle-Marx, R. **752**, 754
Burne-Jones, E. 176, 263
Burnet, J. 476
Burnham, D. H. 224 ff, **230**
Burr 11
Burton, D. 22
Butler, S. 140-1

C

Cabet, E. 152, 155
Cabiati, O. 562
Cagnola, L. **xxix**
Cairns, B. S. **672**
Calcaprina, C. 712
Calini, L. **716**
Cambridge
  Churchill college **820**
  St John's college 55
Cambridge (Mass.) **197**

Canberra **345**, 346, 378
Cancelloti, G. 567
Candilis *équipe* 821, **829, 832**, 833
Canina, L. **163, 166**
Canova, A. 28
Capelletti, C. V. 771
Capponi, G. 566
Cardelli, A. 712, **713**
Caré, A. **713**
Carlu, J. 581
Carlyle, T. 128
Carrà, C. 390
Cartwright, E. 39
Castagnola, U. 564
Castellazzi, M. **716**
Castiglioni, E. **721**
Cato, C. 476
Cendrars, B. 406
Cendrier, F.-A. 103
Ceradini, G. **713**
Cerda, I. **80**, 81
Cézanne, P. 147, 257, 258, 393
Chadwick, E. 24, 47, 48, 49, 170,
  343
Chagall, M. 581
Chamberlain, J. 507
Chandigarh 762 ff, **762-3, 766-9,
  771, 793-5**
Chandler (Ariz.) 672, 673
Chareau, P. 576, 594
Charley 20
Charlottesville, Jefferson's villa 201,
  202
Charton 106
Chartres cathedral 20
Chateaubriand, F. 29, 55
Chatsworth 22
Chelsea, Levy house 588
Chemnitz, Schocken stores 454, **457**
Chermayeff, S. 588, 591
Chesterton, G. K. 358
Chiarini, C. 722
Chicago 219-50, **220-3, 230**, 346,
  378, 785
  auditorium **236**
  campus of I.I.T. 663, 664, **665,
  838**
  Carson, Pirie & Scott building
  237, 238, **240-1**
  Chicago Tribune building **474**
  Crown Hall **665**
  Federal center **806**, 807
  International Life Assurance Co.
  636
  Lake Meadows 834, **836**
  Lake Shore Drive apartments
  666-8
  Leiter building **226**
  Marshall Field building 234
  Masonic Temple **230**
  People's Gas building **230**
  Promontory apartments **666**, 668

Reliance building 228, **229**
silos **388**
Tacoma building **227**
Clark, H. P. 671
Coalbrookdale, bridge **14**, **15**, 19;
ironworks **128**
Cobden, R. 170
Cobden-Sanderson, T. 182
Cocteau, J. 581
Coignet, F. 322
Cointreaux 24
Colbert, J. B. 9
Cole, H. 96, 102, 164, 168, **169**, 170,
284, 630
Colne valley **131**
Cologne 733
cathedral 56
exhibition **299**
Feinhals villa 288
theatre **277**
Werkbund exhibition (1914) 384,
386, **387**
Columbia 835
Como, Casa del Fascio 569–70, 571,
595
Comte, A. 93
Concord (Mass.) 655
Condor, J. 773
Condorcet, A. 6
Contamin 35, 106
Conway straits bridge **18**, 20
Copenhagen **697**, **701**, 808
Bellavista housing estate **612**,
613
Gentofte school **704**, **705**, 808
Rodovre town hall 808, **809–10**
S.A.S. headquarters 808, **811**
Coppée, F. 113
Coquart, E. G. 120
Cornell & Ward **496**, 588
Corot, J. B. 143
Costa, L. 750, 754, **756**, 758–60,
794
Coste, P. 87
Cottancin 106
Coulomb, C. A. 6
Courbet, G. 95, 143
Crane, W. 164, 182, **183**, 186, **260**,
263
Crawley new town **692**
Croce, B. 255, 565
Cumbernauld 813, **819**
Curjel, R. 618
Cuypers, P. J. H. 306

D

Dahlem, Sommerfeld house 420
Dailey, G. A. 671
Daly, C. 120
Daneri, L. C. 595, **598**

Darby, A. 19
Darmstadt, Matildenhöhe 290 ff,
291–4, **379**, 381
d'Aronco, R. **314**, 316, **317**
Dastuge, M. **584**, 585
Daumier, H. 95, **142**, 143–4
David, J. L. **xvi**, **xxxiii**, 28
Davioud, G. A. 105
Day, L. F. 182
de Baudot, A. 109, 322, **323**
de Boinville, C. 773
de Cessart & Dillon **17**, 20
de Dion, H. 105
Defoe, D. 9, 133
Deilmann, H. **734**
de Klerk, M. 309, **311**, 364–5, 458,
459
de Konnick, L. **496**
de Laborde, L. 170
Delacroix, E. 143
Delannoy, M. A. 87
Delaunay, R. 390
del Debbio, E. 567
Delstern crematorium 384
de Mars, V. 671, **672**
de Morgan, W. 182
Derain, A. 389
Desprez, J. L. 608
Dessau
Bauhaus 424 ff, **425–8**, 514
Törten district 514, **516**, 525
de Tocqueville, C. A. **xxii–xxiii**,
xxxiv, 24, 357
Detroit 207, **209**; General Motors
building **677**, 679
Dex, J. F. **551**
Dickens, C. **xxi**, 100, 129–30,
132–3
Dinwiddie, J. E. 671
Diotallevi, I. 595
Disraeli, B. 85
Döcker, R. **478**, 479
Doehlmann, K. 392
Dondel, J. C. **584**, 585
Doré, G. **142**, 144
Dow, H. P. 671
Drancy 509
Muette district **596–7**
Dresser, C. 182
Drew, J. 764
Duchamp, M. 403
Dudok, W. M. 456, 460, 462 ff, 599
works: Hilversum, Minchelers
school **467**; Rembrandtlaan school
467; town hall **468–9**; Valerius
school **470**
Dufy, R. 581
Durand, J. L. N. 28, 31 ff, **32**, **33**,
34, 123, 629
Düsseldorf, Mannesmann offices **735**
Dutert, C. L. F. 106 ff
Duthilleul, J. **830**

E

Eames, C. **680**
Eck 20
Ehn, C. **510**
Ehrenburg, I. 406
Eiffel, G. 29, 35, 103, 105, **118–19**,
121–2
Einstein, A. 424, 454, **455**
Elberfeld stores **545**
El Tablazo 813
Eluard, P. 406
Emberton, J. 588
Ende, H. 773
Engel, G. L. 608
Engels, F. 47, 51, 128, 136, 140, 156
Ensor, J. 263
Epstein, J. 406
Ernst, M. 403
Erskine, R. 702
Eydoux, L. 104

F

Fahrenkampf, E. **545**, 547, 555
Feininger, L. **376**, **413**, 414, 420,
651
Feld, J. 786
Ferraris, G. 375
Ferry, J. 135–6
Fiedler, K. 254–6, 257
Field & Sons 217
Figini, G. 564
Finsterlin, H. **401**
Fiorentino, M. 712, **713–4**, 722
Firminy 797
Fischer, J. **496**
Fischer-Essen, A. 476
Fisker, K. 703
Flagg, E. 218
Flaubert, G. 120
Florence 80, 81, **568**, 723
Focillon, H. 581
Förster, L. 84
Fontaine, P. F. L. *see* Percier &
Fontaine
Fonthill Abbey 55
Formigé, J. 106
Forshaw, J. H. 686, **689**
Fort Worth **833**, 834
Foscini, A. 567, **572**
Foster City 835
Fourier, C. 151–2, 156, 732
Frank, J. **478**, 479
Frankfurt-am-Main 382, 511, **512**,
546, **734**
Franklin, B. 193
Frette, G. 564
Frey, A. 671
Frézier, A.-F. 27
Fribourg, bridge 20

Friesz, O. 389
Fry, E. M. 587–90, **589–90**, 764
Fuller, B. 671

G

Gabriel, A. J. **xviii**, 68
Gailhabaud, J. 87
Galileo 5, 6
Gamberini, I. 566, **568**
Garches, house 445 ff, **446–8**
Gardella, I. 595, 718, **719**, 720, **721**
Garnier, C. **86**, 91, 113, 120
Garnier, Tony 320, 321, 331 ff,
334–5, 340–2, 362, 436
    Lyon **336–7**; industrial city **332–5**
Gaudi, A. 318, **319**
Gauguin, P. 257, 258
Gauthier, T. 87
Geddes, N. B. 651
Geddes, P. 357, **360**
Geneva
    bridge **625**, 626
    Clarté building **528–9**, 530
    League of Nations building
    475–7, **475**, 791
Genoa, bank **717**; houses **598**
Gherassimov, V. **557**
Giertz, L. M. **696**
Gilly, F. 28, **29**
Gimson 182
Ginain, L. 120
Ginzburg **558**, 560
Giolli, R. 565, 711
Giroux, M. R. **579**
Glasgow
    Art school **278**
    Hill House **279**, 281
Gleizes, A. 390, 393
Godin, J. B. 152, **153–4**
Gollia & Co. **315**
Goodwin, P. 671
Gori, A. F. xxiv
Gorio, F. 722
Goulet, N. 24
Gounod, C. 113
Graham, J. 834
Gréber, J. 634, 635, **681**
Greendale (Wisc.) **673**
Greenough, H. 207, 629
Greenwood 507
Griffin, W. **345**, 346
Grinnell (Iowa) **236**
Gris, J. 390, 393, 577
Gronovius xxiv
Gropius, W. 301, 304, 389, 435,
471, 802–3; and Bauhaus 274, 412,
414 ff, 449; and state 498; and
Weimar school xi, xii; and
Werkbund 381, 385–6, 415
    quoted: 389, 420, 522, 525, 653,

661; on Bauhaus 429, 472, 652;
on architecture 398–9, 494, 499,
652, 783 ff; on teaching
architecture 415, 416, 421 ff, 654,
738
    works: Adler motor car **385**, 386;
    competition buildings **474**, 487,
    488; factories **382–4**, 385–6, **387**;
    houses **485**, 486, 654, **655**, **657**,
    659; in England 588, **589–90**; in
    U.S.A. 612 ff, **655**, **673**; town
    planning **478**, 479, 511, 514 ff,
    516, **518**, **521**, **524**, 673
Grubemann, J. U. **8**, 11
Gruen, V. **833**, 834
Grünberger, A. 549
Guadet, J. 123–4, 288
Guarnieri, S. 566, **568**
Guevrekian, G. 549
Guimard, H. **314**
Guise, 'familistère' **153–4**
Gurlitt, C. 255
Gutbrod, R. 736
Guthrie, J. 278
Gutkind, E. A. 357

H

Haefeli, M. E. 618, **622**
Hälsingborg 611
Häring, H. 546, 547
Haesler, O. **543**, 546, 547
Hagen, Springmann house **277**
Hague, the 365
    Gemeente museum **310**, 364, 598
    Shell building **581**, 585
Hall, R. V. 671
Hamburg, Chilehaus **541**, 546
Hamilton 477
Hankar, P. 265, 271
Hardy, L. 104
Harlow new town **690–2**, 813
Harris, H. H. 671
Harrison, W. K. 671, **674–6**, 677–8
Hartmann, E. 253, 255
Harvard, arts centre 797
    graduate centre **660**
Hauck, G. 392
Hauptmann, G. 424
Hausen, M. **734**
Haussmann, G.-E., Baron 52,
61–95, 134–6, 341
Heckel, E. 390
Hedquist, P. 611
Heine, H. 133
Helfreich, W. G. 477
Helsinki, Pension bank **698**
Hemel Hempstead new town **692**,
813
Hengelo, Kleine Driene district 819,
825

Hennebique, F. 35, 322
Herbst, R. 576
Herculaneum xxiv
Herriot, E. 336 ff, 348, 576
Hetsch, G. F. 608
Hilbersheimer, L. **478**, 479, 492–3,
519, 651
Hildebrand, A. 255
Hill, A. H. 671
Hill, O. 85
Hilversum 462 ff
    Minchelers school **467**
    Oranje school 463
    Rembrandt school 463, **467**
    town hall 467, **468–9**
    Valerius school **470**
Hiroshima Peace Centre 777
Hittorf, J. I. 68, 91, 92
Hoban, J. 204
Hodler, F. 263
Höger, F. **541**, 546
Hoffmann, J. 292–8, 366–7, 424,
546, 549, **551**, 555
    works: Palais Stoclet **295–7**, 365;
    Purkersdorf sanatorium **299**
Hoffmannstahl, H. von 424
Hoffstadt, F. 56
Holabird, W. 224, 225, **227**, 231,
636, 669
Holford, W. 758, 812
Holzmeister, C. 547
Hood, R. M. **633**, 636–7
Hook 812, **817**
Hooke, R. 5
Hook of Holland, housing 410,
460–1, **463–4**
Horeau, H. 96
Horiguchi, S. 775, **776**, 777
Horta, V. 263 ff, 325, 476, 791
    works: Horta house **269**; Maison
    du Peuple **267**; Solvay house
    269; Tassel house **266**
Houston (Texas), housing **656**
Howard, E. 351 ff, **352**, **356**, 357–8
Howe, G. **633**, 638
Howells, J. M. **633**
Hubacher, C. 618, **622**
Hugo, V. 55
Hulsenbeck, R. 403
Hunt, R. M. 234
Huntsmann, B. 19
Huszar, V. 406
Hutchinson, H. 55

I

Ichiura, K. 775
Imai, K. 775
Imatra, church **700**, 703
Impington, village college 588,

589–90
Indianapolis 207, **209**
Ishimoto, K. 775
Isozaki, A. 799
Ito, C. 774
Itten, J. 414

J

Jacob, M. 406
Jacobsen, A. 613, 703–5, **704**, 808, **811**, 811–12
  works: Aarhus town hall **614–15**; Bellavista estate **612**; Rodovre town hall **809–10**; Soholm housing **701**
Jancu, M. **496**
Japan 766–82
Jappelli, G. **54**
Jeanneret, P. 436, 437, **439**, 444–5, **446–8**, **475**, 476, **500**, **531–3**, 557, 764
Jefferson, T. **xxix**, 196, 199 ff, **202**, 229
Jenney, W. Le Baron 35, 220, 224, 225, **226**, 234
Jofan, B. M. 477, 560
Joltowsky, N. B. 477
Jones, O. 86, 168, **169**, 170
Jourdain, F. 576
Justi, L. 424

K

Kagawa, Prefecture **777–9**, 780
Kahn, L. 671, 683
Kamakura museum 780
Kamiya, K. **777**, 799
Kandinsky, W. 390, 397, 398, 414, **418**, 420, 424, 434
Karlsruhe, Dammerstock district 515, **518**
Kassell, state theatre 736
Katsura, imperial villa **772**
Keck, G. F. 671
Kern, G. I. 392
Kerr, R. 87–90
Kew Gardens 22
Kharkov, theatre **557**
Kiesler, F. 671
Kigo, K. 774
Kirchner, E. L. 390
Kishida, H. 775
Klee, P. 258, 390, 398, 414, **419**, 424, 430, 434–5, 516 ff, **517**
Klein, A. 515, **519**
Klenze, L. **xxx**
Klimt, G. **289**
Koch, A. 280, **315**
Kocher, A. L. 671

Koechlin 112
Koh, H. 799
Koike, S. 775
Kok, A. 406
Kokoschka, O. 424
Koppel, N. and E. 703
Krahn, J. 595
Kramer, P. L. 309, 365, 458
Krantz, J. B. 103
Krefeld, Lange house 451, **452**
Kreis, W. 553
Kressler, R. **543**
Kubin, A. 390
Kubitschek, J. 755
Kurokawa, N. 799

L

Laasan, bridge 20
Labrouste, H. 68, 91, **93**, 95, 322
Lagrange, J. L. 6
Lambot, J. L. 103
Lancia, E. 562
Langhorst, F. 671
Langley, B. 52
Lanza, M. 722
Laplace, P. S. 6
Larco, S. 564
Larderello, houses **724**
La Rochelle 729, 796
La Sarraz, conference 495 ff
Lassus, J. B. A. 55, 59
La Tourette, monastery 797
Latrobe, B. H. 203, 205
Laugier, M.-A. 31
Lavedan, P. 23
Lavery, J. 278
Lavirotte, J. **313**
Le Chapelier, I. R. G. xvi–xviii, xxxiii–xxxiv
Leconte de Lisle, C. M. 113
Le Corbusier (C. E. Jeanneret) 320, 435–49, 789 ff, 798–9; and Behrens 381; and Cubism 406; and P. Jeanneret 437, 444; and Loos 301; and modern movement 412
  quoted: 7, 341, 797, 798; on architecture 437, 444–5, 594; on art 498; on education 472; on skyscrapers 634; on town planning 530, 536, 594, 732; on the UNESCO building 795–6
  works: Algiers plan **533**; Chandigarh 764 ff, **771**, 791, **793–5**; Clarté apartments **528–9**, 530; drawing **839**; houses **403**, **439**, **441**, 445 ff, **446–8**, **473**, 499 ff, **500–1**, **528**, **592–3**; League of Nations building **475**, 476–7, 791; Marseilles 728 ff, **730–1**, 796; Moscow **557**; Paris 440 ff, **443**,

532, **533**; pavilions **583**, 749; Rio de Janeiro **534**; studio **442**; Stuttgart (Weissenhof) **478**, 479, **485**, 486; Tokyo 782, **789**; United Nations building **674**, 677, 679, 792–3
  competitions: Geneva (1927) 268, 475, 476, 791; Chicago (1922) 474, (1931) 477; Paris (1937) 585
  town planning: 156, 361, 440, 530 ff, 728–33, 796
Lecointe, J. F. J. **79**
Ledoux, C.-N. **xix**, 28, 29, 148 549, 629
Leeuwarden, plans 819, **825**
Léger, F. 390, **403**, 577
Le Havre **725**, 728, 729
Leibnitz, G. W. 5
Lemasquier, C. 476
Lenci, S. 722
L'Enfant, P. C. **203**, 205, 207, 213, 231
Lenoir, V. 20
Le Play, P. G. F. 128
Le Raincy, church of Notre Dame 326, **329**
Leroux, M. L. 578, **579**
Lescaze, W. **633**, 638
'Les XX' 263, 312
Letchworth **352–3**, 355, 358
Lethaby, W. R. 182, 186
Lhote, A. 393
Libera, A. 564, 566
Lindhagen, A. 84
Ling, A. 813
Lingeri, P. 595
Linz, factory **542**, 546
Lipchitz, J. 577, 581
Liverpool, cathedral 283
Lockwood & Mason 85
Lods, M. 509, 594 ff, **597**
Loewy, R. 651
Londberg-Holm, K. 474
London 47 ff, 133, 686–9, 812–13
  Bethnal Green 47
  British Museum xxv
  Carlton House Terrace 20
  Chester Terrace **xxxi**, **36**
  Crystal Palace 9, 23, 96 ff, **97–100**, **162–3**, 168
  City of London 50
  docks **45**; St Catherine's dock 20
  Hampstead Garden Suburb 354, 357
  Highpoint **587**
  Houses of Parliament **53**, 55
  Housing 50
  King's Cross station 46
  Ludgate Hill **137–9**, 140–1
  Park Crescent **36**
  Park Square **35**
  Piccadilly Circus plan 812

Regent Street **30**
St Paul's Cathedral **137**
underground **46**
Loos, A. 261, 288, 298 ff, 474
works: Karma house **300**;
Michaelerplatz house **300**; Moller
house **304–5**; Schen house **302–3**;
Steiner house **300**
Loring, S. E. 225
Los Angeles **836**
experimental school **642**
nursing home **640**
Loughborough estate 812
Louis, V. 12
Lubetkin, B. **587**
Luckhardt, H. **520**, **544**, 547
Luckhardt, W. **402**, **520**, **544**, 547
Lübeck **734**
Lugli, P. **722**
Lurçat, A. 576, **578**, 594
Lusanna, L. 566, **568**
Lutyens, E. 346
Lyon 335 ff, 436
Abattoirs de la Mouche **336**,
337–8
E. Herriot hospital 338, **339**
Olympic stadium **337**, 338
Quartier États Unis 338, **342**

M

Maaskant, H. A. 602, **603–4**, 606,
741
Macadam, J. 11
McCarthy, F. J. 671
Mackim, C. M. 234
Mackintosh, C. R. 60, 261, 276 ff,
278–82, 313
Mackmurdo, A. H. 181, **260**
Macnair, H. 278
Madrid 361
Maekawa, K. 775, 782
Maillart, R. 619–26, **624**, **625**
Malevich, K. 390, **404**
Mallet-Stevens, R. 564, 576, 585,
594
Malthus, T. xxi, xxii, 9
Manchester 19, 40, 47
Manet, E. 141, 145
Manguin 389
Mannheim 194
Mansart, J. H. 68
Marat, J.-P. xvii
Marc, F. 390, 397, **402**
Marcel, G. 581
Marcks, G. 414
Marescotti, F. 595
Marey, E. J. **264**
Margarethenhöhe (Essen) 346, **354**,
357
Marinetti, F. T. 396, 402

Mariotte, E. 5
Markelius, S. 611, 702, 794
Marquet, A. 389
Marseilles, unité d'habitation **730–1**,
796
Marx, K. 156
Massy-Antony **830**
Mathes, house **592–3**
Matisse, H. 389, 581
Matsushita, K. **777**
Mattern, T. 736
Maupassant, G. de 113
Maupertuis, house **28**
Mauriac, F. 581
May, E. 511, 535
Meissonnier, J. L. E. 113
Melograni, C. 722
Melun, Count of 24, 51
Menai bridge 20
Mendelsohn, E. 453–6, 587, 651
works: **455**, **458**, **475**;
Columbushaus **504–5**, 506; Palace
of the Soviets **475**; Schocken
stores 454, **456–7**
Menichetti, G. 722
Mesnil, J. 392
Metcalf, J. 9, 11
Mexico City 81
Meyer, A. 414; Fagus works 382 ff,
382–4, **387**
Meyer, H. 429, **474**, 476
Meyer, Mme **473**
Michelucci, G. 566, **568**, **716**, 719,
720, **723–4**
Middlesbrough **131**
Mies van der Rohe, L. 381, 389,
424, 449 ff, 807–8
quoted: on role of architect 451;
on education 662, 664; on
skyscrapers 449; on Wright 250
works: in Chicago 586, 662 ff,
663, **665–8**, 785, **806**; exhibition
buildings **491**; houses 451, **452**,
489, 502, 503; skyscrapers **450**,
669, **670**, 678, 803, **804–5**, 807;
Weissenhof **478–80**, 481, 486
Milan
Cesate district **721**
Fiera campionaria **600**
Porta Ticinese **xxix**
Torre Galfa **724**
Torre Velasca **719**, 720
Universitá Bocconi 595, **598**
Milhaud, D. 406
Milinis **558**, 560
Milizia, F. 28
Miljutin, N. A. **558**
Mill, J. S. 134, 170
Millet, J. F. 143
Mills, R. 206
Milwaukee (Wisc.) 834
Minoletti, G. 595

Mique, R. **xviii**
Moholy-Nagy, L. 414, 424, 429,
431, 490, 651
Moller, E. 613, **614–15**
Molnar, F. **496**
Mondrian, P. 258, 406, **407–8**, 409,
461, **773**
Monet, C. **143**, **144**, 146
Monge, G. 6, 11, 12
Monier, J. 104, 322
Monticello (Va), Jefferson's villa
201, **202**
Montmagny, church of St Teresa
326, **330**
Montreux, Karma house **300**
Montuori, E. 567, **716**
Morancé, A. **388**
Morpeth, Lord 49
Morpurgo, V. 567
Morris, I. 278
Morris, W. xii, xiii, 60, 148, 164,
170, 176–81, 186, 258, 263
quoted: x, xi, 140; on
architecture 177; on machines
180
works: chintz **175**, **178–9**;
ornamental design **174**; Red
House **175**
Moscow
buildings **706–7**
Centrosoyus **557**
plans **559**, **707**
underground **559**
Moser, K. 476, 618
Moser, W. M. 618, **622**
Mount Vernon, Washington's house
196
Muche, G. 414, 424
Mühleim, church **545**
Münster, theatre **734**, 736
Münter, G. 390
Muggia, A. 476
Mumford, L. 357
Munch, E. **260**, 263
Munich
Brown House **554**
Glyptothek **xxx**
Propylaea **xxx**
Muthesius, H. von **271**, 274–6, 318,
381, 424
Muzio, G. 562

N

Nantes 797
Naper, H. **314**
Napoleon I 11, 52, 55
Napoleon III 65 ff, 103, 120
Narjoux, F. 68, **70**, **71**
Nash, J. 9, 16, 19
works: Chester Terrace **xxxi**, **36**;

Park Crescent **36**; Park Square
35; Regent Street **30**
Nassau (N.Y.) 834
Navier, L.-M. 6, 20
Nelson, G. **680**
Nervi, P. L. 6, 29, 595, 722
Neuilly, bridge **10**, 12
housing 68
Neutra, R. 302, 639–43, 671
works: houses **644–5**; Los Angeles
nursing home 639, **640**
New Delhi 346, 378
New Kensington (Penna) **673**
New Lanark 149–51
New York 210–18, **210–11**, 630
Broadway **214**
Brooklyn bridge **216–17**
Chase Manhattan building **805**,
807
Daily News building **633**
Equitable building **632**
Guggenheim museum **648**
Lever house **677**, 785
Manhattan **215–17**
Rockefeller center **636–7**
Seagram building 669, **670**, 803,
804–5
Telegraph building **631**
United Nations headquarters
674–5, 792–3
Niemeyer, O.
works: in Brasilia 756 ff, **756**,
759, **761**; in Rio de Janeiro 750,
751, 754
Nîmes, Maison Carrée 201
Nolde, E. 390
Normand fils **58**, **79**
North Easton (Mass.) **233**
Nouguier 112
Nuremberg, Schocken stores 454

O

Oak Park 243 ff
Cheney house **248**
Fricke house **249**
Moore house **244–5**
Robie house **243**, **248**
Unity church **249**
Oe, Hiroshe 780
Oki, T. **777**
Olbrich, J. M. 60, **289**, 290, **291–4**
Olmsted, F. L. 231
Orbeletto 595
Osborn, F. J. 685
Osborn, M. 424
Ostberg, R. 608
Osterley Park **xxix**
Otani, Y. **777**
Oud, J. J. P. 250, 258, 301, 410–11,

420, 424, 460–2, 498, 599–601
works: housing at Hook of
Holland **463–4**; Oud Mathenesse
460, **462**; Scheveningen 409, **410**;
Tusschendijken 460, **462**;
Weissenhof **483**, 486; Shell
building **581**, 585; town planning
461–3, **465**, **478**, 479
Owen, R. xii, 148–51, 156, 351,
358, 732
Ozenfant, A. **403**, 406, 437, **442**,
577

P

Padua, Pedrocchino 54
Paestum, temples xxiv, xxv
Pagano, G. 566, 571 ff, 595, 711
works: Rome, Institute of Physics
567; Milan, Universitá Bocconi
598
Paimio, sanatorium 616, **617–18**
Paine, T. 19
Palanti, G. 595
Palos Verdes, Beckstrand house **644**
Panofsky, E. 392
Papadaki, S. **496**, 758
Paris 52, 61–95, **79**, 133, **142**;
plans **62**; (1853) **64**; (1873) **66**;
(by Corbusier) 440 ff, **443**, **533**
Bibliothèque Impériale **93**
Bois de Boulogne 68
Bois de Vincennes 68
Boulevard du Temple **69**
Champs Élysées **21**, 22, **27**, **326–8**
Cité du Refuge 530 ff, **532**
Cité Universitaire 530, **531**
École Voltaire 71
Eiffel tower 112–13, 116–17,
118–19, **121–2**
Esder's tailoring establishment
321
Étoile **74**, 78
exhibition halls 103 ff; (1930)
487–8
Galerie des Machines (1878) 106
ff, **110**; (1889) **111**, **114–15**
garage in rue Ponthieu **325**, 326
Halle au Blé 20
Halles Centrales **90**, **91**, 92
Houses: **313**; Porte Molitor **528**;
rue Franklin 322, **323–4**, **328**;
Savoye house 499 ff, **500–1**;
studio house 440, **441–2**;
weekend house **592**, 594
Jardin des Plantes 22
lunatic asylum of Ste-Anne 71
metro station **314**
Museum of Modern Art **584**, 585
Museum of Public Works **580**,
585

Notre-Dame 55
old people's home of Ste-Perine
70
Opéra **86**, **88–9**
Parc Monceau **69**, **146**
Pont de la Concorde **10**, 12
Pont des Arts **17**, 20
prison of rue de la Santé **70**
rue de Rivoli **34**, 160
rue Rochechouart 68
St-Denis 55
St-Jean de Montmartre 322, **323**
Ste-Geneviève (Panthéon) 5, 12,
13; library **92**
steam engines at Chaillot **73**
store (Lafayette) **314**
UNESCO building 794–5
Parker, B. **352**
Parma, INA building **717**
Passy, house **58**; wells **73**
Patte, P. 23, 28
Paxton, J. 9, 22, 23, 35, 96, 101–2
Payerbach, Khuner house 306
Peabody, G. 85
Peel, Sir R. 165
Percier & Fontaine 20, 22, 28, 160,
163
works: design for bed **158**; rue de
Rivoli **34**; wall motif **159**
Perret, A. 29, 320, 322 ff, 327–31,
341, 378, 619, 728
works: Amiens **727**; Champs
Élysées theatre **326–8**; Esders
321; garage in rue Ponthieu **325**;
house in rue Franklin 322–5,
323–4, **328**; Le Havre **725**; Le
Raincy church **329**; Montmagny
church **330**; Museum of Public
Works 327, **580**, 585
Perret, G. 322 ff
Perriand, C. 576, 780
Perronet, J. R. **10**, 12
Persico, E. 571, 711
Peterson, C. 608
Pevsner, N. 147, 181, 284, 591
Philadelphia 194, **197**, 681, 834
bridge over Schuylkill 11
exhibition hall (1876) 109
Savings Fund Society building
633, 638
Philip & Lee 19
Piacentini, M. 563–4, **572**, 574
Picabia, F. 403
Picasso, P. 390, **391**, 393, 581, **584**,
585
Piccinato, L. 567
Pickens, B. L. 786–7
Pickering, E. 787
Pierron 106
Piranesi, G. B. **xxiv**, **xxv**
Pissaro, C. **86**, **145**
Pistoia, market **716**

Pitt the younger, W. xx
Pittsburgh, ALCOA building **675–6**, 678
Poelzig, H. 424, 546
   works: Festspielhaus **400**;
      Weissenhof **478**, 479, **543**
Poggi, G. 81
Poissy, castle **58**
   Villa Savoye 499 ff, **500–1**
Poleni, Marchese 5
Pollini, G. 564
Polonceau, A.-R. 20
Pompeii xxiv
Ponthieu, J. L. **70**
Ponti, G. 566
Ponti, P. 562
Popp, A. **542**
Portaluppi, P. 562
Porter, G. B. 127
Portland (Oregon) 834
Port Sunlight 351
Potsdam, Einstein tower 454, **455**
Poulsson, M. 608
Prague, Müller house 306
Predaval, G. 595, **598**
Pritchard, T. F. **14**, 19
Proudhon, P. J. 134
Pugin, A. W. N. **57**, **130**, 165, **167**
Purdom, C. B. 685, **688–9**
Purkersdorf, sanatorium 294, **299**, 301
Puy, J. 389

Q

Quaroni, L. **713–15**, 722
Quatremère de Quincy, A. 28
Questel, C. A. **71**

R

Rabut, C. 322
Racine, Johnson works **646**, 649
Radburn (N.Y.) 357
Radiconcini, S. 718
Rading, A. **478**, 479, **544**
Ragghianti, C. L. 565
Ralston, A. 207, **209**
Rapisardi, G. 566
Rastrick, J. 19
Rathenau, E. 406
Rava, C. 564
Rave, P. O. **734**
Rawlinson, R. **57**
Ray, M. 403
Raymond, A. 775, 780
Reading (U.S.A.) **198**
Redgrave, R. 170
Redwood Shores 835
Reich, L. **489**

Reidy, A. E. 750, **752–3**, 754
Reinhardt, M. 424
Renacco, N. 712
Renan, E. 109
Rennie, J. 19
Renoir, A. 263
Reston 835
Richardson, B. W. 157
Richardson, H. H. 60, 224, **233**, 234
Richmond (Va), Capitol **xxix**, 201
Richter, H. 406
Rickman, T. 55
Ridolfi, M. 595, **598–9**, 712, **713–14**, 720, 722
Riegl, A. 255
Rietveld, G. **405**, 406, **407**, 409–10, **550**
Rio de Janeiro 535, 751–4, 755
   civic centre **752**
   Ministry building **751**
   Pedregulho complex **753**, 754–5
   plan **534**
Rizotti, A. 712
Roberto, M. & M. 758
Roche, M. 224, 225, **227**, 231, 669
Rockefeller, J. D. 377
Roebuck, J. 9
Roehampton estate 812, **814–16**
Rogers, E. N. 794
Romano, G. 595
Rome **xxvi**, 346, **573**
   Augusteo **572**
   Città universitaria 566, **567**, 595
   Colosseum **xxvii**
   E42 573, 595
   exhibition (1937) 571
   INA-Casa Tiburtino district **714**, **721**, 722
   library in via Veneto **598**
   Monte Sacro 357
   Musei capitolini xxv
   Palatine xxiv
   St Peter's 5
   SS Pietro e Paolo, E42 **572**
   Stazione Termini **713**, **716**
   Vatican museums xxv
   via S. Valentino house **599**
   Villa Borghese **xxviii**
Ronchamp, church **792**, 797
Rondelet, J. B. **8**, 12, 23, 24, **25**, **26**
Root, J. W. 224 ff, 228, **230**, 636
Rossetti, D. G. 170
Roth, A. 618, 619, 626, **672**
Roth, E. 618, **622**
Rotterdam 365, 740 ff, **742–3**
   Alexanderpolder **744**, 819
   Bergpolder **602**, 606
   Kiefhoek 410, 461, **465–6**
   Lijnbaan **743**
   Montessori school **744–5**
   Oud Mathenesse 410, 460, **462**

   Pendrecht 819
   Plaslaan **603–4**, 606
   Tusschendijken 460, **462**
   Van Nelle factory **601**, 602
Rouault, G. 389, 581
Rouen 51, 55
Rouhault 22
Rousseau, J.-J. xxxiii–xxxiv
Royston, R. 671
Rudolph, P. 683
Ruff, L. **545**
Ruhnau, W. **734**
Runcorn 813
Ruskin, J. xii, 85, 101, 140, 164, **173**, 170–6, 187, 264–5, 630
   quoted: on Gothic 59; on materials 172; on ornamental work 172, 641; on town planning 351
Russell, B. 133–4, 377
Russell, G. 186
Russell, S. 104

S

Saarinen, Eero 638, **677**, 679
Saarinen, Eliel 613, 638, **677**, 679
Sabaudia 567
Saint Dié 729, 796
Saint Gaudens 729, 796
St Gotthard tunnel 375
St Louis, Wainwright building 235, 238
Sakakura, J. 775, 778, 780, 782
Salt, T. 85
Saltaire 85
Salvisberg, O. 546
Salzburg, Festspielhaus **400**
Samoná, G. 566, 718, **723**
San Francisco **192**, **232**, 346
San Mateo (Calif.) 834
Sant'Elia, A. **395**, 396–7, 402
Sao Paulo 535
Sardou, V. 113, 134–5
Satie, E. L. 406
Saulnier, J. 104
Sauvestre, S. J. 113
Säynätsalo, town hall **699**, 703
Scalpelli, A. 567
Scarpa, C. 718, 719
Schäffer, P. **526**
Schaffhausen, bridge 11
Scharoun, H. **478**, 479, **482**, 486, **518**, **544**, 552
Schasler, M. 253, 255
Scheffer, L. S. P. 607
Scheper, H. 424, 429
Scherchen, H. 421
Schevengingen, housing 410
Schinkel, K. F. **16**, 28, **53**
Schlemmer, O. 414, **417**, 424

Schmidt, H. **622**
Schmidt, J. 429
Schmidt, K. 318, **417**
Schmidt-Rottluff, K. 390
Schmitthenner, P. 553
Schneck, A. **478**, 479
Schneider, K. **544**
Schneider-Esleben, P. **735**, 736
Schönberg, A. 424
Scholl, I.-A. 738
Schonko, V. A. 477
Schoussev, A. V. 561
Schumacher, F. 546
Schwarz, R. 595
Scott, B. 281
Scott, G. G. 256
Séguin, M. 20
Sekino, T. 774
Semper, G. 170, 284
Sens, cathedral 55
Serrurier-Bovy, G. 263, 265, 271
Seurat, G. P. 257, 263
Severini, G. 390
Shaftesbury, Lord 39, 49, 85, 343
Shankland, E. C. 228
Shaw, G. B. 141
Shaw, R. N. 182, 186
Sheffield 56
Shepherd, T. **30**
Sicily, power stations **723**
Sirén, H. & K. 703
Sirén, J. S. 608
Sitte, C. 213, 214, 348–51
Sive, A. 758
Skidmore, Owings & Merrill 679, 803, **805**, 807, 834, **836**, **838**
Sloane, Sir H. xxv
Smith, A. xx ff, 41
Snow, G. W. 219
Soane, Sir J. 28
Sobotka, W. **551**
Soholm, housing **701**
Solna, school hall **696**
Sommaruga, G. 316
Soria, A. 358 ff
Soriano, R. S. 671
Soufflot, J. G. 5, 12, **13**
Southwood Smith 49
Speer, A. **554**, 555
Staal-Kropholler, M. 458, **459**
Staines, bridge **15**
Stam, M. **478**, 479, **484**
Steiger, R. 618, **622**
Stephenson, G. 9, 44
Stephenson, R. 59, 96, 170
Stevenage new town 813
Stockholm 84
    crematorium **610**
    exhibition building **609**
    library **609**
    Torsviks district **695**

Stölzl, G. 429, 548
Stone, E. 671
Stonorov, O. 671
Strasbourg, Aubette dance hall **407**, 411
Straub, H. **545**, 548
Strawberry Hill, Walpole's house **53**, 55
Street, G. E. 176
Strnad, O. 548, 549, **551**
Strzygowsky, J. 424
Stuttgart
    Liederhall 736
    Schocken stores 454, **456**
    Weissenhof 477 ff, **478–85**, 486
    Zeppelinbau **543**
Sudermann, H. 424
Suez canal 377
Sully-Prudhomme, R. 113
Sullivan, L. 231–5, **236–7**, 238–40, 635
Sunderland, bridge **14**, 19

T

TAC **660**, 662, **739**
Tange, K. 444, **777**, 780–2, 799–802, **800–1**
Taniguchi, Y. 775
Tatlin, V. E. **557**
Tatsuno, K. 774
Taut, B. 381, 386, **402**, 423, **478**, 479, 493, 546, 775–7
Taut, M. 474, **478**, 479
Tazikawa, M. 775
Teague, W. D. 651
Telford, T. 9, 11, **18**, 19, 20
Teltscher, G. **417**
Tengbom, I. 476, 608
Terragni, G. 564–5, **569–70**, 571, 595, 711
Tesc, N. **696**
Tessenow, H. 553
Thorwaldsen, B. 28
Tivoli xxiv
Tokyo
    City Hall 780
    Museum of Western Art 782, **790**
    Nippon Songo bank 780
    Olympic pool **781**, 782
    Pensioners' hospital 780
    plans 444, 799, **800–1**
    Readers' Digest offices 780
    School of Dentistry **776**
    Wasaka house **776**
Toulouse-le-Mirail, plans 821, **830–1**, 833
Tournon, bridge 20
Trélat, E. 120
Trésaguet, P. M. J. 11
Trigier 103

Troost, P. L. 553, **554**, 555
Tsuboi, Y. **777**
Turin, exhibition 270, 316, **317**
Turner, J. M. W. 143
Tusculum 331
Tuy Medio 813
Tweed, bridge 20
Tzara, T. 403, 406

U

Uccle, house 124, 263, **273**
Unwin, R. **352**
Upton, Red House **175**, 176
Ure, A. 127
Uthwatt, J. 686
Utrecht 365
Utzon, J. 703

V

Vaccaro, G. **721**
Valencia 835
Valori, M. 722
Valtat 389
Van den Broek, J. H. 602, 741, 815 ff, 820–1
    works: Amsterdam-Pampus **826–8**; Hengelo **824**;
    Leeuwarden **825**; Rotterdam **742**, **744–5**
Van der Leck, B. 406
Van der Mey, J. M. 458
Van der Vlugt, L. C. 462, 601–6, 815
    works: Van Nelle factory **601**;
    Bergpolder **602**
Van de Velde, H. 124, 255, 258, 263, 265, 271–7, 312
    quoted 265, 272, 276
    works: furniture etc **271**, **274**, **275**, **277**; house at Uccle 124, **273**
Van Doesburg, T. 258, 406 ff, 420, 424
    works: Aubette dance hall **407**; house **409**
Van Eesteren, C. 406, **409**, 607
Van Eyck, A. 815
Van Gogh, V. **254**, 257, 261
Van Osdel, J. M. 220
Van t'Hoff, R. 406
Van Tijen, W. 462, 601–2, 606, 741
    works: Bergpolder **602**; Plaslaan **603**, **604**; Alexanderpolder **744**
Vantongerloo, G. 406
Van Traa, C. 741
Vasconcellos, E. 750

Vaucresson, house **439**, 440
Vaudoyer, L. 234
Vaudremer, J. A. E. 68, **70**, 265
Venice, hospital 797, **798**
Venuti, R. **xxvi**
Versailles, Marie Antoinette's village and Petit Trianon **xviii**
Vesmin, A. L. and V. **557**, 560
Viara, P. **584**, 585
Viel, J. M. V. 103
Vienna
  exhibition (1873) 104, **108**
  housing block **286**
  Karl Marx Hof 509, **510**
  Michaelerplatz house **300**, 301
  Moller house **304–5**, 306
  plan (1856) **82–3**, 84
  Postal Savings Bank **287**
  Primavesi house **299**
  Scheu house **302–3**
  Secession building **289**
  Steiner house **300**, 301
  Stift house **289**
  technical school 9
  underground **284–5**
  university library **287**
  Werkbundsiedlung housing 549, **550–1**, **578**
Vignon, P. 20, 22
Viipuri, library 616, **620–1**
Vijdeveld, H. T. 365, 458, 476
Villejuif, school **578**
Villeurbaine **579**
Violich, F. 671
Viollet-le-Duc, E. E. 59, 95, 322
  quoted: 120
  designs: **94**, **264**
Vitellozzi, A. **716**
Vitruvius xxiii
Vlaminck, M. 389
Voit & Werder 103
Von Burghaus, Count 20
Voysey, C. F. A. 164, 182, **184–5**, 186, 187

W

Wachsmann, K. **658–9**, 661–2
Wagner, O. 284–8, 301, 312
  works: housing **286**; Postal Savings Bank **287**; Steinhof church **286**; underground stations **284**, **285**; university library, Vienna **287**
Wakefield (Va), Washington's house **193**
Walpole, H. **53**, 55
Walton, E. A. & G. 278
Warchavchik, G. 748, 750
Warndorfer, F. 313
Washington D.C. **203**, 205
  Capitol **208**
  White House **204**
Watanabe, S. 799
Watt, J. 19, 39
Webb, P. **175**, 176
Weimar, monument 420
Welwyn Garden City 352, 355, **356**, 358, **359**, 507
Werfel, F. 424
Wettingen, bridge **8**, 11
Weyland, Chamberlain house **655**
Wheatley 507
Whistler, J. A. McN. 187, 263
White, A. T. 217
Wiebeking, K. 12
Wieringermeer polder **746**, 747
Wilberforce, W. 39
Wilkinson, J. 9, 19
Williams, E. 671
Williams, E. Owen 588
Williams, W. **128**
Williamsburg (Va), Raleigh Tavern **194**
Wils, J. 406, 409
Wilson, H. 813
Winckelmann, J. J. xxv–xxvi, 28
Windsor Castle 55
Wittwer, H. 476

Wölfflin, H. 255
Wokingham **694**
Woodville (Calif.) 672
Woodward, B. A. 207, **209**
Wren, C. **137**
Wright, F. L. xii, 60, 224, 231, 239 ff, 247–50, 643 ff, 649–50
  quoted: 241, 246, 650; on Japanese art 770
  works: Cheney house **248**; Fricke house **249**; Guggenheim museum **648**; International Life Insurance building **636**; Johnson works **646**; Martin house **249**; Moore house **244–5**; Robie house **243**, **248–9**; Unity church **249**; Wright house **647–8**
Wulfen 819
Wurster, W. 671
Wyatt, J. 55
Wyatville, J. 55

Y

Yale, university library **208**
Yamada, M. 778, 780
Yamaguchi, B. **776**
Yamasaki, M. 683
Yokogawa, T. 774
Yonago, town hall 782
Yorke, F. R. S. 591
Yoshino, S. 774
Yuba City 673

Z

Zadkine, O. 581
Zevi, B. 718
Zola, E. 113
Zuiderzee, reclamation 747
Zurich, Neubühl district 619, **622–3**